Immigration raises a number of important moral issues regarding access to the rights and privileges of citizenship. At present, immigrants to most Western democracies do not enjoy the same rights as citizens, and must satisfy a range of conditions before achieving citizenship. Ruth Rubio-Marín argues that this approach is unjust and undemocratic, and that more inclusive policies are required. In particular, she argues that liberal norms of justice and democracy require that there should be a time threshold after which immigrants (legal and illegal) should either be granted the full rights of citizenship, or be awarded nationality automatically, without any conditions or tests. The author contrasts her position with the constitutional practice of two countries with rich immigration traditions: Germany and the United States. She concludes that judicial interpretations of both constitutions have recognized the claim for inclusion of resident aliens, but have also limited that claim.

Ruth Rubio-Marín is Professor of Constitutional Law at the University of Seville.

Immigration as a Democratic Challenge

*Citizenship and Inclusion
in Germany and the United States*

Ruth Rubio-Marín

CAMBRIDGE
UNIVERSITY PRESS

PUBLISHED BY THE PRESS SYNDICATE OF THE UNIVERSITY OF CAMBRIDGE
The Pitt Building, Trumpington Street, Cambridge, United Kingdom

CAMBRIDGE UNIVERSITY PRESS
The Edinburgh Building, Cambridge, CB2 2RU, UK   www.cup.cam.ac.uk
40 West 20th Street, New York, NY 10011–4211, USA   www.cup.org
10 Stamford Road, Oakleigh, Melbourne 3166, Australia

First published 2000

Printed in the United Kingdom at the University Press, Cambridge

Typeset in Plantin 10/12pt [VN]

A catalogue record for this book is available from the British Library

Library of Congress Cataloguing in Publication data

Rubio-Marín, Ruth.
   Immigration as a democratic challenge: citizenship and inclusion in Germany
and the United States / Ruth Rubio-Marín. – 1st ed.
      p.   cm.
   Includes bibliographical references and index.
   ISBN 0–521–77152–8. – ISBN 0–521–77770–4 (pbk.)
      1. Citizenship – United States.   2. Citizenship – Germany.
3. Democracy.   I. Title.
K3224.R83   2000
342.73'083–dc21   99-16899   CIP

ISBN 0 521 77152 8 hardback
ISBN 0 521 77770 4 paperback

To my mother, Joana Marín

Contents

Acknowledgements

This book, which was completed in March 1999, is the result of several years of work in which I have benefited from the inspiration, the support and the teachings of many people.

For inspiration on the subject that animates the book I would like to thank Volkert Ohm who first offered me the opportunity to look into the immigrants' world at close range.

I would like to thank Rory O'Connell for permanent support, lively discussions, teachings and friendship in my years of dissertation work, which ultimately led to this book.

To Leslie Green, Christian Joppke, Steven Lukes, Gerald Neuman, Eric Rakowski, Helmut Rittstieg and Manfred Zuleeg I owe a debt for insight and helpful comments or discussions on parts or all of the preliminary work. Luis Díez Picazo and Massimo Latorre, as my dissertation supervisors at the European University Institute, have always given me important input and encouragement. For sharing the enthusiasm of this project I would like to thank Javier Pérez Royo. I want to thank Pedro Cruz Villalón for his trust and unconditional support throughout the years.

I am especially grateful to Will Kymlicka for all his theoretical teachings and practical help in the making of this book. His generosity with time and knowledge has been an incredible treasure.

From an institutional point of view I want to mention the European University Institute in Florence, the University of California at Berkeley and the University of Seville. The administration and colleagues in each of these places have made this enterprise possible.

John Leslie Ezell has had the patience to read and discuss the whole manuscript, line by line, and has also helped me with the final edition of the book. Sharing the passion and the uncertainties of this project with him has been a 'most excellent' experience.

Finally, my mother, Joana, to whom this book is dedicated, has been the greatest source of inspiration and encouragement in my professional path. I am aware of the costs in terms of geographical separation that my work has meant for us and want to express my infinite love and gratitude to her.

1　Introduction

Postwar international labour migration to affluent and industrialized Western countries has generated some social realities that need to be questioned if the commitment of these societies to liberal democracy is to remain alive. Such a commitment currently ties membership in the polity to the enjoyment of equal political freedom. However, both in Western Europe and North America, increasing numbers of non-national residents, who have by now consolidated their residence, remain excluded from the sphere of civic equality, a sphere which has been reserved thus far for national citizens. This realm of civic equality currently sets the external boundaries to liberal democratic membership. Inclusion in the realm of civic equality refers to the sharing of a space in which political equality is preserved by the equal recognition of freedoms and rights to political participation, as well as of those other rights (e.g. civil and social) and duties recognized as relevant for that purpose. Clearly the causes, but also the degrees and kinds of exclusion of non-national residents differ largely from case to case. Generally, non-citizens are not totally excluded from the sphere of civic equality, as defined here. They enjoy many of the rights that nationals do. In spite of this, full equality is everywhere reserved for national citizens only. Although some voices have started celebrating the consolidation of a new post-national order, nowhere has nationality completely lost its importance as a source of claims of rights.

The exclusion of non-national residents from the sphere of civic equality in spite of their permanent coexistence with nationals provokes concerns about the legitimacy of the public authority and the laws that shape their lives in an increasingly pervasive manner. It is these concerns that I will mainly address. That such an exclusion has not been given great attention in modern studies on political justice may have to do with the fact that many of these studies start out from the image of closed societies, an image which appears to be less and less adequate to confront realities of mobile societies and which only more recent work addressing the moral and political issues raised by immigration in modern democracies has started to question (Barbieri 1998; Kymlicka 1995; Schwartz 1995; Bauböck 1994a).

In Western Europe, a large proportion of the non-national residents today present were recruited as immigrants during the economic expansion of the late 1950s and '60s. They were initially perceived as guest-workers but instead have settled for good. Many of them have by now consolidated a somewhat satisfactory legal status with the recognition of almost the same civil and social rights that citizens have. They have access to the courts, and enjoy most social benefits and services as well as a legally protected and stable residential status (Hammar 1990a: 21).

However, access to some of the main avenues of political participation (e.g. voting rights in national elections or public office) is still generally closed to non-nationals (and sometimes to their descendants too) almost everywhere.[1] Also, no matter how well consolidated their residential status, non-nationals remain, to a greater or lesser extent, subject to deportation. The fact that access to national citizenship, either through naturalization or birthright, is made difficult in some countries, such as Germany, contributes to this 'democratic legitimacy gap' by allowing for the long-term coexistence of people with less than equal political rights. Although official labour recruitment and mobility outside the framework of the European Union has practically stopped in Western Europe, family reunification policies, the European economic and political integration process, and refugee influxes make it likely that the proportion of the population excluded from civic equality will remain a major issue for the foreseeable future.

If we shift our attention to North America, a traditional immigration region, we find that things look different. Although there have been some guestworker programmes to provide for unskilled agricultural labour (Bosniak 1994: 1076), as a general rule, labour migration there has not been understood as temporary in nature. From the moment they are admitted and given the status of immigrants, newcomers are usually set on the route to naturalization. Naturalization is generally granted on easy terms and as a matter of right. Moreover, access to nationality through birthright citizenship following the criterion of the place of birth (*ius soli*) as opposed to that of descent (*ius sanguinis*) has predominated in immigration countries, preventing the problem of the non-citizen second and third generations.

None the less, the fact that in some countries, like the United States, some groups of immigrants have proved less willing to naturalize as soon

---

[1] Exceptions to this rule include full voting rights for resident aliens in New Zealand and full voting rights for Irish and Commonwealth citizens in Britain.

as they have consolidated a fairly secure residential status and gained access to most of the social rights and benefits granted to citizens has also raised concern about non-citizen residents' exclusion from the sphere of civic equality. In the United States, until they naturalize, resident aliens do not achieve an equal political status, lacking the right to vote, the right to serve on federal and many state juries, and the right to run for certain high elected offices and to be appointed to some high appointed offices. Also, they are generally barred from federal employment and they have a lesser right to sponsor their family members for immigration. Last but not least, they remain vulnerable to deportation. Although it is commonly said that the deportation provisions are only few in number, in actuality there are more than one thousand different grounds upon which a foreigner could be removed from the United States. The reduction of state and federal social benefits not only to illegal immigrants but also to legal immigrants over the past few years in the USA also warns against celebrating too fast the loss of importance of national citizenship as a source of claims of rights (Schuck 1997).

Furthermore, mostly in North America, but increasingly in Europe as well, international labour migration is occurring through illegal paths. It seems that neither the official closing of borders in European countries to non-EU national labour, nor stricter immigration policies in the United States are likely to stop completely a labour migration which proves sensitive to economic factors. Clearly, illegal immigrants are also excluded from full membership in the democratic polity. This is not to say that they have no rights at all. Often they too enjoy some of the rights and guarantees that national citizens (or legal resident aliens) enjoy, such as the protection of the courts or public education. Still, in their case, it is not only the lack of political rights or of some of the social and civil rights generally granted to *legal* immigrants that excludes them from civic equality. Rather, their absolutely precarious residential and working status is the main reason why they are placed in a vulnerable and exploitable position and relegated to a socioeconomic sphere in which even the enjoyment of those rights and guarantees theoretically granted to them is often practically impossible.

All this results in an increase in politically vulnerable and disenfranchised communities of socially involved individuals who participate in the social and economic life of the communities in which they live in a myriad of ways. Permanent resident immigrants, both legal and illegal (the latter especially so if they are in great numbers and integrated in the economic forces of the host country), participate in the labour and housing markets and in the cultural life of the community. They pay taxes, bring up their families, send their children to state schools, and often plan to stay permanently in countries which they seem to have more or less consciously accepted as the centre of their existence. Occasionally, they represent a high proportion or even a majority of the population of the local communities in which they live. And yet they are excluded from the political realm. As a result, civil and political society becomes split. It is this reality that threatens the democratic stability and legitimacy of some Western countries (Layton-Henry 1991; Hammar 1985a).

However, as we shall see, not everyone agrees in identifying what we could call the dichotomy between socioeconomic and political member-ship as a democratic concern, at least in the strict sense. For some critics, inclusion in the realm of civic equality requires citizenship, and the definition of the citizenry is something prior to and not essentially con-nected to the polity's commitment to a liberal democratic order. Often, the denounced exclusions are covered by traditional assumptions about the sovereignty of nation-states. According to these, nation-states are assumed to be independent political entities in the international political system. Apart from minimum standards set by general principles of international law and by general norms of human rights (which do not generally refer to the most politically sensitive areas anyway), states are supposed to have full power to decide on matters within their territory. This includes the question of whether or not foreign citizens should be admitted or, if they have been admitted into the territory, allowed to stay, and granted a more or less comprehensive legal status. Therefore, in principle, every state is entitled to pursue an immigration policy which is founded on its own interests, and hence, free to rule on the paths through which any alien, including immigrant workers, can gain access to the different degrees of membership. Immigration, citizenship and natural-ization laws are thus generally referred to as expressions of such sovereign powers.[2] Part of the effort here will be dedicated to showing why this is not fully acceptable, and why it is increasingly important to link Western societies' commitment to liberal and democratic constitutional orders to the degree of inclusiveness of their citizenries. This seems to be especially relevant at a time in which the coexistence of national and non-national residents is becoming a more common reality, proving that some of the

---

[2] Typically, there are three hurdles at which immigrants (or potential immigrants) can be excluded from access to full membership within the state (Hammar 1990a: 12–18, 21): the first is the entry into the territory; the second is usually the acquisition of the legal status of permanent resident which allows the individual to enjoy residence and employment permits free of restrictions and to bring her family to live with her (Layton-Henry 1991: 113); and the last gate opens the path to citizenship through naturalization and hence, to the full enjoyment of rights and duties, including full political rights which are generally reserved for this stage.

assumptions of the traditional construction of the nation-state are increasingly outdated.

On the other extreme some critics would denounce the central concern of this book as already obsolete. Many have seen in the extension of most social and civil rights and even some political rights to resident aliens, which has been the general trend during recent decades, one of the most significant signs of the devaluation of national citizenship and of the progressive and overall decay of the nation-state construct. The reservation for citizens of voting rights in parliamentary elections is portrayed as the 'final bastion and expression of nationhood' (Layton-Henry 1990a: 16), which, more than anything else, retains a purely symbolic value (Jacobson 1996: 38; Soysal 1994: 131). The central role that the enjoyment of political rights and residential stability play in the traditional conception of democratic citizenship is thereby demeaned, and so is the need to guarantee these rights as a way of ensuring the non-reversibility of whatever other rights (e.g. social rights and benefits) may be recognized at any given moment in time. Also, those who speak about the complete devaluation of national citizenship often do not seem to take fully into account the increasingly important phenomenon of illegal immigration, and the legitimation concern that the related exclusions pose. The general precariousness that residential instability introduces into illegal immigrants' legal status is sometimes relegated to second place and the main focus is directed on to the fact that even illegal immigrants are now sometimes granted social benefits and basic human rights. This, they claim, confirms that nationality has already ceased to be a valid source of claims for the allocation of rights and duties in the modern world (Soysal 1994: 131–2).

Those who have instead regarded the splitting of the civil and the political societies as worrisome from a democratic point of view have suggested several paths to overcome it. One is to extend all of the rights citizens currently enjoy, including political rights, to resident aliens. Another is to encourage naturalization by liberalizing naturalization policies (Hammar 1990a). The possibility of granting resident aliens an automatic and unconditional second citizenship, which I will defend here, has generally been discarded. Still, the problem, in reality, is not so much one of choosing between competing alternatives, but rather one of growing aware of the situation and perceiving it as a democratic legitimacy concern. This is clear from the fact that those states which are not willing to encourage naturalization have been also most resistant to granting political rights to permanent resident aliens. Nevertheless, each of these paths raises interesting political issues that need to be discussed.

Also, thus far, the attention of the scholarly debate has largely concentrated on the exclusion and self-exclusion of legal permanent immigrants from the equal enjoyment of civil, social and political rights. Some references to illegal immigrants are occasionally made but, generally, only at the margins and without a deep exploration of the conceptual link binding the exclusions of legals and illegals. Yet setting the limits of what is democratically tolerable seems more important now than ever, as the general animosity towards those who stay in the country in contravention of the law increases and new measures against illegal labour migration are being taken, such as restricting illegal immigrants' access to social bene-fits and public services (Wihtol de Wenden 1990: 27). Some of these measures will presumably affect people who have been living in a country for years with their families and work there; people who have become a socially and economically active sector of the ordinary population. Should the societal integration of illegal immigrants be given any signifi-cant weight in pondering the legitimacy of the means to fight the phenom-enon?

In this context, this book is meant as a contribution along the lines of those who have defended the need to overcome the democratic legitimacy gap posed by the splitting of civil and political society as a result of international labour migration. I will argue that all those who live on a permanent basis in a liberal democratic state ought to be considered members of that democracy and thus share in the sphere of civic equality with the equal recognition of rights and duties. Moreover, I will claim that, to the extent that the enjoyment of a full and equal set of rights and duties within the political community of the state remains attached to the recognition of the formal status of national citizenship, after a certain residence period permanent resident aliens, both legal and illegal, ought to be automatically, and thus unconditionally, recognized as citizens of the state, regardless of whether or not they already enjoy the status of national citizens in some other community, and hence, whether or not that second citizenship makes of them dual or multiple nationals.

In an effort to interrelate the political, philosophical and legal debates concerning immigration and the incorporation of immigrants to the host societies, I will then contrast these normative claims with the constitu-tional practice and scholarly debates in two Western countries, Germany and the United States, both of which have significant immigrant popula-tions and are committed to constitutionally proclaimed liberal democ-racies. And the reader may ask: but why the *constitutional* debate? And why Germany and the USA?

It is generally accepted that a constitution is the part of the legal system that most clearly embodies the commitment of the polity to the founda-tional principles of power legitimation and so, in the cases I analyse, to a liberal democratic order. Unlike statutes, constitutions are not simply the expression of the country's ordinary and changing political options. So, for instance, in the field that occupies us here, immigration and citizenship laws embody the main ordinary mechanisms for a community to decide on the composition of its society and citizenry, but constitutions actually set constraints on the range of political options from which the ordinary legislator can pick. They do so for the sake of the community's commitment to more general and lasting legitimation principles. On the other hand, constitutions do not remain static whether they undergo express reforms or not. Constitutions have to be interpreted and the changing social realities to which they apply are always a renovation stimulus in the process of constitutional interpretation. Those who have the last word in constitutional interpretation, the constitutional courts, more or less consciously and overtly bring in political and moral considerations whenever they interpret the constitution in the light of the changing social and political circumstances so as to keep the polity's foundational commitment to a liberal democratic order updated.

This explains my interest in exploring how the constitutional courts and scholars in the USA and Germany have been reacting to the consolidation of a permanent sector of non-citizens among the ordinary population living under the state jurisdiction and whether, and to what extent, they have perceived this phenomenon as challenging, as I claim it does, some of the traditional assumptions about the democratic state order. Moreover, since not only would-be immigrants but also resident aliens have been traditionally excluded from the ordinary political process, the constitutional realm is especially appropriate for the analysis of the way in which foundational principles of power legitimation can set limits to the range of exclusions. Thus, the questions I have asked myself have been: What do constitutions have to say about the consolidation of a nonnational sector among the ordinary population of self-proclaimed liberal democratic states? Has this been seen as generating inconsistencies within the liberal democratic order which is constitutionally sanctioned? If so, how have the constitutional scholars suggested that we should compensate for such inconsistencies? What have the constitutional courts actually done? Have they forced the community to inclusion even against its own will as expressed in its immigration and naturalization policies? On what grounds?

Analysing the constitutional debate in Germany and the USA seemed therefore an ideal framework to study the basic adaptation of the legal order to the challenges of an increasing post-national order. In the discussion that follows, I will try to show that the norms and principles I defend have been recognized in American and German jurisprudence, albeit in a tentative and truncated form, and that, with some significant exceptions, the courts in both countries are increasingly moving towards the position on inclusion that I defend. Just as important for the reader will be the realization that where scholars and the courts have been most resistant to inclusion they have more or less consciously rested on certain political and philosophical assumptions that I question here. The arguments that I use when discussing these assumptions theoretically could thus be used in an attempt to move towards relevant constitutional interpretations in both Germany and the USA.

Overview

The book begins with an outline of the main normative claims. Chapter 2 constitutes the core of the positive argument in favour of the incorporation of immigrants into the political community. The argument involves two steps. First, I argue that any attempt to determine who should be included as citizens in a particular political community must include all those who are members of the society governed by that community. Second, I argue that long-term residents meet this test of 'social membership', even if they retain citizenship in another state. They are therefore entitled to full civil and political equality with native-born citizens.

Chapter 2 refers also to various mechanisms for achieving this goal. I begin by discussing the most common mechanisms which appear in the literature and suggest then a more novel approach which may at first sight strike many people as infeasible or indefensible. According to this approach, (a) permanent residents could be granted full inclusion 'as aliens' – that is, the right to vote and to permanent residence, as well as whatever other right may be in principle reserved for citizens only, could be granted to all long-term residents without granting them citizenship (which would then become a purely symbolic status which does not affect one's rights or duties); or (b) permanent residents could be 'automatically' granted citizenship – that is, citizenship could be ascribed to all residents after a certain number of years, even to those who would not choose to opt for naturalization under a voluntary naturalization approach. Both of these mechanisms will, in different ways, ensure the automatic incorporation of permanent residents.

Some of the objections that these suggestions may encounter are discussed in chapters 3 and 4. Chapter 3 will explore the fairness objection against granting resident aliens the whole set of benefits of political membership. This objection rests on a view of the state as a mutual benefit society which requires a fair balance between the distribution of benefits and burdens. Many critics argue that including permanent residents as citizens upsets this balance, particularly if these permanent residents retain citizenship in their country of origin as well. Because of their link to the country of their nationality these permanent residents might enjoy certain 'citizen-prerogatives' not available to native-born citizens or they might be able to avoid certain 'citizen-duties' which native-born citizens cannot avoid. For these and other reasons, the link between resident aliens and their country of nationality is seen as an obstacle to their inclusion. I dispute the empirical accuracy and norma- tive relevance of these claims, and argue that critics have vastly exag- gerated the extent to which permanent residents would be in a privileged position *vis-à-vis* native-born citizens if they are granted full inclusion. Indeed, at the end of the chapter I argue that, rather than setting obstacles to full inclusion, fairness considerations may actually undermine the legitimacy of the exclusion of immigrants, questioning the possibility of having separate economic and political schemes of cooperation peace- fully coexisting.

Chapter 4 instead explores the possibility that the degree of openness and inclusiveness which the claim to automatic incorporation implies might pose a threat to the absorptive capacity of liberal democracies, and thus damage liberal democratic institutions where they already have a foothold. This has to do with the fact that inclusion in my claim is achieved by nothing more than residence regardless of the conditions which are generally expressed in the laws on the access to the territory or on naturalization. Critics argue that preserving a certain degree of commonness and homogeneity to enable understanding, cohesion and solidarity is essential for the functioning of social and liberal democracies and recommend more selective inclusion. Yet here again, I dispute both the empirical accuracy of the assumptions on which this objection commonly rests, and the normative conclusions to which it is generally said to lead. I then turn the question around to explore the possibility that automatic inclusion would help solve, rather than aggravate, some of the tensions and strains that appear to threaten cohesion in increasingly heterogeneous countries with immigration.

Even those people who argue for the inclusion of legal immigrants show strong resistance to the incorporation of illegal immigrants who have entered the country without the polity's consent. Chapter 5 will deal specifically with the issue of illegal immigrants, and will discuss the additional problems that arise when applying the claim of automatic incorporation to this group. My main argument is that while legal immi- grants may indeed have valid grounds for expecting 'faster' incorpor- ation, both legal and illegal immigrants share certain morally relevant commonalities which give them a compelling case for eventual inclusion.

The modalities of inclusion are addressed in chapter 6. In fact I will concentrate here on the more novel idea of automatic membership according to which permanent resident aliens should be automatically and unconditionally granted the status of citizens in the country of residence. This may appear to be an illiberal and freedom-restricting approach, especially when contrasted with the much more widely supported alternative of optional naturalization. However, I will defend this approach, exploring the conditions for its valid application, and discussing some specific objections that can be raised for the sake of either immigrants' or the general society's interests.

The discussion on the constitutional implementation of the normative claims comes next. Chapters 7 and 8 describe the debate on the constitutional status of resident aliens in the USA and Germany. Briefly, the question to be answered in both chapters is whether and to what extent sharing residence in the common geopolitical space of the state has implied equal constitutional protection for aliens and citizens, either directly (through the access of aliens to an equal status of rights regardless of nationality) or indirectly (through their access to national citizenship). The possible answers are that the constitution in each of these countries: (a) mandates equality for resident aliens (in the way that I have defended from a normative point of view); (b) allows equality for resident aliens; or (c) forbids equality. I will respond to this question by exploring court cases regarding the constitutional status of resident aliens (both legal and illegal), and their access to citizenship. I will try to show that while both the German and the US constitutions deny equality to resident aliens, there has been an increasing questioning of alienage as self-explanatory grounds for distinguishing between the constitutional status of citizens and aliens, as well as an increasing recognition of the importance of residence and societal integration in determining such a status.

The case-studies: United States and Germany

In selecting the empirical cases to describe the constitutional implementation of the normative arguments, my basic aim when I started this project was to pick out countries with sufficient and relevant commonalities but also with significant and telling differences. Apart from having a contrasting point of reference for each of the countries analysed, I hoped that this would bring to the surface the whole set of complexities and difficulties of the issue. Yet at the same time, if, in spite of the initial differences, I could identify analogies in the legal responses of both countries to the concern regarding the incorporation of immigrants, these analogies would probably support the validity of the conceptualization of the relevant problems in the theoretical chapters.

Germany and the United States seemed therefore good candidates. Among the essential commonalities is the fact that they are two of the Western countries with the largest immigrant populations and that both are thoroughly committed to a liberal democratic order sanctioned in their constitutions. Both of them offer relevant constitutional case law and doctrinal discussions, generally within the framework of political debates on related matters. All of this is clearly useful to determine to what extent, and through which legal instruments, the USA and Germany have read the long-term exclusion of resident aliens from the realm of civic equality as threatening the country's commitment to liberal democracy.

The relevant differences have to do with Germany's and the United States' specific immigration traditions and different conceptions of nationhood or citizenship. These deserve a few words here to set the constitutional discussion in its proper historical and cultural context. As regards Germany, the country's major experience with immigration started only with postwar labour recruitment. Recruited as guestworkers from 1945 to the mid-1970s from countries such as Italy, Greece, Turkey, Morocco, Portugal, Tunisia and Yugoslavia, these immigrants were initially seen as temporary workers who would eventually return to their home countries.

Immigration debates started to become most relevant when, following the oil crisis of the mid-seventies, Germany officially signalled the end of its labour recruitment policy which had lasted for over two decades. However, both political and moral constraints kept the political elite from forcing immigrants back to their home countries. As it became clear that the schemes introduced for voluntary repatriation were not successful, gradually, and not without hesitation and inconsistency, Germany officially came to accept first the need to allow for, and only later, also to encourage immigrants' social integration. Family reunification was essential to this process of settlement.

Although during the postwar period it became one of the largest immigrant-receiving countries in the world, Germany has never regarded itself as an 'immigration country' and still does not. Thus, the guestworker immigration experience has always been described as a historical episode that was not to be repeated. And this may help to explain why there has never been an official and comprehensive immigration policy in Germany. The legal regime of aliens has reflected this conception of immigrants as 'temporary guests'. During the first years of guestworker immigration, old Nazi regulations established the legal framework for handling the presence of foreign workers in Germany, and only in 1965 was this regulation replaced by the Aliens Act (*Ausländergesetz*). However, even this statute lacked distinct residence permits and provisions for anything more than temporary stays on German territory (Joppke 1999a: 66). Until 1978 there was no residence status similar to USA legal permanent resident status. After 1978 the permanent residence status was created but only by administrative regulation. Also, the 1965 Aliens Act did not contemplate rules for family reunification. Detailed rules for reunifying foreign families were not instituted until 1981.

This explains why so many celebrated the 1990 Aliens Act (*Gesetz zur Neuregelung des Ausländerrechts*)[3] which covers in a systematic way all the aspects that had thus far been regulated through a variety of *ad hoc* administrative rules and policies which did not add up to a coherent whole. The new Aliens Act, which went into effect in January 1991, was supposed to replace executive discretion with respect to individual rights mainly by putting into the form of law the already existing administrative rules and legal constraints, many of which had been upheld by activist courts (Joppke 1999a: 84). It did not, however, entail a fundamental change in Germany's concept of its foreigner policy and still conceives the recruitment of guestworkers as a historical event, seeking to prevent the permanent immigration of non-EU nationals in the future (Franz 1990: 8).

The split between political and civil society generated by immigration was accentuated by the fact that the legal mechanisms of civic incorporation in Germany have traditionally been quite restrictively defined. The 1913 Nationality Act (*Reichs- und Staatsangehörigkeitsgesetz*), which is still in force, allows for the acquisition of German citizenship at birth using the criterion of descent only. This rejection of the criterion of the place of birth has allowed for the emergence of second and third generations which do not have German citizenship and are still commonly described as 'immigrants'. Also, under the 1965 Aliens Act, naturalization in Germany has traditionally been conceived as a discretionary act of the state in which process only public interest was taken into account and residence permits were granted rather discretionally and required periodical renewal for a long time before resident aliens could consolidate a secure residential status. Although, as reformed in 1990, the Aliens Act has amended this and provides now also for a naturalization which has lost part of its discretionary nature, the reform has not been sufficient to achieve the expected increase in naturalization rates.[4] This explains why

---

[3] BGBl. I 1354.
[4] Germany has traditionally had one of the lowest naturalization rates among European countries. Hammar gives an annual naturalization rate of 0.3 per cent for 1987 (Hammar 1990a: 77). According to a report by the Federal Government's Commissioner for

the possibility of facilitating naturalization even further and including some *ius soli* elements in the definition of ascriptive citizenship as a way to facilitate the integration of aliens has been on the political agenda over the past decade. Since the appointment of the new Social Democrat government in November 1998 the issue has again become most salient.

The resistance to accepting the immigration phenomenon as something more than a simple hazard of a concrete moment of Germany's economic development is often connected to a conception of nationhood which has been said to prevail in Germany. According to this, German nationalism (which preceded the political organization of the German nation-state, and thus was not initially identified with any specific state or with the idea of citizenship) is rooted in the concept of the people as an organic ethno-cultural entity marked by a common language. The state, then, is the political representation of the *Volk* (the people) or the nation (Jacobson 1996: 22–4; Brubaker 1992: 1–6). Also, as in all European nations, large-scale immigration came after the nation-building experience in Germany, so that immigration has not become part of Germany's national self-definition (Joppke 1999a). And yet, immigrants' proportionately higher birthrates, Germany's persistently restrictive regulation on access to citizenship, the still significant immigration flow (especially through asylum policy and family reunification), and, more recently, the increasing rates of illegal immigration are (together with the European integration process) important reasons to believe that the phenomenon of a non-national population has become a permanent German reality.

This ethno-cultural concept of nationhood was probably reinforced by the outcome of World War II (Joppke 1999a: 63). Thus, in contrast with its attitude of not welcoming immigrants, after the war the Federal Republic defined itself as an incomplete nation-state and committed itself to both rebuilding the broken national unity and to hosting all Germans in the communist diaspora (ibid.). Telling in this regard is the fact that the Federal Republic always saw East Germans as sharing a common German citizenship with West Germans; that it committed itself constitutionally to the reunification of Germany; and that it has viewed as Germans, and not as 'immigrants', the many millions of ethnic Germans who have migrated to West Germany from Poland, the Soviet Union, Romania and other formerly German-occupied areas since World War II. This has all found constitutional coverture. Apart from providing for the reacquisition of German citizenship by former Germans and their

Foreigners' Affairs on the Situation of Foreigners in the Federal Republic of Germany in 1993, we find that the percentage has increased to 0.5 per cent in 1991 (cf. Neuman 1994: 237, 274, ns. 118 and 119). Notice however that naturalization rates in Germany have started to increase significantly over the past few years (Joppke 1999a: 205).

descendants who had been deprived of it during the Nazi regime due to political, racial or religious reasons, when defining who are 'Germans' within the meaning of the constitution, it makes a distinction between German nationals or citizens (*Staatsangehörige*) on the one hand, and people of German stock (*Volkszugehörige*), also known as 'Status-Germans', on the other. Apart from those who possess German nationality (which used to include both East and West Germans), the constitution (German Basic Law) of 1949 recognizes as German those who 'have been admitted to the territory of the German *Reich* within the frontiers of 31 December 1937 as a refugee or expellee of German stock or as a spouse or descendant thereof'.[5]

In principle, one could expect the significance of this constitutional provision to be rather limited. Included among the transitional clauses of the Basic Law, it was intended to give a provisional solution to the problem of a postwar German state hosting, among its population, a large number of persons of German ancestry with some Eastern European nationality, who had been expelled from their countries or had fled as a result of measures of retaliation or dispossession directed against them as people of German stock. In actuality, the implemented legislation has served to facilitate the incorporation of ethnic Germans and their descendants into the body politic. However, since 1990 Germany has passed legislation (*Aussiedleraufnahmegesetz* in 1990 and *Kriegsfolgenbereinigungsgesetz* in 1992) which conceives of this kind of immigration as a late consequence of World War II, restricts the numbers of ethnic Germans who can resettle in Germany by quotas, limits ethnic Germans' rights (including their access to German citizenship) and, more importantly, sets an end to future ethnic German immigration: after 2010 ethnic Germans born later than December 1992 will no longer be entitled to ask independently for admission to Germany (Münz and Ulrich 1997: 71–2). Not surprisingly, some have seen this phasing out of the privileged category of ethnic Germans as an opportunity for Germany to transform its ethnic-priority into a general immigration policy (Joppke 1999a: 96). However, in general, it seems that the constitutional reflection of Germany's incomplete nation-stateness and the problem of the ethnic German diaspora in the East have allowed the perpetuation of the ethnocultural tradition, which was nominally delegitimized by Nazism and World War II.

In contrast to this is the US experience where immigration has traditionally been welcomed and perceived as integral to the formation of the country. The notion of American citizenship also came from a different

---

[5] See Art 116.1 of the German Basic Law.

setting. The American Revolution, it has often been claimed, sought to fashion a nation legitimated through the aggregate of the individual citizens' consent rather than the passive and imputed allegiance of subjects to the Crown. There was a basic coincidence of the political and the national revolution: the political identity (broadly expressed in the Constitution) was central to the American identity. Identity was not so much a function of one's bloodline (with the significant exceptions of black and native Americans) as a function of ideas, of ideology. An alien was one who rejected the premises underlying American nationhood (Jacobson 1996).

This concept of citizenship has made the line between citizens and aliens more permeable in the USA. Entry into the country has historically been relatively easy. And with some significant exceptions, naturalization was easily available to all whites who fulfilled the residency requirement and took an oath of loyalty. Also, from the beginning, aliens admitted as immigrants knew they had been granted the status of permanent residents. The underlying belief was that almost anybody could be assimilated into American society and that the USA was essentially a nation of immigrants. However, as Joppke points out, 'next to the liberal tradition of a nation defined by an abstract political creed and immigration, there has also been an illiberal tradition of alleged "Americanism" which has hypostatized an ethnic core of protestant Anglo-Saxonism which had to be protected from external dilution' (1999a: 23).

Prior to the late nineteenth century, immigration into the United States was unregulated. After that, various laws were passed excluding certain categories of immigrants (lunatics, idiots, anarchists, Chinese) and starting from 1921 a system of ethnically discriminatory quotas was used which favoured Northern European immigrants for the sake of racial homogeneity and Anglo-Saxon superiority. The system was only fully repealed in 1965, through an Immigration Reform statute which put an end to the national-origins system, opening for the first time the door to large-scale immigration from Asia and Latin America.

In 1952 the Immigration and Nationality Act, known as the McCarran–Walter Act (still in force though with a great deal of modification), revised, codified, and repealed nearly all existing immigration law. Enacted at the height of the cold war, it contained ideological and security provisions mainly to protect the USA from communism. These ideological concerns weakened in 1980, as the Refugee Act of that year shows, and became marginal in the Immigration Act of 1990. This latter Act reaffirms the principles of the 1965 Immigration Act which, for the first time, made the holding of professional and high skills and family ties with the country of central importance in immigration matters.

It has been noticed that, in contrast to European restrictionism after the first oil crisis, USA immigration policies have remained quite liberal and expansive (Joppke 1999a: 29). Indeed, in 1965 the USA embarked on a course of liberalization which resulted in the greatest increase in mass immigration since the beginning of the twentieth century (ibid.: 54). At the same time, the country's immigration slots have been insufficient to cope with immigration pressure and American public opinion has turned increasingly restrictionist in recent years. From the mid-1970s onwards the problem of illegal immigration became important.

Since the turn of the twentieth century Mexicans have migrated north to the United States to work on railroads and in agriculture, and restrictions were practically unenforced until the time of the Depression. The diversion of labour to the World War II effort created an urgent need for labour and in 1942 brought about the Bracero arrangement for the recruitment of Mexicans as temporary agricultural workers which was to last for twenty-two years. This programme allowed other Mexicans to learn about work opportunities in the United States and hence gave a strong impetus to illegal immigration, especially after it was suspended in 1964. Although already in the mid-eighties there was the pervasive sense that the United States had lost 'control of its border', the first measures to fight seriously against it came in 1986 when Congress passed the Immigration Reform and Control Act (IRCA).

The early but limited success of IRCA was followed by reports of an upswing in illegal migration and by mid-1992 it had become evident that IRCA was not deterring undocumented aliens. In the end, it legalized the status of about three million undocumented immigrants while failing to stop the inflow of new illegal immigrants. Together with the geographical conditions of the country and the institutional limitations of the American government, the existence of lobbying groups, particularly civil rights groups, ethnic and business interest groups, is essential in an explanation of why the effectiveness of attempts to legislate and implement laws has been so low (Jacobson 1996: 43, 69).

As we will see, the control of illegal immigration has been central to the new anti-immigration movement which has spread eastward from California, expressing the frustration of those states which are most severely affected by illegal immigration and putting pressure on the Federal Government to assume responsibility in the matter. The recent adoption of legal measures to increase the control of illegal immigration and set limits to legal and illegal immigrants' access to social benefits has to be seen as an expression of this new restrictionist spirit, much of which has been spurred by illegal immigration (Joppke 1999a: 55).

Some preliminary remarks

It is important to observe that the book does not purport to indicate the global attitude that Western liberal democracies should have towards current immigration pressure from neighbouring and less well-off countries. Although I concentrate almost entirely on domestic inclusion, in a world in which economic resources and political stability are unequally distributed, one can hardly defend the claim that the commitment to egalitarian liberalism allows states to face only their moral obligations to those who are already within their jurisdiction. Rather, the delimitation of the subject rests on the two following assumptions. The first assumption is that the case of permanent resident aliens presents both legal and moral specificities which justify its specific treatment here. The second and more important assumption is that, in spite of appearances, no obvious correlation exists between domestic and external 'inclusive attitudes'. In other words, there is no concrete evidence that the inclusion of settled immigrants necessarily has to be at the expense of a more rigid attitude to protecting the state against the outside world.

Also, my discussion will not refer to all of the forms in which economic migration currently takes place. Economic migration is increasingly adopting new and more mobile forms, and settlers, which are my main concern here, are only one type of migrant. Together with them, one can find not only 'sojourners' – migrants who return to their country of origin after a relatively short period of time – but also daily commuters who legally or illegally cross the border on an almost daily basis to work, and people who go back and forth for shorter or longer periods of time every year and, thus, can hardly be said to have any single country as the centre of their economic and personal development.

Admittedly, these forms of migration present specific problems and pose some interesting challenges to some of the assumptions which have been commonly made on economic migration thus far. Yet these new modalities, which an interrelated and well-connected world has prompted, have come as an addition to, and not to replace the settlement model. And it is likely that this will continue to be so in the future. Leaving aside a cosmopolitan elite, I believe that people are generally inclined to set down roots in specific residential habitats (in which they make long-term investments) and to rely on specific institutional, social and cultural frameworks to lead a meaningful existence.

It is important to stress that this study does not contemplate either, more than collaterally, the moral and/or legal specificities of some qualified groups of resident aliens, such as political refugees or aliens enjoying a special status which derives from some supra-national process of regional integration. This distinction is most relevant for the German case, as political refugees have traditionally enjoyed a special constitutional status under the German Constitution. Also, a significant proportion of Germany's non-national population is formed by citizens of other Member States of the European Union who enjoy a privileged status of rights and freedoms. Nevertheless, most of the issues that will be raised here can also be of general interest for these groups of aliens. Whatever their more specific constitutional and legal status, political refugees and EU Member States' nationals can also share in the condition of being a permanently settled alien population with their economic and social existence rooted in the country of residence and yet excluded from the realm of civic equality.

I should also warn the reader that the book does not present a theory of constitutional interpretation which specifies what should be the importance of political philosophy for constitutional adjudication. There is a long tradition of authors, to which I subscribe, contending that political philosophy does play a role in constitutional interpretation whether constitutional scholars or courts are willing to accept it or not. Moral and political reasoning should therefore help us, from a normative point of view, in our attempt to read constitutions in their best light.[6] But here this thesis is not specifically addressed. The normative discussion takes place first and the case-studies that follow describe the actual constitutional experiences of the USA and Germany. The description tests whether there has been progress in the advanced position on inclusion and whether or not inclusion has proceeded on the moral and political grounds that I defend or on competing grounds. To the extent that inclusion has not been constitutionally sanctioned it also identifies and conceptualizes from a theoretical point of view the remaining obstacles. Those who believe in the relevance of political philosophy in constitutional interpretation will therefore find material here to strengthen and exemplify their thesis. Those who share the conviction that our liberal democracies need to become more inclusive will find here arguments as to how constitutions can be interpreted in their best light so as to respond to the new democratic challenge posed by the ordinary and permanent coexistence of citizens and non-citizens.

The main characters of the book, people who are settled in countries without being citizens or nationals there, will be called many different

---

[6] See, for example, Dworkin 1986; Alexy 1989; Habermas 1992; Rawls 1993; Nino 1993; Dyzenhaus 1993.

names.[7] These include 'legal and illegal immigrants and aliens', 'resident immigrants', 'permanent resident aliens', 'undocumented aliens', 'resident aliens' and 'non-citizen and non-national residents'. This results partly from adopting the different terminologies in common use in the disciplines of social and political science and law. It also has to do with the different perceptions of the people I am concerned with in Germany (where they are more commonly referred to as aliens or foreigners) and in the USA (where they are generally referred to as immigrants). Finally, it derives from an attempt to avoid the link between these people and any of the predefined set of features and/or purposes which the use of any of the above mentioned labels commonly triggers.[8]

[7] The terms 'citizenship' and 'nationality' I will use interchangeably, meaning the legal relationship recognizing the membership of individuals to different states of the international community, although I am aware that, for that purpose, the former is more commonly used in the USA and the latter in Europe. Admittedly, the term nationality in the German context is often used to express more than the simple holding of a German passport. Thus, as we know, many read into it the membership of a national community with a distinctive character shaped by linguistic, cultural, historical or even ethnic commonalities. I will use more specific terms or expressions to refer to this more substantive meaning of nationality.

[8] I am aware of the pejorative resonance of some of the terms referred to here. Thus, as Raskin rightly notes, the word 'alien' has pejorative if not extraterrestrial connotations. At the same time, as he points out, the term possesses a legal significance which makes it difficult to replace (Raskin 1993: 1393 n. 11). Much more pejorative may be the use of the term 'illegal alien' since it tends to convey the idea of aliens as outlaws and to criminalize their personalities. Often, it is not even clear what the term legally means, there being many ways and many reasons for which an alien can be in a country without a clearly defined legal status. Here, I will use it to refer to all those who are in a country in contravention of its immigration laws. I hope that using the terms 'alien' and 'illegal alien', while arguing for the right to equality of the affected individuals, might help to advance the questioning of the stereotypes to which such terms are often attached.

2 A democratic challenge

The gradual development of the principle of equality is therefore a providential fact. It has all the chief characteristics of such a fact: it is universal, it is lasting, it constantly eludes all human interference, and all events as well as all men contribute to its progress.

A. de Tocqueville (1963: 6)

The claim that I would like to advance and explore is that states claiming to be committed to liberal democracy ought to regard as full members of their organized political community, all those who reside in their territory on a permanent basis, being subject to the decisions collectively adopted there and being dependent on its protection and recognition for the full development of their personalities. Full inclusion in this sense implies their incorporation into the realm of civic equality that unites the citizenry in an equal status of rights and duties, including also a right to be allocated a share in the common public space (the right to remain indefinitely in the territory) and a right to political action (political rights and freedoms). These are rights from which permanent resident aliens have been, at least to some extent, generally excluded.

Moreover, to the extent that being a national citizen is required as a condition for inclusion in the realm of civic equality the claim is that, after a certain residence period, permanent residents ought to be automatically and unconditionally recognized as citizens of the state. This might well imply a restriction of the state's power to define itself as a nation by freely deciding about its members. But this, I will argue, is one of the restrictions that a commitment to liberal democracy requires in the light of both increasing human and labour mobility and the prevalence of territorially organized power structures. It is a restriction that the commitment to democratic citizenship sets on the very definition of national citizenship.

From a strictly normative stand we could thus talk about a main claim and a secondary claim. Although the relationship between the two will be discussed at length in chapter 6, basically the main claim tells us to open the path to the enjoyment of equal rights and duties. This path will be identified as the *path of full inclusion*. Only if a sufficiently compelling case is made to prove that such an enjoyment can be best ensured for all by binding it to the recognition of the status of national membership does the secondary claim come into play. The secondary claim tells us that if this is so, then such a status ought to be granted automatically to all those who are in the position to expect, according to the first claim, full equality in the enjoyment of rights. This secondary claim will be identified as the *path of automatic membership*. Since both these mechanisms will, in different ways, ensure the automatic incorporation of permanent residents, I will refer to both of these as forms of *automatic incorporation*.

Social membership as a path to inclusion

The claim to automatic incorporation relies, first of all, on the relevance of social membership for defining the bounds of the relevant democratic polity. Its main normative thrust was already captured by those who, like Carens, argued that 'people have a moral right to be citizens of any society of which they are members. States that prevent members of their societies from becoming citizens act wrongly' (Carens 1989: 32; Walzer 1983: 60). The basic idea is that membership is first, and above all, a social fact, determined by social factors such as living, working or raising a family and participating in the social and cultural life of a community. The moral relevance of this social fact and what it implies (dependency on society for the protection of rights and the development of a meaningful life project, as well as subjection to the decisions collectively taken in it) is the fundamental basis for the claim to full inclusion.

This takes us to the notion of social membership. There seems to be no neutral way of defining social membership, for even though facts might be more or less undisputed, 'social membership', after all, is a concept that needs to be constructed. 'The purpose guiding the search for its definition will probably determine the result' (Bauböck 1994a: 210). In this case, our concern is with the kind of social membership that ought to be considered politically relevant in a liberal democracy, or, in other words, which defines the group of people who can claim a right to inclusion in a liberal democratic polity.

As relevant notions I have included long-term subjection to the collectively binding decisions adopted in a polity and dependency on a given societal framework associated with permanent residence. I will elaborate on their moral foundations later. First we need to define both what is meant by residence and what is meant by permanent. Starting with residence the distinction between domicile and residence made by the Committee of Ministers of the Council of Europe in 1972 seems useful.[1]

---

[1] Taken from Hammar 1990a: 193–4.

Whereas the notion of domicile 'imports a legal relationship between a person and a country governed by a particular system of law', '[t]he residence of a person is determined solely by factual criteria; it does not depend upon the legal entitlement to reside'. The relevant factors in defining residence are habitual residence (actually dwelling in a place for a certain period of time whether one was born in it or not) and other indications of ties between the person and the place of her residence, such as the work and professional or school environment, the possession of property, the contribution to and reliance on social services, engagement in associations, trade unions and in the cultural life, family and other types of affective ties (Bauböck 1994a: 216; Hammar 1990a: 194–5).

It follows that in the case of immigrants, their qualification as societal members does not correspond to any legally defined immigration status, but rather refers to the actual reality of people who migrate and come to live and work in a place in which they naturally develop a set of attachments and which, after a long residence period, they are likely to make the centre of their existence in practical terms. This is why both legal and illegal immigrants are included in my claim. This explains also why the different terms used here (e.g. 'permanent resident alien workers', 'resident aliens', 'immigrants') do not refer to any of the specific and legally defined categories by which states generally describe the group of aliens who are to enjoy an indefinite right to residence and work in the country, but rather to a social fact whose accuracy and moral relevance can be disputed.

However, by making the distinction between legal domicile and factual residence, the problem of definition is not solved. In fact such a problem seems unavoidable, since between the category of permanent residents, which is our main concern, and that of short-term sojourners there might be a whole range of medium-term residents whose attachments and interests remain centred in their country of origin, while they are in the process of creating a new set of attachments and interests. Probably only one thing is clear: the urgency of the case for full inclusion varies directly with the strength of social ties and thus, normally, with the length of residence. This rule may be already significant in judging the exclusionary practices of some countries. One could say as a general criterion that, whatever the necessary exclusions, it is better that they are imposed before rather than after entry: 'whatever right the state might have to limit non-citizens' stays or full political inclusion must be exercised sooner rather than later so that failure to exercise it within a reasonable period leads to its expiration' (Brubaker 1989a: 19. Also Hammar 1994: 196–7; Carens 1989: 42).

Nevertheless, it might be useful to offer an approximate time limit to help us in setting the presumption that social membership exists and that a right to be recognized as a full member should therefore follow. I suggest that the criteria to orient us in translating into time the moral constraints on the state power to exclude could be given by taking the residence period that Western states have required to accord the legal status of 'permanent resident aliens' to even those people who were initially recruited as temporary guestworkers, and adding to it the time of residence that has generally been required by those states with large-scale clandestine immigration in order to qualify for their amnesty programmes. This would bring us close to ten years.[2] Such a time might be an indicator of when Western societies have felt compelled to recognize unambiguously as full members both those who were initially admitted but only as a temporary labour force, and those who gained access to social membership without the express permission of the polity.

Admittedly, there may be practical difficulties in registering individual periods of residence. But these should not be overestimated. Amnesty programmes for undocumented aliens are a common practice. They generally provide for the regularization only of those who gained access to the territory of the state before a certain date and have been living there on a regular basis ever since. Continued residence over ten or more years should therefore not be too difficult to prove, not even for undocumented aliens (Hammar 1994: 194).

Regular amnesties have taken place in countries with large populations of illegal immigrant workers and no large-scale deportation of immigrants has taken place even in those European countries which have never admitted to being immigration countries and which recruited immigrants as guestworkers. Granted, there is a whole range of practical inconveniences associated with the sending back of socially and economically integrated people which may explain why those countries choose to grant amnesties. However, these actions could also prove that, at least to some extent, Western liberal democracies have already given signs of tacitly accepting certain moral constraints in this direction (Layton-Henry

---

[2] The duration required for permanent residency in the European countries which have been the main focus of immigration ranges from two to ten years (Soysal 1994: 121, 126). Two years seems to be the exception. Most countries require a minimum of four or five years. Thus, we could take five or six as a reasonable compromise and to that we would need to add the time generally required for the regularization of illegal residence. In the United States, the latest amnesty programme for the legalization of illegal immigrants was adopted in 1986 in the Immigration Reform and Control Act and it allowed for the naturalization of all those who had illegally entered the country before 1982, hence of all those who had been residing in the country for at least four years (Weissbrodt 1992: 22).

Note that since most European receiving countries stopped recruiting new workers in the early 1970s, most of the legally resident adult aliens in these countries have been present by now for ten years or more (Carens 1989: 42).

1990c: 190; Wihtol de Wenden 1990: 31, 45; Carens 1989: 44).[3] And once the first step is overcome and resident aliens are accepted as permanent residents full inclusion seems almost inevitable. Allowing for the long-term consolidation of a second-class citizenship is probably something liberal democratic states will find much more difficult to justify (Wihtol de Wenden 1990: 45).[4]

The time limit set above may initially seem excessively long, but the function it is supposed to serve has to be clear. By no means does it imply that countries may not have the legal (or moral) obligation to grant both legal and illegal aliens access to some rights even much sooner than that. So, for instance, legal resident aliens might use consent-based arguments (such as the fact that they have been expressly accepted as permanent residents) to claim a right to naturalize after five years, and illegal resident aliens could use other kinds of arguments to claim a right to regularize their status after only five years, even if their access to the full rights of citizenship has to wait for an additional five years to compensate for the fact that they broke the rules on admission. What the claim rather does is set a democratically founded threshold that obliges the state to recognize those who belong to the community socially, as full members of the polity

[3] Referring to the German experience Hammar recalls that in the 1980s generous compensation schemes were offered to Turkish people who volunteered to return for good, so it was clear that Germany was very interested in their departure. However, even in that context, mass deportation was not considered (Hammar 1994: 18). On the other hand, in the United States' past, one finds the forced repatriation and mass deportation of illegal, and even legal, immigrants of Mexican descent (López 1981: 632–3, 637). However, most commentators agree that today such measures would be clearly considered illegitimate as well as politically inadvisable (Jacobson 1996: 43, 63).

[4] Other related proposals have suggested longer and shorter periods. Hammar has proposed a gradual system of incorporation, whereby the regularization of an alien's illegal entry, her transition from temporary legal resident to permanent legal resident (which he calls 'denizisation') and finally, her access to citizenship through naturalization would follow as gradual steps to be accomplished within certain time limits. He suggests from ten to fifteen years of residence as the time limit for 'denizisation' and from fifteen to twenty for naturalization (Hammar 1994: 190). Here I am concerned with setting a time limit to exclusion from full membership (either through access to the formal status of citizenship or through direct access to civic equality) of all members of society, regardless of their immigration status. Hence, in a way, I am concerned with Hammar's last step. But I consider the fifteen or twenty years Hammar proposes for the regularization of the illegal status to be far too long, not to mention the fact that the transition from the phase of regularization to that of full equality would require even more time under his proposal of gradual inclusion.

Referring to the right to inclusion which, in his opinion, can be expressed by granting aliens the right to naturalize, Carens has proposed the time period of five years (Carens 1989: 31, 42). This coincides with the time of legal residence many states require for regular naturalization. Since the claim that is advanced here is not a claim to naturalization, generally framed in conditional terms, but to automatic and unconditional incorporation, and given that it encompasses both those who have come with the consent of the receiving society and also those who lack at least a formal expression of such a consent, I think that the time period should be longer than five years, and closer to the ten years suggested here.

(or demos) and hence, as entitled to whatever rights and freedoms are granted generally, regardless of whether or not they have been expressly accepted. And this without subjecting them to any further condition expressed in naturalization requirements (or in any other way), other than the conditions (e.g. duties) that ordinary citizens are required to comply with as well. It thus expresses a threshold after which the law cannot legitimately make distinctions in recognizing rights using the criterion of national citizenship. Since inclusion is detached from formal acceptance, legal and illegal resident aliens are in principle equally included. Again, this does not mean that the consent of the community should not be given any moral relevance. It can still be the source of other moral claims which ought to be reflected in the country's immigration and citizenship policy. After all, what we are exploring here is only one of the possible limitations that the commitment to a liberal democratic order imposes on the state power of self-determination concerning membership and the distribution of citizen rights.

Defining the bounds of the political community as a liberal democratic concern

The demand for full inclusion of permanent resident aliens challenges the common assumption that those holding the legal status of national citizens at any particular moment are the only ones who deserve to be regarded as full members of the polity. If national citizenship is not a self-sufficient notion to settle limits of the democratically relevant polity, what are the alternatives? How can we define, from a liberal perspective, the democratically relevant polity? In answering this question I want to argue first of all that the inclusiveness of a community affects its claim to being a liberal democracy, since the question of what constitutes a demos and who must be included in a properly constituted demos is essential to a democratic system. The commitment to liberal democracy already requires a certain degree of inclusiveness, and sets limits not only on the political procedure but also on the range of exclusions that the polity can legitimately make.

Democratic ideas have often yielded a rather ambiguous answer to the question of inclusiveness. Democracy promises rule by 'the people', but the theory of democracy is generally not taken to imply any specific set of arrangements for political membership (Raskin 1993: 1391). In this respect, Schumpeter seems to be an exception. He maintained that 'we must leave it to every *populus* to define itself', arguing that 'what had been thought and legally held to constitute a "people" has varied enormously among "democratic" countries' (Schumpeter, 1976). In fact it is quite a widespread opinion that democracy simply presupposes that the membership of a political community has already been determined. Who can belong to the community is not, in itself, a question of democracy (Hailbronner 1989: 76; Whelan 1988: 30–1). On this view, the democratic state is the dutiful child of the pre-existing demos. Literally, '[d]emocracy does not create its people, rather a people decides to give itself a democratic form of government' (Quaritsch 1983: 9).

This perspective assumes that the definition of the criteria for belonging to the community can only be decided after the creation of the community. There is no political commitment that foundationally compels a certain degree of inclusiveness. The differences in the degrees and modes of inclusion in the different countries depend only on their understanding of their own interests and result from their sovereign exercise of self-determination and self-definition through the ordinary political process.

Dahl shows us the absurdities to which the absence of any criterion for defining the demos of a democracy may lead (Dahl 1989: 121–2). To do so, he defines two different kinds of propositions:

system X is democratic with respect to its own demos;
system Y is democratic in relation to everyone who is subject to its rules.

In principle, Schumpeter's conception of democracy would follow the first proposition. However, Dahl points out the unacceptable consequences of this proposition. If a people is free to define itself, and democracy only compels the self-defined people to establish democratic rules of government to be applied among themselves, then democracy is conceptually, morally and empirically indistinguishable from other forms of government (ibid.: 122); for, apart from the internal democratic rules of government among the 'people', is there not also 'some number or proportion of a population below which a people is not a demos but rather an aristocracy, oligarchy, or despotism?' (ibid.: 121).

In his book *Transnational Citizenship*, Bauböck has directly confronted the issue of the degree of necessary inclusiveness of a democratic polity. He rightly points out that it all depends on what we understand by 'democracy'. If we take what he calls a 'minimalist notion of democracy', as referring to a procedure of aggregating individual preferences to make collectively binding decisions (Bauböck 1994a: 179), there is no way to solve democratically the issue of membership. If, following Dahl's second proposition, we allow those who are subject to the rules to take part in their elaboration, that means that they will have already been included so that there is no further point in deciding that question through democratic procedures. If we simply follow the first proposition there does not seem to be any principled way of determining who ought to be included in the demos, since that is something that will simply depend on whatever the outcome in the political process is. Who gains access as a member (or who is excluded from membership) will depend only on the result of what the recognized majority at any given moment decides. So we find that, unless we are ready to accept that an oligarchic, aristocratic or even a totalitarian system can be democratic as long as it has been grounded in majoritarian procedures for decision making, we will have to agree with Bauböck that settling the question of membership must to some extent precede any democratic deliberation (Bauböck 1994a: 179). This is why the qualification of democracy as liberal democracy is such a relevant one for limiting the range of valid exclusions through some fundamental constraints on the majoritarian decision making.[5]

However, the claim that the definition of the political community is not a liberal democratic concern in the strict sense is not uncommon. Although Western constitutional regimes see themselves as being committed to a liberal democratic order, when it comes to deciding on inclusion, too often all of the common assumptions on the nation-state construct are simply taken for granted and seen as unrelated to the state's commitment to a liberal democratic order. Among those assumptions is the one that only national citizens constitute the referential political community for legitimation purposes. These nationalistic assumptions have enabled people to work with the image of the communities which form the states as natural pre-existing entities, the fruit of history's unfolding revelation and endowed with a sovereign right to self-determination on membership matters (Quaritsch 1983: 1, 8; Schachtenschneider 1980: L150). Such a particularized perception excludes the claim of anyone who does not belong to whatever is recognized as the historical foundational community, to be accepted into the political forum in which the community's self-determination is to be decided.

Such a conception not only tends to overlook the short history of nation-states as political structures but is generally also bound to conceptions of the political community which emphasize its ethnic, cultural or linguistic elements, or, as Habermas has put it, the ethno-cultural

---

[5] Only on these grounds can we claim that Western liberal countries have now achieved a more perfect democracy than that of Athens, at least in terms of its inclusiveness. Recall that in Athens not only women and slaves were excluded from the political realm, but also the so-called metics. The metics were free men, attracted to Athens by the economic opportunities it offered, some of whom reached a good social position. Nevertheless, as Athenian citizenship was transmitted through links of blood only, the metics were excluded from all political rights, and so were their children. The similarities that this group presents with permanent resident alien workers is striking (Walzer 1983: 42).

substance of citizenship (Habermas 1992: 658), over its political or constitutional construction. Relegated to second place is the potential of
democracy as an old ideal (actually much older than nation-states) expressing the need for political equality as a condition for the legitimate
political coexistence of human beings, in whatever political unity serves as
a realm for political interaction, legally and institutionally regulated.
Ultimately, we have to keep in mind that 'although the development of
democracy and the nation-state may have been parallel in time, they were
not the result of the same political ideas, interests and alliances' (Hammar
1990a: 59).

Limits to exclusion in a liberal democratic state

Even if one agrees that somewhere there must be a limit to the exclusions
that can be made in a democratic order, the normative position defended
here still needs to justify what makes permanent residence qualify as a
sufficient condition for claiming full inclusion in a liberal democratic
polity. In other words, what is it that makes social membership a morally
compelling path to civic equality?

Residence and subjection to the laws: the narrow sense of subjection

When discussing the question of how to define the demos in a democracy,
Dahl seemed to be suggesting that subjection to the laws should be the
relevant criterion (Dahl 1989: 121–2). Indeed, such a criterion finds
strong support in modern egalitarian liberalism. Grounded on the idea of
equal moral autonomy and freedom of the individual, egalitarian liberalism cannot accept someone's right to rule over others based on a claim of
intrinsic superiority (Rawls 1993: 29; Ackerman 1980: ch. 1). Political
equality is essential. Everyone's interests are to be attributed the same
intrinsic value, and everyone is in principle to be treated as being best
qualified to judge upon his or her own interests. Permanent coexistence
in less than equal rights and the exclusion of a group of the population
from certain rights which are essential to the achievement of political
equality are therefore incompatible with these demands. So in our case
the political vulnerability, and thus, the democratic legitimacy concerns,
would derive not only from the fact that this population lacks the most
important political rights (e.g. voting rights) and residential security, but,
more generally, from the lack of equal rights that puts them in a disadvantaged position *vis-à-vis* national citizens when trying to develop freely and
fully their individuality relying on the necessary means and protection to
do so (Bauböck 1994b: 202).

Dahl qualifies his criterion with the exclusion of transients who, just like tourists, are likely to leave the community before the political decisions and the laws that their participation might have helped to create can affect them. He also recognizes that this exclusion remains always a potential source of ambiguity (Dahl 1989: 128 n. 11, 129). However, Dahl's criterion of permanent subjection to the laws (which can be understood in a broad sense as subjection to the public authority of the state expressed in any of the branches of government) still has a strong intuitive appeal. Clearly, not all the laws of a country will necessarily affect all of its residents and some of these laws may greatly affect transients, tourists or, increasingly, non-residents. However, it seems that territorial sovereignty, still a basic instrument of political organization in a world of nation-states, frames geographical, institutional and regulatory spheres of jurisdiction, defining the global conditions for human interaction through political freedom in particular societies. One could therefore expect that individuals permanently living in these societies will share common concerns in that they will more often and more pervasively be affected by the collectively binding decisions taken in them.

We could possibly try to accommodate resident aliens' political vulnerability through other means. Some citizens would presumably use their own political rights to articulate the interests of those who lack them. Also, resident aliens preserve a sphere of protection attached to their country of citizenship. Countries with large rates of emigration are likely to show concern for the interests of their citizens abroad and to enter into negotiations with the country of residence. Finally, while in a foreign country, aliens may enjoy the diplomatic protection of their states, dedicate their energies to home-oriented politics or engage in whatever forms of political action they are permitted in the country of residence.

Nevertheless the help immigrants can derive in such circumstances from either the protection of their countries of origin, from other groups of citizens in the country of residence, or else from the exercise of lesser forms of political activities may be insufficient. Leaving aside practical difficulties which pose interesting questions of political efficiency, a right to equal protection which is linked to a right of individuals to equal concern and respect demands that resident aliens be granted equal political power there, where they are more pervasively affected by the political process. It also requires that individuals be recognized as the best judges of their own interests and as having the capacity to take direct responsibility for their ends to ensure, among other things, that their protection will not be instrumentally used by other political actors or even by their own state.

Important as they are, the need to protect one's interests and one's capacity to be recognized as the best judge of one's interests might not be all that is at stake here. It is certainly essential if one starts out from a merely protective version of democracy. This version of democracy strives to offer the maximum protection to the individual sphere of freedom against the tyrannizing temptation of a politically organized majority and sees in political participation one of the essential control techniques existing in modern democratic politics (Dahl 1956: 83).[6] However, competing with this protective model there is also a developmental-participatory model of democracy. According to this, the moral commitment to equality and freedom that democracy is supposed to embody is best fulfilled when society strives for the maximization of human powers, understood as the development of man's natural capacities. Among these capacities political participation plays an essential role through the possibility it offers for growth in self-awareness and self-respect, by allowing people to meet in a public sphere of equal and mutual recognition (Macpherson 1977: 44–8; Pateman 1970).[7]

Holding political assets in a society different from the one in which one ordinarily lives, being able to exercise some, but not all, of the forms of political participation, and ultimately enjoying civic equality in another country are bad substitutes for a model that sees that not only equal power but also equal recognition is at stake. They are also bad substitutes because the model enhances the importance of political activity as an exercise which contributes to a continuous process of individual development. The sharing of a social setting and of experiences which enable a common physical world and common political language to flourish may be essential for political participation when perceived as a communicative process bringing individuals into touch with their social environment.

---

[6] Note that not only the core political rights which are commonly denied to resident aliens (e.g. suffrage and the access to public offices) are essential in this regard. Ensuring resident aliens' protection against tyrannizing majorities might also require some other rights and freedoms. This is most clearly the case with the right to reside but also the right to work in the state of residence, both of which are often granted to resident aliens only partially and/or conditionally. Residence and work permits of short duration, and discretionary decisions about prolongation of permits, are major hindrances to the political mobilization of immigrants in the host countries. They also set obstacles to the effective exercise of all other civil liberties legally and constitutionally recognized when such an exercise may, for whatever reason, displease the government. After all, we should not forget that staying in the national territory is a precondition for the enjoyment of whatever opportunities the society provides for and whatever rights and benefits the legal system makes available.

[7] Under this developmental approach the exclusion of permanent resident aliens from other non-political rights and freedoms might also be essential. First of all, because there might be an instrumental connection between them and political participation (e.g. right of residence and work are essential to avoid intimidatory effects on political participation). And second, because these other rights and freedoms might be essential in themselves to ensure the full human development.

Residence and societal integration: deep affectedness

Presumably, not every committed liberal will agree with the strong substantive and possibly moralistic approach of the developmental model. Even if one takes liberal democracy to express a commitment to the achievement of a free and equal society, the assumption that these values can best be achieved by allowing every individual to develop fully her specifically human capacities is likely to be controversial. There might be also some dispute about the claim that having the possibility to engage in political action is very important, if not essential, to the achievement of a fully human existence, especially if placed in a context in which it is compared with the importance of having access to a minimally promising labour market.

Let us therefore stick for now to the more widely accepted protective model. Here, the alleged violation of democratic principles can be more disputed. Resident aliens' very presence in the country (sometimes even unwanted presence) can essentially be said to express their preference and hence their autonomous judgement as to what is in their best interests. If only the long-term and pervasive subjection to the laws is what generates the democratic legitimacy concern, allowing for non-nationals to remove themselves from the sphere of territorial sovereignty might be a sufficient remedy. In principle, this is something non-nationals have a right to do, in the sense that there is a corresponding obligation on another state to accept them (assuming that they are not stateless). Hence, one could say that the legitimation gap, if there is one, arises only from their individual will to place themselves where they know they will not enjoy equal rights. The legitimizing consent of the individual is still at the root of the situation, although differently expressed.

However, we feel intuitively that having a right to go somewhere else, and thus to 'evade' subjection to the national laws and state authority, is not equivalent to having a right to participate in their generation process. Looking for an explanation as to why long-term residence should be judged relevant for setting the boundaries of a liberal democratic community, I want to suggest that this is so because residence, and the social integration that normally comes with it, helps to define the relevant referential political community for legitimation purposes and, connected to it, a deeper sense of affectedness than that implied by the subjection to the laws.

The residential habitat usually provides the individual with a context for the conception of meaningful life options. In principle, liberal societies are said to be committed to the notion of individuals as capable of having equally worthy conceptions of the good life which they can question and redefine in the light of new experiences and information (Kymlicka 1995: 81). Included among the features which define the citizen in a liberal polity is a capacity for a conception of the good which they can not only form but also revise and pursue (Rawls 1993: 19). If this is so, these societies should recognize the possibility for permanent resident aliens to rely on an opportunity, equal to that of any other societal member, to redefine their life projects in the light of their local experience. And this is not only in abstract terms, but also through the preservation of whatever attachments and ties they might have developed, and within the proper cultural context for the interpretation of these bonds. Such a context one can reasonably expect to be, at least to a sufficiently significant extent, the society in which they have been formed. It would go against this liberal notion to view a proportion of the population as not 'independent from and not identified with any particular conception' (ibid.: 30), but rather as permanently and essentially attached to a predefined set of purposes, be they of economic or of any other nature.

One of the problems with labelling non-nationals who come with the original purpose to work in a foreign country as 'immigrants' indefinitely (and hence, regardless of the length of their residence, of their willingness to stay for good, of their degree of social integration, of whether they are the first, second, or even the third generation in the country, and so on), is that it assumes and reproduces a teleological image which connects them to a certain set of predefined purposes (i.e. working, improving economic conditions, or earning enough to go back). While in the territory, resident aliens are not shut off from the context of choice nor generally from the possibility of accomplishing the projects such a context offers. And if what should be preserved is their possibility of really choosing and not only of conceiving of new options, then it seems essential that they should be able to preserve whatever they have gained as a result of the options previously encountered. We would not be satisfied with a liberal order that allowed us to have a family, a professional career, and a home but preserved for itself the possibility of giving us alternative families, homes, and professional careers for which we would be asked to exchange our present ones. 'It is this home, this career and this family that I want', we may respond. 'It is for them, and not just for having some kind of family, home, and career that I have invested time, energies and efforts.'

There are two ways in which the right to preserve one's ties and attachments may require the possibility of remaining in the social community in which these have been conceived. The first is when the ties are not removable in a physical sense. Some ties are simply not easy to 'take away'. A family may be more mobile than a piece of land or a house. The ties to a school system, to associations, and to neighbours and friends might easily count among those that are difficult to 'take away'. Also, some life options simply seem to require long-term commitments and our lifetime is limited.

One may think that I have partly mispresented the real issue. Thus, one may argue that in many cases such ties and attachments simply should not have been made to start with. This is especially so when the resident alien knows or can be expected to know that she cannot rely on the right either to establish such ties (e.g. by developing a professional activity in the country of residence) or to preserve them for the future (e.g. by planning a life-long professional career in the country of residence). But the relevant question is still whether people can be endlessly denied such rights. In other words, can we legitimately expect people to be indefinitely attached to a certain set of aims and purposes and simply ignore the fact that long-term residence, however it is generated, will inevitably bring with it the possibility that certain ties and attachments and new conceptions of the good life connected with them will emerge?

The second way in which ties, attachments, and, more generally, life projects can be said to be socially linked has to do with the fact that, along with a material and geographical space, social spaces often correspond to cultural spaces. These cultural spaces generally provide us with the tools to interpret the worth of our life options (Kymlicka 1995: 84 ff). In a certain sense it is familiarity within a culture that determines the 'boundaries of the imaginable' (Margalit and Raz 1990: 439–61). This might explain why the option to leave our society does not appear to most of us a sufficient expression of free consent to its laws. We do not just value freedom and equality in abstract terms but rather within our cultural context.

From the foregoing, we can derive the view that, assuming one should always keep the freedom to question the value of one's commitments and attachments, one ought not to be forced to abandon them or to lose the sociocultural framework which feeds their meaningfulness. Granted, a family might be more mobile than a piece of land. However, the very option to found a family may to a greater or lesser extent depend on the broader circumstances of the community in which one lives.

It is in this deeper and more complex way that long-term residents' stake in their residential community needs to be conceived. Direct subjection to the laws justifies the need for them to be able to participate in the democratic process. Dependency on the social and/or cultural environment in the way described above is a determinant of what I call here their 'deep affectedness'. It founds the individual's stake in the overall society and hence in the political system shaping and defining its present and future functioning.

The notion of deep affectedness is also useful in understanding why democracy generally does not involve giving an equal political voice only to individuals who are equally affected by the specific issue being decided (e.g. why the right to vote on fishing policy is not just limited to those with a special interest in fishing). Rather, the sharing of a sociopolitical space is seen as creating a community of concerns in which all the members can share in a more global sense. Such a presumption of a shared interest in the polity is also useful in explaining why one should be careful in making assumptions about permanent resident aliens' capacity to engage in responsible political action. Thus, although permanent resident aliens could theoretically evade their political responsibility by eventually leaving the country, one would expect that, with time, the assumption either that they need to stay or at least, if they ever leave the country of residence, that they might need to rely on the possibility of coming back replaces the assumption that sooner or later they will resettle completely in their countries of origin.[8]

Some cautionary remarks

Some additional remarks about the nature of societal integration are needed. It is first of all important to be clear that the social acculturation that the present account rests on does not necessarily imply non-national residents' complete abandoning of their old culture or their assimilation into the dominant culture of the receiving society. The cultural experiences that they will have will in fact differ from case to case. Their overall impact will probably depend on how different the societies they come from really are. In some cases the cultural experiences will be more directly related to the fact of being exposed to the dominant culture. This is likely to be the case with second generations. For some others the experiences in endogenous immigrant communities might be the crucial factor. Also, the degree of social mobility in each society is just as likely to have a significant impact on immigrants' processes of acculturation. What I suggest here is that, whatever the concrete experiences, long-term

[8] The fact that even after a long residence abroad many immigrants seem to retain the hope of returning to their home countries should not be interpreted directly as a sign of lack of attachment to the societies of residence. This is supported by the fact that few actually do return after a long absence and that many of those who declare an intention to return cannot give precise dates as to when and how they expect to carry out their plans to go back. According to Hammar, the lasting wish to return to the place, region or country of origin is explained by the great role of our first locus in life. It represents the place in which the first experiences in life and the primary socialization have taken place. A common human need for a certain sense of continuity may also partly account for it (Hammar 1990a: 203).

residence and social integration will expose the individual to new social practices and new cultural contexts which may alter, in sufficiently significant ways, the perception of oneself and the value of one's ends. Preserving the links with the society which has offered the context of reinterpretation might be strongly connected to the very possibility of undertaking whatever the individual redefines as a meaningful life project.

It is just as important to stress that the argument does not rest on the assumption that, after a certain residence period, well-settled aliens will only be able to carry out a meaningful existence in the society of residence. Experience shows that, even after a long time abroad, many immigrants choose not to give up their original nationality to take up a new one. One can easily deduce from this that many of their ties and loyalties remain attached to the society of origin. In fact, it is the original society that often serves as a context of interpretation for some of the experiences and ties acquired in the country of residence. So the point here is that, due to their specific life histories, settled immigrants' referential social frameworks might have become broader so as to encompass, to different degrees and in different ways, both the society of origin and that of residence (Neuman 1994: 277; Hammar 1990a: 205). This is why cutting the links with the country of origin should in principle not be required (e.g. by asking for renunciation of previous citizenship) as a condition for the inclusion within the realm of civic equality.

One could still argue that, occasionally, some long-term immigrants conceive of their immigrant experience, of no matter what duration, just as a bracketed experience which only has meaning for them with reference to life projects shaped in the societies of origin. The relevant question, though, is whether the receiving society should expect this to be so and act accordingly. The claim here is that people cannot simply be expected to go indefinitely without developing ties and attachments, without engaging in long-term commitments which may come to be essential for them, or without taking from the cultural and social context in which they live the necessary tools for interpreting their meaningfulness.

Underlying the criterion of affectedness are a concern with residence and certain assumptions about the likelihood that most of us will generate ties and attachments which are connected to a social environment delimited by a certain territorial space, and that we rely, at least to an important extent, on the cultural specifics in that social environment to interpret their meaningfulness. Certainly, we may also imagine attachments and cultural spaces that are created across frontiers. We can think of people who conceive of their life projects by being exposed to a socialization process that is not necessarily territorially confined. However, for most people, long-term residence is an essential element precisely because it sets the main framework for social and political interaction without which their specific life projects can hardly be pursued, even if those projects were previously defined by the acquisition of non-territorially linked cultural idioms.

To sum up, the main thrust of the argument is that a liberal democratic society should look at all of its permanent residents as potential citizens who are equally dependent on it for the protection of their rights and the development of their persons. It should not relegate a proportion of them indefinitely to a specific function or set of purposes, such as that of being only immigrant workers. This implies recognizing that permanent resident aliens are equally entitled to aspire to whatever life options the society generally allows for and presents as meaningful. Whether these aliens actually start to conceive of the country of residence as the relevant framework to measure their status of political equality will partly depend on their self-perception which, in its turn, will be largely influenced by their experience of the country of residence as a new social and cultural space. Immigrants might remain indefinitely attached to their societies of origin as the main context for interpretation of their experiences and commitments. Yet the relevant question is whether the receiving society should expect this to be so, and act accordingly. Answering this seems crucial, to the extent that, like self-fulfilling prophecies, the answers might well have an influence on what actually happens.

The protection of legitimate expectations: a competing foundation?

It is not uncommon to find arguments supporting inclusion resting on the need to protect immigrants' legitimate expectations. When expressly allowed in for a long period, or for shorter periods one immediately after the other, or even indefinitely, isn't it reasonable that there will be generated on the part of immigrants an expectation that they will be able to remain indefinitely, achieve a full status of rights and, eventually, citizenship? Even if initial entry into the country was without permission, doesn't the long-term tolerance of residence (and hence, arguably, a sort of tacit consent) ground a similar expectation?

This kind of concern seems to underlie Hammar's claim for inclusion (Hammar 1994: 196). According to him, there should be time limits on the state's right to deny permanent resident aliens the entitlement to improve their immigrant status, and eventually, to have access to citizenship. He defends this claim by appealing to the general interest in justice being done within a reasonable time. Applying such an interest to resident aliens, Hammar argues, would mean that a state would have to make a decision about the immigrant status within a reasonable time instead of postponing it endlessly.

Admittedly, such an argument is very useful in strengthening the claim for inclusion. What is not so clear, though, is that it can by itself do the job of sustaining the claim to automatic incorporation. At first sight the notion that justice should be done within a reasonable time seems mostly an argument to set time limits to the state's right to punish illegal entrants for their infringement of the law. The idea that certain crimes cannot be prosecuted after a certain lapse of time is common in many countries and we will come back to it. However, it is not clear that this argument can take us all the way to the desired result. Hammar talks about the individual and society as having an interest in decisions about immigrant status being taken within a reasonable time (ibid.: 198). But why should this be sufficient to support a claim about the specific content of such decisions? For instance, the receiving state could express, again and again, its intent not to allow illegal immigrants to regularize their status or to grant citizenship to legal residents. To claim that the demands of justice are not fulfilled by such repeated signs, one would need more than the merely procedural argument that justice should be done within a reasonable time. One would have to say that even if the state is clear about the immigration status it is willing to accord to long-term residents, and repeatedly makes them aware of it (i.e. sets express limits to their expectations), the terms defining the status might become unfair if indefinitely maintained. The unfairness would have to be asserted on grounds other than that of the state not having done justice in time. What is precisely at stake is the question of what is required by justice.

Admittedly, one could always question the relevance of the expressed signs denying full inclusion when, at the same time, aliens are being tacitly allowed to remain. Think of the case of illegal immigrants whose continued residence, in spite of the official immigration policy and discourse, often appears to be welcomed by the state. It is not clear, though, that the principle of protection of legitimate expectations would by itself cover illegal immigrants' claim to full inclusion, or even that of legal residents. For even if one accepts that they are actually allowed to stay in the territory, this does not mean that they are allowed to exercise all the rights connected to citizenship and it is not clear why they should expect that this will eventually be the case.

National sovereignty and automatic incorporation: limiting the scope of the claims

It is important at this point to limit the scope of the claims advanced thus far. The main limitation comes from the realization that, rather than challenging the state's prerogative to treat national membership as an outcome of sovereign self-determination, the claim to automatic incorporation questions only the scope of such a prerogative and purports to identify at least one of its limits. What this means is that the claim to automatic incorporation does not in principle question the legitimacy of nation-states' control over access to membership through traditional means. Stating that liberal democracy requires a degree of inclusiveness regarding those permanently settled within the territorial boundaries of the polity is not to say that the exact shaping of the community has to be decided following only liberal axioms set a priori. Even if the range of legitimate exclusions is limited by such axioms, the existing community might still be able to decide about the rules of membership following majority-based democratic procedures of self-determination. If the criteria of subjection in a narrow sense and of deep affectedness were the only valid ones to set the limits of the relevant political community, we would have to question the legitimacy of most immigration policies designed, as they are, to serve the different national interests (e.g. the recruitment of professionally qualified aliens) as defined through the ordinary political process. Many of these policies imply the incorporation of new members who are neither subject to the state jurisdiction nor deeply affected by its political process. Likewise, if subjection and deep affectedness were the only valid criteria for defining membership in the liberal democratic state, we would need to question whether we should allow nationals who are absent from the country for a sufficient period to lose any significant connection with it (or their descendants) to preserve their originary citizenship.[9]

As long as we recognize the liberal legitimacy of the existing order of states, even if with the necessary corrections, to a large extent the distribution of membership will essentially remain a matter of democratic self-determination and will presumably be guided by national self-interest (Walzer 1983: 40). This self-determination will be exercised through immigration and naturalization laws and requirements which are the traditional mechanisms to make the most relevant decisions concerning the national composition. As such, it will depend upon choices concern-

---

[9] In fact, this is not a new claim. Some scholars have questioned the legitimacy of allowing membership through descent to generate the endless inclusion of non-resident citizens, at least in the political decision-making process. See, for example, Bauböck 1994b: 222.

ing what kind of community a given polity wants to re-create. It is not something that can be decided through independent criteria mandated directly by the constraints of democratic legitimacy.[10]

On the other hand, this does not revert to the thesis that the definition of the political community or demos (and hence, the decisions on inclusion or exclusion) is in no respect a liberal democratic concern in the strict sense. Rather, the claim for automatic incorporation advanced here allows for a compromise between extremes. Instead of completely cancelling the state's bounded dimension, as far as membership is concerned, the commitment to liberal democracy takes priority but also has the more limited task of setting the legitimate constraints within which the state can adopt what it perceives as necessary exclusions. It allows for the recognition that every state has the legal authority to pursue its own national interests, whether they be economic well-being, political and social cohesion and solidarity, national security, maintenance of the national language, or anything else. This the state can do by shaping its laws regarding citizenship, immigration, and naturalization. However it also obliges states to expand the very notion of 'national interest' to encompass also permanent residents' needs and claims. It therefore denies that such choices are morally unconstrained. It exonerates liberal democracies from the task of defining, anew, the distribution of political membership abstracting from all of the existing particularities, but it still sets liberal democratic limits within which states must operate when advancing their distinctive national interests.

As a matter of definition, the requirements of immigration and naturalization laws are not imposed as conditions for access to the realm of civic equality on those recognized as citizens at birth, that is, on those who, either by descent or birthplace, somehow 'inherit' membership. The claim here is that, similarly, none of these should be imposed on those who have 'acquired' membership as permanent residents. This does not necessarily mean that the state ceases to have a 'right to self-determination' in this respect. It only means that those who are shielded by the claim of full inclusion should be seen as already belonging to the 'self' and thus, as necessarily protected from the screening process. Whether immigrants hold the status of legal or illegal residents or whether they comply

[10] Alternatively, one could simply question the whole legitimacy of the system of states and its justice in allocating membership to differently endowed political communities, or even the legitimacy of the existence of such differences among states. But to the extent that the current system is at least minimally accepted, whatever the rectifications recommended, they will have to come about through and not at the expense of the existing political communities (Walzer 1983: 31–63; Ackerman 1980: 69–103). And if this is so, a meaningful right to self-determination in relation to membership seems essential to the preservation of distinct political communities.

with the statutory naturalization requirements loses its relevance as soon as automatic incorporation is morally and constitutionally mandated. This is not to say that legal and illegal residents are put on exactly the same footing. Legal residents may have other bases on which to strengthen or accelerate their claims to full inclusion, or to question the legitimacy of some of the naturalization requirements. They may find that the required level of economic sufficiency is too demanding, that the residence time before they can naturalize is too long, or that the cultural assimilation requirements are too narrowly or strictly defined. What this means is that liberal democracy sets a limit on the time both legal and illegal immigrants can be kept outside the realm of civic equality.

This is how the character of the enterprise here is qualified. I am not looking for the single set of criteria that are to guide the pattern of inclusion in democratic societies. Rather, my purpose is to check whether the specific exclusion that concerns us, that of the population that is affected in a deep sense by the ruling process in a political community, should be tolerated in a liberal democracy. And my argument has been that it should not.

It is also important to note that it is not suggested that the criteria of narrow subjection and of deep affectedness are the only ones that may qualify as liberal constraints. Clearly, there may be limitations concerning not only those whose interests need to be taken into account, but also what kinds of interests can legitimately qualify as such from a liberal democratic ethos. Could, for instance, the interest in preserving a racially homogeneous community qualify as a legitimate one? A different but related question is whether the considerations on which deep affectedness rest could morally require acceptance or prioritization of certain individuals from outside the territory. If this is so, somebody who is not permanently subject to the laws could perhaps invoke her attachment to the society (e.g. through family members) or could claim that she needs it as a relevant cultural context (e.g. dispersed ethno-cultural minorities) to advance either a right to be accepted as a full member of the political community or at least preferential treatment (Bauböck 1994a: 210–11).

Summarizing, the claim to automatic incorporation challenges not the traditional state prerogatives on membership so much as their scope. However a country ranks the importance of economic prosperity, public order, civic loyalty, and cultural homogeneity, these things must be calculated by taking into account the entire population and not only that which has inherited membership. Admittedly, even after a long period of residence immigrants might still have an irregular residential status or a low socioeconomic status, or be recognized as national citizens by the state of origin. They may diverge from whatever cultural patterns or morally required standards are considered to express the community's parameters. But, the claim goes, in that case they have to be considered as the community's illegal, poor, cultural dissidents, dual citizens, and moral dissenters.

3   Fair to whom?

It is time now to focus on the objections the claim to full inclusion is likely to encounter. This and the following chapter will be devoted to the analysis of some of them. One powerful objection to my account of the political exclusion of immigrants, and the one which I will discuss now, is that it presents immigrants only or mainly as resident workers asking for full inclusion in the community of residence while neglecting the fact that their alien status usually implies their inclusion in another political community. Implicitly, this may suggest that, for my argument, only the bonds that exist between the individual and the community of residence are morally and legally relevant. But it could be argued that the actual and legal bonds between aliens and their country of nationality are also of essential importance in deciding on the fair distribution of benefits among citizens and non-citizens within each state.

Underlying the concern with the distribution of rights and duties are basic notions of fairness grounded on the moral imperative of equality, requiring that similar individuals be treated equally. Aliens and citizens are not equally situated as far as duties and commitment to the state are concerned, and, to that extent, allocating them equal rights would be unfair *vis-à-vis* the body of citizens. The exclusion of aliens from political rights and from the full right to residence would thus be required to preserve for citizens the distinctive place they deserve within the national community.

I now intend to explore in more depth this fairness claim as a possible objection against the full inclusion of permanent resident aliens. I thereby hope to bring to the surface the assumptions on which this 'fairness objection' rests and discuss both their validity and current relevance. But first, I will present a fuller account of the terms in which fairness-related claims can be set out. At the end of the chapter I will turn the argument around to explore, only briefly, whether, rather than setting obstacles to full inclusion, fairness considerations may not actually undermine the legitimacy of the exclusion of immigrants. The specific problems that the inclusion of illegal resident aliens poses from the point of view of fairness will be addressed in chapter 5.

Setting the fairness objection

National citizenship serves an allocating function in the international order of territorial states. It assigns individuals to geographically bounded states (Brubaker 1992), states that one could also imagine as internal schemes of cooperation or 'mutual benefit societies' (Miller 1988: 652). This probably explains why, when treating the issue of fairness as a source of political obligation within the state, the schemes of cooperation are simply assumed to include only citizens as relevant members (see, for example, Simmons 1979: 137). Within these schemes, citizens have access to a wide range of goods such as public order, national security, pollution control, access to a labour market, a complex array of rights and freedoms, including intangible 'goods' such as a feeling of belonging or collective identity (Brubaker 1989a: 20). Most importantly, citizens enjoy a stable residential status within the national territory as the main precondition for having access to whatever other public goods are distributed within it.

As a counterpart, citizens are expected to contribute to sharing the burdens or restrictions on their liberties that make the provision of these benefits possible in the first place. Among the duties of citizens we find obedience to the law, paying taxes, and some others which are said to imply a certain degree of personal sacrifice for the sake of the state, like the duty to contribute personally to its military defence (Soysal 1994: 130; Miller 1988: 648) or, more generally, the duty of allegiance to the state (Dagger 1985: 143).

Permanent resident aliens, on the other hand, enjoy only some of the benefits full membership consists of, and, accordingly, owe only some of the duties to the state. The degree of inclusion varies according to the alien's legal status (mainly, legal v. illegal; temporary v. permanent residence permit). But a line seems to be drawn between social and economic inclusion on the one hand, and political inclusion on the other. Thus, while resident aliens, to a greater or lesser extent, are supposed to share in the benefits and burdens of social and economic membership, only citizens share in the benefits and burdens of political membership.[1]

---

[1] Note, however, that there are relevant differences between countries. Thus, some authors have contrasted the fact that Western European countries have historically had comprehensive public benefit schemes combined with restrictive immigration and citizenship policies, with the United States' having had fairly liberal immigration and naturalization policies, combined with relatively stringent benefits policies (Johnson 1995: 1523). Some of this may be explained by the inevitable relationship between immigrant access to public benefits in a country and that nation's general disposition toward such benefits (Soysal 1994: 263, 173–6). Still, that permanent resident aliens enjoy most of the social benefits has generally been the case in both European countries and the USA. As we will see, recent statutes restricting immigrants' access to means-tested federally funded social pro-

Burdens such as the general duty to abide by the law or to pay taxes have a territorial application and hence cover all permanent residents, including non-citizens. However, since non-citizens are allocated to a different political community they are generally exonerated from those duties that are said to be more 'politically charged', such as, typically, the duty to serve in the military defence of the state but also the duty to serve on a jury. Accordingly, while physically present, resident aliens enjoy most of the benefits distributed in the community. Some of them, like national defence, the system of public highways, law and order, are open or non-excludable goods so that no resident can in fact avoid benefiting from them; once generated, they benefit everyone (see Klosko 1992: 35). Permanent resident aliens enjoy most social benefits,[2] especially, though not only, if they are legally present.[3] However, some other benefits or privileges are expressive of the specifically political dimension of membership, and thus reserved for citizens who are the only ones bound to the state by 'ties of allegiance and obligations of service' (Brubaker 1989a: 23). Among them are, first of all, the right to vote in national elections, as that which carries the strongest symbolic meaning in terms of national sovereignty (Soysal 1994: 131), but also the right to hold public office involving the exercise of public authority (Brubaker 1989b: 161).

At first sight this scheme supposedly represents a fair balance which takes into account the different degrees of membership. In the economic sphere the main distinction is not between aliens and citizens, but be-

grammes in the USA have made the gap between the status of citizens and that of permanent resident aliens more significant.

[2] A basic distinction is nevertheless generally made according to the kind of benefit. Those deriving their meaning and justification in reference to work and intended to replace lost income when a person is unable to work because of injury, involuntary unemployment, or old age are generally financed through employer and employee contributions and are generally granted to all workers, unemployment insurance and social security being relevant examples. Most people would probably agree that anyone granted access to the labour market should qualify for such directly work-dependent benefits (Brubaker 1989a: 21 ff). Other social benefits have a different meaning, in that they are financed out of general revenues and thus find their justification with reference to membership and to the need for some form of mutual aid. Family allowances and housing assistance are examples. Here membership might be interpreted restrictively to mean citizenship only, but it generally applies to all resident aliens, thus excluding only those illegally or temporarily present. Finally, a third type of benefit is justified with respect to urgent need and this includes emergency medical care and emergency assistance generally. These are usually extended to all persons in need, whatever their membership status, including illegal immigrants.

[3] Regarding illegal workers Brubaker notes that although 'increasingly eligibility rules include references to legal status, social insurance benefits based in part on workers' contributions tend to be paid regardless of legal status, once the beneficiary is in the system and has paid contributions which have been credited to his account. Most states are trying to prevent illegal aliens from registering for social insurance programs, but sometimes the regulation is easy to circumvent' (Brubaker 1989b: 159–60).

tween those aliens who have an ordinarily irrevocable right of permanent residence and the others. Only the former are allowed to take any job they wish (except certain public-sector jobs) or to go into business for themselves, and, with a few exceptions, to be eligible for social benefits on the same terms as citizens (Brubaker 1989a: 27). In the political arena, though, the most relevant distinction remains that between citizens and non-citizens. Granting resident aliens access to full political membership, as a means to implement their full inclusion within the community, would break the delicate equilibrium and introduce unfairness into the system.

According to the classical formulation of the principle of fairness that Hart gave in 1955, we can say that, 'when a number of persons conduct any joint enterprise according to rules and thus restrict their liberty, those who have submitted to these restrictions when required have a right to a similar submission from those who have benefited by their submission' (Hart 1955: 185).

Therefore, fairness tells us that whenever a claim for the extension of benefits is made, the burdens are closely scrutinized, so as to make sure that the balance between the enjoyment of benefits and the bearing of burdens is well preserved. Only this ensures that the mutuality of restrictions, as the moral basis of the principle of fairness, is maintained and that no free riding is facilitated (Klosko 1992: 34).

Now the reason why the full inclusion of resident aliens could break the delicate equilibrium has to do with the fact that they supposedly belong to the political community of their country of nationality. Agreeing to aliens' political inclusion would imply that they are allowed to codetermine the political destiny of the state while at the same time they are both able to evade their political responsibility by returning to their state of origin, and exonerated from the burden to defend the state from inimical forces risking their lives when this is required by a state of war (Döhring 1963: 37). In other words, the link between resident aliens and their country of nationality prevents the state from possibly accommodating, on the side of burdens, the expansion that full political inclusion would entail on the side of benefits. There are two sources of inequalities which have been commonly alleged in this respect. Both of them give content to the expression of 'exclusive allegiance link' which is often used to describe the bond between the citizens and the state. I will call them 'citizen prerogative' and 'citizen duties'.

As regards the first, it is commonly accepted that international law compels every state to accept its citizens into its national territory if no other state – in principle having no obligation to do so – wants to host them (Berber 1975: 404; Wengler 1964: 1002). Full residential rights are given to citizens alone and states have full powers to regulate length of stay and to expel any foreign citizens when it is in their interests to do so (Hammar 1990a: 12). For the individual this means a 'citizen prerogative' to always have, as an asset, a political community to turn to: a geographically and politically allocated space in the world of states. In our case, the fact that immigrants (whatever their bonds to the country of residence) may always rely on the possibility of 'going back home' places them in a privileged position *vis-à-vis* national residents. For although, as a matter of fact, the latter may also evade their political responsibility by leaving the country, they lack, in principle, a claim to be accepted by any other state. This is why it is sometimes argued that only citizens are ultimately bound to their state, even though in practical terms this does not require that they spend a single day of their lives in their country, as may be the case of second- or third-generation aliens (Isensee 1974: 93). This has often been the grounds for defending citizens' over aliens' concern with the state community of interests. Since, ultimately, only the former are bound to the destiny of their state, only they may fully identify their interests with those of that state, and this should be relevant for preserving their distinct political status.

The second alleged source of inequalities has its origin in the so-called 'citizen duties' and is related to the sacredness of the link generally assumed to qualify the citizen–state relationship, citizens' duty of loyalty to the state (Hammar 1990a: 30). The greatest expression of such an expected loyalty is the duty to contribute to the military defence of the state, even at the expense of exposing one's own life in warfare. Some authors have also included among the 'citizen duties' all those that imply not only 'performing a service for the state, but acting for the state itself' (Jellinek 1992: 425; Berber 1975: 409). For them, jury service, honorable offices, and similar civic duties would presumably also be included in such a category (Birkenheier 1976: 66).

Briefly, the stated inequalities are linked to the existence of an international order of states in which national citizenship plays an allocating function, and allegedly justify the resistance to the full inclusion of resident aliens in the name of fairness. Supposedly, entitling resident aliens to equal political codetermination would imply running the risk of having citizens' lives constrained by the political determination of those who are not bound to remain in the state or to risk their own lives for its sake. And hence there is the fear that in the exercise of their political rights aliens might advance the interests of the country of nationality over those of the community of actual residence (Birkenheier 1976: 62; Döhring 1974: 37; Isensee 1974: 93). Either directly (because of the existence of a 'citizen burden' that does not apply to resident aliens) or indirectly (because of the existence of a 'citizen prerogative' that puts permanent resident aliens in a position of advantage with respect to citizen residents), the citizen–state link operated by the status of nationality determines the specificity of the situation of aliens as aliens with respect to the scheme of cooperation binding the national citizenry internally. Thus, the fairness-based opposition to the egalitarian interpretation of democracy advanced through the claim of inclusion purports to rest on the constraints set by the principle of equality itself, taking into account the connection of resident aliens to their country of nationality and the resulting inequality between national citizens and resident aliens.

Exploring the fairness objection

As shown, the fairness objection rests on a split between the economic and political spheres of the state community, and distinguishes, accordingly, two schemes of cooperation and two membership statuses developing within the national territory simultaneously: one, with political relevance, which is more restrictive and includes only citizens, and another, mainly of a socioeconomic character, which encompasses aliens also, at least to the extent that they are legally recognized as permanent residents.

Indeed, the consolidation of different kinds and degrees of membership seems to adequately portray a reality of Western countries of immigration over recent decades. The problem is that this split between economic and political membership might be contrary to democratic principles in the long run (Brubaker 1989a: 27). In the following pages, I will test my argument for inclusion against the fairness objection. To do this, I will argue that the fairness objection rests on two assumptions that deserve closer scrutiny. The first is that immigrants actually and necessarily hold something like a 'privileged' position within the community of residence which justifies their exclusion from full political membership. The second is that maintaining the situation (limited commitment = limited inclusion, so to say) is the only way to preserve the equilibrium that fairness requires.

Regarding the latter, it might be useful to anticipate some notions here. Following Klosko:

if A benefits from the effort of individuals associated with cooperative scheme X without making similar sacrifices, a just distribution of benefits and burdens requires that he participate in their cooperative activity. In cases of this sort, fairness can be achieved in three different ways:
(1) if things can be arranged so that A does not receive the benefits in question;
(2) if the other members of X can also be freed from the burdens of cooperation (i.e., if the benefits are not supplied);
(3) if A comes to bear burdens similar to those of the X-ites. (Klosko 1992: 35)

We may imagine A to be the immigrant and the X-ites to be the national citizens. As presented above, the fairness objection seems to simply assume the impossibility of alternative (3) and jumps directly to alternative (1) without even considering alternative (2). It takes for granted that immigrants cannot come to bear the same burdens citizens do, and does not explore the possibility of freeing citizens also from their burdened status. It simply advances the solution of excluding resident aliens from some of the benefits of full political membership as if it were the only alternative. Since the fairness objection is presented as opposing the claim of full inclusion we need to explore, above all, alternative (3), namely whether 'citizen burdens' can be imposed on permanent resident aliens as well. But let us first consider the validity and the relevance of the assumptions underlying the global view that resident aliens hold a 'privileged' position within the state of residence.

The duty to defend the state as a 'citizen duty'

It is true that, usually, immigrants have not been asked to perform military service in the country of residence. But from this it seems, to say the least, exaggerated to conclude that immigrants are placed in a privileged or less burdensome position *vis-à-vis* the whole body of resident citizens. To the extent that conscription is still imposed on the latter, which we know is no longer always the case, it is also a common fact that a large sector of the citizen population is also excluded from military duties. Usually conscription only affects fit young males with no special reasons for exemption. Generally exempted are, for example, women, who represent more than half of the population, handicapped citizens, conscientious objectors. And yet all of these enjoy in principle the benefits of a secured residential status and full political membership within the state (Neuman 1994: 272; Zuleeg 1974: 348).

Granted, the exoneration of some members from burdensome cooperation does not necessarily question the very existence of the scheme of global cooperation. One could always say that some things are required from some members and other things are required from others. After all, in order to produce a certain benefit or public good, e.g. national security, it is only necessary that 'the cooperation of some (generally most) but not all individuals [be] required to produce the benefits' (Klosko 1992: 34). But still, one would want to know why exonerating some, but not others, from the burden to cooperate would put only some and not all of the exonerated in the position of 'free riders' on the scheme of cooperation if all of them are equally allowed to enjoy the benefits of full membership.

Moreover, the increasing professionalization of the military in many

Western countries, often accompanied by the abolition of military conscription, stresses more the (alien-encompassing) duty of contributing to the defence of the state by means of tax paying. And even where conscription still exists taxes are still essential for the funding of the whole national security system. Also, the fact that supra-national regional integration processes are increasingly curtailing the sovereignty of the state is relevant (Hammar 1990a: 27). One very important aspect of regional integration is peaceful conflict resolution which forecloses the use of force to settle disputes among the members of a security community (Hammar 1989: 92).

Even if it were true that the existence of such 'citizen duties' implied the privileged position of resident aliens one would have to look for alternative responses to preserve fairness. In this respect, some authors have claimed that imposing on resident aliens duties, such as the duty to perform military service, or to fight in war to defend the state, or to perform some other kind of civic service, would go against commands of international law, since it would mean an infringement of the personal jurisdiction of the country of nationality (Verdross 1984: 803). And yet neither the general principles of international law nor international customary law seem to support the existence of such a rule, except maybe for the specific and unlikely case in which aliens are compelled by the country of residence to fight in a war against their own country (ibid.: 990; Wengler 1964: 1006). In fact, although most do not, some countries enforce conscription on permanent resident aliens or have done so in the past and many more require their active involvement in helping the state out of non-military national catastrophes.[4] The fact that many states accept non-citizens as volunteer soldiers in wartime cannot be neglected either (Hammar 1989: 92).[5]

[4] This is the case of the United States where foreign residents would be liable to be drafted if general conscription were to be introduced. On the topic see, generally, Fitzhugh and Hyde 1942: 369 (tracing and defending the USA policy of subjecting resident aliens to military service) and Roh and Upham 1972: 501 (updating the analysis to the Vietnam War). Often, though, it is claimed that the USA is an exception because it is an immigration country that conceives settlement as a first step towards the expected result of naturalization.

   As for Germany, art. 2.1 of the Military Service Act foresees that aliens coming from a state in which Germans are obliged to perform military service may themselves be obliged to perform military service under the same circumstances (see Birkenheier 1976: 65).

[5] To this it has been objected that most states object to military service by their emigrants in the host state and that, in fact, often those who serve in a foreign army are automatically denationalized. However not many Western states contemplate automatic denationalization for ordinary military service. Many states do not include anything related to this in their denationalization provisions (e.g. Germany, France) and others will only denationalize their citizens when this service is performed against their express will (e.g. Italy, Spain). Finally those that do denationalize their citizens for performing military service in a foreign nation have specific provisions for dual nationals (e.g. Austria).

Ultimately, whatever the obstacles to the direct extension of 'citizen duties' to aliens from an international law perspective, we cannot forget that the state is always free to define its citizenship rules. So it could decide that granting citizenship automatically to all those who are permanently settled in the state is the best way of solving the problems generated by their exclusion from the scheme of cooperation embodied in the set of citizen rights and duties.[6] Since the state lacks the power to dissolve permanent resident aliens' previous nationality, this path would almost inevitably lead to dual or multiple citizenship.[7]

One may argue that dual citizenship is a rather poor solution to the problem. It makes the internal realization of fairness-based schemes of cooperation extremely difficult. Citizens may belong to two schemes of cooperation at the same time and a subsequently imperfect correspondence between the restrictions and benefits in either one or both of the communities may follow. Not surprisingly, there is a widespread opinion that dual citizenship allows people to take the best of two countries (e.g. taxation, social benefits, old age pensions, etc.) and becomes therefore a source of complaints and envy (Hammar 1990a: 118). True as this may be, it is not clear why the disruptions would necessarily always be to the advantage, rather than to the disadvantage of the double citizen. Dual citizenship brings about situations of both multiple protections and obligations (Neuman 1994: 271–2). The likely proliferation of social benefits, or the possibility of enjoying a double set of political rights (voting rights or right to public office) which may go to dual nationals' advantage, needs to be considered jointly with the burdening possibility of dual taxation and dual military obligations (Hammar 1990a: 116).[8]

[6] Note, however, that international law does not force a state to grant its nationality to anyone regardless of that person's degree of connection to the state, or to accord her the same rights it accords to its citizens (Berber 1975: 387; Wengler 1964: 989).

[7] Under general international law no state is obliged to take away citizenship from any of its citizens when they lose their effective connection with the state, spend a certain amount of time in another state, or acquire another citizenship (Berber 1975: 377).

[8] Note, however, that, as a matter of fact, the denounced imbalance will not be very relevant since dual citizens often cannot exercise the rights they have been formally accorded in both countries (Hammar 1990a: 103). Concerning political rights, distance makes participation, information, and engagement difficult. Some countries do not allow voting by mail or in embassies (e.g. Greece, Italy, Switzerland). Also, sometimes the exercise of political rights depends on residence anyway (ibid.: 118–19, 186). The enjoyment of socioeconomic benefits often does not depend on citizenship so much as on domicile (ibid.: 118). Most of the problems with dual citizenship are perceived not *vis-à-vis* the country of residence anyway (for people have to fulfil their obligations there according to the law), but *vis-à-vis* that of origin. Each state is in principle free to apply its legislation and disregard the legislation of other countries. It is the country in which the dual citizen is not a resident that may have problems in either extending its protection (e.g. diplomatic protection) to or enforcing the obligations (e.g. military service) on its citizen abroad when they are also recognized as nationals in the country of residence (ibid.: 115).

What this means is that to remain internally committed to a principle of fairness, the states will have to act so as to avoid having members that are either over-burdened or over-privileged with respect to their citizen peers. But this applies to all those who are dual nationals, including those who derive such a status as a natural result of the birthright citizenship regulation of the state. The proliferation of bilateral or multilateral conventions may be the best way to advance in this direction (Hammar 1990a: 117; Berber 1975: 379) and, as a matter of fact, the problem of dual obligations for military service has been considered one of the main obstacles to dual citizenship and has therefore been addressed through international conventions.[9] There is the option of restricting the simultaneous exercise of political rights by resorting to the technique of 'passive–active citizenship'. This means that dual citizens will have only one 'active' citizenship at any one time (usually the citizenship of the country of habitual residence).[10] This technique represents an effort to define relevant state interests as narrowly and concretely as possible, and thus appears to be more adequate from a liberal perspective (Bauböck 1994a: 132). It refuses to recognize the exercise of voting rights or public office as an indication of exclusive loyalty towards one state which is incompatible with being a citizen of another state.

Most of the time it is suggested that imposing 'citizen duties' on aliens, even if not directly prohibited, is practically inefficient because such duties require, for their effective fulfilment, a 'loyalty' bond to the political community that cannot reasonably be expected from either foreigners or dual citizens. This seems related to the fact that, more than just ordinary duties, some of the so-called citizen duties appear to be nation-building symbols. Nations are built by the flag, national anthem, solemn oaths, military service, and active service in war (Hammar 1990a: 205). Nevertheless, it is not clear what exactly such a duty of loyalty would

---

[9] The 1963 Strasbourg Convention on the Reduction of Cases of Multiple Nationality and of Dual Military Obligations developed a solution based on four simple rules contained in articles 5 and 6: (1) a plural citizen has to fulfil military obligations only in one of the states of which he is a citizen; (2) dual citizens will be drafted in the state of their habitual residence; (3) nevertheless, until the age of nineteen, individuals have a right to choose to serve in the army of one of these states; and (4) each state will accept that dual citizens who have already served in the army of another contracting state are no longer liable to be drafted.

[10] This rule would appease the fear that in exercising their political rights in both states dual citizens could represent the interest of another state rather than of the local population (Bauböck 1994a: 132). Spain and some Latin American countries have signed conventions stipulating that civil and political rights shall be exercised only in the country where their dual nationals have chosen their effective residence (Hammar 1985b: 447). Likewise, Martin refers to the technique of what he calls 'effective nationality' as opposed to 'dormant nationality' as a principle to solve conflicts in cases of dual nationality (Martin 1994: 309).

comprise, if not simply the generally required compliance with the law and the shouldering of burdens (i.e. taxation, jury service, military service, etc.) (Neuman 1994: 271).

Hammar draws a distinction between the two kinds of loyalties which citizens are generally taken to owe to their state (Hammar 1989: 88). Internal loyalty requires that citizens accept decisions that are constitutionally valid, even when they personally disagree with them, and thus falls within the category of obedience to the law in a broad sense. External loyalty is tested in international crisis situations, when the core interests of the state, sometimes even its survival, are threatened by other states. Citizens are then obliged to set aside internal conflicts and unite in defence of their common interests. To say that loyalty cannot be expected from resident aliens in this second sense seems to imply that for some specific reason resident aliens cannot be expected or trusted to defend the state in situations of international crisis. But this seems not to take into account the fact that their interest in developing a meaningful existence may well depend on the state's political destiny.

It is rather pointless to look for empirical evidence supporting the claim of resident aliens' disloyal behaviour. For when such a claim is made, instead of reference to empirical evidence of any kind one generally finds reference to some sort of spiritual or sacred bond which is said to bind the state and its citizens in an exclusive and profound way. And yet to the extent that such or any similar connection can exist it is difficult to see why a status like that of national citizenship, which, in most cases, is simply ascriptively acquired by birth, should express it. Why shouldn't the actual relationship, familiarity and dependency bonds, which are likely to come with time and residence for both citizen and non-citizen residents, lead to a similar degree of attachment?

Occasionally, the argument becomes even more ridiculously sophisticated. Thus, it is not resident aliens' good intentions or personal disposition but the vulnerable position in which the holding of the old nationality allegedly places them *vis-à-vis* the country of origin that is said to justify the doubts about their loyalty, and hence a concern with security risks. The country of origin could put pressure on resident aliens to gather information that might advance its own interests by using express or implied threats to the relatives and property left behind. As Hammar rightly notes, to the extent that they exist at all, these risks do not depend primarily on citizenship status, for they could apply as easily to naturalized aliens, to dual citizens or to other cases (Hammar 1989: 92).

In most cases the notion of loyalty is paraphrased through other expressions, such as those declaring that only citizens are bound in a 'community of interests' which makes them advance, through their own personal interest, the nation's interest. When performing such delicate functions, like military defence, it is important, the argument goes, that resident aliens will not give priority to the interests of any other nation over those of their own.[11] However, once more, to the extent that anything like an all-encompassing 'national interest' can be identified, presumably it would refer to everything a community may want to have, whatever else it desires. One could mention peace, prosperity, or public health. But permanent resident aliens actually live, work, and raise their families in the country of residence. What is more, if born there, they may have no ties to any other country. It is not clear how these things could not be in their interest as well.

The difference, one could argue, is that aliens may go back to their country of origin, and in fact many seem to cherish such a hope. This would hold true even for dual citizens. It is in this respect that citizens, and not aliens (or dual citizens), are often said to be bound in a 'community of destiny' which ensures their external loyalty to the state. In the case of a conflict (especially, though not only) with the state in which aliens enjoy the status of citizens, one might expect them not to commit themselves as strongly as citizens, or even to give priority to the defence of their national state. After all, the common assumption is that 'the territory of the state is [the citizens'] territory; indeed the state itself is their state. It is their well-being for which the state is responsible' (Hammar 1989: 87).

Nevertheless, there seems to be something wrong with taking, as a norm, what may be only an exceptionally rare situation to make it the normal justification for immigrants' ultimate exclusion. Dual loyalties *per se* are neither unusual nor improper. They can be held not only by resident aliens but by citizens as well. In fact it seems that in an increasingly interrelated world of states, double attachments should be recognized as something other than a pathology in a system of perfectly delimited communities. On the rare occasions when dual attachments may cause problems (e.g. an international crisis between the state of residence and that of the alien's nationality) the state may find it necessary to use extraordinary methods with respect to groups whose loyalty is deemed to be uncertain. But in the normal course of events, dual loyalties are not mutually exclusive (Spiro 1997; Hammar 1989: 89). It seems simply unfounded and, when put forward to justify exclusion, rather dishonest, to assume that dual citizens (or resident aliens) lack the

[11] In this respect, it has been said that the problem of dual loyalty is not only relevant in the situation of direct conflict between two states (typically, in the case of war), but rather has to be understood in a broader sense: it implies that the individual – when making any kind of political decision – should be mainly motivated by the interests of her own state. A kind of 'indivisible loyalty' is thus expected from her (Quaritsch 1980: L137 ff; Döhring 1974: 20).

required internal and external loyalties. More effort needs to be put into coming up with new formulas to address the few concerns that the exercise of traditionally conceived citizen rights by dual citizens may seriously raise now that notions such as that of exclusive loyalty or allegiance are increasingly being desacralized (Spiro 1997: 1482–3).

The possibility of leaving the state as a 'citizen prerogative'

What about the alleged mobility advantage of aliens? It supposedly enables aliens to evade the country's political destiny, and thereby also their political responsibility by going back at any moment to their country of nationality. Does this kind of mobility advantage really and necessarily place aliens in a sort of privileged position?

It is important to start by noting that the absolute right to leave the country does not generally assist resident aliens. Usually, there are grounds on which the country of residence can also prevent aliens from departing, especially in the case of infringement of other duties (e.g. criminal conduct), or for any other reason related to the order and security of the state (Berber 1975: 410). On the other hand, most liberal democracies are constitutionally and internationally committed to allowing their citizens to leave the country too. Thus, the 'inseparability' or 'inescapability' of citizens, a common concern among German critics, does not really seem to be such. After all, the citizens' right to exit is a necessary foundation of consensual government and thus no less important than the aliens' right to return. The Universal Declaration of Human Rights, the International Covenant on Economic, Social and Cultural Rights, and the European Convention on Human Rights all support this view.[12] Also, at a regional level, projects like the European Union are creating new political spaces that make this right to exit more meaningful by allowing citizens not only an abstract right to exit but also a concrete right to settle permanently somewhere else (Sasse 1974: 55). Practically speaking, citizens of Western receiving countries enjoy much greater mobility opportunities than alien immigrants from non-Western states who are subject to visa regulations in many more countries.

---

[12] Article 13.1 of the Universal Declaration of Human Rights, art. 12.2 of the International Covenant on Economic, Social and Cultural Rights, and art. 2 of the Fourth Protocol to the European Convention on Human Rights all guarantee a person's right to leave any country including her own. Also, in the German context, art. 2 of the German Basic Law, as interpreted by the Federal Constitutional Court, recognizes the right of German citizens to leave their country. Similarly, art. 13.2 of the Universal Declaration of Human Rights, art. 12.4 of the International Covenant on Economic, Social and Cultural Rights, and art. 3.2 of the Fourth Protocol to the European Convention on Human Rights guarantee nationals' right to enter their own country.

More importantly, a characteristic of the Western constitutional states is also that they are among the affluent countries which are generally able to guarantee safe and worthy lives for their citizens. No wonder that they have become targets of immigration flows (Scanlan and Kent 1988: 65). Being 'bound' to these states in any significant way in a world with great disparities concerning national wealth, the control of disease, and life expectancy, as well as the amount of political freedom and social equality, appears to be more a blessing than any kind of significant burden. Let us be clear. It is precisely in these well-off countries that the situations of life-threatening political or economic instability seem today more remote. And only these situations would sustain the claim that citizens are really disadvantaged by being bound to the state's destiny. Finally, the commitment, constitutional in some cases, and international in others, to offering asylum to seriously persecuted individuals, fortunately, questions the notion of being 'ultimately bound to one's country of nationality' as applied to any individual at all, no matter the situation.

If we simply assume that aliens really are in a privileged position because of their 'mobility advantage', what seems foreclosed is the possibility of finding an alternative path to preserve the balance between benefits and burdens. Since the 'mobility advantage' is an advantage aliens (but also dual citizens) derive from being citizens of other states, there would not really be anything the state of residence could do to remove aliens from this 'privileged' position *vis-à-vis* its own citizenry. At least nothing that would not violate the internationally recognized sovereignty of each state to define who its national members are, together with the also internationally recognized duty of the state to open its borders to its nationals when they are expelled from any other state.

However, for that very reason, taking for granted that resident aliens have a privileged position *vis-à-vis* the community of citizens because they can in theory rely on the possibility of going back to their home country seems misleading. This is most clear from the fact that a stateless alien does not, in principle, enjoy such a prerogative. But it is also clear from the fact that many other reasons may effectively prevent immigrants from returning to the countries they come from, even when they hold on to their old nationalities, not to mention those countries they have never been to as could be the case if they are second- and third-generation aliens. We know that immigrants often preserve identity and affective links with their countries of origin. This is why their initial departure and non-returning after a relatively short period of time, if anything, creates a presumption against the easy feasibility of returning.

Ultimately, the actual possibility of resident aliens returning to their country of nationality seems to depend on features that lie outside the control of the state of residence (e.g. that the home country is or has become a more stable and prosperous place in the meantime, so enabling returning citizens to carry out meaningful life projects there). To a certain extent, it is therefore misleading to count on this possibility when making assumptions about the stake immigrants might have in the political community of the country of residence. After all, it can hardly be said that the right to leave the community one has been born into or that one has actively sought as a means to advance one's life chances is a relevant asset if compared with the power of the community of residence to end that residence more or less at will. Also it seems that aliens' marginal mobility advantage which comes from their right to be admitted in one other country would be more than outweighed by their weaker right to return to their country of residence.

Looking at fairness from the other way round

Thus far, fairness has only been considered as a possible objection to the claim of full inclusion which was advanced in favour of settled immigrants from a democratic concern. There has been no discussion of whether the situation of assumed equilibrium (according to which permanent resident aliens may have access to social and economic membership but not to political membership) actually accords to the demands of fairness. It is time now to look at fairness from the other way round so as to question the legitimacy of the exclusion of resident aliens from full membership. The following considerations present some of the arguments and concerns that a defence of the current situation's fairness would need to take into account.

More concretely, such a claim would need to respond to the demand that until full inclusion and, hence, equal recognition of rights and duties is upheld, fairness cannot be attained. Presumably, this would actually mean different things for the different kinds of resident aliens. For those with a secure residential status and indefinite working permits it would be mainly a demand for political inclusion, at least in those countries in which legal permanent resident aliens are already granted full access to social benefits. As for those with temporary permits and, above all, for those illegally present it would be also a demand for the enjoyment of all the relevant civil liberties and social and economic benefits. The defender of the *status quo* would then need to show that, as things are, each of these groups is already getting its fair share. Leaving aside for the moment the discussion on illegal residents, which I will specifically address later, let us briefly focus on legal residents. We will assume here that they have a consolidated residential status and full access to social benefits and public services so as to concentrate on the exclusion common to all: the exclusion from full political membership.[13]

If we recall, when justifying resident aliens' equal duty to support the legal order, the public institutions, and the welfare net, notwithstanding their reduced political status, the claim was that fairness so commands. Resident aliens are expected to do their share by contributing to the social scheme of cooperation simply because they derive from it some benefits as well. After all, these benefits are made possible by similar restrictions on the freedom of citizens. Among them one can find not only highly valuable public goods (e.g. a secure and healthy environment and a promising job market) but also, and more specifically, the benefits that derive from a legal system that preserves for aliens a sphere of individual freedom and ensures their inclusion in a social welfare scheme. This is the institutional framework resident aliens must accordingly help to sustain, even when they are not allowed to participate in its definition through political codetermination.

As I have noted in passing, the fairness argument concerns the moral impermissibility of free riding. A typical case of free riding is presented by Simmons (1979: 126–7). He asks us to imagine a neighbourhood of people that has problems with the water supply and, to solve them, decides in a meeting by a majority vote to dig a public well near the neighbourhood to be paid for and maintained by the members of the neighbourhood. Some are in favour of the proposed scheme and some are not, and one in particular, Jones, expresses clearly that he does not want to have anything to do with it. Once the well is built, though, envying the benefits of fresh and clear water that all the others are getting, Jones gets up in the night, and knowing that the water will not be missed, takes some for the next day. The principle of fair play would say that Jones has a duty to do his part and contribute to the scheme of cooperation because he accepts the benefits it generates thanks to the contribution of all the other members who participate in the scheme. So in our case too, immigrants seem to have a duty to do their share when they are getting the benefits that derive from a scheme of cooperation.

Yet things may not be as straightforward. The advocates of immigrants' fairness-based duty to contribute would need to explore whether what immigrants receive as their due share corresponds in fairness to what they contribute. More precisely, they will have to argue that the duty

[13] Clearly, the advocate of full inclusion would also question the legitimacy of permanent resident aliens' less than full 'socioeconomic inclusion'. It is therefore not surprising that those opposing the most recent curtailment of social benefits to legal immigrants in the USA have called upon fairness-based arguments (see Abriel 1995: 1627; Legomsky 1995a: 1464–7).

to act fairly allows for the peaceful coexistence of an economic and a political scheme of cooperation, in the name of which resident aliens are supposed to be excluded both from the benefits and from the burdens of political membership only.

Those willing to question the *status quo* will probably find that the consolidation of different kinds of membership within the state represents a purely theoretical and far from neutral approach to the alien–state relationship, an approach that hides relevant facts. Among these, first of all, the fact that immigrants integrate into the labour force of the state and contribute by myriad ways to both the social and political configuration of the state they live in. Second, the fact that the size and nature of whatever economic benefits immigrants receive and have to contribute to are precisely decided through the political process from which they are excluded. To a large extent the harmless and clear-cut schism between political and economic membership is therefore nothing but a fiction (Walzer 1983: 58). When applied to political communities, the idea of a scheme of cooperation needs to be that of a grand-scale scheme where public rules are designed to regulate activities in ways which accrue to all equally.

The benefits that a society derives from the presence of immigrants cannot be reduced to the economic sphere or clearly disentangled from the political.[14] Resident aliens' obedience to the law will strengthen the stability of laws and institutions and thus the political structure of the community. Their tax contribution will help the financing of social benefits but also the system to ensure national peace and order. Their cultural diversity will open up new markets and enlarge the social and cultural range of options for citizens, but also help to strengthen the foundations of a pluralistic and tolerant democracy. Their readiness to accept unqualified and low-paid jobs that are necessary, though often despised by citizens, will keep the economy going but will also allow for others to make what they perceive as more meaningful life options.

To deny resident aliens the benefits of political cooperation is often impossible, as many such benefits (e.g. national security or public order) are non-excludable goods open to all residents. But even concerning excludable benefits, such as the exercise of political rights, it might also be manifestly unfair to the extent that it denies both the political relevance of the contribution of immigrants and the economic relevance of immigrants' political exclusion. Where, if not in the political arena, will it be

---

[14] Also, one would have to face the additional problem of individualizing the contributions. To mention an example, it has been rightly asked: 'Yet how can we say that a criminal or revolutionary who is also a citizen participates in a joint enterprise in a way an industrious, law-abiding refugee does not?' (Shacknove 1988: 144).

decided what social benefits will be distributed and in what languages, or what the rules on labour and housing markets should be like, or whether a war should be fought or not?

Clearly the contributions of resident aliens have the effect of restricting their freedom, as their duty to pay taxes and, more generally, to obey the law shows. Aliens have to shape their lives according to the restraints set by laws which others have decided, and this is the kind of restriction that enables democracy to function. Fairness, one might say, makes it compelling that citizens also be subjected to the freedom-restricting burden of allowing resident aliens to enjoy the same social and economic rights and civil freedoms, but also the same political rights, to prevent citizens from acting as 'free riders' on their contribution.

4   Safeguarding liberal democracy from itself

Democratic pluralism assumes that members of society will not organize around single interests of race, class or gender but will explore and discern their commonalities, coming together around certain issues and diverging on others in constantly changing configurations. Deliberate lies which deny these commonalities divide groups which might otherwise organize around mutual interests, and instead forge loyalties based on artificial and reified . . . identifications that do not permit society to perceive and pursue its various goals.
(*R v. Zandel, per Cory and Iacobucci JJ.*, p. 232, in 95 Dominion Law Review 4th, 202 (1992))

The claim to automatic incorporation sets certain limits on the freedom of a country to define the terms of admission of newcomers. More concretely, it questions the validity of indefinitely making the incorporation of permanent resident aliens to the body politic a matter of arbitrary discretion or of conditional access subject to the fulfilment of criteria, such as those generally recognized in naturalization laws and in the laws on the initial admission of aliens. Permanent resident aliens already belong to the polity. If anything, they should be part of the body which is legitimately authorized to decide about the incorporation of further members, instead of outsiders who first need to comply with certain conditions to gain recognition as members.

Rather than being deprived of its right to 'self-definition' concerning membership, I argue that the national community cannot exercise such a right *vis-à-vis* those whom it should consider full members according to democratic principles. In practical terms, we saw that this forces the nation-state to a certain degree of openness. More than just a fixed entity deciding sovereignly about its future composition, the national community becomes an ever-changing entity which has to take account of the social realities already operating within its territory.

This raises the question as to whether, by allowing the political community's continuous reshaping, without retaining at the same time a certain control over who is given political voice and who is allowed to remain unconditionally, the basic elements that allow for the existence of a liberal democratic society might be put in danger. Preserving a certain degree of commonness and homogeneity to enable understanding, cohesion and solidarity may prove essential for the functioning of social and liberal democracies.

This is basically the concern that I address in this chapter under the 'democratic objection'. After setting out in more detail the terms in which this objection is expressed, I will proceed to analyse the validity and the relevance of the assumptions on which it appears to rest. Finally, as I did with the 'fairness objection', I will turn the question around to explore briefly the binding potential of inclusion and its capacity to solve, rather than aggravate, some of the tensions and strains that threaten the cohesion of increasingly heterogeneous countries with immigration.

Setting the democratic objection

The 'democratic objection' critic will question whether automatically according equal political rights to people who may lack a common identity, a common language, a proper knowledge of the political institutions, or similar socioeconomic status or political conceptions, is compatible with preserving the basis for liberal democracy. Moreover, there is the worry that some of the interests held by automatically incorporated individuals who may have preserved their attachments to other political communities could conflict with essential interests of the receiving state as a territorial entity in potential competition with other states. Some of the political conceptions or attitudes introduced might embody a direct threat to the most basic democratic premises if the newcomers are not sufficiently committed to the democratic order. Finally, there is the concern that bringing together diverse cultures and languages might pose serious problems not only to the creation of a common identity but also to the understanding and trust that living together in equal freedom requires. So basically, could the lack of admission and naturalization requirements testing newcomers' knowledge, their social status, or their personal character endanger either the state or its liberal institutions (Bauböck 1994a: 96; Hammar 1990b: 76)? Could any kind of democratic system preserve itself under the conditions of inclusiveness advanced here?[1]

---

[1] Among the cognitive abilities most commonly required for either naturalization or the consolidation of a stable residential status are knowledge of the language, the constitution, history and geography and the institutions of the country. As for the requirements which make reference to the applicant's economic position and personal disposition, one commonly finds employment, sufficient income, standard housing, absence of a criminal

This concern has to do with the limits of the absorptive capacity of any liberal state. And this is a well-founded concern, much more so than the concern with fairness. Hence the need to explore it in greater depth. In principle, it seems hardly possible to give a comprehensive answer to all of the questions that the 'democratic objection' raises. In each actual case the answer would probably depend on a great number of considerations. When talking about the potentially disruptive effects of the automatic incorporation of resident aliens we may want to know how many (in proportion to the national population) we are talking about; how ethnically or culturally different and how naturally assimilable they are; how ethnically or culturally composite the national community already is; whether the state where they come from is or is not hostile to the receiving state and hence, whether national security concerns may be involved; what the political culture in which immigrants have been primarily socialized is like; how mature and stable the democratic commitment of the receiving society proves to be in terms of tolerance to diversity; and how healthy the economy and strong the welfare system of the receiving societies are. All these features should therefore be taken into account, as prudential considerations, when adjusting the normative conclusions advanced in this work to the practical conditions of feasibility in each situation.

Nevertheless, exploring the democratic objection might be useful to shed some light on the validity and democratic relevance of the assumptions on which it often appears to rest. Such assumptions, I will claim, are often false and, when taken as if they were not, the path to less exclusive alternatives appears to be naturally closed.

Exploring the democratic objection

Let us first of all discuss the accuracy of the assumptions on which the democratic objection often relies as well as the normative conclusions to which it is generally said to lead.

record, good moral character, loyalty to the political ideology of the state or to the state itself. Thus, in Germany, naturalization generally requires lengthy residence, good moral character, linguistic skills, adequate housing and means of support, as well as commitment to Germany's constitutional order. Naturalization policy also emphasizes the elimination of multiple citizenship (Hailbronner 1989: 67–81). Basic criteria for naturalization in the United States include admittance to permanent residence; five years of continuous residence (three if the alien was married to a USA citizen throughout the period (8 USC'1430 (a) Supp. V 1993); good moral character (ibid., '1427 (1988 'Supp. V 1993)); ability to speak, read and write English; knowledge of the 'fundamentals' of US history and government ibid., '1423); attachment to constitutional principles; being 'well-disposed' to the good order and happiness of the United States (ibid., '1427 (a)): and an oath expressing allegiance to the United States and renouncing all prior allegiances (ibid. '1448).

Homogeneous body of citizens v. homogeneously different body of permanent resident aliens?

Rules for naturalization (or for the consolidation of a stable residential status) often require that the applicant be able to prove some kind of cultural or political aptitudes. Common examples are competence in the dominant language of the country, some knowledge of the country's institutions or history and some sort of commitment to its fundamental values or constitutional culture. Underlying these requirements is a concern with either preserving a distinct national identity as a common bond linking the political community, or else with protecting directly the basis of the political system from being internally eroded. I will distinguish between the concerns with cultural assimilation and national identity on the one hand, and those with political assimilation on the other.

The concern with preserving a common national identity (and the fear that naturalization by itself may not be sufficient to achieve the required commonalities) explains why some states have either not encouraged naturalization at all, or else demanded an absolute break with the country of origin, usually in the form of renunciation of prior allegiances, as a precondition for full political inclusion (Layton-Henry 1991: 115). In many countries (e.g. Germany) this requirement seems to account for the low incorporation rate of permanent resident aliens into the citizenry. Citizenship is often considered an expression of individual identification. And since among first-generation immigrants this sense of personal 'belonging' is often focused on the country of origin and its language and culture, many of the immigrants are reluctant to acquire the new citizenship, something which some of them would actually perceive as an act of treason (Hammar 1990a: 205).

Clearly, this line of argumentation has influenced the naturalization practices of European states more than those of North America. The idea of national citizenship as exclusive membership in a homogeneous nation-state, and thus, to some extent also the concern with dual citizenship as an expression of dual identities, has not carried much weight in North America 'where citizenship has rather meant membership in an ethnically heterogeneous state regardless of linguistic, cultural or religious conformity' (Hammar 1989: 94). However, some of the requirements mentioned above (such as the command of the language and the renunciation of prior allegiances) have been set as conditions for naturalization also in the USA. And some critics have expressly stressed their unifying potential (Schuck 1989). Also, it is of interest to note that the discussion on dual citizenship has gained in relevance in the USA in recent years. Thus, whereas European states seem to have become more relaxed about dual citizenship, there is now a growing debate about dual citizenship in the USA since Mexico has introduced the policy of allowing its citizens to naturalize without losing their Mexican nationality.[2]

Claiming the importance of preserving a culturally or ethnically homogeneous polity in this context seems to rest on a certain assumption, namely, that present democratic societies are actually functioning because of their internal homogeneity. However, despite their nation-building efforts, modern states are seldom homogeneous nation-states based on one national group, one language, a common origin, one religion, and so on. Most states are heterogeneous in language, religion and ethnicity (Kymlicka 1995: 2; Hammar 1989: 91). Even in the European context the narrative about homogeneous nation-states has now lost much of its appeal. Postwar immigration has transformed Western European states into multicultural and multiracial states with substantial non-European minorities. And even before that, the old idea of the nation-state may have been no more than a myth. Although many European states have traditionally considered themselves homogeneous nation-states, in fact they all have included indigenous and other minorities (Hammar 1990a: 108; Miller 1988: 655–6; Weber 1977).

Also, the phenomenon of multiple identifications and mixed identities is not an exclusive feature of the immigrant population, or a phenomenon linked exclusively to cultural diversity. Rather, multiple identifications and mixed identities are the norm in modern societies (Spiro 1997: Hammar 1990a: 117). Identifications following different criteria, such as gender, age, religion, ethnic group or professional category, all seem to cut across one another. And, as Hammar has put it, it is precisely this cross-cutting that often 'works to take the edge off intergroup conflict' (Hammar 1989: 90–1; Scanlan and Kent 1988: 62). All of these criteria of identification, and presumably some others too, are just as likely to apply to the immigrant population. It should therefore not be judged as a homogeneous whole.[3]

---

[2] To follow some of the scholarly discussion on the topic, see Schuck (1998), ch. 10 and Spiro (1997).

[3] Hammar explains that in Sweden one of the most common fears before aliens were granted the right to vote in local elections was that they would alter the whole political picture by establishing new political parties and substantially altering the equilibrium between the already existing political forces. In fact, there were not many attempts in this direction and those few failed. Immigrant voters did not see themselves as a single group of 'immigrants'. In the end, almost 100 per cent of the new electors voted for parties already represented in the Swedish Parliament. Also, immigrants with longer residence in Sweden voted more like the Swedish electorate than relative newcomers did (Hammar 1985a: 95). In a later study reflecting a more comprehensive analysis of local elections in different European countries, Hammar confirms the conclusion that on most political issues immigrants share more or less the same concerns as other voters and hold specific class-related claims (income, employment, taxes). At the same time, they appear to be especially sensitive to some issues, such as education, ethnic culture or religion (Hammar 1990a: 167).

Presenting the incorporation of resident aliens who do not undergo the naturalization process as a menace to internal cohesion and as a source of cultural disintegration seems to support a narrative in which not only are citizens perceived as a homogeneous body but also immigrants are seen as an equally diverging and threatening element. Their relative differences, but also citizens' and resident aliens' relative similarities, are thereby hidden. Acculturation and resocialization processes which naturally take place with long-term residence and social integration, as well as with the exposure to the majority culture and language, should not be under-estimated. The narrative hides even stronger realities. For second and third generations the country of residence may be the only place in which they have experienced a process of socialization and acculturation. Final-ly, the original culture and national identification are often progressively supplemented with – and not simply replaced by – a new identification with the language and the culture of the host nation (Hammar 1989: 90).

Cultures seem to be always changing. Neither the culture of the coun-try of origin nor that of the country of residence remains static. Nor do immigrant communities stick eternally to the cultural patterns of the home-country. As Spinner has put it, 'a biological connection to our grandparents does not translate into a cultural connection' (Spinner 1994: 65). As cultures change they redefine identities. Among well-settled immigrants (not to mention second-generation 'immigrants') 'hyphen-ated' cultures and identities are likely to come across as something rich, and irreducible to any of the elements that have contributed to the generating process (ibid.).

Let us imagine now that our concern is not so much with cultural assimilation and the preservation of a common national identity, as with political attitudes (see, for example, Ackerman 1980: 93–5). Now the objection would be that letting every kind of resident alien have a political voice would endanger a democratic system by allowing political power to be used to corrupt the very democratic structure from the inside. This concern is hardly a new one. Thomas Jefferson expressed worries about the preservation of American republicanism, and the possibility that it might be undermined if an excessive number of immigrants, unfamiliar with its principles, were enfranchised (cf. Whelan 1988: 17–18). Now-adays, we could say that ensuring that immigrants are law-abiding (i.e. checking that they have no criminal record) and that they will remain loyal to the fundamental values, the constitutional culture or the specific interests of the state (especially if these clearly compete with those of another state), are among the reasonable functions which many states

Presumably, the more heterogeneous and ethnically mixed a nation is, the less immigra-tion-related such concerns will be.

expect immigration and naturalization laws to serve. They are also among the reasons why dual citizenship is sometimes looked upon with special antipathy. Citizenship is said to involve loyalty to the state and support for the fundamental principles of government and for its basic shared values. Those who join the political community and have a say in shaping its future should be committed to defending the state and its constitution and institutions.

Now the relevant question here is whether for some specific reason it can be reasonably assumed that resident aliens are likely to be a greater danger to the political order than citizens. If the matter depends on political socialization, as with cultural socialization, this too is not genetic and can be acquired with time and social integration, as well as with participation in civil society and public political life (Bauböck 1994a: 92). Assuming that citizens, by the mere fact of being citizens, are more likely to be law-abiding seems as wrong as assuming that aliens, simply because they are aliens, will have more difficulty in accepting the constitutional order. In fact, since serious criminal offences are generally grounds for deportation, if anything, the continued presence of aliens should rather create a presumption of law-abidingness.

However, if what is at stake is not so much law-abidingness as loyalty to the state, things may look somewhat different. The presumption against loyalty, or at least against exclusive loyalty to the state in the case of international conflict, may appear somewhat more justified (Martin 1994: 318–19). The assumption now is that only citizens can be expected to be loyal to the cause of the state and willing to make the necessary sacrifices in critical periods. Aliens are suspected of being less trustworthy (Hammar 1990a: 28–9). The fact that they preserve their old citizenship may be potentially disruptive for a system of states as political units which are always somehow in potential competition and which must always be prepared for the worst (Bauböck 1994b: 205; Whelan 1988: 21).

Such a perception can be more or less justified depending on what exactly one takes loyalty or allegiance to imply. If it means a readiness to defend the state's interests against those of other states, one should recall here that resident aliens often make the country of residence the centre of their existence, if it has not always been so. If this is the case, once again, an interest in defending the state's interests should be expected (Legomsky 1994: 294; Scanlan and Kent 1988: 78). There is evidence that immigrants who remain proud of their heritage are among the most patriotic citizens (Kymlicka 1996: 119).

Thus, maybe only a smaller presumption can be supported: that in the rare case of direct conflict between the country of residence and that of their citizenship, immigrants will not be as loyal to the state of residence.

But here again let us not forget that national citizens may also be dual citizens and also that naturalized citizens may retain relevant bonds to their countries of origin. Hammar explains that eligibility to become a legislator has often been said to be restricted to citizens because it may imply gaining access to secret information and taking part in deliberations of great importance to the state's security and defence. However, Hammar remarks, few states have actually excluded dual citizens from eligibility or voting rights, and naturalized aliens are allowed to vote and be elected even though they may have preserved similar attachments to their countries of origin (Hammar 1990a: 185–6).[4] Finally, any citizen may lack allegiance or exclusive loyalty to their country for a great variety of reasons, whether or not they feel strongly committed to the defence of its interests (Spiro 1997; Legomsky 1994: 296; Aleinikoff 1986: 1478). Federal governmental structures, international organizations and regional arrangements can also provide simultaneous loci of loyalties and they need not necessarily conflict with each other (Neuman 1994: 270).

Briefly, the formal status of citizenship seems a bad proxy for judging who may and who may not be a risk to the state (Hammar 1990a: 185–6). Once again, there are no empirical studies on the behavioural modes characteristic of the different categories of residents (native citizens, naturalized citizens or resident aliens) in relation to loyalty to the country (ibid.: 208). Before admission to the territory, aliens are screened for security problems. And in some countries, like in the USA, the government is prepared to draft resident aliens into the military if conscription were to be reintroduced. This shows that they are not regarded as disloyal (Legomsky 1994: 295–6). A narrower tailoring would be needed if our goal is to include only trustworthy people.[5]

Also, even if we assume that some differences in terms of political or

---

[4] Note, however, that in some countries naturalized citizens can be excluded from certain political or security-sensitive offices: in the USA the President must be a native-born citizen; in Britain naturalized citizens may be excluded from some positions in the armed forces (see Layton-Henry 1991: 118).

[5] According to Hammar, security risks are best evaluated in individual cases and not on the basis of formal criteria. Thus, he argues, the risk involved in enfranchising resident aliens depends on a wide range of features such as a country's position in the international political power structure or its evaluation of its international security. Under conditions of peace and little external threat, objections to national voting rights bear less weight than in situations of international tension or threat of war. Also between friendly neighbouring states there is less risk. A less restrictive alternative for the rights of aliens could be for national voting rights to be granted to citizens of friendly neighbouring states, and during high-risk periods for resident aliens not to be allowed to vote (Hammar 1990a: 209, 217; Spiro 1997). According to Hammar, paradoxically, the fear that foreign policy conflicts will be imported seems more justified in countries that have excluded foreign residents from politics for a long time, since such an exclusion encourages immigrants' focus for political agency to be indefinitely attached to home politics. It thus becomes a self-fulfilling prophecy (Hammar 1990a: 167).

cultural integration are likely to persist between settled immigrants and national citizens, we would want to be certain that the measures taken to ensure the necessary degree of social cohesion are at least effective. We would have to know to what extent performing actions such as swearing loyalty to the country, its laws and institutions, or giving up the formal status of prior citizenship for the sake of a new one, are effective means of ensuring future loyalty and law-abidingness or shaping new identities around common cultural elements. Many scholars have shown their scepticism on the matter (Note 1997: 1825–6; Legomsky 1994: 294; Schuck 1994: 326; Aleinikoff 1986: 1501). And numerous historical examples prove that the acquisition of citizenship has often not been sufficient to overcome the prejudices against former aliens' cultural or political 'strangeness'. Just to mention one example, following the Wall Street Crash of 1929, xenophobic notions surfaced in the USA forcing the deportation and repatriation not only of hundreds of thousands of documented and undocumented Mexicans working and living in the United States, but also of American citizens of Mexican descent (López 1981: 663). The internment of naturalized US citizens of Japanese descent during the Second World War (which was upheld by the Supreme Court in Korematsu v. United States)[6] is another example.

The democratic relevance of heterogeneity

Judging the degree of accuracy of the factual assumptions or the effectiveness of the means proposed to solve what is perceived as a democratic threat does not solve the question as to whether we really face a democratic threat. To do this we would want to know what normative conclusions can be attached to the fact that certain political and/or cultural differences may persist in characterizing settled or second- and third-generation 'immigrants'. And this depends partly on a prior judgement on the general relevance of heterogeneity in a liberal democratic state. In this respect, it has been argued that requiring cultural assimilation in addition to ordinary and consolidated residence, as a condition for inclusion, is unacceptable because it collides directly with the idea of democratic pluralism (Zuleeg 1974: 348). As Carens has put it, 'to require "integration" beyond residence, as a precondition for the granting of citizenship is to violate the principle of toleration and respect for diversity to which all liberal-democratic states are committed and to call into question the equal status of current citizens who differ from the majority' (Carens 1989: 40). The notion of equal citizenship in our liberal democ-

---

[6] 323 USA 214 (1944).

racies does not allow for discriminations in the public sphere which are based on identities.

Rather than suppressing differences, it appears that a liberal democracy is required to recognize differences and to adjust its institutions to the best possible form of coexistence under terms of equal recognition. Also, one should consider the fact that immigrants' claims for specific recognition are generally claims for recognition within the main public institutions and not so much aspirations to develop alternative and separate institutional frameworks. And yet only the latter could be a serious threat to internal cohesion (Kymlicka 1995: 98).

Let us now shift our concern from the cultural dimension to the more political. Here again, we may start by granting that resident aliens (at least first-generation immigrants) are as a group more likely to maintain old allegiances and less likely to be familiar with the laws and institutions of the country of residence. But the question now is what relevance should these features be given in terms of political inclusion or exclusion?

We have seen how the concern with dual allegiances is often put forward to justify either the non-recognition of political rights to aliens, or else the renunciation requirement for naturalization. To a large extent, though, this concern falls into that of dual national identities and presents strong similarities to that of cultural pluralism. Foreign-born immigrants preserve many ties to their countries of origin. Some of these might be passed on to their descendants. They may maintain contact with relatives and friends still living there, and they may follow the news from the old country with interest. But if this is so, it is probably true regardless of their national citizenship status. Naturalized citizens who have given up their old citizenship may retain exactly the same sort of attachments to the old country as persons with dual citizenship. We could describe these attachments as a sort of loyalty to the old country. But does this loyalty exclude loyalty to the state of residence, or is it rather a strong affection which can be perfectly compatible with the internal and external loyalties required for citizenship in the country of residence?

The relevant question here is why dual national identifications should not only be naturally expected but also naturally accepted in a liberal democratic polity. Identity seems to be tied up with our memories (Neuman 1994: 277; Hammar 1989: 89). Thus, abandoning an old identity might be like denying a part of ourselves. The greater importance we attribute to individual identity as a personal matter and to its connection with the basis for individual self-esteem, the more we will want to question the legitimacy of asking the individual to give up an essential part of it as a condition for political inclusion. As Spinner recognizes, 'who we are depends on who we were . . . [and although] we may sometimes want to change our identity, this means reflecting on who we were; it means react[ing] to our memories' (Spinner 1994: 65).

Going back to the case of immigrants, it might be true that their identities are in some sense tied up with their memories (especially if they are first-generation immigrants), and hence, with the customs and traditions of their native land. The possibility for them to react to their past depends, at least to some extent, on the possibility of preserving those memories and attachments. But this becomes difficult when they are asked to break with their past by giving up their old citizenship. On the other hand, cultures are always changing; they are always moving along a path. 'National identity is not a zero-sum-game' (Hammar 1985b: 449). Rather than being fully rooted in the home country's culture, immigrants often stand between two cultures. And this is why dual national citizenship may be the most reasonable legal acknowledgement of their specific, composite social and cultural identification.

One could still argue that the concern with dual identities is not the only and certainly not the most disturbing feature about dual loyalties and that it does not capture their relevance in a liberal democratic polity. The greater concern, one could say, is with allegiance. In a world largely organized around a Hobbesian view of international relations as a latent state of war, it seems that admission to the polity must remain under the control of the receiving state. Also, it is only natural that in such a world one essential qualifying criterion for naturalization has to be a credible change of loyalty. Whatever their identities, until formally accepted by the state, aliens can be presumed to favour their original state's interests over those of the country of residence.

The problem is that such a conception of states as sovereign polities that need to be not only externally bounded but also mutually exclusive is more and more at odds with modern liberal conceptions of democracy and with an increasingly interdependent international order. Once again, one has to accept that multiple loyalties are neither unusual nor improper in the pluralistic societies of a world grown smaller, and are not only held by alien residents but by citizens as well (Hammar 1990a: 89; Carens 1989: 47; Aleinikoff 1986: 1497; Levison 1986: 1648). Also, at this point, a basic distinction needs to be made between allegiance as loyalty to the state and allegiance as a commitment to the basic principles of its democratic and constitutional order. If allegiance is understood in the latter terms, then aiding in the overthrow of an unconstitutional government, for instance, would indicate no loss of allegiance in the relevant sense (Martin 1994: 306; Aleinikoff 1986: 1493, 1500–1). One would want to know more about what is specifically at stake in each conflict.

The concern could strictly be with the preservation of the laws, institutions and constitutional values of the state. But, clearly, the liberal state simply does not allow for certain behaviours that pose a direct threat to its basic political principles, its institutions or its territorial integrity (e.g. religious persecution or violent secession). The fact that some immigrants may hold undemocratic or illiberal views does not leave them in a position essentially different from that of rebellious or dissenting citizens. The liberal rejection of religious intolerance is a non-confessional rejection. Granted, when resident aliens become citizens, the state loses the option of deporting them if they act as rebellious or dissenting citizens. But one can expect the system to have other defences against those attitudes and, more generally, against all of those who break the law or engage in criminal activities, and to use them in an equally energetic way whenever it feels threatened (Bauböck 1994a: 99; Neuman 1994: 259). The idea of constitutional limitations imposed on the exercise of political rights and freedoms for the sake of protecting the structure of the political system is generally accepted. Why those limitations should be stricter for resident aliens than for citizens is not quite clear.

Maybe the relevant question is: why should we rely only on repressive mechanisms to protect democracy? Scrutinizing and testing those who cannot be assumed to have acquired the attachments, abilities and knowledge that make the system work or those who, during their stay in the country, have already proved not to be fully compliant with the laws, might be justified precisely as a preventive measure against the erosion of democracy. Ensuring that immigrants who are to join the body politic are fully loyal to the system, generally law-abiding and that they have a minimal knowledge and acquaintance with the country's institutions and language could precisely be seen as this kind of preventive measure.[7]

There seems to be no easy answer to the issue of the limits of heterogeneity or integrative capacity of a pluralist society. But let us assume that we found a plausible one. What necessarily derives from it is not the urge to exclude from the democratic process those citizens and permanent resident aliens who presumably lack the required skills. After all, either as a matter of right or as a matter of fact, many will nevertheless not abandon

---

[7] In a neo-republican understanding of citizenship, Herman van Gunsteren has also included the criterion of competence to act in a particular community, expressed as knowledge of the language and respect for the laws (van Gunsteren 1988: 736). Also referring to the concern of having a common language as a common medium of political discourse, see Neuman 1994: 265. Van Gunsteren adds to this the condition of having access to an *oikoa*, a reasonably secure access to means of existence so as not to be forced to sell one's judgement. This last requirement could be interpreted as requiring a limitation on the number of poor that the community can accept, since admitting more would make the community poorer as a whole and less able to take care of its least fortunate members. However, excluding the poor from the polity does not exclude them from society. And sending back those who have lost their independent income has become unacceptable in democratic welfare states in which social rights have gradually come to be attached more to residence than to citizenship.

the country. Rather, to the degree that these skills are perceived as essential to the health of the overall system, it should be ensured that those who may have had fewer opportunities to acquire them naturally do so now on an equal basis. It becomes thus not a question of excluding but of strengthening the mechanisms of practical functioning. Offering facilities and, in general, encouraging the acquisition of the required knowledge should be the path to follow. As a class, resident aliens cannot be perceived as essentially unable to behave as citizens of liberal democratic states. 'The capacity to be a citizen should in principle be ascribed to any person who has not given strong evidence of the contrary in speech or deeds' (Bauböck 1994a: 92).

A slightly different problem is posed when it is not the lack of evidence but precisely the existence of negative evidence (e.g. past criminal conduct) that the conditions for political incorporation try to discover. But why, when naturalization applicants have broken the law in ways that are not significant enough to justify their deportation, should they now be denied access to citizenship? And also, if they have already been punished and have completed their sentence, on which additional grounds should they be denied political incorporation? The argument against automatic incorporation of resident aliens who are convicted criminals serving their sentence also seems to lose part of its strength when one considers that prison inmates are deprived of active citizenship anyhow (Bauböck 1994a: 100).

This does not mean that some exceptional measures can never be applied. Yet if they are, they ought to be as narrowly tailored as possible and rely on the absence of less restrictive means. This would imply for example that, rather than generally applying the renunciation requirement as a condition for the naturalization of permanent resident aliens and hence, for their enjoyment of political rights and duties (e.g. voting or military conscription), special guarantees of loyalty would be sought only in those cases where resident aliens' exercise of political rights and duties could compromise essential interests of the state. This could for instance be the case if the state of residence was in a situation of war against an alien nation (Hammar 1990a: 89; Aleinikoff 1986: 1497).

As a general principle, one could say that whatever the requirements found to be compelling for the survival of a democratic society, they should apply equally to all its members. When the issue of inclusion or exclusion as a fundamental right is at stake, overbroad presumptions are extremely inadequate. Ultimately, cohesion should not be selectively safeguarded. The example of loyalty oaths, for instance, is an interesting one. Levison reminds us that such oaths have been required in the United States in critical periods to ensure citizens' loyalty (Levison 1986: 1450). As that author rightly mentions, liberals might be unhappy with a state that inquires into the political views held by its members. But at least then we do not have the additional problem of discriminating between the members by asking only some and not others to express such commitments.

Compulsory education raises an interesting issue as it applies to native-born citizens. It forces native-born citizens to undergo a number of years of schooling with a curriculum that includes notions of the country's main language, history and institutions. Hence, it could be read as legitimating the requirement for resident aliens to prove an equivalent knowledge as a condition for full inclusion. Now, there is the fact that an ever-increasing number of citizens attend school in a foreign country. But leaving that aside, the truth is that compulsory education exists and that one of the purposes it is expected to serve is that of facilitating the communication and the trust that social cohesion and a participatory democracy require to ensure citizens' responsible exercise of their duties.

This argument might partly support the selective inclusion of resident aliens, an inclusion which could, for instance, depend on proving some degree of knowledge of the dominant language of the country. However, we should note two things. First, that when native citizens disregard their duties with regard to compulsory education, this does not generally imply that they are either expelled from the country or prevented from participating in its political process. Second, that, if we set compulsory education or proof of a certain knowledge as a necessary condition for the inclusion of resident aliens, we find that those who do not comply with it will still preserve their residence. Once again, the alternative for resident aliens will be residence without citizenship or equal rights. And this is likely to have a marginalizing effect which serves even less well the proclaimed public interest of ensuring understanding and cohesion.

In general, the basic idea is that, rather than asking only immigrants to prove some kind of cultural assimilation, loyalty or political aptitude as a condition for the full enjoyment of political rights (either directly or through naturalization), the system should be ready to impose the same requirements on its citizens as a condition for the exercise of political rights.[8] Clearly, this is probably where the voices claiming that the very

---

[8] But see Bauböck 1994a: 96–7; Schuck 1994: 326. According to Bauböck, the fact that many citizens would not comply with naturalization requirements cannot be considered of equal relevance because admission does not have to be symmetric with expulsion. The conditions on which admission is based need not be the opposite of those for expulsion. After all, voluntary entry and involuntary exit are not comparable situations. Moreover, the involuntary exit of citizens violates the substantial norm of justice whereby promises ought to be kept. An association that has pledged to protect its members ought not to deprive them of this protection without serious and well-defined reasons. Connecting this position to the one defended here, I have to say that, to the extent that inclusion is attained through direct access to the full enjoyment of rights and freedoms, membership in the national association to which Bauböck refers would not even be necessary. But if

survival of democracy is at stake are likely to become more cautious. 'Asking for a certain degree of cultural assimilation or political loyalty is problematic if the requirements apply equally to everyone' (Carens 1989: 38). But this is precisely what ought to be done if permanent resident aliens are to be seen as part of the community (as I have claimed they should). Seen from this angle the problem ceases to be that of a society trying to defend its democratic system against any possible external harm, and becomes that of a society trying to face the challenge of integrating the claims of its diverse population. Whatever freedom-restricting measures need to be applied for the sake of preserving democracy (and that will be in itself a highly contested issue), these should be applied to all equally given that the political freedom of all the concerned individuals deserves equal respect.

Most likely, the incorporation of people holding different political interests, having different cultural backgrounds and economic positions will raise the level of difficulty in reaching a general and common good. However, if it is really the common good that we want to reach (and assuming that this must somehow accommodate conflicting interests and conceptions of the good), this cannot be done at the price of leaving out the dissenting voices of those who just appear to be too unprepared, too different, too dangerous, or too poor.

Inclusion as a path to integrating differences and ensuring cohesion

Exclusion to encourage effective inclusion

Of the assimilation requirements I have mentioned, there is one type which can be democratically relevant, not for the sake of protecting the larger society, but rather for ensuring resident aliens' well-being. I am referring to knowledge of the dominant language. Presumably, one could say something similar about a minimal knowledge of the country's institutions and political system. These requirements have the benefit of ensuring that people included in the body politic will have the necessary skills to enjoy effectively the opportunities offered to them and to their children in civil society and in the political process. The threat to the

membership in the national association is made a precondition to the enjoyment of essential political rights, something Bauböck seems ready to accept (Bauböck 1994b: 227), then the subsidiary claim of automatic membership would question the validity of applying the conditions to permanent resident aliens only and, more generally, of using in this context concepts such as those of admission and expulsion which, I argue, assume what needs to be decided to start with, namely, the relevant boundaries of membership in the political community.

stability and well-being of American society but also to their own well-being posed by the increasing failure of many Hispanics to master English is a recurrent theme in the USA (Schuck 1989: 63). Immigrants who do not master the language will probably experience exclusion even if they are formally accorded full civic equality (Bauböck 1994a: 99). Moreover, the language naturalization requirement is probably an effective method. A language test at the time of first immigration would lead to a very narrow selection, and after immigration only school children can be exposed to compulsory learning of the national language. Thus, imposing the linguistic requirement seems the only effective way to test whether adult immigrants really meet this basic requirement for active citizenship.

On the other hand, one should remember that, generally, it is immigrants themselves who are most interested in acquiring competence in the dominant language. It will allow them and their children to be included in the economic, social, academic and political life of the country (Kymlicka 1995: 15; Neuman 1994: 265). If, contrary to what one would expect to best serve their interests, settled aliens do not acquire the relevant skills, one needs to weigh up the benefits of using exclusion as a stimulating mechanism against the likely effects of exclusion in the long run if the mechanism fails (Legomsky 1994: 295). Often the real alternative is that of remaining perpetually excluded (Bauböck 1994a: 102). And the permanent exclusion of *de facto* members of society from civic equality might have a more detrimental effect on them and on the society overall than the inclusion of persons who are perhaps not ideally qualified. Such an exclusion can bring about a two-tiered society in which those who are most vulnerable are deprived of the political means to fight against the social conditions that may have made the access to the relevant qualifications so difficult for them to start with. Ultimately, one should not forget that the more demanding the conditions for inclusion, the greater their deterrent potential (Bauböck 1994a: 99).

Be that as it may, the main thrust of the argument is still that deriving normative conclusions from the nobility of the ends and the effectiveness of the means is not sufficient when the very legitimacy of the means is doubtful. It may be true that to be able to effectively exercise certain rights (like the right to vote and to participate in the political debate, or the right not to be discriminated against in hiring practices), as a matter of fact, one needs to acquire certain abilities (like the ability to communicate well in the dominant language). However, this does not necessarily justify the practice of requiring such abilities as preconditions to having formal access to the rights at stake. Rather, it could be said, it only shows that granting everybody an equal status of rights is sometimes insufficient to accommodate the specific needs of a sector of the population and hence, to safeguard effective inclusion. To live up to its commitment to equality of opportunities, formal freedom is a necessary precondition which needs to be supplemented sometimes to ensure real equality where it is most crucial, such as in the political process.[9]

If this is so, we can conclude that it might not be sufficient for the liberal state to tolerate languages other than the majority language. Positive measures to ensure equal freedom might be required. Incentives and opportunities should have priority over selective naturalization (Bauböck 1994a: 99; Legomsky 1994: 295). These may range from offering bilingual public education for the children, to offering instruction in the majority language in work places and bilingual information about the political system and the national institutions. All these seem adequate positive measures to encourage integration while respecting rather than penalizing differences.[10] In any case, what one should not do is take the actual requirements for enjoying a right effectively, and make of them requirements for the entitlement of the right, especially since enjoying rights in an effective manner can be assumed to be in the interest of their holders. Some language and cultural groups may be simply too small or dispersed to support alternative public cultures. But to the extent that the leading concern is equality of opportunities, at least in the political arena, it should be served by recognizing and allowing for the expression and accommodation of differences rather than by ignoring or penalizing them.[11]

The hope is to reach integration by reversing the path. When this is done, the political inclusion of permanent resident aliens ceases to be perceived as the terminus of an assimilation-based integration process

[9] This is why the requirement of economic sufficiency, which can also be connected to an interest in ensuring equality of opportunities in both civil society and in the political game, is also defective. Most of the time, and even concerning illegal immigrants, the alternative is not that immigrants will be motivated to improve their socioeconomic condition. I would imagine that this they already have a private interest to do. The alternative is rather that they will remain excluded from civic equality and that, in the long run, this exclusion will introduce further internal tensions into the system (e.g. with labour unions), and prevent immigrants from gaining the power they need to alter the social roots of their actual exclusion. A dynamics of exclusion could thus easily be generated.

[10] More doubtful, from a liberal perspective (where civic virtue cannot be presumed), would be imposing compulsory education on adults (Neuman 1994: 266). The choice might depend, first of all, on whether one thinks that the overall interest in achieving a free and equal society through a participatory democracy justifies this kind of freedom-restricting measure to ensure that everyone has the necessary skills to engage actively in the political process. One possibility would be that of allowing people to choose between proving a minimum knowledge of the language and agreeing to some kind of compulsory education. Finally, the legitimacy of imposing compulsory education will also depend on empirical evidence, such as whether a second language has or has not become so widespread that it can serve as a valid instrument for political communication.

[11] Although the effort here has been concentrated on the need to provide facilities to acquire the necessary linguistic skills, similar efforts might be needed to fight patterns of social discrimination and prejudice, so as to ensure that immigrants' rights are effectively enforced (Kymlicka 1995: 114).

and becomes the starting point for pluralistic integration. In response to those who argued against extending suffrage to the working class because the working class was not politically astute, John Stuart Mill responded in his *Considerations on Representative Government* that the working class would never become politically informed until it had the vote. Likewise, one would expect the expansion of voting rights to have an encouraging effect on the political participation of immigrants (Hammar 1990a: 150).[12] The risk of not trying out this possibility is always that of entrenching social exclusion in the law and deepening divisions within society by denying recognition and representation to certain cultural and religious groups (Bauböck 1994a: 101).

That immigrants themselves will give up their minority language and culture with time as they become increasingly influenced by the mainstream culture is only one possibility, though in many situations, it is the most likely one. Another possibility is that enough people come to speak a second or third language so that an alternative public language emerges. This possibility will probably depend on empirical questions such as the economic disadvantage suffered by monolingual speakers, and the efficacy of political communication across the language divide (Neuman 1994: 268). In any event, the preference for one official language can never represent the effort of a group to reserve power for itself (ibid.: 267). The identity of the political community may change over time, even dramatically so (Spinner 1994: 181).

What effective inclusion requires

Thus far, the issue has been whether resident aliens should be accorded special and provisional rights that help their integration into the mainstream society. A different question is whether they should also be granted specific national rights, permanent in nature, which allow them to retain their original culture, re-creating their homeland culture in the country of residence. Among these could be a right to institutions of self-government or to public services in their mother tongue, maybe similar to those a country's native ethno-cultural minorities sometimes enjoy.

---

[12] Layton-Henry explains that in Sweden it was hoped that by granting voting rights to resident aliens, ethnic and racial conflicts would be reduced (Layton-Henry 1991: 120). Since many of the immigrants had insufficient knowledge of Swedish the information about the new rights and the election system had to be translated for the first time into many different languages. Post-election studies have shown that the government authorities, political parties and labour organizations that produced information materials were able to draw increased attention to the election, even among those who had been indifferent prior to the campaign. For the first time foreign citizens in Sweden received political information in their own languages. Political parties translated their programmes and appealed to the immigrants at meetings and in brochures (Hammar 1985a: 94).

According to Kymlicka, although people should in principle be able to live and work in their own culture, these rights can be waived, and immigration could be one way of doing this. By voluntarily uprooting themselves immigrants may be giving away some of the rights that go along with their original national membership. This means that immigrants might legitimately be denied the legal status and resources they would need to become new national minorities in the countries of new residence (Kymlicka 1995: 95–6). Note, however, that Kymlicka makes a distinction between voluntary and involuntary immigration. He admits that in the case of involuntary immigrants, e.g. refugees, one could hardly say that they have freely decided to give up their culture. The problem is that the rights of refugees to stay and give expression to their culture are mainly rights against their own government. When they are not respected, the question as to what other country should redress that injustice becomes a difficult one (ibid.: 98).

As Kymlicka rightly argues, the fact that the line between involuntary refugees and voluntary immigrants is difficult to draw in a world with massive injustice in the international distribution of resources and with different levels of respect for human rights complicates things even further (ibid.: 98–9). However, if with Kymlicka we agree that most people accord great value to their own culture and are not easily ready to relinquish it (ibid.: 84 ff), a presumption on the involuntariness of its renunciation should be set for the cases in which immigration appears to be backed by a desire to overcome a situation of strong economic deprivation. Kymlicka is ready to admit that these kinds of considerations might make us more sympathetic to the demands for national rights of immigrants at least as long as the situation of unjust international distribution of resources is not rectified (ibid.: 99). But this, he argues, will not be sufficient to redress the injustices that must ultimately be solved in the original homeland (ibid.: 99–100).

One should add here that, with regard to settled resident aliens, it is especially relevant to recall that a long time of residence may, among other things, bring about a process of resocialization. This may render the new societal culture an essential referent for resident aliens, especially for second- and third-generation aliens. When this happens, one can hardly expect these immigrants to claim a right to the re-creation of the national culture they left behind. And it would probably also not be legitimate to coerce already-settled and half-integrated immigrants through a well-intentioned effort to re-create the context of their alleged national identity (e.g. through the geographical reallocation of immigrant groups to enable self-government).[13]

[13] This encourages us to distinguish between newly arrived immigrants and well-established immigrants. However, this distinction not only is practically difficult to establish but,

However, dual identities are more likely to occur, rather than just the straightforward replacement of one old identity linked to a specific societal culture by a new one. Hence, probably, resident aliens' need to preserve certain ties with both societal cultures. Even after long-term settlement, such a need would legitimize at least certain demands on the country of residence. Such demands could refer to bilingual education; to changes in the academic curriculum to include history and culture of immigrant groups; to the formal recognition of dual citizenship; or to the need for the country of residence to engage in international agreements with the countries of origin to facilitate the preservation of dual identities and attachments. Unlike the claims for self-government of many autochthonous national minorities, it seems that most of these measures need not be perceived as seriously divisive.

In any event, whatever the means necessary to guarantee integration, the alternative of exclusion from civic equality and, especially, from the democratic political process should be abandoned. For those who stress the general integrative potential of democracy, the inclusion of permanent resident aliens must be necessary. It obliges the community of citizens to address and therefore to become aware of this sector's needs and concerns in the process of defining the public good. Moreover, it encourages immigrants themselves to participate, forcing them to grow in responsibility and to become aware of their position in relation to the community of citizens, as well as to learn and contribute to a common political language. And this can only promote their support for laws and institutions that they will no longer see as merely imposed on them (Raskin 1993: 1446, 1452).[14] After all, it is a claim for inclusion in the mainstream society and not for separation that motivates, on most occa-

---

above all, may be regarded as fictitious to some extent. The process of social acculturation that immigrants may have experienced while in the country of residence and which is now taken as a reference to define their needs will probably be very different if, from the beginning of their stay, immigrants are afforded a right to reproduce their national culture and institutions in the new society.

[14] The integrative potential of democratic inclusion can be strongly supported by Pitkin's views about the interactive nature of the democratic process. Paraphrasing her, in a democracy citizens must explain why they think a certain policy should be implemented, and to do so they need to appeal to public standards in a public language. Thus they are forced to create a common language of purposes and aspirations, which, more than serving just to hide their private outlook in public disguise, makes them grow aware of their public significance. Citizens need to try to make the larger political community understand their reasons and needs if they want to convince others that they should support a specific policy. Citizens have to think about what kind of appeals to the larger community will work. This will make them think about the larger community, its problems and its needs. Thus, citizens will become directly involved in the definition of standards of justice and grow aware of the importance of such standards for the overall community. As citizens change the way they think, their identity also is likely to change. Thus, 'citizens become part of the larger community even as they battle parts of it' (Pitkin 1981: 347–8).

sions, immigrants' proclamation of their differences (Kymlicka 1995: 98). It is the desire that the common institutions be really common in that they allow for the expression of their cultural, linguistic or religious differences (ibid.: 118–19).[15] One should rather fear that exclusion and separation will come to hinder integration and to encourage minority politics, generating greater possibility for ethno-cultural conflict (Hammar 1990a: 167, 174).

Granted, democratic inclusion may not be a panacea for ensuring perfect integration. Greater efforts to ensure social justice will also be required. As Spinner notes with a certain cynicism, economic domination and oppression are a sure route to cultural pluralism because preventing members of certain groups from having access to the dominant institutions of society will almost certainly make them retain their different culture or construct an alternative one (Spinner 1994: 63). Just as an example, we could mention the generalized overall exclusion of resident aliens from public sector employment. As we will see, the traditional justification for it has always been that non-citizens, whatever their degree of economic and social integration, have not joined the political community. Therefore, their ultimate loyalty to the state cannot be presumed, and hence the need to exclude them from the exercise of public authority. However, as Brubaker observes, the wholesale exclusions made in the name of the need to preserve the basic conception of the political community often seem much more motivated by a mere desire to monopolize in favour of citizens the access to certain attractive and secure jobs (Brubaker 1989b: 153).

To those who fear democratic 'disintegration', one could say that, if anything, the democracies of the affected countries are actually strengthened by learning how to integrate cultural pluralism into their broader political culture. Democratic citizenship, in this respect, should not permit one official version of citizenship to deny equal citizenship for the rest of the population (Bauböck 1994a: 101; Spinner 1994). 'The demand [of liberal citizenship] to accept others as equal citizens is constantly evolving' (Spinner 1994: 75), for 'whenever citizens . . . face new practices they dislike, the real meaning of nondiscrimination comes to light; when liberal principles are tested, citizens come to understand their real meaning' (ibid.: 73–4).

---

[15] Some modifications of the institutions of the dominant culture might be needed to accommodate the needs of immigrants. Kymlicka mentions exemptions from Sunday closing legislation for Muslims, the right of Sikhs to exemption from motorcycle helmet laws and bilingual public education as examples of cultural adaptations that may be required to accommodate ethnic differences in the institutions of the mainstream society (Kymlicka 1995: 96–7).

5   Inclusion without consent

In the previous chapters the inclusion of resident aliens has been discussed in general terms only. No distinction was made between the different categories of resident aliens. It was only required that these be social members. And this merely implied having lived in the country for a number of years, turning it into the centre of one's personal and social experiences. But what about the so-called illegal resident aliens or illegal immigrants? Does their permanent subjection to the law and their being affected by it ultimately trigger their automatic and unconditional inclusion as well? There seems to be a general conviction that it does not. Let us explore why and whether it is morally defensible that this be so.

The exclusion of illegal resident aliens

In principle, if what disturbs our democratic spirits is the long-term coexistence of people with less than equal rights, the inclusion of illegal immigrants can only be more urgent than that of legal aliens. Granted, illegal immigrants are often accorded a whole variety of rights and guarantees. Among them, typically, are the right of access to the courts and appeal against deportation, the right to be treated humanely and usually also some essential social rights, like public education or minimum medical care. After all, we know that in many Western democracies these rights are constitutionally accorded to the person, and not to the citizen. Nevertheless, illegal immigrants' exclusion from civic equality is usually more severe than that of aliens legally residing in the country. In the case of illegal immigrants it is not primarily the lack of political rights reserved for citizens that prevents their equality, nor is it the lack of some of the social rights and civil liberties which are generally granted to legal immigrants. Rather, it is their absolutely precarious residential and working status that places them in a vulnerable and exploitable position from which even the enjoyment of those rights and guarantees theoretically granted to them is often practically impossible (Neuman 1996: 185; Layton-Henry 1990a: 15–16). It is widely known that the fear of being discovered and deported makes illegal immigrants underuse the social benefits and services to which they are entitled and prevents them from seeking redress of civil and criminal wrongs. No wonder that they are permanently exposed to exploitation. The pervading link binding illegal immigrants to their countries of origin (where one simply assumes they 'belong') works as a Damoclean sword. They may be entitled to some rights and benefits but if they make use of them they make themselves noticeable and risk deportation. For the illegal residents, who otherwise might come to regard the country of residence, where they have family and work, as the centre of their existence, this has a clear inhibitory effect.

So, we find that although illegal resident aliens' exclusion from civic equality is in principle more serious, the claim for their full incorporation has been much less explored. Within the discussions on their legal status often lurks a merely instrumentalist logic. Illegal immigrants' residence and life conditions are addressed in the public debate mainly in terms of whether the country derives more benefits from their presence (e.g. when there is a shortage of labour in some sectors of the economy) or more losses (e.g. when the social benefits this sector requires for a 'worthy' existence are said to drain the public economy more than the extent to which their work and tax money contribute to it). The most general justification in the public discourse for granting rights and benefits to illegal immigrants is that depriving them of some social rights and ser vices, such as education or health services, may affect the interests of society as a whole (criminality, public health, etc.). The wider interest is deemed to take priority. However, if we look at the competing interests that make up the wider one, we find that illegal immigrants are not treated as self-authenticating sources of valid claims.[1] In other words, their own needs and interests do not count as such but only to the extent that they may affect those of the larger society in which they live (López 1981: 626, 630).

The fact that public opinion and scholarly discussion have sympathized less with the inclusion of illegal aliens is to a large extent understandable. It seems related to the most basic concerns and assumptions about national and territorial sovereignty and to a view whereby membership, according to the liberal tradition, requires mutual consent (Schuck 1989; Schuck and Smith 1985). In the case of legal immigrants, we may be more ready to discuss whether some of the conditions set on their access to full or partial membership are adequate or fair from a liberal point of view.

---

[1] Rawls stresses the need for citizens to be viewed as self-authenticating sources of valid claims as one of the ways in which persons are seen to be free and equal in a constitutional democratic regime. By that he means that they are to be seen as able to make claims on the institutions to advance their own conceptions of the good (Rawls 1993: 30).

But nobody questions that the consent of the receiving community of citizens is always present. As a matter of fact, it is usually statutorily expressed. After all, legal immigrants have been allowed into the territory in the framework of the country's immigration policy. It is the law that sets the conditions for their naturalization or allows them to remain in the country as permanent resident aliens (Schuck 1989: 60). In contrast with this, in the case of illegal immigrants, consent is at most unilateral and hence, in principle, insufficient. Moreover, illegal entry is an infraction of the law. At stake is the minimum required for the preservation of the autonomy of the state as a sovereign territorial entity: its right to control who has access to its territory. Here, one would say, it is not the modality but the very capacity of the polity to determine itself concerning membership that is questioned. And it is questioned to the detriment of those would-be immigrants who patiently 'wait in the line' showing respect for the laws of the country.

Automatic incorporation of illegal resident aliens

At the same time, the phenomenon of illegal immigration is growing in scale and becoming institutionalized in more and more countries. This is the case in the United States, where millions of illegal immigrants are permanently settled and actively present in the labour market and in the public institutions (e.g. education and health systems).[2] In such cases, perpetuation of exclusion and inequality is regaining relevance as a proper concern of liberal democratic societies. For one thing, the alleged lack of consent becomes suspicious, when there has not been any serious attempt to prevent illegal entry or to deport illegal aliens before they consolidate their existence in the new society. After all, illegal migrant workers appear to be, in many respects, an ideally exploitable source of labour (Neuman 1996: 185). They are poorly paid, often unorganized and, for good reasons, uncomplaining (Wihtol de Wenden 1990: 42). Their availability and precarious position render them the ideal source of manpower to meet the fluctuations of the labour market.

More generally, there is an increasing dissatisfaction with confining the debate on the status of aliens to consent-based arguments. As we saw, a line of argument questions the distinctions in the status of rights within

[2] Under a legalization programme, which took place in 1986, the Immigration and Naturalization Service in the USA granted legal status to more than 1.2 million aliens who had unlawfully entered the country and more than 250,000 who had entered lawfully and overstayed their visas. Some estimates calculate that more than one million aliens enter the United States illegally each year, of which some 250,000 to 300,000 individuals remain in illegal status more or less permanently, producing an illegal population now estimated at over 5 million (Schuck 1997: 4).

the population when taken to apply to individuals who appear to be similarly situated as regards their integration into, contribution to, participation in, and dependency on the society and institutions of the state. And, increasingly, such considerations apply to the social realities that large-scale clandestine immigration is generating. Claims such as the following one (which were once made with the concern about legally settled aliens in mind) seem to hold true for both legal and illegal permanent resident immigrants in an increasing number of societies:

> [they] are certainly members of the states, participating in the labor and housing markets, paying taxes, bringing up families and sending their children to school . . . They contribute to and receive welfare benefits, and are involved in the social and cultural life of their local communities. (Layton-Henry 1991: 108, 118)[3]

As with the claim to inclusion advanced here in general terms, the main problem with confining the debate to a consensual rationality is that, when this is done, the consenting parts are generally assumed rather than discussed or justified. Now clearly, to the extent that we accept the existence and legitimation of states as separate and distinct units, we will always have recognized body politics entitled to decide on future incorporations. Yet the question is who should belong to such body politics and whether this decision is morally constrained or not. The claim advanced here is that at least all those who are permanently subject to the law and deeply affected by the political process should be automatically and unconditionally included. As societal members, settled immigrants (whatever their legally recognized status) qualify for full democratic membership. In other words, we could say that illegal resident aliens share with legal resident aliens sufficiently compelling moral grounds to claim recognition as part of the would-be consenters rather than the would-be consented. Claiming that in a liberal polity consent for inclusion has to be mutual does not solve the problem if we do not first explain and justify who the consenting parts are. The commonly made distinction between the morally constrained modality of inclusion (the 'how') and the morally unconstrained decision on inclusion (the 'whether'), on which the different perceptions on the treatment of legal and illegal resident aliens seem to rest, becomes thus an artificial one.

Now let us be clear. The main thrust of my argument is that whether

---

[3] Layton-Henry is referring to the need to include permanent resident immigrants in the political realm from which they are commonly excluded. For analogous claims, though referring expressly to illegal immigrants, see Carens 1989: 44: 'people who live and work and raise their families in a society are members of that society regardless of their legal status . . . Their presence may be against the law, but they are not criminals like thieves and murderers. It would be wrong to force them to leave once they have become members, even when we have good reasons for wanting them to go and to prevent others like them from coming.' Similarly, Jacobson 1996: 63 and Hammar 1994: 190.

immigrants hold a legal or illegal status or whether they comply with the statutory naturalization requirements loses its relevance as soon as automatic incorporation is morally and constitutionally mandated. But this is not to say that legal and illegal workers are put on exactly the same footing. Legal residents may have other bases on which to strengthen or accelerate their claims to full inclusion. They may still want to question the legitimacy of some of the naturalization requirements or the actual way in which these are applied. None the less, there should still be a limit on the time both legal and illegal immigrants can be kept outside the realm of civic equality. The time of residence that has been suggested here should therefore not be seen as a necessary condition for full incorporation. Rather, it should only be regarded as a sufficient condition to operate the automatic incorporation of both legal and illegal resident aliens. Hence the suggestion to calculate its length by adding the residence time that Western states have required to accept legal aliens as permanent residents to the period of time they have generally required for the 'regularization' of illegal entries. In other words, we are aiming to define a threshold after which the law cannot make legitimate distinctions in the recognition of rights by using the criterion of national citizenship or immigration status (similarly, Hammar 1994: 190, 196).

If immigrants qualify as societal members it is not because of a legally defined immigration status. Rather, this responds to the actual reality of people who migrate and come to live and work in a place in which they naturally develop a set of attachments, a place which, after a long residence period, they are likely to make the centre of their existence in practical terms. And this is why the criteria for inclusion (subjection and deep affectedness) also apply to illegal immigrants when they become well-settled societal members. Nevertheless, to make a convincing argument for the inclusion of illegal resident aliens we have to explore whether some specificities significantly strengthen the objections against inclusion in their case. So let us explore now how the 'fairness' and 'democratic' objections could specifically apply to illegal resident aliens. In doing so I hope to bring to the surface and discuss some of the most widespread assumptions lurking in the general public debates on illegal resident aliens.

Fairness and the inclusion of illegal resident aliens

Illegal immigrants are in principle subject to the laws and have to comply with the duties set out in them. However, their clandestine existence often excludes them in practical terms from some duties other than those which have traditionally been considered 'citizen duties'. Typically, the clandestine nature of their work not only facilitates but actually encourages tax evasion as one other means by which to remain unnoticed by the public authorities. The claim to full inclusion as applied to illegal aliens would therefore have to deal with such additional imbalances. But it would probably find it easy to do so, as it defends equality in rights and duties: make them pay all their taxes but let them effectively enjoy the whole set of benefits and services, as well as the civil rights and political freedoms citizens enjoy.

The truth is that criticism against inclusion generally focuses not so much on the fact that illegals do not contribute enough to the social well-being but rather on the fact that they do not contribute at all. Thus, the common claim is that illegal residents are actually a perturbing element, that they simply do not belong to the social scheme of cooperation. If they do get some rights it is not because they deserve them as their due share, but simply because not doing so would make the general society worse off. If anything, fairness makes exclusion mandatory. Exclusion not only from the political sphere, but also from the enjoyment of social benefits and services to prevent the exhaustion of the limited resources of the welfare system, and ultimately, exclusion from the country. This is why the case of illegal aliens presents certain significant peculiarities from the point of view of fairness. It is their contribution to the societies in which they live clandestinely that is questioned. The general view is that citizens and illegal aliens are not bound together in any kind of social cooperation scheme. And this supposedly justifies, in terms of fairness, the almost absolute exclusion of illegal immigrants from political, and also from other civil and social rights.[4] Only self-protection and the most basic humanitarian demands demand granting illegal resident aliens any rights at all.

Many people find it strange to even discuss the rights of illegal immigrants and unauthorized workers, because they have no right to be present in the country or at least should not be working. They have jumped the queue in which other people may have been waiting years to be lawfully accepted. Moreover, they often have committed criminal offences by avoiding immigration controls and/or by taking up work without permission. As wrong-doers, why should they have a moral claim to receive services from the very government whose laws they are transgressing (see Legomsky 1995a: 1468)? This explains why in the political

---

[4] Alternatively, one could claim that by not doing their fair share, i.e. not complying with the law, illegal immigrants are actually excluding themselves from the scheme of cooperation. But this might lead us to a circular argument in the sense that the reason why illegal immigrants are not allowed to participate fully in the scheme is that they are defined as not belonging to it to start with.

debates concerning the access of undocumented persons to public benefits and services they are often portrayed as 'outsiders by definition, as
non-part of the community' (see Johnson 1995: 1531, n. 83, 1538).

Yet, also in the public debate, one can find arguments in support of
illegal resident aliens' contribution. Thus, illegals are often described as a
positive resource taking unpleasant, low-paid work that native-born
workers refuse to do. They are generally law-abiding and independent,
and they often do not even dare to ask for the benefits to which they may
be entitled, and may well have contributed to through taxation (Johnson
1995: 1538; Wihtol de Wenden 1990: 42; Martin 1983: 202). The question would be whether this contribution, if persistent through time,
should not give illegal workers a fairness-based claim to full economic and
political inclusion. The fact that states often have ambiguous and even
contradictory attitudes towards illegal workers, allowing them to enjoy
some social benefits, might indicate that to some extent they recognize
such a duty towards them. At the same time, we know that mere self-
interest might also justify the granting of those rights. Jealous of their
border control as they are, states have been very reticent to admit the
consolidation of claims of illegal immigrants as a matter of right.

There may be no single way to respond to such a complex issue.
Nevertheless, it might still be worth the effort to conceptualize some of
the arguments that the fair play principle, as applied to the rights of illegal
immigrants, would need to face. Basically, as we have seen, these arguments turn on two different questions: first, whether illegal immigrants
generate benefits in the scheme of cooperation and second, whether these
benefits are relevant to tie illegal immigrants, on the one hand, and
citizens and legal immigrants, on the other, in one single scheme of
cooperation.

Concerning the first, generalizations are inadequate. We have already
seen that the claim that illegal immigrants make a significant contribution
in the country of residence is likely to be disputed.[5] Their work may
indeed be cherished by a sector of the population, such as the entrepreneurial sector, while being strongly opposed by some other sectors, such
as the national workers and their labour unions who fear the weakening of

---

[5] To follow the debate in the USA, see López 1981: 634–8, 713–14 (referring to the
cost/benefit analysis of Mexican illegal immigration in the USA). Whether illegal
immigrants are a net cost to the USA is a subject of continuing controversy. See also
Johnson 1995: 1531 (arguing that, generally, the public outcry about the stereotypical
undocumented immigrant on welfare in the USA is, to a large extent, misplaced, since
undocumented persons are ineligible for the major and most costly public assistance
programmes). Also see the bibliography quoted in Neuman 1996: 181, n. 86. See also
Reich 1995: 1588–94 (citing case law in the USA where courts have held that undocumented aliens should receive certain benefits due to their important role in the
nation's economic and social system).

their bargaining power and the loss of scarce job opportunities. On the other hand, illegals take lower status jobs that native-born workers will not. Although in many cases illegals pay taxes, their covert presence means that this is often not to the same extent as regular residents. Also, one would think that illegal immigrants' depressed socioeconomic position makes them especially likely to avail themselves of certain public services like public health or education. But the fact is that behind the large-scale flows of illegal immigration often lurks the awareness of a market of opportunities more than the hope of living exclusively and indefinitely at the public's expense. Illegals often, through fear of deportation, do not claim the benefits to which they may be entitled. Finally, while they may be generally law-abiding, their presence in large numbers contrary to the law may constitute in itself a source of instability and delegitimation of the system.

The question as to whether illegal immigrants contribute in society has therefore no easy answer and the factors that need to be taken into account to address the issue will change from case to case. However, as a general remark, we should note that it is not uncommon to find that the dangers and costs associated with the presence of illegal aliens are often overemphasized in the public debate and assumed, rather than thoroughly discussed. Take, for example, the previously mentioned argument that the very presence of illegals brings instability and delegitimizes the system. By repeatedly being referred to as 'outlaws' or 'lawbreakers', illegal immigrants become globally 'criminalized' (Johnson 1995: 1531; Neuman 1995: 1441). And yet the fact that they have broken immigration laws does not mean that one can only expect from them a career of unremitting delinquency. Admittedly, illegal immigrants have broken immigration laws as many people break other laws (e.g. tax laws). But this does not mean they should be globally described as criminals or outlaws. Citizens, by definition, cannot commit the crime of breaking immigration laws in order to gain access to their own country. The fact that this is therefore perceived as 'immigrants' criminality' does not justify its being 'stigmatized'.

We should also recall that the legal orders whose legitimation and validity we are trying to ensure, generally do not focus only on the punishment of illegal conduct. In many countries the idea that there should be time limits on the punishment of illegal conduct or the prosecution of criminal acts is common (Hammar 1994: 196). There are competing explanations for this principle of prescription according to which a penalty cannot be exacted or a crime prosecuted after an excessive lapse of time. Two have to be mentioned here as most closely related to our concern (Mir Puig 1995: 770 ff). The first has to do with the need to ensure a minimum of legal certainty. Briefly, the argument is that one has to take into account the expectations that the lack of prosecution of an illegal conduct will generate on the infractor after a long time. In other words, the latter should not endlessly be expected to bear the uncertainty of knowing that at any point in time she could be punished for an action she committed in the past. This is especially relevant when the punishment can have a tremendous impact on the person's life – as seems to be the case with deportation – and when – as happens with the breaking of immigration laws – the criminal conduct constitutes no offence to the most essential legal values, such as the life or integrity of human beings. In fact, one could even consider the threat of punishment over such a long period of time, and the uncertainty that necessarily goes with it, to be a sufficient punishment for the person's illegal conduct. This applies especially in the case of illegal immigrants where, as we know, this 'punishment' is likely to be aggravated by the fact that society at large often takes advantage of their illegality to subject them to systematic exploitation.

Another justification for the principle of prescription asks us to consider which social purposes the punishment serves and whether they can still be achieved when the punishment is inflicted long after the illegal conduct took place. In this respect, we should not forget that one of the main aims of criminal punishment is the general deterrence of criminal conduct. So, in our case, punishing illegal entrants would probably deter other would-be illegal immigrants. However, would this aim be achieved if deportation comes after an excessively long time? Or will other would-be immigrants gamble on the high probability that they will never be caught, or if they are, only after a very long period of time? In other words, does the deficient enforcement of immigration laws undermine the potential deterrent of the repressive mechanisms, thereby defeating the very purpose that inspires them? If so, who should be blamed then for the delegitimation of the system?[6]

Interesting as it may be, the discussion on the extent to which illegal immigrants benefit from or contribute to the public scheme of cooperation might not even be needed. Let us assume what seems likely, namely, that to a greater or lesser degree they do contribute. Does it necessarily follow that citizens and illegal immigrants are, in any relevant sense, members of a scheme of cooperation that unites them in the conduct of some kind of joint enterprise in which fairness claims can arise? We know that this will probably be denied by the country that hosts them, even if we limit ourselves to the case that most concerns us here, namely, that in

---

[6] Another explanation for the principle of prescription focuses on procedural rather than substantive grounds and questions the likelihood of guaranteeing the prosecuted a fair trial, given that the relevant evidence for the case may have disappeared or weakened with time, allowing for a greater risk of judicial error.

which illegal immigrants are numerous and actively integrated in the national labour force.

This takes us to the question of acceptance of the benefits. One of the strongest arguments against the existence of a duty of fair play *vis-à-vis* illegal immigrants is that whatever the benefits that derive from their residence and work in the state, they have not been accepted in any relevant way by the community. After all, for a fairness-bound duty to do one's share to arise, it is not enough that the benefits are simply produced; they also need to be accepted by the individual. Otherwise, one could simply be an 'innocent bystander of [a] scheme built around [oneself]' (Simmons 1979: 120). Going back to the neighbourhood well example used in chapter 3 to deal with the question of free riding (see p. 57), it seems that to be bound by a duty of fair play Jones needs to accept the benefits of the scheme, as he clearly does by taking the water. We might have felt very different about him if, after he refused to cooperate, the others had none the less supplied him with the facility to use the well, and, in spite of him not having made any use of such a facility, they had still expected Jones to pay his share on the grounds that the facility had been granted to him.

In the case of illegal immigrants one could say that whatever benefits are generated, they are generated against the community's will as explicitly expressed in its rules. To explain the difference between receiving and accepting benefits let us take another example that Simmons provides. This time he asks us to imagine that 'a stranger sneaks into my yard while I am out of town and mows my lawn', and then compares it with the case in which a stranger 'asks me if I'd like to have my lawn mowed, and proceeds to mow it after receiving an affirmative response. In both cases I have clearly received a benefit (in fact, the same benefit), but only in the latter would we say that I had "accepted" that benefit.' And 'it seems equally clear that this distinction may play a crucial role in determining whether or what obligations arise from my having benefited' (Simmons 1979: 108).

Thus the question in our case would be whether the host society not only benefits from illegal workers' contribution, but whether it also accepts such a contribution in some relevant sense for 'it would be peculiar if a man, who simply going about his business in normal fashion benefited unavoidably from some cooperative scheme, were told that he had voluntarily accepted benefits which generated for him a special obligation to do his part' (ibid.: 131).

Different authors have presented different interpretations as to how the acceptance requirement should be understood. Simmons claims that to have accepted a benefit an individual must have either 'wanted the benefit

[he] received, or have made some effort to get the benefit, or at least not have actively attempted to avoid getting it' (ibid.: 108). For Klosko the goods need not be accepted in the strict sense. It is sufficient if they are 'presumptively beneficial goods', e.g. goods that one can assume that everybody wants whatever else they may want (Klosko 1992: 39 ff). Now, in the case of legally accepted or recruited immigrant workers it seems clear that society has calculated and wanted the benefits it is going to receive from this pool of labour. It is often the case that immigration has been actively encouraged by the receiving state. Also, the granting of permanent residence and working permits is generally accompanied by requirements seeking to ensure the future law-abidingness of the concerned individuals (e.g. good moral character or absence of criminal records) and even their economic sufficiency and social integration.[7] In contrast, the case of illegal immigrants is more doubtful and seems closer to that of the stranger who sneaks into the owner's yard without his awareness, mows his lawn and comes later to ask for his share. Not even the main benefit that society could be said to derive from illegal immigration – the availability of a cheap labour force ready to take jobs rejected by the rest of the population – must necessarily be seen as a benefit the country has actively promoted.

This, however, need not be conclusive. As long as the benefit is produced, we feel intuitively compelled to check that it is really true that it has not been accepted by the society that benefits. One would probably feel different about the case of our lawn-mowing man if, in clear contravention of the regulations of a neighbourhood, he had adopted the regular habit of coming and performing his mowing activity in many of the yards of the neighbourhood, without there being any serious attempt to prevent him from doing so. In this case, probably, we would not feel that the benefits are being imposed on the neighbourhood (as opposed to being accepted by it). This is why in the case of illegal workers' alleged contribution we may want to ask ourselves how active the state has been in

---

[7] This is why one can always say that *legal* resident aliens have been considered worthy of community membership. In the USA, for instance, it is a general practice for entry to be conditional on immigrants' potential economic self-sufficiency and to limit their access to public benefits during the initial years after entry as a way of ensuring 'that those who come are worthy of community membership and are likely to contribute economically to its betterment' (Johnson 1995: 1538–9).

Note, however, that this does not necessarily imply that, for the acceptance requirements to be satisfied, all the possible moral consequences of the transaction must have been taken into account and wanted. If this was so, fairness would collapse into consent (see Simmons 1979: 117). And yet the distinction is relevant. In some cases the recruitment of immigrant workers might have been initially conceived in the form of a temporary guestworker programme and only later, and as a result of moral imperatives, might the guestworkers have been allowed to stay as permanent residents.

attempting to avoid it. As a matter of fact, in those countries facing the reality of large-scale illegal immigration, it is not uncommon to find the government criticized for a tacit attitude of toleration (Bosniak 1994: 1083; López 1981: 707–8).

On the other hand, in discussing the requirement of acceptance, we would also need to take into account the degree of difficulty and effort that the effective refusal of the benefits requires. So, going back to our lawn-mowing man, we might feel different about his fairness-based claim on the neighbours if he sneaks in and works during the times he knows everyone is away on holiday (even if the neighbours are informed by someone not belonging to the neighbourhood about the man's activities), rather than when all the owners are at home and see him work day after day. Acceptance of the benefit would be more likely to be presupposed in the second case.

Returning to the phenomenon of illegal immigration, it seems clear that the consideration of many different factors is required. The dimensions of the problem, the degree of social awareness, the active adoption of measures to stop it (like border controls, but also sanctions on employers) and the seriousness in enforcing the required measures are some of the relevant considerations. The ease or difficulty of enforcing control mechanisms should also be pondered. The easier it is to isolate oneself from the benefit-generating contribution, the stronger the case for not seeing the contribution as merely incidental and hence, the stronger the case in favour of the fairness-based obligation to give illegal workers their due share. One would assume that the larger the dimensions of the social phenomenon, the more difficult and costly its eradication. In other words, the larger the number of illegal immigrants, the less well founded the claim that their toleration in the country hides an attitude of hypocritical and tacit acceptance. Rather, one would tend to think that the costs of eradication of the phenomenon are simply higher than those of its passive toleration. Now it is obvious that the costs of eradication or prevention will be larger where the phenomenon has already reached large dimensions. But on the other hand, one should not forget that the larger the phenomenon, the more suspicious its spontaneous generation in the first place (see López 1981: 669).[8]

---

[8] When the phenomenon is widespread and reaches large dimensions interesting questions about intergenerational obligations arise. Thus, López (1981) argues that illegal immigration from Mexico was actively encouraged by the USA throughout history and that, due to this, new generations of Mexicans grew up relying on this possibility which they considered they had somehow 'inherited'. See also Legomsky 1995a: 1469.

Illegal resident aliens and the democratic objection

As applied to illegal resident aliens, the claim of automatic incorporation could also imply certain additional problems arising from a concern with preserving the liberal democratic order. On the one hand, the resulting change for the benefit of illegals is more significant than for aliens who have been accepted into the country but have not passed the citizenship test that would allow them to share in the political process shaping the polity's destiny. What illegal resident aliens have to gain from full inclusion is much more than unconditional and automatic political inclusion. In their case societal recognition will make the greatest difference, meaning the allocation of a public space where they can live and work in the open. Unlike the case of legal resident aliens the choice here is not between remaining with less than equal rights and gaining full inclusion. At stake is illegals' actual chance to remain at all, in no matter what conditions.

However, on the other hand, if we look at it from the receiving society's point of view we also find some significant differences between the cases of legal and illegal immigrants. Legal resident aliens have at least overcome some selection processes: one which controls who has access to the country and one which defines who is entitled to establish his or her residence in it. Presumably, these decisions are taken in the awareness that they imply a choice on the future composition of the society. Thus, the receiving country can try to ensure, already at this stage, that the newcomers will not place too great a strain on the absorptive capacity of the liberal state and its institutions. To this purpose would-be immigrants are often asked to give an indication of their present and future economic self-sufficiency (e.g. adequate professional skills) and of their political aptitudes (e.g. absence of criminal record). Now what distinguishes illegals is precisely the fact that they do not pass this initial scrutiny. Their automatic and unconditional inclusion would therefore question even more deeply the community's right of self-determination concerning membership (both social and political). It would also force it to a larger degree of openness with more unforeseeable consequences. Hence the worry that it might imply a significantly greater threat to the health of the social and democratic institutions of the liberal state.

Such a worry seems well founded. To the extent that the capacity to remain bounded spaces is essential to the very functioning of liberal democratic states, the automatic incorporation of illegal immigrants would clearly imply a more serious threat. After all, it would sanction the practice of systematic disregard for the mechanisms through which that boundedness is commonly ensured. Moreover, it might actually encourage other would-be immigrants to freely join in the community in the awareness that, in due course, they too will gain full recognition as equal members. The right to collective self-definition concerning membership would thus be seriously curtailed, and with it, the capacity to choose those newcomers who, culturally, economically and politically, might pose a lesser threat to social and political cohesion, understanding and solidarity.

Serious as this objection may be, it should be clear that it is not the right to self-definition, but only its scope, that the claim to full inclusion questions even when applied to illegal resident aliens. The polity is still entitled to have an immigration policy containing the criteria and the priorities for new incorporations. Coercive measures can be legitimately adopted to enforce such a policy. On the other hand (and this is where the claim comes in) such a prerogative has to be limited in time. For affected by it will not only be recognized citizens but, more and more, those non-recognized members who, in the meantime, have set down roots and integrated socially. In other words, both possible extremes are unacceptable: denying the polity's right to enforce its immigration laws and allowing people to live endlessly in the precariousness and exploitable condition in which illegal immigrants exist.

What about the alleged encouraging effect? In principle, the awareness that one will be set on the route of citizenship as soon as one gets into the country (even against its express will) might indeed render illegal entry more appealing. On the other hand, it seems that the existing possibilities in the job market are the main pull factor in societies with large communities of clandestine aliens. The full set of social rights and benefits or the access to the polls that would come with citizenship could improve the living conditions of the affected immigrants. But this does not mean that these are the things that actually have a strong appeal for them, especially when compared with the importance of being able to make a living. Also, one should not forget that illegal immigrants' access to these rights and benefits would be deferred in time and equality would come only after about ten years.

However, the possibility that inclusion might provide an incentive for further large-scale immigration could be relevant in deciding on the modality of incorporation of illegal immigrants. Thus, we could distinguish between collective amnesties and individual regularization. Collective amnesties may become necessary when a large stock of illegal immigrants has built up and presents serious social and economic problems. But their negative consequences are considerable. They present an incentive for further illegal entries or an occasion for tightening immigration control. These effects are considerably weaker when regularization is continuous and comes after a longer time of residence. So, even though ironically Western states have been much more willing to repeat the exercise of collective amnesties rather than to fix a general time period after which illegal entry would no longer count as a reason for deportation or differentiation in the recognition of rights, the latter seems to be a better alternative to meet the demands of justice and yet minimize the possible costs that the inclusion of illegal immigrants may trigger.

At this point we should also mention the possibility of intangible damages to the receiving society. Among them, most clearly, is the risk of the gradual loss of credibility of a system that ultimately allows people to gain benefits from their infringement of the law. This is a common claim in the debates on illegal immigrants. But it lacks, first of all, accuracy. Whatever the benefits illegal resident aliens derive *from* their inclusion and recognition, these do not derive from their infringement of the law but only *in spite of* their infringement of the law. Thus, the claim here is that with time the importance of having entered the country and established one's existence in it without the permission of the community should decrease and allow for subjection and affectedness to develop their inclusive potential. Also, one should say that even if we take the concern with the general credibility of the system to be a serious one, a parallel question cannot be avoided: how much does this credibility suffer from the *de facto* consolidation of a second-class citizenship which is formed by an exploitable labour pool of thousands of people who live and work in the dark?

Nevertheless, when confronted with the case of legal immigrants, the inclusion of illegals into the social and political schemes of cooperation has at least one additional particularity. This particularity may be especially significant in liberal democracies which are committed to a certain idea of distributive justice resting on a shared sense of solidarity. In the case of legally accepted or recruited immigrant workers, as we said, the society has presumably calculated and wanted the benefits it is going to receive from a pool of labour whose economic sufficiency it has probably tried to ensure first. This has little in common with the uncontrolled aggregation of what is often only poor and unskilled labour. As poor and unskilled labour, the inclusion of those citizens who have joined in illegally might be a potential source of conflicts, especially of conflicts with the native groups at the lower edge of the social scale.

In this respect, the inclusion of illegal immigrants inevitably raises a whole set of sensitive issues. And once again, generalizations may be deceiving. The underlying concern with the draining of limited resources and the tensions that would come with it can be more or less justified depending on the concrete situation. It is not uncommon that, whatever the price that a certain society needs to pay for the sake of including marginalized or oppressed groups, it will be unevenly distributed among the population, affecting more seriously those in a weaker position. We should not oversimplify this. If our concern is with social benefits and public services, we know that, already, as illegal residents, immigrants might be entitled to some of them. The argument that this does not really count because fear of deportation prevents them from actually using them is self-defeating in a discussion that is led in the name of preserving our liberal democratic institutions. Also, we have to take into consideration that, as citizens, former illegal immigrants who abandon the realm of the country's submerged economy would probably have to contribute more to the social net.

After all the calculations, which would lead to different results depending on each case, we may still find that the inclusion of illegals is not economically 'profitable'. We may find that it still introduces additional social and economic strains and that these strains would affect the deprived classes of citizens more seriously. Would this justify exclusion? Or would it rather imply that the better-off classes who, in principle, are those who gain the greater benefits from exploiting illegals in the first place, would now have to contribute more to pay for their 'citizens' suits'?

The concern with the scarcity of job opportunities and with how inclusion would affect in this respect citizens at the lower edge of the social scale is easier to address. The truth is that, to the extent that citizens are really willing to do the kinds of jobs that illegals take up, competition exists already before inclusion. As a matter of fact, inclusion would only imply that competition would occur with fairer terms to the advantage of citizens. It is clear that the clandestine labour market commonly functions precisely because illegal immigrants know and willingly agree to take jobs in infra-legal conditions. It is easy to see how this can affect the bargaining power of citizen workers. Setting limits to this might curtail the flows of illegal immigration as it would make this labour force less attractive to the entrepreneurial sector. But this would probably be the only way to really cut down the tensions with native workers and labour unions.

This raises an interesting issue. Some may argue that, if given the choice, illegal immigrants might be willing to forgo some rights and freedoms and accept indefinite exclusion to be able to enter the country and find a stable source of income there. After all, they may find 'exploitation' in the country of residence more freedom-enhancing altogether than having no other option but remaining in their countries of origin. So, once again, if given a choice, they might prefer the system as it is over one with more rigid control mechanisms that would prevent them from entering the country or consolidating their existence there but would treat them as equals once they do. However, the right to consolidate an equal status of rights with time cannot be waived. It cannot be waived at least as long as we are not ready to generally accept the legitimacy of one of the following: one, a two-tiered society with a second-class citizenship (and then, the question becomes why we should limit this 'option' to illegal immigrants only), or two, an ultra-libertarian order which knows of no borders but also of no social rights for anyone, whatever their citizenship or immigration status.

It is important to recall at this point that full inclusion implies not only that illegal immigrants will have a right to stay and thus to regularize their *de facto* social membership. It also implies that they will be included in the body politic automatically, circumventing the filter of both entry regulation and naturalization criteria. Does this raise additional concerns of the kind expressed under the democratic objection? Two things might be relevant here. First, one could argue that in the case of illegal resident aliens, by definition, the presumption of law-abidingness that we argued should apply to legal resident aliens can no longer hold. Illegal immigrants' presence in the country is a continuous infringement of the law. Second, relevant also might be the fact that illegals' precarious residential and working status presumably reduces the chances they have to participate in civil and political life and, with it, the chances of exposure to the legal and political institutions in the country of residence. This might render their political and cultural assimilation significantly more difficult and hence make automatic and unconditional political inclusion more problematic.

However, the fact is that with the obvious exception of immigration laws, well-settled illegal immigrants are often known to be generally law-abiding. It is obvious that they have a special interest in being so. Being law-abiding is often what allows them to remain in the dark, and to preserve their work and family life in the country. So, the question becomes: should the breaking of immigration laws be taken as a proxy for general criminal conduct and justify the compellingness of preventive exclusion? Or should the consolidation of long-term residence, the fact that the alien has not made herself noticeable through ulterior criminal conduct and hence, has not been deported, set a contrary presumption of general law-abidingness? The presumption would be reinforced by the fact that, increasingly, states are embracing policies of prioritizing the deportation of those illegal immigrants who do commit crimes. Ultimately, the claim of automatic incorporation does not imply that repressive mechanisms against general criminal and illegal conduct should be given up. Nor does it imply that the filters that are commonly used to prevent criminals from exercising political rights or functions should not apply. Basically, only the possibility of deporting illegal immigrants as such is given up, and this only with time. But after such time, if they are punished for some criminal activity which is not related to their immigrant status, what justifies the fact that they also endure the additional punishment of being cut off from their social and cultural environment? They may still be criminals, but why should we endlessly consider them 'someone else's criminals'? The harshness of sending criminals to their countries becomes most evident when it is applied to second- or third-generation aliens who may have never been to 'their' country of nationality before and may not even speak its language.

As for the risk of an aggravated lack of cultural and/or political socialization due to a lesser exposure to the legal and political institutions of the country of residence, such a risk exists and concern is justified. But once again we are faced with the question of which normative conclusions should be attached to it. Since the ultimate right of inclusion, as defended here, does not depend on any kind of proof concerning the degree of cultural or political assimilation, the conclusion can only be that, to the extent that social and political harmony really rest on those grounds, positive and encouraging measures should be taken to help those who have had fewer chances to acquire the necessary skills and knowledge, partly because of their prior exclusion.

This links up with the concern about the damaging potential of exclusion that was mentioned in passing. In more and more Western countries we find well-established communities of illegal immigrants. Whether because of the undesired insufficiencies of enforcement mechanisms, or a more or less tacit and hypocritical attitude of tolerance, the fact is that many of those immigrants will never be deported from those countries. And this forces us to ponder also the socially marginalizing effects that the legal measures restricting illegals' access to social benefits or to the political process can have (Legomsky 1995a: 1465; Raskin 1993: 1466–7; Bosniak 1988: 998–1006, 1019). For illegal residents exclusion implies a more serious deprivation of rights and protection than it does for legal resident aliens. The latter, as we know, enjoy at least most of the social rights and benefits granted to citizens. The marginalizing effects of keeping the former out of the realm of civic equality can therefore only be more severe also because their social, economic and cultural background places them especially in need of inclusion.

6 Keeping nationality relevant

Having presented and defended the claim to the automatic incorporation of resident aliens and explored some of the strongest objections against it, it is time now to analyse the specific modalities of inclusion embraced by the main claim to full inclusion and the secondary claim to automatic membership.

Disentangling rights from citizenship v. encouraging naturalization

Two paths have been most commonly proposed to overcome the increasing dichotomy between socioeconomic and political membership in those countries with large communities of permanent resident aliens. One way is to extend all the rights citizens currently enjoy, including political rights, to immigrants. The second is to encourage naturalization by liberalizing naturalization policies (Hammar 1990a). Generally, such paths are explored to ensure the incorporation of legal resident aliens only.

The alternative of encouraging naturalization has been said to be more in accordance with the generalized conception of democratic citizenship as membership, not just in any polity, but in the still dominant political unit in the international community: the nation-state. Such a conception is supposed to serve an inherently egalitarian ideal, according to which the members of the nation-state are united in a single status of membership.[1] The international system already defines an external membership

---

[1] As defined externally from the perspective of the international system, citizenship, or nationality, as it is more often called in this context, binds all those who are admitted into it in a state of reciprocal and permanent protection and allegiance. It defines as citizens those who have an absolute right to return to the state (Legomsky 1994: 300) and cannot be deported (on the international limits on a nation deporting its own nationals see International Convention on Civil and Political Rights, art. 12.4, 999 UNTS 171, 176, adopted by the UN General Assembly as Res. 2200 (XXI) on 16 December, 1966; Starke 1984: 330). It also refers to those who can enjoy that state's diplomatic protection when they are maltreated or endangered by other states while abroad (Lillich 1984: 8–17); to

status which is based on national citizenship. Whereas democratic membership is based around the idea of political equality and ensures only that the rights and duties which are essential for preserving political equality are recognized to all on equal terms, national membership derives a certain substantive content from the framework of the international political system. By making membership in the democratic polity and in the nation-state go hand in hand, we obtain a single status of membership which is characterized by the sharing of a realm of bounded political equality both internally and externally defined (Legomsky 1994: 298). National citizenship has inevitably both an excluding and an including potential (Brubaker 1992: 21–50).

Tying nationality and democratic membership together has been said to encourage a sense of identity and hence, a spirit of solidarity and readiness to sacrifice for the sake of our peer compatriots. Narrowing the gap between citizens' rights and those of resident aliens may bring about an entitlement mentality which devalues citizenship and makes mutual sacrifice more difficult (Schuck 1989: 60 ff). A mere rights-based membership might not prove to be a sufficient link to bind people together, especially in times when few duties are specifically required from national citizens anyway. Feelings of belonging, exclusiveness, solidarity and sacrifice can be of extreme importance to encourage civic virtue and the responsible exercise of rights and freedoms. The proper functioning of social democracies and the prospering of the state, which remains the most encompassing protective framework, might well depend on them. Preserving full and equal rights for national citizens only may well be the expression of group preference, a group preference which may appear illicit in a liberal morality, but, at the same time, may be central to civic morality in healthy democracies (Whelan 1988: 31).

Clearly, there is always the option to look for other possible sources for such feelings. But whether alternative membership feelings can be constructed on different grounds or institutions, as some authors have suggested (Legomsky 1994: 293), remains merely speculative. For many the usefulness of engaging in the search for alternative paths to ensure communal bonding is, to say the least, doubtful. The fact that other institutions could play an equivalent role to that of citizenship is not sufficient to

those whom the state can refuse to extradite in the absence of a specific treaty obligation (Starke 1984: 330); but also to those who owe a duty to perform military service for the state or, at least, cannot be forced by another nation to fight against it in the case of war (see Convention Respecting the Laws and Customs of War on Land, 18 October, 1907, art. 23,36 Stat. 2277 (1911)), or, finally, to those who can be subject to the jurisdiction of their own state of nationality for acts committed abroad (Starke 1984: 224). So a derivative status of membership and a set of rights are inherent to the relationship of national and state as assumed in the international order.

make a persuasive case for downplaying an institution that already accomplishes the useful task of evoking civic virtue. One should at least be quite sure that those other institutions are adequate to fill the void beforehand (Martin 1994: 303). National citizenship has this function, and, at the same time, 'can be defined in quite open and non-invidious terms' (Schauer 1986: 1515). It is therefore important that it should not be devalued.

Some of those who defend the path of naturalization stress also that the membership feeling that national citizenship conveys should not only be judged instrumentally. Many people take it to provide for experiences that are valuable in themselves (Whelan 1988: 32; Schauer 1986: 1504–6). National citizenship, it has been said, has provided a 'focus of political allegiance and emotional energy on a scale capable of satisfying deep human longings for solidarity, symbolic identification, and community', serving as an 'enclave to define oneself and one's allegiances more locally and emotionally' (Schuck 1997: 8; 1989: 65; Note 1997). A strong sense of communal membership has built around it, and nothing better protects a sense of 'relatedness and mutuality' (Walzer 1983: 29).

The main problem with recognizing alternative paths to the full enjoyment of rights and duties within the political community, but outside the boundaries of national citizenship, is that it might cut off fundamental parts of the concept of citizenship (Hammar 1990a: 198) and practically devalue the meaning of national membership. In order for it to preserve its community-bonding function, certain tangible benefits or entitlements might need to turn on citizenship (Schauer 1986: 1516).[2] Granted, such a devaluation could be seen as a new victory for the liberal principles of inclusiveness and equality given the current reality of large percentages of non-citizens integrated as part of the ordinary population of the state (Soysal 1994). However, the dangers that such a step might bring to the liberal project should not be neglected. If the significance of national citizenship declines, we might expect 'people's more parochial loyalties [to] loom correspondingly larger and to be asserted with greater intensity' (Schuck 1989: 65). Historically, neighbourhoods have turned into closed or parochial communities whenever the state was open (Walzer 1983: 38). In societies that are already pervaded by inequalities of all kinds (ethnic, wealth, religious, gender and linguistic), losing the common ground of nationality might not be without its dangers (Martin 1994: 307; Schauer 1986: 1516; Walzer 1983: 62–3). Ultimately, nation-states are still relevant

---

[2] Note, however, that the contrary argument has also been held, namely, that in order to preserve its meaning national membership should be disentangled from the rights of citizens so as to avoid an instrumental approach to the former which undermines its capacity to express community affinity (Note 1997).

as social, institutional and cultural spaces allowing individuals to meaningfully enjoy the rights and freedoms granted to them in a liberal order (Kymlicka 1995: 84 ff).

On the other hand, the alternative of encouraging or facilitating naturalization by liberalizing naturalization policies has not gone uncontested. First of all, it might not be a good way to go about disentangling rights from citizenship. Liberalizing naturalization policies generally implies reducing the qualifications necessary and/or reducing the degree of administrative discretion in application procedures to render naturalization more like a real choice (Hammar 1990a: 212–15). However, for the same reason that opening the path to citizenship rights without requiring naturalization may devalue the meaning of citizenship, making access to citizenship through naturalization too easy may have similar results.

I will criticize this alternative from the other extreme, that is, as not inclusive enough. Indeed, even if facilitated and encouraged, the alternative of naturalization might not solve some of our initial concerns. Typically, the alternative of naturalization as a right addresses only the concern of legal immigrants, rather than of illegal. Also, when presented as a right, a whole set of conditions are generally defined as requirements that must be fulfilled before the consolidation of such a right. Finally, even if the right to naturalization was fully unconditional and phrased in terms which allowed for the inclusion of illegal immigrants, there would still be many resident aliens who would not apply for naturalization. And this could be troublesome if we take our concern to refer not only to the exclusion but also to the self-exclusion of resident immigrants from the political realm and its likely effect on both the individual well-being of immigrants and the broader democratic society that we are trying to preserve.[3] Both the fear of losing some valuable assets by acquiring a new nationality (e.g. property rights, a certain sense of identity, or the possibility of returning to the country of origin), and what might be perceived as mere political apathy might account for such attitudes of self-exclusion.

The alternative of automatic incorporation

If we recall, the claim to automatic incorporation of permanent resident aliens is organized into a main claim and a secondary claim. The main

---

[3] Easy and encouraged naturalization has brought about a rather successful incorporation rate in countries like Canada. However, in other countries in which naturalization is conceived as a right, such as the USA, the naturalization rate of some communities, such as the Hispanic, had been declining over the past few years. The recent reintroduction of citizenship as a legal condition for having access to some social benefits has dramatically altered this trend. This may prove the soundness of the argument that disconnecting rights (e.g. social rights) from national citizenship discourages political incorporation through naturalization.

claim tells us to open the path to the enjoyment of equal rights and duties (the path of full inclusion). Only when a sufficiently compelling case can be made to prove that such enjoyment is best ensured for all by binding it to the recognition of the status of national membership – something which may prove to be the case now but not necessarily in the future – does the secondary claim come into play. The secondary claim tells us that such a status ought to be granted automatically to all those who deserve, according to the main claim, full equality in the enjoyment of rights (the path of automatic membership).

The claim to full inclusion coincides with one of the discussed alternatives, that of disentangling rights from national citizenship. The secondary claim admits (though does not necessarily endorse) the thesis that, as today, there might be compelling reasons not to split democratic citizenship from national membership. However, it departs from what has traditionally been perceived as the natural alternative: recognizing resident aliens a right to naturalization, preceded by a right to amnesty and regularization for those illegally present (Bauböck 1994b: 226–7; Hammar 1990a; Carens 1989: 32, 47; Walzer 1983: 58). Instead, it advocates the automatic and unconditional granting of national membership.

The difference should be perceived in its proper terms. Clearly, the more the right to naturalization (and, eventually, to regularization) is recognized unconditionally and as a matter of right, the closer we will come to meeting the requirements grounding the claim to full inclusion. Practice has shown that it is accepting naturalization as a right, not to mention as an unconditional right, that states have most strongly resisted. Instead, they have considered naturalization as an essential expression of their sovereign nature and have always referred to some requirement in addition to residence. However, the need to go one step further and proclaim automatic access to citizenship is not irrelevant. It rests on an important conceptual difference. More than a right to naturalize (or regularize), what is claimed is the right to be recognized as a legitimate holder of all the rights granted to citizens. When the latter is linked to the status of national citizenship for some compelling reason grounded on the preservation of the liberal system, then resident aliens are automatically recognized as national citizens. So the ascription of nationality encompasses all those who, following the normative constraints set on citizenship, should share in the sphere of civic equality.

Underlying this notion of an autonomous claim to membership is the idea that permanent resident aliens have to be seen as belonging to the constituent community already. What they need from the politically empowered community is not permission to enter it fully and on equal terms, but mere recognition. Their belonging derives from facts – their permanent subjection to political authority and their social integration –

made morally relevant by means of a commitment to liberal democracy. If we were to phrase the debate in consensual terminology we would state that, in principle, the consent of the 'recognized community' (the community formed by those who at any given moment are legally recognized citizens) is expressed through the conditions it sets on 'newcomers' for their access to the different membership and right entitlements. The idea suggested here is that, once again, such a consent becomes irrelevant because the duality of roles that it assumes (the 'consenters' and the 'consented') loses significance in front of the claim that the would-be consented in fact belong already to the group of the would-be consenters. Hence, the strong symbolic implications of using one path or the other to ensure inclusion.

In general terms embracing this modality of incorporation would help adapt the overall structure of citizenship allocation to face a reality it did not conceive when it was shaped (i.e. the reality that the tissue of the state would be increasingly made up of people who were not born in the country and who hold dual attachments and identities), helping the notion of citizenship preserve its meaningfulness as a protective asset in liberal democracies. Too often the realization of the deficiencies of the old notion of the nation-state in our modern and mobile societies makes scholars jump into the cosmopolitan alternative which views the international order and human rights instruments as a substitute for national citizenship-based claims of rights and state protection. This work tries to explore another path which allows for the fact that the nation-state may still prove to be an indispensable protective framework for individual freedom. Not belonging exclusively to one state does not mean not belonging to *any* state, nor belonging to *every* state. It may mean belonging to two states. Hence the interest in, instead of giving up fully the concept of national citizenship, exploring new paths which, at a large scale, will lead to normalizing 'multiple national citizenship' and helping it to become a notion which is more open and plural and less exclusive.

It is time now to analyse in depth this more original path of automatic membership. In normative terms the first thing one may want to know is why exactly, when full inclusion is linked to nationality, a purely optional right to naturalization (and regularization, in its case) does not help the inclusive purpose animating the claim to inclusion equally well, if not better. This, in fact, is the position thoroughly defended by Bauböck in his book *Transnational Citizenship*. It is by referring to his thesis that I will defend here the path of automatic membership. In principle, Bauböck accepts as equally valid (from a liberal democratic point of view) two alternatives, the first equating the legal status of resident aliens to that of what he calls 'nominal citizens' (which is how he refers to national citizens) and the second making access to democratic decision making depend on prior naturalization (Bauböck 1994b: 227). In the second case, he specifies, naturalization needs to be optional rather than discretionary or automatic (Bauböck 1994a: 88–102).

In this chapter, I will first address the freedom-restricting implications that the method of automatic membership seems to have, especially when compared with the alternative of optional nationality. To do this I will, first of all, elaborate somewhat further on the conditions for its valid application so as to make clear what the reach of the claim is. I will then discuss three concrete objections to the automatic granting of national membership. The first relates to immigrants' freedom and questions whether it is valid to impose nationality on resident aliens. The second is concerned with preserving a meaningful sense of nationality and asks whether this interest is served by a system that apparently requires no individual commitment from newcomers. Finally, I will briefly address a few issues of feasibility, concentrating on the problems of the automatic recognition of nationality from the perspective of international law.

Conditions for the valid application of automatic membership

Two conditions must be met for the valid application of the claim to automatic membership: that it comes into play only secondarily and that nationality is granted absolutely unconditionally. Starting with the first, it has already been argued that the method of automatic recognition of membership should only come into effect if sufficiently strong reasons prove the necessity of keeping the full enjoyment of rights and duties attached to the status of nationality. Such a necessity has to be related to the preservation of the liberal democratic order, something which may require different things in different times and circumstances.

This brings us to the second condition. It is also necessary and most important that nationality is granted absolutely unconditionally. In practical terms the unconditional granting of nationality means that resident aliens will not be asked to change or assimilate in order to become nationals in the new country of residence. They will simply be recognized as they are: no cultural assimilation requirement, no competence criteria, no renunciation of a previously held national citizenship. Any of these requirements could result in the new nationality being perceived as an imposition. Instead, the real challenge here is to redefine the new nationality in terms that are broad enough to include all societal members whoever they are.

Forcing resident aliens to acquire a new nationality, if it implies for them acquiring something they lack or giving up something that they have and may value, could indeed be a freedom-restricting imposition. Under such circumstances we can imagine that many would choose to remain partially excluded from democratic citizenship rather than pay the price for inclusion. This does not happen with unconditional inclusion. If conditionally defined, automatic nationality would imply a different burden for those whose acquisition of the required conditions implies a greater sacrifice. And as we saw before, full inclusion and commonality should not be reached at the cost of treating unfairly those whose interests and concerns have not been sufficiently taken into account when defining the parameters of commonality in the first place.

An interesting issue remains whether or not the possibility of voluntary expatriation should be available for resident aliens once they had automatically become nationals. My view is that, here again, the treatment given to them should be analogous to that of native-born or otherwise naturalized citizens. However, the same treatment will probably not imply the same thing and, as matter of fact, the possibility of voluntary expatriation is likely to be much more accessible for resident aliens. In general, the possibility of expatriation is subject to some minimal conditions. The most widespread one is that before expatriating themselves people must have acquired another nationality to replace the first one or at least have the formal agreement of another state that it will accept the applicant as a citizen. The main purpose of this is to avoid statelessness (as in Germany, Austria, Belgium, Spain and France). With this in mind, we may imagine that expatriation would simply be much easier for resident aliens. However, sometimes further conditions are set (such as not having a pending criminal case which could entail the deprivation of freedom). And here, the argument goes, whatever these restrictions may be, to the extent that they are backed by legitimate concerns from a liberal democratic perspective, they should apply also to our dual nationals. In other words, only if, by becoming a dual national, the concern which originally motivated the restricting condition for expatriation is automatically removed (e.g. a concern with statelessness) should such a condition be removed as well.

This opens up an engaging question. Should former resident aliens who have given up the automatically acquired citizenship still be able to remain within the country? Now, together with the acquisition of a foreign citizenship, residence abroad is another condition which some states set for voluntary expatriation (e.g. Spain). Two different sorts of concerns have been put forward to support such a condition. The first has to do with the problem of fairness and free riding on others' contributions. The argument is as follows. By expatriating themselves without leaving the country, expatriates could be opting out of important obligations (e.g. loyalty and service). To the extent that such restrictions are justified from the perspective of a liberal democracy, and one could always discuss whether they really are (see Bauböck 1994a: 147), it is not clear why they ought not to be maintained for everyone equally.[4]

Another justification for the residential requirement for voluntary expatriation has to do, not with the interests of the state, but with what Bauböck identifies as the liberal democratic demand for 'consent in government and for substantial rights of citizenship' (Bauböck 1994a: 147). Bauböck is worried about the consequences for the value of citizenship if individuals could not only expatriate but could also choose the citizenship of a state in which they do not live. According to him, this would, in practical terms, mean enhancing the freedom of choice regarding membership at the cost of devaluing what is chosen. The idea is that by choosing a different citizenship, people would lose some of the rights and obligations of citizenship (e.g. the rights to vote, military service) 'while not gaining anything of comparable importance for their status as members of a political community' (ibid.: 147). The overall result would be a 'general devaluation of the substantial aspects tied to nominal citizenship' (ibid.).

Initially, these considerations may not apply with equal strength in the case of immigrants who can think of their citizenship abroad as a most valuable asset. They may have plans to return to their countries of origin at some time in the future. They may therefore be interested in not losing touch or their voice in the political life. However, as time passes and the actual chances and/or intentions to go back diminish, a similar concern about preserving a formal status of citizenship might advise a similarly cautious attitude towards the possibility of allowing for expatriation before the actual return.

Some objections against the path of automatic membership

Even if done automatically and absolutely unconditionally the granting of automatic nationality may encounter objections related to either the

---

[4] A slightly different issue is whether the condition of dual citizenship ought to remove dual citizens from some specific duties, such as the duty to fight against their country of birth. Even when granted, such an exemption would not necessarily remove the broader duty of service to the state. So, for instance, dual citizens could still be required to defend their state *vis-à-vis* a third state. What we have here is not that the condition of dual nationality automatically removes the concern backing the restriction (in this case, the duty to defend the state) but rather, that it introduces the possibility of burdening in an unequal manner individuals who are, in the relevant sense, differently situated. Nevertheless, as we saw, this concern with fairness is also present with native-born dual citizens. Whatever the best solution to this problem from a liberal democratic perspective it should apply to all kinds of dual nationals equally.

interests of resident aliens, those of the receiving society, or simply
general feasibility conditions. Let us briefly turn to each of them.

Automatic membership as an imposition on immigrants

From the perspective of resident aliens there may be reasons to prefer
optional naturalization to even fully unconditional and automatic nationality. But this is no oddity. If the claim to full inclusion is qualified by the
necessity of membership (sanctioned in the secondary claim), it is also
because more than just the expression of individual preferences is taken
into account. Once a sufficiently strong argument exists for binding civic
equality to nationality (and this is a precondition for applying automatic
membership instead of full inclusion and must come from a concern with
preserving the liberal democratic state), there might be similar interests
which support having the whole of the state's ordinary resident population (and not only those who have acquired citizenship at birth) included
within the body of nationals and thus within the sphere of civic equality.

The general use of the rule of ascriptive nationality at birth is rightly
seen as helping a liberal purpose. It ensures a maximum degree of
inclusiveness of the resident population in the context of the existing
national authorities which territorially assert their powers most directly
over the body of residents (Bauböck 1994a: 36–7) and it ensures intergenerational continuity. Citizenship, unlike many other forms of membership, is just not voluntary. Citizens might be free to quit the state, but
not to renounce their citizenship. As a matter of fact, in many places
renunciation is not accepted (Hammar 1990a: 30–1). So access to nationality by native born is not commonly triggered by individual choice. Yet
we are used to recognizing that it serves a liberal purpose.

The claim here is that the automatic access to nationality when applied
to permanent resident aliens should be seen as serving a similarly inclusive purpose. Such a claim is grounded on two considerations. First, it will
be argued that embracing automatic membership through residence as a
rule is most likely to enhance the freedom of permanent resident aliens.
Second, the focus will be on the general interest of society. The possibility
of individual 'self-exclusion', the argument runs, opens up the potential
for having large sectors of the population permanently excluded from
civic equality (i.e. disenfranchised, or in a permanently precarious residential status). This is a valid legitimation concern because it can have a
diminishing effect on the overall level of civic commitment, thus eroding
the society's commitment to a free and equal society, even if it results
from rational individual choices. Inclusion and equality can thus be of
overriding importance for liberal democracy. Along similar lines, the

possibility of self-exclusion may pose interesting questions as to the evasion of certain duties which may be essential for the preservation of the community.

Self-exclusion and individual interests   Focusing on the interests of resident aliens, since the granting proceeds unconditionally and they do not have to give up anything they value, it seems that, in principle, automatic membership can only have freedom-enhancing results. One can hardly question the fact that adding residential stability and the possibility of exercising the whole set of political rights and freedoms, as well as whatever other rights a system may in principle reserve for its citizens, will have such an effect. On the other hand, there are studies showing that legal resident immigrants actually make little use of the political avenues that are already open to them. This and the fact that, having the right to, they may still decline the option of naturalizing (which is the whole point here), could be presented as evidence against the idea that permanent resident aliens will perceive automatic inclusion as necessarily having freedom-enhancing effects. If resident aliens show a genuine political apathy it is not clear that full incorporation, whether through full inclusion or through automatic membership, will add to their status anything which is really meaningful to them.[5]

Now one should probably avoid deriving normative conclusions from such evidence too fast. Granted, some immigrants may be genuinely uninterested in the political debate because they expect to leave sooner or later. But this factor would presumably lose strength as time passes (Hammar 1990a: 146). There are many reasons to account for the apparent political apathy of permanent resident aliens, some of which are commonly shared by other sectors of marginalized citizens. As we saw, in the case of illegals, it is clear that any open effort to engage in political activities exposes them to the risk of deportation and sometimes those legally present do not enjoy a fully stable residential or working status either. Also, the existence of strong social bias in the practice of political participation may account for much of the phenomenon (Birch 1993: 83). Non-citizens tend to be over-represented among persons with the characteristics that usually lead to low participation, such as being young,

---

[5] Some of the evidence generally quoted to support the thesis of aliens' self-exclusion is that in those countries where resident aliens have been granted local voting rights, their participation seems to be lower than that of the citizen population (see Hammar 1990a: 165). Also, in some countries where naturalization is encouraged and facilitated the rate of naturalization is low. Finally, according to some scholars, emigration can be seen as a political act, in that, instead of trying to achieve improvements within the political system of their country of origin, emigrants decide to leave their country, hoping to find individual solutions in other countries (Tung 1981; Hirschman 1970).

unmarried, newly arrived, but also with low education and low income (Hammar 1990a: 146). Significant also is the fact that many immigrants have a faulty knowledge of the electoral system and the relevant political issues, which is often aggravated by their lack of language ability and social isolation as well as by the fact that immigrant issues are not disputed in party politics and do not play a role in electoral campaigns.[6]

Even if immigrants' low levels of political participation were a sign of genuine political apathy, no direct normative conclusion could be derived from it (Bauböck 1994a: 102). Liberal democracy requires the recognition of political rights to citizens regardless of how politically apathetic they actually are. So, even if low participation is taken as a genuine expression of immigrants' apathy this does not mean that resident aliens do not need residential stability (which, as we have said, is a condition for the fully free exercise of the rest of the rights and freedoms) and the access to the political process. The latter seems essential for the defence of their interests and concerns just as for those of any other sector of the population, if not more, given their special vulnerability. Political apathy might prove that the right is not sufficient but not that it is not necessary. Political power is worthy in itself and constitutes a protective asset even when not fully used. Granting resident aliens nationality automatically implies that they will hold the full status of rights thus far reserved for citizens. Even if later they decide not to use them (e.g. not to vote) there is a protection that derives already from the power which is linked to the entitlement.

But maybe we have started from the wrong assumption, namely, that

---

[6] As for the low interest in naturalization, Hammar offers a comprehensive explanation of the different factors that can account for it. They should be taken into account before rushing to the conclusion that low naturalization rates are a genuine sign of political apathy (i.e. the acquisition of political rights does not sufficiently motivate aliens to apply for naturalization). Certainly, the personal projects of the immigrants are relevant, and thus, depending on whether they see their stay as a temporary phase or whether they plan to stay permanently in the new country, they will probably show different degrees of interest in naturalizing. Generally, a cost/benefit analysis precedes the decision. Gains and losses of rights and prerogatives are likely to be pondered. Political rights can be seen as a gain, but so may some of the social and economic rights to which the alien might not have had access until she naturalizes. Losses, however, count as well, especially when naturalization implies giving up the previous citizenship. The loss of the right to inherit or to own property, or the duty to pay back to the state the costs of previous education, are some of the consequences that can flow from giving up an old citizenship. Together with these internal factors coexist external factors, some of which clearly affect the shaping of personal projects and perceptions. Among them, Hammar refers to the emigration/ immigration and citizenship policies of the sending and receiving countries. These, he explains, may induce the migrants to perceive their stays as 'temporary' stays abroad even if they are not, and are also likely to have a strong influence in their perception of what citizenship implies in terms of national identity and hence for the nation-building process. As a result, they can also encourage or discourage naturalization (Hammar 1990a: 97–105).

resident aliens' change of status (with the rights they will gain from it) necessarily has to be seen as freedom enhancing. Is it really the case that resident aliens will not lose something in the process? In answering this question maybe we should not be looking only for tangible benefits or damages. The automatic recognition of nationality could, for instance, be seen as imposing on resident aliens a certain identity with which they may not feel comfortable.

However, we find that the fewer the conditions on which naturalization is granted, the higher the naturalization rates are. In particular, there seems to be a clear correlation between naturalization rates and naturalization systems that do not require aliens to give up their old citizenship. Thus, far from imposing a certain identity on resident aliens, it seems that the granting of automatic nationality in the absence of cultural or political assimilation and loyalty requirements could be a way of redefining nationality so as to encompass the actual plurality of identities, attachments and loyalties already coexisting within a given state. If a common identity should connect all the individuals sharing a political space, to be really common, such an identity has to acknowledge the existing differences rather than suppress them. But if it does acknowledge the existing diversity, resident aliens would probably find themselves recognized in it. Granted, accepting resident aliens as nationals just as they are would presumably end up making the concept of nationality thinner. In composite societies its ethno-cultural connotations would be weakened, and with them, the fear that the automatic recognition of nationality might be perceived as an unjustified imposition of identity.

Let us assume that neither material damage nor symbolic harm to resident aliens follows from automatic membership. It is conceivable that some resident aliens would still not want to become nationals whatever the benefits doing otherwise might imply. Isn't it pure paternalism to insist on automatic membership as being best for them? And why should this paternalism be now justified? We saw that imposing some naturalization requirements, such as competence in the dominant language, may be useful to encourage resident aliens to acquire the skills to effectively enjoy the rights, freedoms and opportunities they are offered in the host society. Is there a contradiction between not requiring those skills as conditions for inclusion (even if we know that this would be to their advantage) and, on the other hand, imposing on resident aliens a nationality they may not want on the basis that it provides for them a necessary degree of recognition and protection in the host society?

There seems to be a slight difference between the two. In the case of naturalization requirements, access to civic equality, which is something resident aliens have a right to, is conditional on the fulfilment of certain requirements. The conditions work indirectly as a threat and have a clear excluding potential. Those who do not acquire the skills to enjoy all the rights and opportunities effectively are simply deprived of some of those rights. Instead, automatic nationality operates unconditionally. It allows resident aliens to retain their old citizenship. And the option of subsequent exit remains open, theoretically, in the same terms as it is for national citizens. Practically, as we saw, the fact that they already have one citizenship and that they may be planning to return to their countries of origin will probably further facilitate their option of exit. Paternalistic as such an inclusion might be, it does not rest on punishment nor can it have the effect of aggravating exclusion.

One should also remember that, after all, the automatic access to citizenship is not the exception but the rule. Ascriptive citizenship at birth is the key rule to allocate citizenship. Native-born nationals are also ascriptively assigned their nationality. If it was really essential for democratic membership that nationality be acquired by individual consent this should apply to national citizens as well. If, on the other hand, what is really relevant, more than just individual consent, is that people get to share in the sphere of democratic membership and that they do so through the status of nationality, then the question becomes why permanent resident aliens should be an exception.

Some people will claim that the comparison is not fully accurate. As potentially freedom enhancing, ascriptive nationality may have a different relevance for aliens and native-born citizens and hence, be backed by justifications which differ in the degree to which they are compelling. Thus, one could argue that inclusion through ascriptive nationality at birth serves the purpose of avoiding statelessness, a status of great vulnerability in a world where personhood and international instruments are still not sufficient to ensure the adequate protection of individual rights (Legomsky 1994: 297–9). In the case of resident aliens though, at least when they hold another nationality, ascriptive nationality could be seen more as an imposition simply because it cannot serve a freedom-enhancing purpose in an equally meaningful way.

There is some truth in this. However, appealing as it is, the soundness of this argument rests on a doubtful assumption. The assumption is that the protection and recognition that one 'enjoys' merely by being a national of a state – even if one permanently resides outside its jurisdiction – are equivalent to those one can enjoy within it. For this to be so, either the protection that the state can give to its non-resident nationals while in a foreign state, or the mere possibility nationals have to return to their country, would have to be sufficient for legitimation purposes. And this may be doubtful.

Another argument for distinguishing birthright citizenship from automatic membership could be that the former applies to children who are unable to consent and purports to give them protective resources even against their parents, who could freely decide that their children would be better off without the nationality of the state in which they were born. However, this argument would not apply to adults. But this does not explain why states have been so sceptical about allowing the expatriation of their adult citizens unless they are also willing to leave the state and in most cases also to acquire another nationality.[7] I do not believe that the inclusive and protective virtue of automatic citizenship at birth is perceived mainly as a result of the transitory protection it grants to those who are unable to consent until they gain full consenting capacity. Otherwise the general rule would be that, at majority, people would systematically be asked to give an express sign to revalidate the citizenship that was ascribed to them at birth.[8]

According to Bauböck, the strongest reason for preserving inclusion, in the form of optional naturalization, over the alternative of unconditional and automatic nationality is that the acquisition of nationality by resident aliens has a different value and meaning from the ascriptive acquisition by citizens (Bauböck 1994a: 89 ff). In explaining this, Bauböck refers to the Rawlsian notion of the worth of liberty to persons meaning how individuals can advance their ends within a framework of equal liberties. Immigrants have a wider framework of social ties of membership and may therefore refer to different states as the focus of their interests (ibid.: 91). Thus, to compensate for the diminished worth of the liberties and rights of citizenship for immigrants, these ought to be given at least the additional liberty to choose their citizenship (ibid.: 89). Bauböck refers to the example of political liberties and explains how the additional freedom to choose for themselves their nationality might be seen as a way of maximizing the political impact of whatever orientation immigrants choose for

[7] Some authors have in fact advanced arguments in favour of the possibility of consensual exit from membership for native-born citizens (see, for instance, Schuck and Smith 1985: 122 ff). But see Bauböck 1994a: 147 (alerting us against the risk of emptying citizenship of its substantive content – and its protective potential – if we decide to make it a purely consensual membership status for all).

[8] From a public interest perspective it could be argued that birthright citizenship is more justified than automatic membership because all polities have to be understood as intergenerational communities in order to create sufficient commitment to pursue political solutions for long-term problems, and automatic ascriptive citizenship at birth sustains this intergenerational continuity. However, there is a similar public interest in having the ordinary population and not just the native-born citizens of the state included in the polity precisely to further their long-term commitment to it, especially when they are a significant part of the population. This point and related issues are dealt with in greater depth in the next section where I address the relationship between automatic membership and the general interest of society.

themselves (ibid.: 90). Nevertheless, as he himself recognizes, this argument loses most of its force when multiple citizenship becomes a rule (ibid.: 91). And this explains why it is essential that the path of automatic membership be pursued with prudence until multiple citizenship becomes generally accepted, as seems to be increasingly the case (Spiro 1997).

The second alleged reason is that the acquisition of citizenship is not only of different value but has a different meaning for aliens too. Here Bauböck refers to naturalization as a way for the alien to make a conscious and public choice about her membership thereby expressing her commitment to a particular democratic state. Whereas native citizens will learn to be committed not only to general democratic norms but to the more specific institutions of the state by continuously participating in public life, such an experience is not available to immigrants in the same way. Thus, for resident aliens optional and voluntary naturalization is to be seen as a specific kind of 'political resocialization' (Bauböck 1994a: 92). More than a test of education in liberal democracy, naturalization allows aliens to state that they have acquainted themselves sufficiently with the political and legal system of the country to decide about their future membership.

However, it is not quite clear what function this process of 'political resocialization' is supposed to serve. In principle, it is not supposed to prove any kind of competence. As Bauböck recognizes, the capacity to be a citizen in a liberal democracy has to be presupposed of every person unless by speech or deeds the person gives evidence to the contrary. Neither is it supposed to prove acquaintance with the concrete institutions of the country, for according to Bauböck migrants catch up with native citizens' political socialization directly by participating in civil society and public political life. In fact, Bauböck explains that the naturalization decision is to take place after experience with the state and its institutions has already been accumulated (ibid.: 93). If aliens do not have to prove anything in terms of political or cultural assimilation, and are supposed to become naturally acquainted with the institutions of the country, it is not clear why a special commitment to the latter, if necessary at all, must be presupposed on the part of the native citizens but not on the part of resident aliens. The expression of such a commitment does not even necessarily portray a preference when aliens are allowed to retain their original citizenship.

Assessing the value and meaning that immigrants would attach to a second citizenship which they acquire automatically is not easy. We cannot simply accept that because it would not be the outcome of an express act of consent immigrants would attach no value to it. Native-born citizens value their citizenship even if they did not choose it and even when, as adults, they become aware that they did not choose it. They value it because of the symbolic community feeling that they develop around it, and because and to the extent that it supplies them with a protective framework which allows them to enjoy rights and freedoms and public goods such as peace, health and a flourishing economy – precisely the kinds of things that move immigrants.

Ultimately, the rules of ascribing citizenship, be it at birth or later, will most likely generate a context from which the very meaningfulness of that status is judged. Adopting the rule of automatic membership through residence would probably produce an incentive for immigrants (who would presumably know of its existence) to see their stay as a continuous path to a citizenship that will necessarily and unconditionally arrive and hence, to align themselves, right from the beginning, with the activities and choices of the nationals of the country. And this may encourage them to understand their experiences, right from the start, as something more than a merely economic enterprise of an indefinite duration. Also, it would force the receiving community to watch and treat immigrants as potential citizens and raise the awareness of native citizens about the fact that, from a liberal ethos, having been born a member of a prosperous and healthy democracy is to a large extent an unjustified privilege. With automatic membership through residence, we would accept that one is not only 'born' a citizen but that one can also 'become' a citizen as a rule, and not only as an exception. I do not deny the value of choice and consent. I claim that choices as to what constitute meaningful life options and projects are made in a certain context that feeds their meaningfulness. My view is that the certainty that becoming a citizen is only a question of time would affect right from the beginning the meaningfulness immigrants attach to their experience as well as their identity formation process while in the country of residence and hence, their future choices too. If immigrants were given a choice, say, after fifteen years of residence, as to whether they want to be citizens of the state of residence or not, would it be relevant for such a decision whether this actually meant (a) renouncing the second citizenship they acquired automatically after ten years or (b) taking up the new citizenship in cases when they had the choice of becoming citizens after five or ten years but had not taken it at that time?

Self-exclusion and the general interest of society   The second set of arguments for favouring automatic over optional naturalization stress the fact that resident aliens' interests might not be all that is at stake here. Concerned with such interests Bauböck has argued that automatic mem-

bership could have the consequence that aliens would be asked to perform some duties that they do not want to. Since for Bauböck the liberal
democratic norm of inclusion only means the recognition of equal rights
(but not necessarily of equal positive obligations) to societal members,
automatic nationality would open the way for imposing non-accepted
duties, such as military conscription. According to Bauböck, although
not every state imposes this obligation on its citizens, even if they do,
resident aliens have a stronger reason not to be drafted than either
native-born or naturalized citizens (Bauböck 1994b: 225). According to
him the obligation to kill or die in defence of one's country requires a
conscious expression of consent. And while under certain conditions of
emergency, conscription of native citizens may be justified by invoking
their hypothetical consent, no such implication can be inferred from the
facts of residence and societal membership of foreigners.

Now it is not clear to me why this should be so. One may wish to discuss
whether conscription should be imposed on anyone at all and if so, under
which circumstances. Bauböck himself argues that with the exception of
just wars or conflicts affecting the territory of the state, military service
should never be an obligation for citizens (Bauböck 1994a: 300). But if it
is imposed on nationals it is not clear why it should not also be expected
from all those 'whose social position durably relates them to a certain
state so that they depend on this state for their protection and rights'
which, according to Bauböck, is the basic standard for inclusion in a
liberal polity (Bauböck 1994b: 205). After all, sharing in an equal sphere
of legal obligations might actually further the sense of belonging that was
a recommendation for keeping national and democratic membership
bound to each other to start with. This is especially the case when the
obligation at stake is linked to the very survival of the polity.[9] When a
conflict really affects the interests of the nation inclusively defined (encompassing therefore the interests of the resident alien population) it is
not clear why resident aliens should not be expected to be equally committed to their defence.

More important, in my view, is the fact that individual 'self-exclusion',
when and if it becomes a large-scale phenomenon, might have a diminishing effect on the overall level of civic commitment, thus eroding the
society's commitment to a free and equal society. Society's interest in
preserving a healthy democracy for the sake of everyone's freedom may
transcend individual interests. Participatory theorists of democracy have

---

[9] Note that the concern with ensuring that resident aliens do not enjoy all the privileges of
citizenship without being subject to equivalent duties has also helped in the past to decide
on the rules of membership. See Brubaker 1992: 85 ff (referring to the French experience
during the nineteenth century and to the extension of *ius soli* rules of citizenship as a means
of subjecting resident aliens to conscription).

insisted that democracy is more than a mechanism to simply reflect a whole sum of individual preferences or to protect oneself from eventual tyrannies. Rather, democracy is thought of as a 'quality pervading the whole life and operation of a national or smaller community' and 'the whole set of reciprocal relations between the people who make up the units in the society' (Macpherson 1977: 6–7).

As applied to our case, this means that we cannot concentrate solely on how an immigrant decides what it is best to do with her political assets. We have to take into account also what effect the rules on the allocation of citizenship may have on political participation and political accountability in general. So, for instance, we must also consider the negative consequences for the rest of society of having communities of politically disenfranchised and apathetic individuals. In believing that the pursuit of material gain often uses few of the human faculties and tends to make individuals concentrate their attention and interests exclusively upon themselves and their families, making them indifferent to public matters, a participatory conception of democracy believes that facilitating relegation to the economic sphere does not encourage civic virtues (Himmelfarb 1963: 230). Immigrants' consolidation of an economic status seems to facilitate (self-)exclusion from the political community. But in the long run this might be incompatible with European and North American immigration countries' 'self-understanding as democracies' (Brubaker 1989b: 162). It is not sufficient that 'most non-citizens are manifestly law-abiding and socially productive . . . [and] presumably no less altruistic than other people' since the fact remains that 'by withholding their participation in and commitment to our civic life, they decline to be public-spirited in the fullest sense. To that extent, they may impoverish the democratic spirit of their communities' (Bauböck 1994a: 204; Schuck 1989: 62).

So, if the moral ambition of creating a society pervaded by freedom and equality is what animates democracy, then the free and equal society must exist for all of those living in it, and must encourage all of them to develop fully. Having a sector of second-class citizens undermines the freedom of all, and not only of those in the worst position (Pateman 1970: 26–7; Michelman 1988: 1495). Hence, to some extent, 'society's interest in the value of citizenship transcends the value that the individuals in that society place upon it' (Schuck 1989: 63). And this not only to achieve a republican order, but also to preserve the basis of a liberal polity concerned with individual liberty, tolerance and substantial equality (Schuck 1994: 329–30).[10]

---

[10] Also, when presented as a moral model containing a moral vision of the 'possibility of the improvement of mankind, and of a free and equal society not yet achieved', the role of democracy cannot be relegated to that of registering the desires of people as they are, nor

The fact that many citizens, and not only immigrant workers, seem to concentrate on their economic progress and exert their political virtues only minimally is not sufficient to rebut this participatory conception of democracy. 'Experience and empirical evidence cannot in themselves lead to value judgements' (Birch 1993: 91). Importing workers without opening up access to citizenship can only exacerbate the already generalized political apathy among citizens. Faced with large streams of newcomers avid to join in what they mainly perceive as an economic venture, Western societies' own perception of what social and political membership is mainly about is also likely to change. It seems that the judgement of others as to what we are worth and what we can offer them is an inevitable input in the process of forging our self-perception.

This raises an interesting issue, namely, whether embracing this more ambitious conception of democracy and grounding on it, at least partly, the convenience of granting resident aliens nationality automatically would not require, as a matter of consistency, taking some measures to ensure not only resident aliens' but also resident citizens' active engagement in politics. Mandatory suffrage would probably be the best example. This too could be described as a limitation on individual freedom set for the purpose of ensuring a healthy democratic society.

However, we should not rush into this conclusion so fast. Maybe, but not necessarily, one could answer. What resident aliens gain through automatic membership is a membership status as well as a set of rights, not the obligation to exercise them. The membership status will presumably facilitate their integration and enhance their feeling of belonging and, with it, stimulate their political engagement. Also, the entitlement to political rights and residential stability implies an additional protection. Granted, there is no guarantee that this consolidated status will bring about the more active engagement of the newcomers in the political process. But the most likely outcome is that it will.

Even if immigrants remain keen on preserving their cultural, linguistic and national identities for themselves and later generations, they will probably realize that this can only be achieved by increased involvement in the host society, especially in the political process. This will result in immigrants' associations and in their members becoming more active

even to that of preserving spheres of protection within which people can decide freely their preferences. Rather, democracy has to contribute to what they might be or might wish to be (Macpherson 1977: 79). And this is also why a participatory account cannot simply accept for democracy the role of capturing whatever preferences immigrants may have, even if presented as reasonable ways to advance their interests and personal development, and must also take into account the need to encourage the exercise of responsible public action which 'enables man to think of any kind of collective interest, of any object or ideal to be pursued jointly with others instead of in competition with them' (Pateman 1970: 31).

participants. It will not escape them that in order to influence the education of second generations, to obtain grants for advice centres and planning permission for religious and community buildings, their associations
need to become active participants in local and national politics (Layton-
Henry 1990b: 109).

Also, as we know, as they become potential voters it is likely that the
system will adjust and take into account the conditions that are needed to
address this new sector as a political audience (e.g. information campaigns in different languages, addressing of their specific concerns and
needs, etc.). One can probably expect an encouraging effect of the expansion of voting rights on the political participation of immigrants. Presumably, if this comes together with them acquiring a second nationality, the
encouraging effect will be even stronger. As long as citizenship carries a
strong symbolic value as an expression of belonging one can expect that,
as fully recognized members, resident aliens' self-perception will also
undergo some significant changes. They will probably stop perceiving
their existence in the country of residence as a time-bracketed experience
which is mainly guided by an economic purpose. Instead, they will
probably start to conceive of a new sphere of interaction which respects
their full humanity just as they are (with no assimilatory intentions),
which is receptive to their specific concerns and aspirations and accepts
their potential for contribution in the definition of the larger political
project. Clearly, recognition and not only power is at stake. Sharing in the
membership status that citizenship expresses certainly implies recognition. And it would not be surprising that an increase in recognition
triggered an increase in the level of active political engagement.

What if we find the stimulating effect of the power and recognition
gained through inclusion to be insufficient to meet the requirements of a
truly participatory democracy? If flows of newcomers avid to join in an
economic venture can alter the receiving society's perception of what
social and political membership is mainly about, the same should be true
the other way round: a politically apathetic citizenry will also condition
the meaning that new members will attach to their new condition as
citizens. This is why, when the level of political participation is generally
low, and this is judged as detrimental to the democratic commitment of
society, we may start considering measures such as mandatory suffrage
for all as a further step.[11] But this does not mean that mandatory suffrage
necessarily follows from automatic membership.

In summary, the main thrust of our argument has been that according
permanent resident aliens an automatic and unconditional second na-

---

[11] Defending the position that the problem of low and unequal voter turnout could at least
be partially resolved through mandatory suffrage see, among others, Lijphart 1997.

tionality in their countries of residence (something which they would probably know before they decided to settle in it) will have mostly freedom-enhancing implications for them. It would definitely help to replace the image and self-image of immigrants as individuals who are conceptually and teleologically linked to an economic function, with that of individuals who, from the start, are encouraged to understand their experiences in a more encompassing way. In this way both immigrants and national citizens of the receiving communities would be challenged to perceive and prepare for their immigration phenomena as what, in the end, they really turn out to be: more of a polity-shaping force and less of an economic arrangement. If there are any freedom-restricting implications at all these should not be judged as very different from those that derive from also ascriptively including native-born citizens in the liberal democratic polity. To the extent that the reasons for binding civic equality to national membership status are valid, they ought to be justified as restrictions on the freedom of individuals for the sake of preserving the liberal democratic state and institutions. Thus, if a minimum of social and political cohesion or solidarity is required and such a minimum can best be achieved by binding equality of rights to nationality and ascribing nationality automatically at birth, rather than by allowing entry and exit from national membership to be purely a matter of individual consent, or full rights to be enjoyed by non-citizens, such a constraint ought to be seen as compelling enough to limit the freedom of both resident aliens and native-born citizens for the sake of preserving the general conditions for freedom.

Nationality and individual commitment

Several objections could be raised to the automatic granting of nationality from the perspective of the state. Even if one concedes that once civic equality and nationality are bound together there might be a liberal concern in making the rule of nationality as inclusive as possible, it could also be that the same interests that recommend keeping civic equality and nationality attached in the first place would not be served (or not be served equally well) if resident aliens' access to nationality was made automatic rather than optional or discretionary. Let us recall that the major concern supporting the marriage between civic equality and nationality was the preservation of a bond of commonality ensuring solidarity and cohesion and binding the polity internally (i.e. binding the members to each other) and externally (i.e. binding the members against the non-members). Unconditional and automatic entry might not be a good way, or at least, not the best way, to respond to such a concern. Optional naturalization, conditional or unconditional, might be a better alternative.

Let us focus on the alternative of optional and conditional naturalization first. The advantage that this kind of naturalization can have over automatic incorporation is that it allows the community to decide what is necessary to preserve the basis of understanding, solidarity and cohesion, by making the access to citizenship selective. In other words, the relevant question is whether, when deprived of substantive content, the status of national citizenship can still serve to bind the polity, especially if in some cases access to it does not even have to be requested by the individual. Allowing accession to citizenship without ensuring at the same time some degree of cultural, linguistic, economic or political homogeneity is unlikely to further the degree of commonality that solidarity and cohesion require. Also, facilitating dual nationality is hardly a good way to preserve a clear system of exclusive bonds of allegiance in the international order. A certain homogeneity and allegiance can be presupposed of native-born citizens who have undergone their political and cultural socialization process in the country of nationality. Automatic membership is thus conceived as a missed chance to prove resident aliens' assimilation and commitment.

Underlying this is again the concern that by allowing a political community's continuous reshaping, without retaining at the same time sufficient control over who is given political voice, the very basis of a democratic society might be endangered. The relevant worry is, therefore, about the adequacy or sufficiency of a nationality status, which is based on nothing more than coexistence within a territorially organized political community, to promote both the subjective attitudes and the objective conditions that the proper functioning of liberal institutions requires.

As I have tried to argue, this concern is a legitimate one, and raises important questions about the limits of inclusion that sustaining liberal democracy requires. I will not go into the discussion again. It might be useful simply to recall here that, as an objection to the automatic incorporation of permanent resident aliens, this concern often rests on exaggerating both the actual degree of homogeneity binding nationals and that of heterogeneity separating nationals from non-national residents. It also reflects an inconsistent approach to the political relevance of difference in a pluralistic democracy and raises the question of why cohesion should be selectively safeguarded. In particular, we saw that while critics focus on the potentially eroding effects of an excessively inclusive policy, they typically ignore the eroding effects of the alternative of exclusion (Raskin 1993: 1446). If our concern is with preserving solidarity we must also consider the risks of not including resident aliens automatically.

But let us now focus on the alternative of unconditional but optional naturalization. We saw that, according to Bauböck, making naturalization an option can be useful to preserve its expressive value of commitment to the legal and political institutions of a specific state as opposed to just any liberal institutions (also Schauer 1986: 1504–17). It could be seen as a way to enhance the binding force of nationality, as a voluntary association, especially if an equivalent right to expatriation, subject to the condition of effective integration into another society, was available to native-born citizens. Moreover, according to Bauböck, this would not even necessarily imply that the full access to equal rights should be postponed until resident aliens have naturalized. Rather on the contrary, Bauböck argues that it would be desirable for resident aliens to be granted citizen rights to acquire practical experience with the political and legal systems before they express a relevant commitment to them. Hence, naturalization would retain only a symbolic value as a formal expression of membership or attachment to the polity.[12]

I have no difficulties accepting this account for it would satisfy the demands of the claim of full inclusion. The problem is that, for Bauböck, equal rights before naturalization (which is what would satisfy the claim to full inclusion) is only desirable, and not necessary. He admits as equally valid the alternative that certain rights, like the right of suffrage in national elections, be preserved only for those who, by naturalizing, show their commitment. But isn't choosing a country of destination and making it the centre of one's personal and professional existence and/or family life a sufficient expression of one's attachment to it? Also, Bauböck makes a distinction between instrumental and expressive approaches to naturalization (Bauböck 1994b: 227). Clearly, what we are after here is the expressive approach. But if it is the preservation of certain rights for naturalized citizens that works as an additional stimulus to enhance naturalization rates, then naturalization will be guided by an instrumental rationality and thus, lose its expressive value which is the whole point here (Legomsky 1994: 292). This is in fact one of the most common criticisms levelled by commentators at state policies which limit aliens' access to social benefits in order to increase their interest in naturalizing (Note 1997). Now it could be argued that the wish to obtain citizenship in order to exercise national franchise is the desire to be a full member of a democratic polity so that the desire to exercise the franchise is the desire to be a full member of the polity. However, aliens could simply express this kind of commitment by actually exercising suffrage and engaging in the political debate. The main problem of using political rights as incen-

---

[12] Bauböck is aware of the fact that a commitment of a purely symbolic nature is always likely to assume a nationalistic tinge but refutes this objection on the grounds that, at the most, such a commitment would express 'a rather harmless kind of patriotic pride' for a liberal democratic polity (Bauböck 1994b: 227).

tives for naturalization is that it may well be that they do not make naturalization appealing enough (as has often been the case when resident aliens consolidated their social status before naturalization) (ibid.: 1824). The risk then is that a large percentage of the population in societies of immigration will remain permanently excluded from civic equality. If automatic incorporation refers to people who are already expected to be acquainted with liberal principles and with the specific institutions and laws of the country and, therefore, need not prove anything additional by naturalizing anyway, the question is whether the symbolic value of the expression of commitment should not be sacrificed for the sake of more inclusive results, especially when such a commitment can be deduced from other signs.

After all, the argument on the symbolic value of naturalization as a form of commitment seems largely counterfactual. Once again, it is difficult to determine to what extent resident aliens who, from the beginning, expected to gain with time automatic and unconditional access to a second nationality would develop a natural sense of commitment to the laws and institutions of a society they could gradually consider fully theirs, especially since it allows them to express their differences. In such circumstances nationality would become a status of political equality, binding residents internally to those with whom they ordinarily interact in the framework of common laws and institutions and externally, against those with whom they do not. Admittedly, the preservation of an old nationality will make an exception and reduce minimally (only *vis-à-vis* the country of origin) the sphere of externally defined singularity. But we have seen that, increasingly, dual citizenship is a common feature among native-born citizens as well. New forms of interconnections can only be naturally expected in an interrelated world which increasingly sees nation-states as giving way to infra- and supra-national political spaces. Once again, whatever the degree of possible commonalities in modern societies, it ought not to be selectively defined.[13]

---

[13] Bauböck gives an additional reason for optional naturalization – namely, that liberalism's goal is ultimately to turn all migration into voluntary movement. If this is so, he argues, denying immigrants the choice as to whether they want to become nationals of the country of residence seems inconsistent. The imperatives of inclusion are not strong enough to override the manifold individual reasons migrants might have to refuse applying for naturalization. However he himself emphasizes that this is only so because citizenship rights and nationality need not be strictly tied to each other (Bauböck 1994b: 226). But this is precisely what makes the difference for our purpose. If they need not be and are not tied to each other the reasons for automatic nationality might indeed not be compelling enough. However, if there are sufficient reasons not to accord resident aliens full civic equality before they naturalize (as Bauböck admits can be the case), then the case for inclusion becomes more compelling and the automatic and unconditional ascription of nationality needs to be judged differently.

Feasibility objections: international law concerns

Finally, there might be objections against the automatic recognition of membership related to its feasibility within the international framework. The concern with preserving the link between civic equality and nationality presupposes an international order which rests largely on the state as the prevalent political unit. It would therefore be preferable if the recommended solutions did not lie outside the realm of what is legitimately feasible according to current public international law standards. Nevertheless, it should also be clear that, ultimately, the normative validity of the arguments presented here depends on the current standards of international law as little as it does on the standards of national law.

From what has been advanced thus far two things could meet some resistance: the automatic granting of a second nationality without the prior consent of the affected aliens, and its multiplying effect on cases of dual nationality. However, international rules are far from clear in this respect. States are generally seen as fully sovereign to define who their nationals are as an essential prerogative linked to their recognized independence in the international community (Berber 1975: 374). Even in those times when the exclusiveness of the bond linking nationals to their states was most emphasized, dual nationalities had to be accepted, if only as a necessary evil to preserve each state's sovereignty on the matter. In most cases, multiple nationality resulted, and still does, from the mere fact that the two most common criteria to ensure the automatic transmission of nationality at birth (*ius soli* and *ius sanguinis*) can, when applied to the same individuals, make of them dual nationals right from the beginning. In contrast, secondary admissions have generally depended on voluntary individual applications (Bauböck 1994a: 34).

On the other hand, no general and clear limitation can be founded on international law concerning the prerogative of the state to recognize as its nationals those aliens who have established their residence in it and have a stable connection to it. If international law does not support a duty of the state to recognize them as its nationals or to accord them the same rights it accords to its citizens (Berber 1975: 387; Wengler 1964: 989), neither does it constrain the state's capacity to consider the existing links as sufficient to ground the recognition of either optional or automatic nationality.[14] In fact, although rather exceptional, auto-

---

[14] Someone may claim that by automatically granting nationality to non-stateless resident aliens a state would be interfering with the personal jurisdiction of the state of origin. However, if anything at all, only a minimal degree of connection binding the individual to the state has been recognized as a possible limit on the capacity of the state to define freely who its nationals are (see, for example, Wengler 1964: 1030; see also the case Nottebohm, ICJ Reports, 1955). There is no reason why long-term residence – not to mention the

matic nationality granted at some time after birth is not completely new. Just to mention some examples the citizenship laws in Belgium, Italy, France and Austria know or have known some form of automatic citizenship after birth (de Groot 1989: 213–15). The aims behind automatic citizenship have been mainly those of protecting the individual and recognizing her attachment to the country of residence. Typically, automatic citizenship has been conceived as a mechanism to avoid statelessness. Thus, sometimes it came right at the moment that the individual would become stateless. At other times it came when the individual performed certain services for the state of residence that could be read as signs of disloyalty by the state of origin and hence trigger denationalization, such as performing military service or entering the civil service (ibid.: 318). Even the practice of linking the automatic granting of citizenship to residence is not new. France reintroduced in 1998 the automatic granting of nationality at majority age to those born of alien parents in France, who have lived in France for at least five years since the age of eleven. Until 1992 Italy had a similar rule. Other kinds of automatic citizenship, such as automatic citizenship at marriage, have generally been abandoned and rightly so. But discriminatory as they were, the past existence of such practices also proves that automatic citizenship at some time after birth is not as new as it may seem. Austria has had a long and singular tradition of granting its citizenship automatically to those aliens with a university chair in the country. There is no reason to see the claims advanced here as a great oddity from the point of view of international law.[15] Ultimately, we can always ask ourselves why taking domicile in a country has to be regarded as a less legitimate ground for making somebody a citizen than

personal, professional and social implications that usually come with it – should not be taken to express a sufficient link binding state and individual. Also it is important to recall that the nationality of origin would in principle not be affected and that if they decided to go back to their countries resident aliens, as dual citizens, could probably just divest themselves of their second nationality. Presumably the reaction of the state of origin to the automatic granting of a second nationality to their nationals in a foreign country would depend on whether or not the democratic purpose of this form of ascriptive citizenship is generally recognized. It would also help if, as I have argued elsewhere, the right to have not just any nationality but the nationality of the country where one is a permanent resident was first recognized as a human right. See O'Connell and Rubio-Marín 1999.

[15] From an international law point of view countries seem to feel rather free to sovereignly decide their rules of national membership. Just to mention an example, in recent years Germany's former Christian Democrat government explored the possibility of installing a so-called 'children's citizenship'. Not known in international law, this was conceived as a provisional quasi-nationality that would not come automatically but only if the parents applied for it before the child's twelfth birthday and would expire on the child's nineteenth birthday if the child did not divest itself of its other nationalities. Not being a full nationality, this 'children's citizenship' did not remove the child from the sphere of application of foreigner law for purposes such as deportation (Joppke 1999a: 207).

the mere chance factor of having been born in it which is generally accepted (Grawert 1973: 224).

Now if we check the history of automatic membership we find that this institution existed until the mid-nineteenth century in some European monarchies, where foreign residents were naturalized after some time without being asked for their consent. However, this historical precedence is not a strong objection because it also applies to the rule of *ius soli* which has its roots in feudal relations. The truth is that, rather than being liberal or illiberal in and of themselves, we find that it is the use of the rules of acquisition of citizenship as applied to different social and historical realities that decides their freedom-enhancing or freedom-restricting impact. The fact that the general tendency over recent decades has been to drop automatic citizenship in favour of optional naturalization does not mean that, with changing circumstances, automatic citizenship could not be embraced again with the liberal and freedom-enhancing purpose of keeping our political communities as inclusive as possible. In a world with increasing human mobility which more and more shows the insufficiencies of simply assuming that people will be exclusively rooted in one country, only the claim of automatic membership through residence advanced here would serve such a purpose. The major rules for allocating citizenship, *ius soli* and *ius sanguinis*, operate automatically. The idea thus would be to introduce automatic membership through residence in order to update the automaticity rule and to keep the inclusive and protective purpose that it serves adapted to a new and increasingly widespread social reality.

Given that states lack the power to dissolve their resident aliens' previous nationalities, and that a condition for the valid application of automatic membership is that the person will not be deprived of her prior nationality, the path of automatic membership would lead to an increase in the numbers of dual or multiple citizenship. Now dual citizenship has sometimes been regarded as something to be avoided because of the conflicts it may generate (e.g. dual military obligations, uncertain legal status and jurisdiction, legal kidnapping, dual taxation and diplomatic protection). As we will see, a widespread opinion among German legal scholars is that dual citizenship is a domestic and international 'evil' which needs to be avoided. However, there is no recognized general principle which forces a state to make the dissolution of a previous citizenship bond a necessary condition for the recognition of a new citizenship (Berber 1975: 378). Neither is there an obligation on the part of the state to expatriate its own citizens when they acquire another nationality (ibid.: 377).[16] Also, there is an increasing general trend to

---

[16] However, quite a number of European countries have such a provision in their laws (de Groot 1989: 282–3). Presumably, this can best be explained by the general desire to avoid

re-evaluate dual or multiple citizenship in a positive way (Spiro 1997). Concerns about dual citizenship have thus far clearly been more important in continental Europe than in North America and even though scholarly debate in the USA has regained some interest in dual citizenship, this has to be seen mostly as a response to the increasing numbers of dual citizens in the country (Spiro 1997: 1414). The truth is that dual and even triple citizenship is increasingly common and that the State Department no longer opposes it in principle (Schuck 1997: 4). Naturalizing aliens in the USA still have to swear that they renounce prior allegiances but this promise is not systematically enforced. In the European context, the 1963 European Convention on the Reduction of Cases of Multiple Nationality and of Dual Military Obligations was opened for ratification in the Council of Europe. Its success though was only limited. Few countries signed it. Besides Ireland and Italy, only immigration countries ratified the convention, so that the contracting states did not bind themselves to apply the principles of the convention in relation to the major emigration countries of the 1960s, such as Portugal, Spain, Greece, Yugoslavia or Turkey. More importantly, all signatories of the convention now officially accept dual nationality. And even in those countries, such as Germany, which have traditionally shown the strongest resistance to dual citizenship the authorities are increasingly generous in allowing exceptions (Joppke 1999a: 205). The increase in dual citizenship is also due in large part to sending countries which, more and more, are allowing their citizens to either retain their citizenship in spite of naturalization or reacquire it instantly if they happen to lose it automatically through naturalization. Similarly, sending countries are also removing all types of restrictions on the legal status of those who take up naturalization somewhere else, restrictions which have traditionally discouraged immigrants from naturalization. There is therefore a general current of toleration of dual citizenship, probably 'reflecting a changed international context, one in which dual nationals pose a diminishing threat both as an encumbrance to cordial bilateral relationships and as a potential source of subversive activity' (Spiro 1997: 1415). Although the actual number of dual nationals is not known, some estimates have been made, according to which, as of 1985, there were more, and possibly many more, than three million dual nationals in Europe (Hammar 1985b: 444). Still in the framework of the Council of Europe, a European Convention on Nationality was adopted in November 1997 with a totally different outlook on

dual citizenship. On the other hand a whole range of additional concerns (e.g. increasing the number of citizens in the country or retaining a maximum number of emigrants as citizens) will be essential to understand fully the individual options adopted by each state (Bauböck 1994a: 127).

multiple nationality from that of the 1963 Convention.[17]

In other words, the idea that people 'should belong to one state and only to one' seems increasingly outdated. We have retained mechanisms for avoiding statelessness and nobody seriously questions their relevance in today's world. The part of the equation of 'belonging at least to one state' still holds. It is the 'and only one state' that is being increasingly questioned. Against traditional assumptions dual and multiple citizenship is perceived less and less as merely an unavoidable pathology of a system that grants states full sovereignty on their rules of ascriptive citizenship at birth (de Groot 1989: 320). Instead, more and more, it is seen as a necessary instrument to preserve inclusive communities and facilitate the integration of people with dual identities and attachments.

As of today, and until dual citizenship is fully embraced, what we have is the realization that one essential validating condition of the secondary claim of automatic nationality does not depend exclusively on the country of residence. The country of origin, with which emigrated citizens might still have strong connections, could still decide to take away their nationality when a second one is acquired. Some states do not while others do. However, most interesting for our purposes is the fact that those states that do denationalize their citizens for acquiring another nationality typically require additional signs of detachment (e.g. Spain), or do so only when the acquisition of this second citizenship is the result of a voluntary action or expresses the actual intent to give up the prior citizenship, and not when such acquisition proceeds automatically, typically as a result of another country's legal system (e.g. USA, Germany, Austria and Belgium).

---

[17] Most significantly, among its provisions concerning the acquisition of nationality the aforementioned Convention provides that: '[e]ach State Party shall provide in its internal law for the possibility of naturalization of persons lawfully and habitually resident on its territory. In establishing the conditions for naturalization, it shall not provide for a period of residence exceeding 10 years before the lodging of an application' (Ch. III, §6.3); '[e]ach State party shall facilitate in its internal law the acquisition of its nationality for persons who were born on its territory and reside there lawfully and habitually (Ch. III, §6.4.e). As for the rules concerning multiple nationality the Draft foresees that '[a] State Party shall allow children having different nationalities acquired automatically at birth to retain these nationalities' (Ch. V, §14. 1.a). Although in the Convention it is foreseen that a State Party may provide for the loss of its nationality when there is a voluntary acquisition of another nationality in its internal law (Ch. III, §7.1.a), it also provides that 'the Convention shall not limit the right of a State Party to determine in its internal law whether its nationals acquiring or possessing the nationality of another State retain its nationality or lose it' (Ch. V, §15.a) or whether 'the acquisition or retention of its nationality is subject to the renunciation or loss of another nationality' (Ch. V, §15.b), and, finally, that '[a] State Party shall not make the renunciation or loss of another nationality a condition for the acquisition or retention of its nationality where such renunciation or loss is not possible or cannot reasonably be required' (Ch. V, §16).

Be that as it may, from a normative standpoint one could always say that the country of origin acts wrongly whenever it does not sufficiently recognize the adequate moral relevance of the ties and attachments that its emigrated nationals might still preserve. From a practical point of view, however, such considerations would recommend prudence and strongly alert us against following the path of automatic ascription of second nationalities until the necessary conditions are given. Until multiple citizenship is generally recognized, as it should be, either disentangling civic equality from nationality or else according resident aliens a fully optional right to naturalize might still be the best paths to overcome the criticized deficit of democratic legitimacy.[18]

---

[18] Note that the same prudence would be advisable if the state of origin reacted adversely to the full inclusion of its nationals in another state, for example by taking away their citizenship when they perform some of the rights or duties traditionally perceived as citizen rights or duties (e.g. military service or political rights), instead of dealing with these issues in the same way as when they apply to other dual nationals, as I claim they should. In all these cases, optional naturalization might still be preferable to any of the forms of automatic incorporation.

7   The constitutional debate in the United States

We now have a normative case for how the inclusion of permanent resident aliens should proceed. But what is actually happening? How have the courts been reacting to the consolidation of a permanent sector of non-citizens among the ordinary population living under the state jurisdiction? Are they advancing through constitutional interpretation in the direction of ensuring the inclusion of resident aliens into the sphere of constitutional equality? If so, on what tacit or express moral grounds are they relying and which constitutional mechanisms are proving most useful? If not, which ones are proving the hardest obstacles to overcome?

Focusing on the constitutional debate is especially interesting in the USA. As a country of immigration, it has traditionally welcomed newcomers. Many of these newcomers were accorded the status of immigrants right from the beginning, and with it came the expectation that they would remain in the country and become citizens through a naturalization which was granted as a matter of course after a certain period of residence in the country. So, given what, with some significant exceptions, appears to be a rich and welcoming immigration *policy,* looking at the Constitution is very revealing. It is revealing because it helps us to identify whether there have been constraints linked to the community's commitment to a constitutionally sanctioned liberal democracy which have forced inclusion even further than has naturally been the result of the ordinary process of political self-determination expressed through the country's laws on immigration and citizenship. Hence the interest in analysing the US debate on the inclusion of resident aliens in the sphere of constitutional equality. Obviously, rather than on a general description of the constitutional status of aliens (which clearly depends on the more general features of the US Constitution) my focus will be on relational equality. So, the question is: to what extent has alienage been a self-explanatory ground for legal differentiation and classifications? Does the US Constitution, as interpreted by the legal scholars and the courts, mandate equality for resident aliens, allow for the equality of resident aliens or else forbid equality?

But first, a brief point on terminology and some preliminary remarks. Our main concern in this work is with permanent resident aliens. As I said, in the USA these are generally aliens who arrive in the country with the legal status of immigrants (i.e. persons admitted for permanent residence). In fact, unless otherwise specified, I shall be referring to them when I refer to 'aliens' or to 'resident aliens', in general terms. Clearly, included in the category of 'resident aliens' or 'resident immigrants' in the previous chapters were also illegal immigrants (provided they had been in the country for a sufficient period of time). For the sake of clarity I will specify when I refer to them or to any other kind of aliens present in the country but without the legal permission to remain indefinitely.[1]

Also, I should start by saying that, as it has been rightly said, the 'American Bill of Rights does not reflect an identifiable theory of the rights of aliens' (Neuman 1990: 76–7). Resident aliens' constitutional status has thus been judicially constructed. The by-default holders of constitutional rights have always been United States citizens within the territorial boundaries of the country. As for aliens, the Supreme Court has held for more than a century now, that aliens *within* the territorial jurisdiction of the United States are in principle covered by constitutional protection and this has generally also included aliens who were unlawfully present.[2] However, more than by this general inclusion, the specific place

---

[1] It may be of interest to explain briefly the typology of aliens in the USA system. Basically, aliens are divided into two groups: immigrants and non-immigrants. A non-immigrant is any alien who can prove that he or she falls into one of the statutorily enumerated categories of (mostly) temporary visitors, such as students, tourists, business visitors or temporary workers (see *Immigration and Nationality Act* (henceforth, *INA*), '101 (a)(15), 8 USC ' 1101 (a)(15)(1994)). All other aliens are immigrants and therefore subject to the more rigorous standards applicable to those who seek permanent residence in the United States.

Apart from regular immigrants, or people 'lawfully admitted for permanent residence' (ibid.: '101 (a) (15), 8 USC ' 1101(a)(15)(1994)) (the so-called 'green card holders'), one can also find illegal immigrants. 'Illegal alien' is a term that rarely appears defined, and when it does, it is generally in a 'context driven and inconsistent manner' (Neuman 1995: 1440, n. 69). The term 'illegal immigrant' can mean a great variety of things. The status of illegality may derive from having entered illegally, overstayed or otherwise violated the terms of their temporary admission.

Finally, there is a hybrid category to which I will not be referring. It is that of aliens 'permanently residing under color of law' (or PRUCOL). It includes several miscellaneous groups such as aliens who have received *asylum* (*INA* ' 208, 8 USC ' 1158 (1994)); some who have been *paroled* into the United States (see *INA* ' 212(d)(5), 8 USC ' 1182 (d)(5), authorizing the Attorney General to 'parole' an alien into the country temporarily 'for emergency reasons or for reasons deemed strictly in the public interest'), as well as miscellaneous others who remain in the United States with the knowledge and permission of the Immigration and Naturalization Service (henceforth, INS).

[2] *Yick Wo v. Hopkins*, 118 US 356 (1886); *Wong Wing v. United States*, 163 US 228 (1896); *United States v. Mendoza-López*, 481 US 828 (1987); *Plyler v. Doe*, 457 US 202 (1982).

of resident aliens in the constitution has been determined by two conceptions of the community which have been competing with each other at
different times and to different degrees.

On the one hand, the polity is portrayed mainly as one political unit in
the world of states and the state is perceived as still largely resting on
nineteenth-century notions of sovereignty. The state is referred to as
sovereign to control access to both its territory and its citizenry. As
members of competing state units, aliens, including permanent resident
aliens, are excluded from the recognized body politic. Whether they may
or may not enter the country, enjoy a more or less rich status of rights,
and, eventually, become citizens, depends on the will of the state and is
largely a matter of political discretion. The courts have little or nothing to
say. Competing with such a conception is that which highlights the polity
as a social sphere of interaction. Most relevant to this view is the fact that
resident aliens are part of the social tissue of the country and that they are
permanently subject to the law. They have generally been expressly
accepted to stay indefinitely and they are usually included in the scheme
of rights and duties that binds citizens too. Depending on which view, the
more political or the more societal, has prevailed resident aliens have been
allocated different constitutional status. Ultimately, the coexistence of
these two notions of the community has generated some contradictions,
which, I will show, reveal the difficulty of having a liberal democratic
order in which the socioeconomic and the political spheres of membership are split.

Resident aliens and the political realm: the unquestioned exclusion

Permanent resident aliens have traditionally been excluded from the
political realm. They have been denied the core political rights (such as
suffrage and the right to hold a public office) almost as a matter of course
and this has only very rarely been questioned as a discrimination of
doubtful constitutional validity. Thus, the possibility that the Constitution, when read in its best light, may require full equality, including full
equality of political rights, has not been seriously considered, either by the
courts or by mainstream legal scholarship. The strictly political dimension of the community has clearly prevailed in the decision on the allocation of political power.

To some extent this undisputed exclusion of resident aliens from the
realm of constitutional equality is probably also related to the fact that
citizenship, both statutorily and constitutionally defined, has been quite

accessible in the USA, making up, to some extent, for the democratic deficit that might have otherwise come about. Typically, naturalization in the USA has traditionally been seen as a right that comes almost automatically after a five-year residence period. Also, entrenched in the Federal Constitution is the principle of citizenship following the place of birth (*ius soli*). Naturalization and birthright citizenship have thus functioned fairly well as paths for the incorporation of newcomers, facilitating their access to national membership, and this might partly explain why so little effort has thus far been made to rekindle the alien suffrage debate in the USA (Neuman 1992: 309).[3] However, the increasing numbers of non-citizen residents due to the continued presence of immigrants, some of whom are not eligible for naturalization (such as, most typically, illegal aliens), and the recent restrictions on resident aliens' access to social benefits proving them to be an easy political target at times of perceived economic hardship (Levinthal 1996: 470), might provide good reasons for reopening the debate. There would be additional reasons if birthright citizenship was restricted so as to prevent illegal immigrants' children from automatically joining the American community or naturalization conditions became more strict to prevent aliens from naturalizing fraudulently, for the wrong reasons or simply too fast. All of these possibilities have been in the political debate during the past few years (Schuck 1997: 2). In other words, if access to national membership becomes more restrictive we can surely expect the alternative path to civic equality, full inclusion, to become more compelling.

However, the reigning consensus thus far has been that, as things are now, aliens can legitimately be discriminated against in the political realm: they can legitimately be denied the right to vote and to run for office at least in national and state elections, the state having an interest in limiting participation in government to those persons within the political community, and aliens not being part of such a community.[4] The exclusion also encompasses aliens' right to serve on grand and petit juries,[5] and, as we will see, the right to have equal access to a fairly broad category

---

[3] Until a few years ago there was a concern because some groups of immigrants, such as, most typically, Hispanics, did not show a great interest in naturalization. Recent years have witnessed unprecedentedly high naturalization rates. Several reasons seem to account for this, among them the fact that many of the illegal immigrants whose status was regularized under the *Immigration Reform and Control Act* of 1986 have only now become eligible for citizenship. The 1996 reforms curtailing permanent resident aliens' access to most means-tested benefit programmes has probably also had an encouraging effect (Aleinikoff, Martin and Motomura 1998: 57). Finally, Mexico's recent policy of allowing its nationals who naturalize in the USA to preserve Mexican citizenship may also have had an impact on the naturalization rate of Mexicans.

[4] *Skafke v. Rorex* (553 P. 2d 830 (Colo. 1976), appeal dismissed, 97 S. Ct. 1638 (1977).

[5] *Perkins v. Smith*, 426 US 913 (1976), *affg.* 370 F. Supp. 134 (D. Md. 1974).

of state and federal public employment viewed as closely related to the process of self-government. Moreover, as a constitutional imperative, only citizens can become presidents of the United States, senators and representatives.[6] This does not mean that aliens are totally banned from the political realm. It is generally accepted that aliens enjoy the guarantees of free expression and association covered by the First Amendment of the Constitution and nobody questions the political dimensions of such freedoms. However, the general understanding is that full political equality between resident aliens and citizens is not constitutionally mandated.

Does this imply that what is mandated is actually inequality? Or could the legislator fulfil the imperatives of liberal democracy by proceeding to the statutory inclusion of permanent resident aliens? In other words, are there any constitutional limits to the legislative authority to enfranchise resident aliens? Raskin and Neuman, both of whom have engaged in a thorough discussion on the topic, tend to agree that, if not mandated, as I have argued should be the case under certain circumstances, alien suffrage is at least constitutionally permissible (Raskin 1993; Neuman 1992). Only Rosberg has advanced the claim that in certain cases alien suffrage is constitutionally *required* (Rosberg 1977b). For Neuman, although what is at stake here is the polity seen as a political community, the Constitution does not provide 'a single conception of a political community' (Neuman 1992: 320). Regarding its power of self-determination, the community can include a variety of non-invidiously defined optional electorates of categories of persons who have interests implicated in its political process. Similarly, for Raskin, the matter of who votes should be decided by citizens through the ordinary political process as a central question in a community's process of political self-definition (Raskin 1993: 1429–40). All of them agree that resident aliens have the necessary stake or interest in governmental affairs and in having a say in the adoption of rules governing their conduct (Neuman 1992: 322). This is at least the case when they are permanently residing in the country and will therefore be pervasively affected by governmental decisions (Rosberg 1977b: 1112). Moreover, there is nothing peculiar about aliens' status that disqualifies them from becoming an optional electorate. Nothing interferes in principle with their ability to vote intelligently or responsibly (ibid.: 1115). Still, the prevailing opinion is that inclusion should be statutorily decided. It is not a constitutional 'must'.

Underlying the discussion is the awareness that, given the historical background, it would be strange to consider alien suffrage an anomaly in

[6] US CONST: Art. I, '2, '3; Art. II, '5.

the United States. Race, gender, property and wealth, not citizenship, were determinant during the eighteenth century. And although the late eighteenth century marked the emergence of a national concept of citizenship, the Constitution having declared that certain political offices could only be held by citizens, the movement away from alien suffrage began only late in the nineteenth century and continued into the twentieth, as the nation's hostility to foreigners increased, reaching its peak with the xenophobic and nationalist feelings preceding and accompanying the First World War. The first election in which no alien participated took place only in 1928, the disappearance of alien suffrage corresponding thus almost perfectly with the end of open and unlimited immigration to the country (Raskin 1993: 1397–1417; Neuman 1992: 292–300, 307–8; Rosberg 1977b: 1093–1100). Whether one interprets it as a triumph of history or of principles, such a long history of alien suffrage makes it unlikely that the Supreme Court would interfere with a state's attempt to restore it if there was one.

The modern Supreme Court has never had occasion to reconsider the constitutional permissibility of the inclusion of aliens into the enfranchised body. Rather, the cases it has had to face deal only with the permissibility of the exclusion of aliens, be it from public employment closely related to the process of self-government or from the right to vote. And although it has often started from the common assumption of the right to vote as a right of citizens and has therefore approved of the permissibility of exclusion of aliens, it has never sanctioned the citizenship requirement as compulsory.[7] Also, the tenor of the relevant constitutional provisions seems at most inconclusive (Bickel 1975: 46). Precisely this inconclusiveness has occasionally allowed for the argument that, when read in its best light, the Constitution actually mandates equality (Rosberg 1977b). The Constitution contains no specific qualifications for voting in state elections and simply borrows from state-created suffrage qualifications to define the federal electorate. The three constitutional amendments dealing directly with the qualifications of voters – the Fifteenth (race), Nineteenth (sex) and Twenty-sixth (age) – all refer to the voting rights of citizens, as opposed to persons. But it is known that the latter two amendments simply track the verbal formula of the Fifteenth Amendment.[8] As for the Fifteenth Amendment, the drafters spoke in terms of citizenship because they were working against the background of

[7] See *Dunn v. Blumstein*, 405 US 330, 336 (1972); *Kramer v. Union Free School District*, 395 US 621, 627 (1969); *Reynolds v. Sims*, 377 US 533, 565 (1964).
[8] The Fifteenth Amendment provides: 'The right of *citizens* of the United States to vote shall not be denied or abridged by the United States or by any State on account of race, color, or previous condition of servitude.' (US CONST. Amend. XV, '1 (emphasis added)).

a famous decision, the Dred Scott decision,[9] which had linked the civil and political rights of blacks with the question of citizenship and had denied citizenship to blacks on the grounds that whites did not consider them appropriate partners in the political community (Rosberg 1977b: 1107; Bickel 1975: 41). Briefly, none of these constitutional amendments purported to declare who was going to be an eligible elector: they only provided that states could not exclude citizens from the right to vote on the basis of certain criteria.

So the first difference when comparing resident aliens' and citizens' constitutional status has to do with their strictly political status. There is a long tradition of alien suffrage in the USA. But the Constitution has not taken a clear stand on this. Thus far, the Supreme Court has not offered a convincing justification as to why the expansive wave of equality should stop short of the political realm. However, it has generally been assumed that citizenship sets the boundaries of the necessary realm of democratic accountability. Only citizens belong to the body politic and thus should be entitled to full political rights. No distinction is made between the different kinds of aliens even though they might have different kinds of interests at stake. On the other hand, entitling resident aliens to the core political right, alien suffrage, has not been seen as infringing the Constitution and some have argued that their subjection to the law and being deeply affected by the political process make them at least an optional electorate.

For the future, both the path of more inclusive ordinary legislation on the matter and that of more expansive constitutional interpretation of the principle of equality are open. Ultimately, only the latter would fully meet the claim of inclusion whereby excluding long-term resident aliens from full political membership should cease to be considered a legitimate option in a liberal democracy. Only time will tell which, if either, of these paths will be activated if the percentage of non-citizen residents continues to increase, widening the gap between the ordinary residential community and that of the politically entitled. As long as the alternative paths to inclusion through citizenship remain fairly accessible (and, as we will see, we can expect the Constitution to react against restrictive attempts in this respect), they will probably make up, to a significant degree, for the democratic legitimation gap that the permanent exclusion of resident aliens from the political sphere entails. Hence the need to keep in mind the connection between the main claim and the subsidiary claim of inclusion.

[9] 60 US (19 How) 393 (1857).

Resident aliens as aliens. Federal classifications on the basis of alienage: the plenary power doctrine

So we find that the Constitution generally applies to resident aliens and that the main exception to this is equality in the enjoyment of political rights, an equality which is not interpreted as constitutionally mandated. What other differentiations based on alienage have been constitutionally tolerated?

To answer this question we have to draw a major dividing line separating the classifications on the basis of alienage that have resulted from the federal government action from those that have derived from the action of the different states. Briefly, when it is the federal government that acts, the political dimension of the community is again underlined and resident aliens are perceived mainly as aliens and thus, as individuals ascribed to competing sovereign political communities. This has justified the courts' general attitude of deference towards the political branches ruling on the subject even when that implied treating aliens, including permanent resident aliens, differently from citizens. In stark contrast, at the state level, a different view of resident aliens has prevailed and they have mainly been seen as residents of the states, more or less equally situated with respect to their citizen-resident peers. And here, the courts have been much stricter in demanding justifications for their differential treatment. So, once again, we find the differentiation between the community as a political and as a residential habitat. The difference is only that, here, what makes the difference is not the kind of right that is at stake but rather which political actor undertakes the measures affecting aliens in the country. The federal structure of the USA has allowed this rigid duality which remains a striking feature of the USA constitutional treatment of resident aliens. But let us see how this has worked, taking one step at a time.

The Supreme Court has in principle been most reluctant to subject any federal measure related to immigration to any substantial review. Far from enforcing constitutional equality between citizens and resident aliens, under the so-called *plenary power doctrine* the Supreme Court has consistently argued, for more than a century now, that the immigration and naturalization policies pertain exclusively to the political branches of the government. Literally, the 'power to expel or exclude aliens [is] a fundamental sovereign attribute exercised by the Government's political departments [which is] largely immune from judicial control';[10] 'over no conceivable subject [is] the legislative power of Congress more complete

---

[10] *Shaughnessy v. United States ex rel. Mezei*, 345 US 206, 210 (1953).

[than over immigration matters]'.[11] Consistently, in its lifetime, it has had the chance to uphold not only the exclusion but also the deportation of aliens on grounds such as race, national origin and sexual or political orientation.[12] Moreover, the problem is that what constitutes the country's immigration policy has been quite broadly defined. Thus, the plenary power doctrine has generally covered the body of laws governing aliens' general status of rights and obligations while in the territory, and not only entry and departure. And this has included measures which seemed most closely related to domestic concerns and most unrelated to the country's immigration policy such as resident aliens' access to welfare and social benefits while there.[13] All that was required was that the measure be a federal measure and that it affected aliens.

Most regrettable for our purposes is the fact that under the common label of immigration matters the Supreme Court has not substantially distinguished between the claims of aliens to enter the country and to remain in it once they had settled. Aliens are aliens no matter how long they have lived in the country. No distinction has been made to accommodate those aliens who have made the USA their main societal habitat. Thus, under the plenary power doctrine, the federal government has enjoyed the largest discretion in the deportation of aliens, something which has left them permanently exposed to the possibility of losing their general constitutional status as residents. Under such a broadly conceived power Congress has traditionally been given almost unfettered discretion in selecting deportation grounds. These could have retrospective effects, and apply regardless of how long ago the offending conduct had occurred,[14] of how long the implicated aliens had been living in the United States,[15] and of how deeply the personal

---

[11] *Oceanic Steam Navigation Co. v. Stranhan*, 214 US 320, 339 (1909).

[12] Under the plenary power doctrine the Supreme Court has upheld the exclusion of Chinese nationals in the late nineteenth century (see *Fong Yue Ting v. United States*, 149 US 698, 713–14 (1893) (upholding an act of Congress authorizing the deportation of Chinese labourers under Chinese Exclusion laws), and *Chae Chan Ping v. United States*, 130 US 581, 609–10 (1889) (upholding the statutory exclusion of Chinese labourers as a constitutional exercise of legislative power)), and the exclusion and deportation of homosexuals and political radicals in the twentieth century (see, e.g., *Boutilier v. INS*, 387 US 118, 120–3 (1976) (holding that the then-existing 'psychopathic personality' ground of exclusion encompassed homosexuals) and *Harisiades v. Shaughnessy*, 324 US 580, 591 (1952) (upholding a statute providing for the deportation of legally resident aliens because of past membership of the Communist Party).

[13] See, for example, *Mathews v. Diaz*, 426 US 67 (1976).

[14] See *Harisiades v. Shaughnessy*, 324 US 580 (1952) and *Galvan v. Press*, 347 US 522 (1952) (both approving deportation of long-time permanent residents – some of whom had been residing in the USA for up to thirty-six years – based on earlier behaviour and/or membership of the Communist Party that was lawful when it was engaged in).

[15] The landmark case in this respect was *Chae Chan Ping v. United States*, also known as the *Chinese Exclusion Case* (130 US 581), from 1889, where a statute excluding Chinese

and family interests at stake could be affected.[16]

Understandably, the plenary power doctrine has been subject to permanent criticism by the constitutional commentators (Neuman 1996: 119 ff; Legomsky 1995b; Aleinikoff 1990: 9; Motomura 1990: 545; Schuck 1984: 4). But its express overruling has not taken place yet. All of the attempts to justify the doctrine share something in common, namely, the view of resident aliens, no matter how firmly settled and integrated in the USA, as individuals who nevertheless 'belong to other states'. Once again, we find the assumption that only citizens have an allocated geopolitical space in their country and, to some extent, also the assumption that the Constitution is only fully their Constitution. Underlying it is often also a Hobbesian concept of the world, which incorporates nineteenth-century notions of state sovereignty. In it, states are portrayed as competing political communities, and aliens, accordingly, as potential enemies.[17]

Not surprisingly the most popular theory in support of the plenary power doctrine has been said to be the one holding that immigration provisions are a political question which affects foreign relations.[18] Related to it is another thesis, the sovereignty thesis, according to which the power to exclude and to deport aliens is inherent in sovereignty, so that Congress's exercise of that power should be immune from substantive constitutional constraints.[19] There is, finally, the guest theory which is clearly connected to the other two (Legomsky 1984). It justifies the plenary power doctrine on the assumption that resident aliens are merely 'guests'[20] who have 'come at the Nation's invitation'.[21] They are guests asserting 'privileges' rather than 'members' asserting 'rights'.

---

labourers was applied to prevent the readmission of a person who had been living and working in the USA for twelve years and had taken a temporary trip back to China.

[16] See, for example, *Marcello v. Bonds*, 349 US 302 (1955) (upholding the *ex post facto* deportation of a narcotics offender with citizen wife and children) or *Galvan v. Press*, 347 US 522 (1952) (upholding the *ex post facto* deportation of a Communist Party member with citizen wife and children).

[17] As the Court once said, the power to exclude aliens is an 'incident of every independent nation' because if a nation could not control its borders 'it would be to that extent subject to the control of another power'. 'To preserve its independence, and give security against foreign aggression and encroachment is the highest duty of every nation.' (*Chae Chan Ping v. United States*, 130 US 581, 603, 604 and 606 (1889)).

[18] Vague references to either foreign affairs or political questions have surfaced in some of the plenary power cases (see *Kleindienst v. Mandel*, 408 US 753, 766 n.6 (1972); *Galvan v. Press*, 347 US 522, 530 (1952); *Harisiades v. Shaughnessy*, 334 US 580, 588–91 (1952); *United States ex. rel Knauff v. Shaughnessy* 338 US 537, 542 (1950); *Fong Yue Ting v. United States*, 149 US 698, 705–6 (1893)).

[19] See *Fiallo v. Bell*, 430 US 787, 792 (1977); *Kleindienst v. Mandel*, 408 US 753, 766 (1972); *Shaughnessy v. United States ex rel. Mezei*, 345 US 206, 210 (1953).

[20] *Mathews v. Diaz*, 426 US 67, 80 (1976).

[21] *Landon v. Plasencia*, 459 US 21 (1982); *Foley v. Connelie*, 435 US 291, 294 (1978).

Admission of aliens is thus depicted as a retractable privilege. The power of Congress to exclude aliens altogether from the United States and that of prescribing the terms and conditions upon which they may come to the country are put on an equal footing.[22] After all, the latter could always be described as 'conditions on entry'.

Most of these explanations sound very anachronistic. The vast bulk of the immigration code which refers to provisions such as those providing for preferences for family members, for the exclusion of persons with contagious diseases, for the deportation of aliens who commit serious crimes, etc. has little to do with foreign policy. It rather focuses on local conditions in the USA and is centred around the relationship between the government and aliens as individuals, and not around the relations between governments (Neuman 1996: 136–7). It looks at immigrants more as potential or actual residents than as members of competing polities. The recognition of an inherent and unlimited power raises by itself a whole set of problems in a constitutional state which cannot simply be set aside by calling on the notion of sovereignty. The federal government does not own the land in the USA. It only has some powers of regulation over it and it has to exercise those powers in compliance with the Constitution (ibid.: 121). Framing the issue in terms of rights and privileges and calling the legal restrictions set on aliens 'conditions on entry' does not take us very far either. After all, it has been argued, if the government can enforce 'conditions on entry' as valid restrictions, it is not because the entering alien agrees to them, but rather because these restrictions are themselves inherently reasonable (Rosberg 1977a: 329). And whether they are 'reasonable' depends on whether or not they comply with the constitutional restrictions the nation has committed itself to respect (Legomsky 1984: 270). Otherwise, 'the government could simply impose the most appalling restrictions on aliens by inducing them to "accept" them as the price for admission to the United States' (Rosberg 1977a: 329).

According to Legomsky, the formation and perpetuation of the plenary power doctrine has not only relied on misconceived doctrinal theory, but also on a range of external forces (Legomsky 1984: 225, 278 ff). Among these he stresses the Court's own perception of its judicial role in the field of immigration, a perception which the Court has expressly incorporated into its rhetoric and then perpetuated by calling on the strict observance of precedent (*stare decisis*). The most clear and commonly quoted example of this is *Galvan v. Press*[23] where the Court stated:

[22] *Lem Moon Sing v. United States*, 158 US 538, 547 (1895).
[23] 347 US 522, 530–1 (1954).

[M]uch could be said for the view, were we writing on a clean slate, that the Due Process Clause qualifies the scope of political discretion heretofore recognized as belonging to Congress in regulating the entry and deportation of aliens . . . But the slate is not clean. As to the extent of the power of Congress under review, there is not merely a 'page of history' . . . but a whole volume . . . [T]hat the formulation of these policies is entrusted exclusively to Congress has become about as firmly imbedded in the legislative and judicial tissues of our body politic as any aspect of our government.

Such a judicial attitude is best understood, Legomsky claims, when related to contemporary social and political forces around 'which a general public opinion of animosity against immigrants has formed and which the judges have then been hesitant to defy' (Legomsky 1984: 286 ff). As he puts it, an increase in the volume of immigration has historically been followed by an increase in the level of anti-immigration sentiment and, accordingly, in restrictive legislation. Restrictive legislation and increasing volume of immigration have produced a higher number of exclusions and deportations and, hence, a greater amount of litigation before the courts. In the midst of general public animosity the courts have been hesitant to overrule the plenary power doctrine and, in doing so, have actually contributed to its consolidation.

Fortunately, things are gradually changing. In recent years the Court has used language that leaves open the possibility of some judicial role in assessing the constitutionality of federal immigration statutes.[24] For our purposes it is interesting to notice that, for the time being, the greatest exceptions to the plenary power rule refer to resident aliens and, more concretely, to the procedural rights assisting them in deportation procedures. Most telling is also the fact that some exceptions have been carved out with regard to exclusion procedures of aliens who, although physically outside the country, had significant ties to the country when they made their claims.[25] As part of the ordinary population living in the

---

[24] See, for example, *Fiallo v. Bell*, 430 US 787, 792 (1977); *Kleindienst v. Mandel*, 408 US 753 (1972); *Hampton v. Mow Sun Wong*, 426 US 88 (1976).

[25] A point on immigration terminology. Until the immigration reform that took place in 1996 through the Illegal Immigration Reform and Immigrant Responsibility Act, 'deportation' generally meant the removal from the country of an alien who had already entered it, lawfully or unlawfully. 'Exclusion' was the rejection of an alien who had arrived at the border but had not yet entered the country, at least as the law defined entry. Traditionally, far greater constitutional protection was accorded to deportation procedures than to exclusion procedures. Although aliens who were outside the country, for whatever reason, were always excludable and not deportable aliens, the Supreme Court developed some mechanisms to ensure that, in their claim to re-enter the country, resident aliens would enjoy the stronger guarantees of deportation procedures. See *Rosenberg v. Fleuti*, 374 US 449 (1963); *Landon v. Plasencia*, 459 US 21 (1982); *Kwong Hai Chew v. Colding*, 344 US 590, 596 (1953). Recently, the boundary line dividing excludable aliens from deportable aliens has been moved. The former category, now called

country, settled immigrants could not endlessly be regarded as visitors about whose residence the government could sovereignly decide at any time. This certainly represents a significant change in attitude if compared with the nineteenth-century doctrines the Court has not dared to defy for such a long time. There is also a promising tendency among some lower courts to apply not only procedural but also substantive norms mostly to deportation cases (Legomsky 1995b).

The Supreme Court has not yet spoken clearly on the issue. There is no doubt that the Court has not been willing to overrule the plenary power doctrine expressly. Presumably, as many scholars have suggested, its dismantling will proceed only gradually and through exceptions and qualifications (Motomura 1994; Rosberg 1977a: 284). The adoption in 1996 by the Clinton administration of the Illegal Immigration Reform and Immigrants Responsibility Act and of the Personal Responsibility and Work Opportunity Reconciliation Act, also known as the Welfare Reform Act, as legal measures which restrict illegal but also legal immigrants' access to a great deal of welfare benefits might present the Court with the occasion to think over some of its precedent. Before 1996 almost all major federally funded public benefits programmes were open to lawful permanent resident aliens (see, for example, Abriel 1995: 1600–5) so that differences between the legal rights of citizens and permanent resident aliens were mostly of a political nature (Schuck 1997: 13). The Welfare Reform Act has widened the legal gap by restricting lawfully present aliens' access to both federal and state public benefits and was initially conceived as applying also to aliens who were already in the country and were already beneficiaries of the affected programmes.[26] It is unclear at this stage how much litigation it will trigger and what the chances are that the cases will reach the Supreme Court, since the Clinton administration restored some of the benefits for resident aliens already in the country in 1997 at the time the law came into force and is

inadmissible aliens, has expanded to include non-citizens present in the country without having been inspected and admitted. Thus, entrants without inspections, previously subject to deportation, will henceforth be considered applicants for admission, subject to the inadmissibility grounds no matter how long they have been in the country. Moreover the distinction between exclusion and deportation *proceedings* has been abolished. Now, all questions about a person's right to remain are adjudicated in a unified removal proceeding even though the difference in the degree of protection of an admitted and an inadmissible alien, in the new terminology, has not been removed.

[26] The aim of this Act has been described as that of 'adjusting unabated mass immigration to a welfare state under siege' (Joppke 1999a: 60). Already a new law passed three months earlier had made most legal immigrants ineligible for federally funded means-tested welfare benefits. The new law added to this the concept of 'deeming' which includes the income of the sponsors of family immigrants in order to calculate the poverty line below which immigrants may benefit from some social programmes and holds the sponsor legally responsible for supporting the immigrant in case of need.

currently considering further restorations. Relevant for our purpose is the fact that among the groups that the law exempts from the exclusion from the social net are aliens who have been working in the country for ten years, as long as they have not claimed public assistance during that time.

Be that as it may, these legal measures raise important theoretical issues. Can they be described as immigration measures simply because the federal powers and not the states have enacted them? If so, should they be left without substantial review or is this the perfect occasion for setting the principle that, whether or not related to the powers of Congress on immigration policy, measures like these which affect aliens who have become part of the social community should be subject to judicial scrutiny?[27]

Resident aliens as residents: resident aliens and state action

Aliens, state action and equal protection

In striking contrast with its deferential attitude *vis-à-vis* the federal government, the US Supreme Court has been much more demanding when examining state measures discriminating against resident aliens unless such measures had to do with strictly political rights and public functions. In these cases the Equal Protection Clause of the Fourteenth Amendment, which provides that no state shall deny to any person within its jurisdiction the equal protection of the law,[28] has allowed resident aliens to be seen more as local residents sharing many of the relevant circumstances with Americans living in the state, than as individuals linked to a foreign nation through the legal bond of nationality.[29] If, at a federal level,

---

[27] New York City, Florida and other plaintiffs immediately challenged the new federal policy for discriminating against aliens. A federal district court in New York, however, has upheld the statute as being rationally related to the government's interest in encouraging both the self-sufficiency of resident aliens and their naturalization, as well as in helping fiscal savings. It should be mentioned that the court expressly stated that, whether or not it was viewed as an exercise of the plenary power doctrine, the statute had to be subject to judicial scrutiny. Applying a rational basis test, it held that the statute did not infringe against the equal protection element of the Fifth Amendment's Due Process Clause. See *Abreu v. Callahan*, United States District Court, Southern District of New York, 1997, 971 F. Supp. 799.

[28] This clause reads as follows: '[N]or shall any State ... deny to any person within its jurisdiction the equal protection of the laws'.

[29] Let us briefly advance some general notions on the equal protection doctrine in the USA as the legal mechanism to fight against discrimination. Several types of judicial scrutiny have generally been functioning under the Fourteenth and Fifth Amendments' guarantees of equal protection. The first is the so-called *rational basis test*. It is satisfied whenever it is possible to identify a legitimate public purpose which is rationally connected to the classification at stake (see, e.g., *Lindsley v. Natural Carbonic Gas Co.*, 220 US 61

the concern with the political dimension of the national community has prevailed, allowing resident aliens to be seen mainly as members of competing nations, at a state level the societal dimension has prevailed binding both citizens and resident aliens through a fairness-based scheme of cooperation at least in the socioeconomic realm.

From the special public interest doctrine to the doctrine of alienage as a suspect classification   Things were not always like this. As early as 1886 the US Supreme Court put to one side the doubts on the applicability to aliens of the Fourteenth Amendment's Equal Protection Clause.[30] However, no significant protection was derived from it for aliens in the first decades. Under the then-prevailing public interest doctrine the allegation of any kind of public interest was all the Court required as a justification for statutes that discriminated against aliens, limiting common property or state resources to the use of citizens. What is more important, the state's concern with advancing the interests and the profit of the citizen body over those of aliens was already accepted as a valid public interest. Briefly, resident aliens' interests and concerns did not qualify as 'public' interests, whereas citizens' did. Resident aliens were thus not fully perceived as self-authenticating sources of valid claims. By definition, their needs simply did not have to be as seriously accommodated by the public institutions as those of their citizen-peers. The possibility of discriminating against aliens followed almost automatically. During the first decades of the twentieth century the Court upheld state statutes which prohibited aliens from owning land, taking or hunting wild game, or working in public employment.[31]

(1911)). Much more demanding is the *strict scrutiny test*. It applies either when the classification is suspect (such as, most typically, classifications on the basis of race (see, e.g., *McLaughlin v. Florida*, 379 US 184 (1964)) and national origin (see, e.g., *Korematsu v. United States*, 323 US 214 (1944)), or else, when the discriminating act significantly burdens the exercise of some fundamental right (see, e.g., *Shapiro v. Thompson*, 394 US 618 (1969) (freedom of interstate movement). Here the judge is not satisfied with the allegation of any kind of interest but requires that it be a compelling one and that the classification be narrowly drawn to achieve it. A third level of scrutiny (sometimes called intermediate scrutiny) is applied to statutes which, while not involving a fundamental right or suspect classification, still restrict important or substantial benefits. These statutes must fairly be viewed as furthering a substantial state interest in order to withstand judicial review (see *Plyler v. Doe*, 457 US 202, at 217 (1982)).

[30] *Yick Wo v. Hopkins*, 118 US 356 (1886).
[31] See *Terrace v. Thompson*, 363 US 197 (1923) (prohibiting aliens from owning land); *Mc Cready v. Virginia*, 94 US 391 (1877) (upholding Virginia's restriction of the right to plant oysters in its rivers to citizens of the state); *Patsone v. Pennsylvania*, 232 US 138 (1914) (upholding a Pennsylvania act excluding any unnaturalized foreign-born resident from wild game hunting); *Heim v. Mc Call*, 239 US 175 (1915) (upholding a provision of the New York Labor Law confining employment in public works to citizens); *Crane v. New York*, 239 US 195 (1915) (upholding a New York statute prohibiting the employment of aliens on public work projects).

It was not until the 1970s that the Court expressly overruled the special public interest doctrine. The landmark case was *Graham v. Richardson*.[32] Applying the equal protection doctrine the Court declared unconstitutional statutes of Arizona and Pennsylvania requiring either citizenship or durational residence requirements for aliens' access to welfare benefits. In *Graham* the Court declared that classifications based on alienage, like those based on nationality or race, are inherently suspect and thus have to be subject to close judicial scrutiny. As a class, aliens were said to be a prime example of a 'discrete and insular minority'. Unfortunately, the Court gave little explanation of its new doctrine. It did not explain why it was calling aliens a discrete and insular minority. The expression had been drawn from another case, *United States v. Carolene Prods. Co.*,[33] where the Court elaborated its doctrine on suspect classifications but which most scholars have seen as more related to race and national origin than to alienage, strictly speaking.[34] Nothing was added in *Graham* to explain in what sense, and on which group characteristic, aliens could be considered a discrete and insular minority.

As the Court saw it, the saving of welfare costs could not justify an otherwise invidious classification. Relying on a fairness-based argument for the inclusion of resident aliens, the Court added that the justification of limiting expenses was particularly inappropriate and unreasonable when the discriminated class consists of aliens because 'aliens, like citizens, pay taxes and may be called into the armed forces . . . aliens may live within a state for many years, work in the state and contribute to the economic growth of the state . . . [t]here can be no special public interest in tax revenues to which aliens have contributed on an equal basis with the residents of the state.'[35]

When controlling state classifications on the basis of alienage the Court has therefore assumed that such similarities in the way resident aliens contribute to the community ground an equal concern for their interests. *Graham* represents thus the first example of a strand of argumentation in which the Court shows a willingness to overcome the formal distinctions between aliens and citizens as allocated members of different national

---

[32] 403 US 365 (1971).   [33] 304 US 144 (1938).

[34] In its famous footnote number four *Carolene Products* stated: 'It is unnecessary to consider now whether legislation which restricts those political processes which can ordinarily be expected to bring about repeal of undesirable legislation, is to be subjected to more exacting judicial scrutiny under the general prohibitions of the Fourteenth Amendment than are most other types of legislation . . . Nor need we inquire whether similar considerations enter into the review of statutes directed at particular religious . . ., or national . . ., or racial minorities . . .: whether prejudice against discrete and insular minorities may be a special condition, which tends seriously to curtail the operation of those political processes ordinarily to be relied upon to protect minorities, and which may call for a correspondingly more searching judicial inquiry' (304 US, at 144 n. 4).

[35] 403 US at 376.

communities, for the sake of applying a more substantive approach which is based on the real differences and similarities between aliens and citizens seen as *de facto* members of the American society. By reasoning in such a way, the Court touched upon the conceptual basis of the special public interest, sanctioning the need to define the 'interest of the nation' (or the 'public interest') by accommodating the interests of all those who are active members in society and not only of those formally recognized as citizens. After *Graham* the Court has relied on the doctrine of alienage as a suspect classification to invalidate many state measures such as those prohibiting aliens from practising the profession of law[36] or public notary;[37] those absolutely excluding aliens from any civil service employment;[38] those denying aliens the possibility of acquiring civil engineer licences;[39] and those restricting the receipt of state financial assistance for higher education to those resident aliens who had filed an intent to apply for citizenship.[40]

Whatever the place that needs to be allocated to resident aliens in the distribution of rights and benefits, why did the Court think it should treat classifications based on alienage as suspect and subject them to heightened judicial scrutiny? Why wouldn't it trust the legislator to perform the proper allocation and control its action less strictly? Some of the later cases, but more importantly the doctrinal debate following them, have in part compensated for the *Graham* Court's parsimony in explaining the doctrine of suspect classification as specifically applied to aliens. Not surprisingly, aliens' political powerlessness has been accepted as the most obvious reason to apply heightened scrutiny to control state classifications based on alienage (Johnson 1995: 1514; Legomsky 1984: 305–6; Rosberg 1977a: 304 ff). The idea is that state legislation must be presupposed legitimate in that, in principle, it expresses the democratic will. Such a will is formed in a democratic process where all groups who are potentially affected by the legislation and whose concerns therefore need to be taken into account must have had an opportunity to express their views and to pursue their interests. Thus, there is the need to grant extraordinary protection when a group is systematically shut out of the political process and is denied an opportunity to form alliances with any other group. On those occasions the Court may have well-founded fears that the injury to the members of the disadvantaged group, more than just a by-product of the state's effort to serve a legitimate interest, was in fact the very purpose of the classification.

---

[36] *In re Griffiths*, 413 US 717 (1973).   [37] *Bernal v. Fainter*, 467 US 216 (1984).
[38] *Sugarman v. Dougall*, 413 US 634 (1973).
[39] *Examining Bd. of Eng'rs, Architects & Surveyors v. Otero*, 426 US 572 (1976).
[40] *Nyquist v. Mauclet*, 432 US 1 (1977).

As applied to aliens, their exclusion from the right to vote already implies that any representation aliens receive in the political process will exclusively be 'virtual' (Ely 1980: 161–2). However, the exclusion of aliens from the political process goes well beyond the denial of the right to vote and to hold a high political or elected office. Many aliens come to the United States from countries where active political participation is not encouraged, so that they may lack a taste for political activities. Moreover, their previous experiences with immigration and other governmental agencies (known for the large amount of discretion with which they generally act) and the awareness of their vulnerability to deportation have all been considered sufficient reasons to chill aliens' willingness to engage in politics (Johnson 1995: 1514; Legomsky 1984: 305). The opportunity to seek the assistance of the country whose nationality the alien holds is often purely theoretical (Rosberg 1977a: 304). Finally, we know that other factors related to the sociocultural condition of aliens might also be relevant to determine their vulnerability in the political process.

What is so interesting about the Supreme Court treating classifications on the basis of alienage as suspect because of aliens' vulnerability in the political process, is that it constitutes a perfect example of the difficulty of separating the socioeconomic and the political as spheres of membership. On the one hand we have that the denial of the most essential political rights to aliens is generally seen as constitutionally valid even though it clearly and necessarily weakens the position of resident aliens in the political process. On the other hand, however, we find that this damages the credibility of the democratic process, a process in which resident aliens' interests need to be fully taken into consideration. As a consequence, the laws that result from it and which should treat resident aliens with equal concern (at least in the socioeconomic realm) cannot be sufficiently trusted any longer and thus, require a stronger control by the courts. Hence, paradoxically, this more demanding control by the courts appears as a guarantee to protect the interests of aliens who lack equal political powers to express and defend such interests in the first place.

For some, the fact that alienage is relevant when political interests are involved, but is usually irrelevant to private activity, might well portray a 'dual aspect of alienage' which is unique. But if this is so, it has been argued, it is only because aliens constitute a unique class.[41] Others have tried to prove the conceptual weakness of the argument of the political powerlessness of aliens (and related to it, of the doctrine of alienage as a suspect classification) by observing that the political powerlessness of aliens is itself the consequence of distinctions that are constitutionally

---

[41] *Toll v. Moreno*, 458 US 1, 22 (1982) (Blackmun, J., concurring).

permissible.[42] And finally, more in line with the normative claims of this book, others have sought to solve the apparent contradiction by pressing the argument from the opposite perspective. If the Court is serious about its suspect classification holding as applied to aliens, it should re-examine state decisions denying permanent resident aliens the right to vote.[43]

Together with aliens' political powerlessness, one can identify a whole set of additional factors further weakening the democratic credibility of the political process in which the legal status of resident aliens is decided. Among these is the fact that the generalizations involved in some classifications based on alienage may be suspected of serving the interests of the decision-makers, most of whom are citizens who have always been such and will never cease to be such (Ely 1980: 158); or the fact that the lack of substantial social intercourse between recent or some kinds of immigrants (e.g. illegal immigrants) and those who make the laws largely eliminates the possibility of overcoming prejudice and ensuring empathy.[44] Also aliens have often in the past been the victims of prejudice and widespread hostility. And this has manifested itself most strongly during times of relative economic uncertainty and hardship.[45] Prejudice has been rightly described as 'a lens that distorts reality', blinding to overlapping interests that may exist, in fact, providing the 'majority of the whole' with that 'common motive to invade the rights of other citizens' (ibid.: 153). Often, prejudice and hostility are not directed against aliens in general, but against a particular national, ethnic or racial group. For instance, many authors connect the fact that both legal and illegal residents have currently become again the special target of the political efforts to reduce public spending with the general animosity towards Latino immigration and especially towards Mexican people (Johnson 1995; Neuman 1995: 1352). Too often alienage labels come to provide a 'code in which ethnically specific appeals can be couched' (ibid.: 1429, 1452).

Some other justifications given to support the doctrine of alienage as a suspect classification seem less conclusive. For instance, involuntariness or immutability of a status or feature (e.g. race or gender) is sometimes taken as a sign that the classification based on it intends to stigmatize the members of the disadvantaged class, who cannot do anything about it, as inherently less worthy than those of the advantaged class. But the fact is that, as we know, after five years of residence almost every permanent

---

[42] See *Toll v. Moreno*, 458 US 1, 39–42 (1982) (Rehnquist J., dissenting).

[43] But see *Sugarman v. Dougall*, 413 US 634 at 647–9 (1973) (where the Supreme Court expressly warns against drawing such conclusions from the doctrine of alienage as a suspect classification).

[44] See *Toll v. Moreno*, 458 US 1, at 20 (1982) (Blackmun, J. concurring).

[45] See *Hampton v. Mow Sun Wong*, 426 US 88, at 102 (1976); *Toll v. Moreno*, 458 US 1, 20 (1982) (Blackmun, J., concurring).

resident alien is eligible for citizenship so that remaining an alien becomes to a large extent a matter of choice. However, in proving the connection between full inclusion and automatic membership as alternative paths to civic equality, we find that if access to citizenship was more restrictively defined so that alienage became more of an 'immutable' status the need for a higher protection by the courts would be reinforced. As things are, this explanation for the doctrine of suspect classification is not convincing. If the fact that the individual cannot change her status was our real concern, the class entitled to special protection would have to be defined much more narrowly and would not include all permanent resident aliens in the United States (Rosberg 1977a: 303). Those aliens who have the least power to change their status, such as aliens admitted as non-immigrants, but also illegal residents, would be the ones with a stronger claim to reinforced protection by the courts. We may agree that this should indeed be the case, but as an explanatory thesis of the USA Supreme Court doctrine of alienage as a suspect classification it fails. Otherwise, how should we explain then that the doctrine has only been applied to immigrant aliens legally residing in the country?

The political function exception doctrine   So we have that resident aliens are denied the main paths of political expression and that this has been seen as introducing distortions, distortions which have justified the fact that, under the doctrine of equal protection, the laws that affect them in the socioeconomic sphere (i.e. enjoyment of social rights and benefits) can be subject to close judicial scrutiny. This split between the socioeconomic and political spheres of membership, on which the suspect classification doctrine implicitly rests, has been confirmed by the so-called political function exception to the *Graham* rule. It was first enunciated in *Sugarman v. Dougall*[46] where the Court stated that while most forms of state alienage discrimination should be subject to strict review, if a case involved matters resting firmly within a state's constitutional prerogative to define its political community, a lesser standard of scrutiny might apply.[47] Thus, the political function exception allows that, in their broad power to define the political community, the states may require citizenship not only for suffrage but also from 'persons holding state elective and important nonelective executive, legislative, and judicial positions' who, the Court says, formulate, execute or review broad public policy and 'perform functions that go to the heart of representative government'.[48] We can see how, once again, the political dimension of the community gains relevance but this time at the state level. Whereas the

[46] 413 US 634 (1973).   [47] Ibid. 643.   [48] Ibid. 647.

national government, as we saw, has the fullest discretion to decide which and under what conditions aliens may come and remain in the country as an exercise of national self-determination and self-definition, states may now enjoy significant discretion in excluding aliens from politically sensitive positions. The exception shows again the limits to the constitutionally required equalization of the status of citizens and resident aliens in the strictly political realm.

Since that early formulation, the *Sugarman* exception has been applied on several occasions. Relying on it, the Court has upheld statutes requiring citizenship of those who intend to become police officers,[49] to teach in the state's public schools[50] and to become deputy probation officers,[51] though notably not to become a public notary.[52] In *Cabell v. Chavez-Salido*[53] the Court articulated a theoretical explanation of the political function exception which, not surprisingly, rested on the distinction between the socioeconomic and the political spheres of membership and, more concretely, on the distinction between the economic and the political functions of government.[54] It reasoned that 'although citizenship is not a relevant ground for the distribution of economic benefits, it is for determining membership in the political community'.[55] When the restrictions at hand implicated the state's definition of its political community, distinctions between citizens and aliens were not necessarily to be discouraged.[56]

The subordination of the rights of aliens to state community interests under this new doctrine has occurred without much of a battle at the level of the Supreme Court (Bosniak 1994: 1114–15). The conflict has rather raged over the question of how broadly or narrowly to interpret the domain of the political (ibid.: 1112–13). And here again we see the difficulty and maybe also the degree of fiction that the schism hides. On balance, the expansive reading of the political function exception seems to have prevailed. And the fear now is that the political function exception may come to swallow up the entire proposition that alienage classifications are suspect (Koh 1985: 63; Rosberg 1983: 400). The rules and

---

[49] *Foley v. Connelie*, 435 US 291 (1978).   [50] *Ambach v. Norwick*, 441 US 68 (1978).
[51] *Cabell v. Chavez-Salido*, 454 US 432 (1982).
[52] *Bernal v. Fainter*, 467 US 216 (1984).   [53] 454 US 432 (1982).   [54] Ibid. 440.
[55] 454 US at 438.
[56] Quoting from the Supreme Court in *Cabell v. Chavez-Salido* (454 US 432 at 439–40 (1982)):'[t]he exclusion of aliens from basic governmental processes is not a deficiency in the democratic system but a necessary consequence of the community's process of political self-definition. Self-government, whether direct or through representatives, begins by defining the scope of the community of the governed and thus of the governors as well: aliens are by definition those outside of this community. Judicial incursions in those areas may interfere with those aspects of democratic self-government that are most essential to it.'

criteria for determining when the exception applies have remained rather uncertain. Far from providing the lower courts and the legislator with more definite guidance the Supreme Court has often appeared to be making the decision on a case-by-case basis.[57] Proving the inconsistencies generated by the exception we find that the position of deputy probation officer – an occupational category which included a large variety of jobs such as those of toll takers, cemetery sextons, fish and game wardens, furniture and bedding inspectors – has been upheld,[58] whereas the ban on aliens becoming public notaries was declared unconstitutional under the same test.[59]

Commentators have interpreted the exception in rather different ways. For some, the political function exception has introduced membership concerns where the *Graham* rule was trying to replace them by a broader notion of constitutional protection based simply on equal personhood (Bosniak 1994: 1112–15). I tend to think that it has rather shown the contrast between the political and the societal notions of community in the United States (similarly, Karst 1977: 45). One thing is clear: the exception has revitalized the notion of the political community stressing the gap between those who belong in the strict sense and those who do not (Martin 1983: 198–9). The disquiet that its vague contours and its expanding force have provoked rests partly on the fear that, with the excuse of preserving the integrity of the political community, old discriminations in the socioeconomic sphere have come to be revived. Granted, the split between political and societal membership might involve some deep contradictions and tensions. But, hopefully, when these are solved they will be so for the sake of more inclusive instead of more restrictive results.

Aliens, state action and pre-emption

Together with the equal protection doctrine under the Fourteenth Amendment, the Supreme Court has relied on the doctrine of federal pre-emption when reviewing the constitutionality of state actions concerning aliens. Generally speaking, this doctrine ensures the respect for the hierarchy of federal over state laws.[60] It has also been interpreted as preventing the states from interfering in the regulation of fields which have been reserved for federal regulation, through either constitutional or

---

[57] See *Ambach v. Norwick*, 441 US 68, at 92; *Foley v. Connelie*, 435 US 291, at 296.
[58] See *Cabell v. Chavez-Salido*, 454 US 432 (1982).
[59] See *Bernal v. Fainter*, 467 US 216 (1984).
[60] This mandate rests specifically on the so-called Supremacy Clause of Article VI, cl.2 of the Federal Constitution. Such a provision provides that '[t]his Constitution, and the laws of the United States which shall be made in pursuance thereof . . . shall be the supreme Law of the Land'.

express congressional mandates. For our purposes, the main fact is that immigration legislation has been entrusted to the federal government,[61] the reasons most commonly advanced to justify this being the need for uniformity in immigration laws (Motomura 1992: 1632–3) and the federal government's better qualification to deal with foreign nations (Abriel 1995: 1609).[62]

In practice, reliance on pre-emption has introduced new complexities and brought to the surface some of the tensions and contradictions of having different notions of membership functioning at federal and state level. In the light of the case law, it is not quite clear what makes the Court decide between the equal protection and the preemption strands of review, when it does not apply both simultaneously. In theory, one could draw a distinction between the legislation that constitutes a regulation of immigration (which is preempted by the federal immigration authority) and that in which the state legislation discriminates against aliens for domestic purposes, such as the regulation of employment, public licences and permits, professional licensing, education, and public benefits and services (which need not be preempted and would have to comply with the demands of the equal protection doctrine). On the other hand, when enacted by the federal government, this kind of measure was said to pertain to the country's immigration policy. Thus, the dividing line is far from clear. Ultimately, the issue is of the utmost importance as long as the application of such different standards of review is made dependent upon whether the acts affecting resident aliens are related to the country's immigration policy, and hence, fall within the realm of the federal political discretion.

In attempts to solve some of these contradictions there has been a highly controversial debate on the degree of conceptual independence of the equal protection and preemption standards of review with respect to each other. Some scholars have argued that the complex equal protection doctrine as applied to aliens is inconsistent with the logical framework of equal protection law and that it ought to be abandoned and completely replaced by a federal pre-emption analysis. States should be able to adopt measures which discriminate against aliens unless, by doing so, they

---

[61] The federal authority over immigration emanates from various sources. Among those advanced in the case law and scholarly debates, Abriel notes the following: the naturalization power granted to Congress under Article I, Section 8, Clause 4 of the Constitution; the Commerce Clause, Article I, Section 8, Clause 3; a view of immigration as closely interwoven with foreign relations; the war power, Article I, Section 8, Clause 11; the 'maintenance of a republican form of government'; and a belief that the power to admit or forbid entry to foreigners is inherent in sovereignty and essential to self-preservation. See Abriel 1995: 1608–9.

[62] For a recent exchange on the pre-emption question in the alienage discrimination context, see Abriel 1995: 1597; Spiro 1994: 121; Motomura 1994: 201; Olivas 1994: 217.

interfere with the federal immigration policy (Perry 1983: 334–5; Note 1980: 940; Levi 1979: 1069–91; Note 1979: 1069). The issue has much practical relevance and reflects the difficulty of having two different standards to measure the treatment of aliens at state and at federal level resting on two competing notions of membership (national-political community versus state-residential community).

There are two possibilities. If it is accepted that the equal protection standard, as applied at the state level, is indeed independent and embodies a constitutional commitment to a fundamental sense of fairness in the state as a residential community, then the question is why at least some of those constraints should not apply also when the federal government makes analogous discriminations, as I think they should (also, Bosniak 1994: 1106–7; Rosberg 1977a: 316).[63] On the other hand, and this would be the other possibility, if every measure affecting aliens at a state level is to be seen as endorsing in one way or another a certain national immigration policy, then the commitment to equality through the notion of fairness loses its constitutional autonomy completely. Then, all we would have is a certain federal immigration policy which could at any time be replaced by a less egalitarian policy. As a consequence, Congress and not the Constitution would decide how broadly aliens can be made vulnerable to mistreatment by the states (Neuman 1995: 1439–40). No notion of constitutionally sanctioned equality would set limits to the ordinary political process. The facts are that the Supreme Court has decided some cases exclusively and expressly on one of the two standards only,[64] and other cases on both simultaneously but expressly giving specific and separate weight to each.[65] The chances are that it will continue to

[63] Note that this does not necessarily imply that the same equal protection standard would be applied to review federal discriminations on the basis of alienage. After all, one has to consider two things. First, that there may be reasons to think that the dynamics of the political process leave aliens more vulnerable at the state level than at the federal level. Among them, Neuman mentions the fact that anti-foreign movements have rarely taken place nation-wide; that aliens have had at least a virtual representation in Washington by means of the foreign affairs establishment; and that states, lacking control over the entry of aliens, might have a tendency to channel their frustration about unwelcome federal policies into hostility toward the admitted aliens (Neuman 1995: 1436–7). Second, that the concerns that motivate deferential review of federal alienage legislation under the plenary power doctrine (e.g. justiciability, commitment to other branches, risks of interfering with the country's foreign policy) have no applicability whatsoever to state discrimination against aliens (ibid.: 1437). The district court that reviewed the 1996 Welfare Reform Act in *Abreu v. Callahan* stated that no strict scrutiny applies to federal alienage classifications, which arguably are not within the plenary immigration powers because of the differences in the language of the constitutional provisions and the different roles of the national and state governments in the federal system concerning foreign relations and war power.

[64] See *Sugarman v. Dougall*, 413 US 634; *In re Griffiths*, 413 US at 718, n. 3.

[65] See, for instance, *Graham v. Richardson*, 403 US 365, 382 (1972).

support the thesis of the independence of the pre-emption and the equal protection strands of review whatever the tensions or contradictions that it may generate.

However, even when the Court has clearly relied on pre-emption grounds, its doctrine has retained obscure aspects. The cases themselves have not offered clear guidance as to when the state's regulation on the legal status of aliens was to be judged as an undue interference with the country's immigration policy. All in all, it appears that the preemption doctrine has strengthened federal over state powers on the subject, and reinforced aliens' legal status against past state efforts to set restrictive conditions on those aliens residing in their territory.[66]

The current relevance of the topic is undeniable and raises concerns on the 'reversibility' of aliens' rights. The 1996 Welfare Reform Act did not only restrict non-citizens' access to federal benefits. It also contained provisions that restrict states from providing non-citizens with state benefits, as well as others giving states the option to provide non-citizens with benefits jointly funded by the federal and state government (see Needelman 1997). So, the question is raised as to whether Congress has the power to authorize states to violate the Bill of Rights, since, as we know, the Fourteenth Amendment's Equal Protection Clause has been read as prohibiting states from discriminating against non-citizens in dispensing public benefits.[67] Also, there is the question as to whether this 'national

---

[66] As interpreted by the Court, the pre-emption doctrine has, first of all, embraced the principle that states could not exclude aliens from those activities and benefits by means of which they can secure their subsistence once they have been admitted to the national territory. Otherwise, it has been argued, the very federal decision to admit them into the territory would run afoul (*Truax v. Raich*, 239 US 33 at 42 (1915)). Also, the Court has shown a tendency to interpret federal statutes concerning the conditions on entry and residence of aliens as a complete scheme of regulation, with which states could not interfere (*Graham v. Richardson*, 403 US 365, 378 (1972); *Elkins v. Moreno*, 435 US 647, 664 (1978); *Toll v. Moreno*, 458 US 1, 13 (1982)). In principle, the Court has stated on different occasions that states can 'neither add nor take from the conditions lawfully imposed by Congress upon admission, naturalization and residence of aliens in the U.S.' (*Takahashi v. Fish and Game Comm.*, 334 US 410, 419 (1948); *Graham v. Richardson*, 403 US 365, 378 (1972); *De Canas v. Bica*, 424 US 351, 358, n. 6 (1976)). Moreover, the Court has not accepted as a principle that the fact that a group of aliens had already been demarcated by a federal statute for its own specific purposes could be a sufficient justification for the state's attempt to impose additional burdens on such a group. Such an attempt, the Court has held, ignores the fact that the federal government has broader constitutional powers in determining the conditions of residence when admitting aliens to the USA (*Takahashi v. Fish and Game Comm.*, 334 US 410, 418, 419 (1948)). Finally, the Court has declared the need to check state action not only against the explicit federal rules on immigration but also against the possibility that such action stands as an obstacle to the accomplishment and execution of the full purposes and objectives of Congress in passing those rules (*De Canas v. Bica*, 424 USA 351, 363 (1976). See also *Toll v. Moreno*, 458 US 1, 14–15 (1982)).

[67] See *Graham v. Richardson*, 403 US 365, 382 (1972) (stating that Congress cannot authorize the states to violate the Equal Protection Clause).

policy to discriminate against aliens in federal programmes' could legitimately cover similar restrictive attempts by the states even if they are not expressly allowed by the Welfare Reform Act. In other words, does today's restrictive federal policy simply exonerate the states from the fairness-based constraints that the equal protection doctrine has thus far set on them? To a large extent this will depend on whether or not the current Court decides to keep both preemption and equal protection as independent standards of review of state action, resisting the temptation to interpret its own equal protection doctrine as a 'federal policy' of better times. The issue would become less relevant only if the Court finally overruled its plenary power doctrine and decided also to subject restrictive federal policies to the demands of equality.

The constitutional status of illegal resident aliens: including the unconsented

The Supreme Court has occasionally stated that some constitutional provisions also protect undocumented aliens in the country.[68] More often, the Court has referred to 'resident aliens' but has not made it clear whether, by such, one should understand aliens holding some kind of immigration status (i.e. 'immigrant aliens' or aliens admitted for permanent residence) or simply 'domiciled aliens' (presumably, as defined by the law of the state, and possibly, encompassing undocumented aliens as well). Although on several occasions it has referred to 'aliens lawfully admitted to the territory',[69] it has avoided specifying to what extent such a reference should be interpreted as excluding aliens who were on the territory but had not been legally admitted.[70] Still, the general consensus has been that although the constitutional provisions, including the Equal Protection Clause, may cover illegal immigrants as well, for equal protection purposes, the suspect classification doctrine applies only to legal immigrants, excluding non-immigrant legal residents (e.g. foreign students, visitors) and, of course, illegal immigrants too.[71]

---

[68] Thus, undocumented aliens have been said to enjoy the protection of the Fourth, Fifth, Sixth and Eighth Amendments of the Constitution in criminal proceedings. See *Almeida-Sánchez v. United States*, 413 US 266 (1973) (Fourth Amendment); *Wong Wing v. United States*, 163 US 228 (1896) (Fifth and Sixth Amendments). But see *United States v. Verdugo-Urquidez*, 494 US 259 (1990) (suggesting, *in dictum*, that the rights of undocumented aliens under the Fourth Amendment had thus far been only assumed and not definitely adjudicated).

[69] See *Takahashi v. Fish and Game Comm.*, 334 USA 410, 418–19 (1948); *De Canas v. Bica*, 424 US 351, 358 n. 6 (1976).   [70] *Toll v. Moreno*, 458 US 1 (1982).

[71] Unfortunately, the one case in which the Court dealt specifically with non-immigrants who were, none the less, *bona fide* residents was solved on pre-emption rather than on equal protection grounds (see *Toll v. Moreno*, 458 US 1, (1982)).

The debate on the constitutional protection of undocumented aliens is related to two important issues. First of all, the case of illegal immigrants represents the test case for the independence between equal protection and pre-emption. To what degree do undocumented aliens ordinarily residing in the state have to be treated as equal residents even though their presence in the country violates by definition the country's immigration policy and one of its traditional sovereignty pillars, such as territorial sovereignty? Second, the debate on illegal immigrants' constitutional status can also shed some light on the question of what justifies, in general, the inclusion of aliens within the realm of constitutional protection. Again by definition, illegal immigrants, at least formally, and unlike legal permanent resident aliens, cannot be said to have been accepted as members of the national community. Does this automatically exclude them from the realm of constitutional equality? If not, on what grounds are they still included?

The doctrinal relevance of such a debate can hardly be denied at a time when both states and the federal government are experiencing with growing anxiety the issue of illegal immigration, and have started to adopt legal measures to curb the phenomenon and to protect the public from the draining of resources by illegal immigrants' and their children's access to social benefits and public services. The Illegal Immigration Reform and Immigrant Responsibility Act, probably the most dramatic change in immigration law and procedure in thirty years, and the Welfare Reform Act were conceived in this spirit. Maybe the best expression of the unrest around illegal immigration at state level is Proposition 187 enacted in November 1994 by the State of California.

Precedence in case law

In the past the Supreme Court has dealt with the issue of illegal immigration quite directly on two occasions. These were *De Canas v. Bica*[72] and *Plyler v. Doe*.[73] In *De Canas v. Bica* the Court faced the challenge of a provision of the California Labor Code which prohibited an employer from knowingly employing aliens if they were not entitled to lawful residence in the USA, when such employment would have an adverse effect on lawful resident workers. The petitioners were not unlawful residents but legal immigrant farm workers who had brought the action against the farm labour contractors on the basis that they had been denied continued employment due to a surplus of labour resulting from the respondents' knowing employment of illegal aliens. The lower courts had dismissed the complaint, holding that the provision was unconstitu-

---

[72] 424 US 351 (1976).   [73] 457 US 202 (1982).

tional because it interfered with the comprehensive regulatory scheme enacted by Congress in the exercise of its exclusive powers over immigration. The Supreme Court, however, upheld the California statute. Introducing limitations to its previous doctrine on pre-emption when applied to illegal immigrants, it maintained that although the power to regulate immigration is exclusively federal, California's regulation could not be called a regulation of immigration even if it could have some purely speculative and indirect impact on immigration. Offering a restrictive interpretation of immigration policy, the Court held that such a policy was 'essentially a determination of who should or should not be admitted into the country, and the conditions under which a legal entrant could remain'.[74] The Court further argued that states have broad authority under their police powers to regulate employment relationships and, more concretely, to prohibit the knowing employment of illegal aliens because the 'employment of illegal aliens in times of high unemployment deprives citizens and legally admitted aliens of jobs' and 'the acceptance by illegal aliens of jobs on substandard terms as to wages and working conditions can seriously depress wage scale and working conditions of citizens and legally admitted aliens [diminishing thereby] the effectiveness of labor unions'.[75] Although the Court acknowledged that 'even state regulation designed to protect vital state interest, must give way to paramount federal legislation',[76] it was not willing to accept that already, from the mere existence of federal legislation regarding the general terms and conditions of entry and residence of aliens, such as the Immigration and Naturalization Act, one could derive the conclusion that Congress had intended to preclude even 'harmonious state regulation touching on aliens in general, or the employment of illegal aliens in particular'.[77] Such legislation, it claimed, referred mainly to the conditions of entry and stay of legal residents.[78]

Much more relevant was *Plyler v. Doe*. It was decided in 1982 and has undoubtedly been one of the most controversial decisions in the field.

---

[74] Ibid.: 355.	[75] Ibid.: 355–6.	[76] Ibid.: 356.	[77] Ibid.: 358.

[78] Thus, the Court limited itself to verifying that Congress's constitutionally reserved powers to rule over immigration and its general legislation on immigration (embodied mainly in the *Immigration and Nationality Act (INA)*) did not pre-empt by themselves the state's regulation on a field that was clearly of the state's interest, even if it could have some effect on immigration. In fact, the very failure of Congress to enact general sanctions against the employment of illegal immigrants was judged by the Court as strengthening the thesis that Congress believed that this problem did not yet require uniform national rules, and, hence, could be appropriately addressed by the states as a local matter (ibid.: 360, n. 9). For the rest, the Court remanded the case to the lower courts. These would have to decide whether the state regulation could still be said to stand as 'an obstacle to the accomplishment and execution of the full purposes and objectives of Congress in enacting the *INA*' or of any other federal law (ibid.: 363).

This time the case was solved on equal protection grounds. At stake was a Texas statute withholding from local school districts state funds for the education of children who were not 'legally admitted' into the United States and authorizing these school districts to deny enrolment or charge tuition to such children.[79]

First, and most importantly, the Court stated that the Fourteenth Amendment's Equal Protection Clause referred to every person in an ordinary sense, and therefore also unlawful aliens. Sanctioning the thesis whereby 'subjection' to the law is essential to the triggering of constitutional protection the Court interpreted 'within its jurisdiction' in a geographical and territorial expansion, including all those submitted to the state laws.[80] Even if the unlawful and unconsented initial entry of a person into a state or into the USA could serve as a reason for expulsion from the territory, this could not negate the simple fact of her presence within the state's territory. And from such a presence derived both the subsequent subjection to the full range of obligations imposed by the state's civil and criminal laws, and the equal protection by the laws of the state. Interpreting the Equal Protection Clause the Court found that 'the equal protection clause was intended to work nothing less than the abolition of all caste-based legislation. That objective is fundamentally at odds with the power to classify persons subject to laws as nonetheless excepted from its protection.'[81]

This, however, was only the starting point of the inquiry. Yet the importance of this starting assumption should not be understated. It can provide what is maybe one of the strongest arguments in favour of the independence of the equal protection doctrine from that of pre-emption. Illegal residents who, by definition, cannot be said to be covered by the federal policy of equal treatment of aliens legally accepted into the country can, nevertheless, be protected by the doctrine of equal protection. It is therefore impossible to read such a doctrine as a mere expression of the federal immigration policy (Bosniak 1994: 1115; Aleinikoff 1990: 25). But having said this, the Court still had to decide whether the equal protection provision had been violated on this particular occasion. To do this, the Court first had to agree on the standard of review to apply.

The Court rejected the claim that illegal aliens were a suspect class. Unlike most of the recognized suspect classifications, entry into the class of illegal aliens, the Court argued, was the product of a voluntary action, such as that of entering the territory illegally. Obviously, the Court did not have in mind those who flee their countries in fear of persecution or compelled by a situation of need, for these do not seem to be really

---

[79] *Texas Education Code Ann. ' 21. 031 (Vernon Cum. Supp. 1981)*.
[80] 457 US 202, 211–15 (1982).   [81] Ibid.: 213.

'voluntary' actions (Bosniak 1994: 1122 n. 319). According to Justice
Brennan, it could hardly be suggested that the undocumented status of an
alien is a 'constitutional irrelevance', for such a status is derived from the
federal government's wide constitutional powers to conduct foreign policy and to control access to the nation, a power which could not be
denied.[82]

Some scholars have criticized these arguments as insufficient to justify
the exclusion of undocumented aliens as such from the broader suspect
class of aliens. After all, it is this subgroup of resident aliens which is most
severely deprived of the possibility to defend its interests in the political
process, as they cannot even come out in the public sphere and voice their
interests and needs so that the enfranchised community may take them
into account. The lack of sympathy due to their foreignness, the common
animosity towards some specific groups among them (such as, currently,
towards Latino immigrants) (Johnson 1995: 1517), but also the states'
frustration at the federal government's inability to enforce the immigration statutes of the country render them especially vulnerable to hostile
discrimination and expose them to mistreatment (Neuman 1995:
1449–51). To this one could add that undocumented aliens have historically been the victims of exploitation and discrimination in the past and
largely continue to be so in the present. The children of illegal immigrants
who have not been born in the USA are even more vulnerable since they
cannot rely on virtual representation by their parents. Finally, the status
of undocumented alien, unlike that of aliens qualified for naturalization,
is one which cannot be altered by individual will. To acknowledge this
and to act accordingly, enhancing the protection of this sector of the
population is not to deny the power of the nation to control access to the
country but to limit it, to the extent that such a power can affect the lives
of those who through time and residence have become part of the USA's
social tissue.[83]

However, even though the Court was not willing to accept that illegal
aliens could be treated as a suspect class as such, moved by a basic
concern with fairness similar to that it had shown in alienage cases since
Graham, it held that the existence of an underclass of millions of illegal
migrants raised 'the specter of a permanent caste of undocumented
resident aliens, encouraged by some to remain here as a source of cheap
labor, but nevertheless denied the benefits that our society makes available to citizens and lawful residents', and it presented 'most difficult
problems for a Nation that prides itself on adherence to principles of

---

[82] Ibid.: 219 n. 19.
[83] For an insight into the different doctrinal positions contrast Gerety 1983: 379, 387–94
with Hull 1983: 419.

equality under the law'.[84] In other words, the Court's interpretation was that, on the one hand, when individually taken, the status of illegal immigrant was only the expression of the community's self-determination in the matter of membership through immigration laws. However, the Court also saw that the consolidation of large numbers of illegal immigrants among the ordinary population of the state raised specific legitimation concerns in a democratic society. In addressing these concerns it reproduced all the relevant considerations for a fairness approach when applied to determine the adequacy of undocumented aliens' exclusion. It decided that the collectivity of illegal immigrants and their children contributed and could contribute to the community.[85] It also pondered whether this contribution could be said to have been relevantly accepted given that illegal immigration was actually encouraged by some sectors of society as a source of cheap labour. But at the same time, stressing the relevance of the lack of express consent by the host country, whose rules on membership had been violated, the Court recognized that the denial of certain rights and benefits to undocumented aliens was an appropriate 'consequence' of their wrongdoing.[86] Finally, the Court held that the concern with 'fundamental conceptions of justice'[87] was most decisively strengthened by the fact that, within the underclass of illegal aliens, it was illegal children who were going to be directly affected by the legal measure.[88] These, Justice Brennan argued, could 'neither affect their parents' conduct nor their own status',[89] being thus the helpless victims of a legislation clearly concerned with their parents' misconduct.

The other element that proved decisive for the justification of the Court's use of a reinforced scrutiny level was the kind of individual and public interests at stake, a public interest which the Court approached from more than a merely instrumental point of view. Although public education was not a constitutional right, Brennan argued, neither could it be considered a mere governmental 'benefit', especially if one took into account the negative effect that its deprivation could have on *both* the children (as individuals and as members of an already disadvantaged class) and American society as a whole.[90] Basically, the Court

---

[84] 457 US 202, 218–19 (1982).
[85] Thus, the majority was unwilling to accept that illegal immigration had an overall negative effect on the state's economy (ibid.: 228). Also, when referring to the community's stake in educating its illegal residents, the Court held that, in spite of their status, many of these aliens were likely to remain in the territory and that, in spite of their exclusion from the political arena as non-citizens, they could still play an important role in other areas of import to the community (ibid.: 222, n. 20).   [86] Ibid.: 220.
[87] Ibid   [88] Ibid.: 219–20.   [89] Ibid
[90] It is important to observe here that the Court relied on both instrumental and non-instrumental arguments when deciding on the degree of constitutional protection to accord to illegal immigrants' children. Among the former, the Court stressed the

recognized the damaging potential of permanent exclusion and faced the fact that many of those children were unlikely to be removed from the country.[91]

Having made up its mind for heightened scrutiny, the Court then proceeded to the analysis of the interests alleged by the state and rejected them as insufficient, one after another, before striking down the measure. First of all, the Court rejected the state's interest in helping the pursuit of the national policy of immigration and with it, the related argument that Congress's disapproval of the presence of illegal children already provided the state with the necessary authority to impose special disabilities upon them.[92] Most significantly, the Court rejected the state's alleged concern with the preservation of its limited resources for the education of its lawful residents. The Court only quoted *Graham v. Richardson* to support its thesis. But the implications of equating both cases are most relevant. As the dissenters pointed out, *Graham* was concerned with legal residents. The Court's equating of *Plyler* and *Graham* supports therefore the independence of the equal protection argument from that of pre-emption. Only aliens in *Graham*, but not those in *Plyler*, could be said to be protected by a federal policy of equal treatment. The fairness-oriented

importance of education in maintaining the nation's basic institutions and its cultural and political heritage as well as in serving as an important socializing institution by imparting those shared values through which social order and stability are maintained (457 US at 222, n. 20 (1982)). It also expressed its concern with the public costs that the creation and perpetuation of a subclass of illiterates within its borders would entail and underlined the insignificance of the savings in public education compared with these (ibid.: 229–30). In his concurring opinion, Powell J. listed some of these costs. Among the measure's most likely negative effects he mentioned an increase in the country's rate of criminality and unemployment, as well as in the demand for welfare benefits (ibid.: 241).

As for the non-instrumental protection of the children, the Court considered that the deprivation of education was likely to have a negative and lasting effect in their lives, bringing about clear disadvantages to their social, economic, intellectual and psychological well-being (ibid.: 221). Furthermore, focusing on the class (rather than on its individual members) Brennan argued that 'denial of education to the children of some disadvantaged group forecloses the means by which that group may raise the level of esteem in which it is held by the majority and sets serious obstacles to the advancement on the basis of individual merit, which is one of the goals of the Equal Protection Clause' (ibid.: 222, n. 20).

[91] Justice Brennan relied on statistics which had been presented to the lower courts, indicating that between 50 and 60 per cent of the alien workers of that time had originally been illegal migrants (457 US at 422).

[92] This was rejected on several grounds. First, it was recalled that states, unlike the federal government, have no authority to rule over immigration and naturalization issues. Moreover, depriving that class of education could not be said to mirror a federal policy. There was no evidence that the conservation of educational resources had ever been a congressional concern in restricting immigration (457 US at 226). The mere deportability of these aliens was also considered an insufficient ground. Given the federal discretionary powers to grant relief from deportation, Texas had no certainty that a child subject to deportation would ever be deported.

interpretation of the equal protection mandate, common to both cases, seems thus to lie at the core of the equal protection doctrine as applied to resident aliens, whatever their legal status. Finally, the Court rejected also the state's alleged interest in deterring the economic and demographic problems deriving from illegal immigration, in improving the overall quality of education and in restricting access to education to citizens and legal resident aliens who, being more likely to stay in the USA, would have more chances to put their education to productive social or political use within the state. From all of these, the Court considered the interest in avoiding the economic and demographic problems related to illegal immigration to be a legitimate state interest. However, it was unwilling to accept that illegal immigration had an overall negative effect on the state's economy given the evidence suggesting that illegal aliens underutilized public services, while they contributed their labour to the local economy and tax money to the state fisc. Ultimately, there was no evidence that the denial of free education to the children was going to be an effective measure in stopping immigrants seeking primarily working opportunities, at least when compared with the alternative of prohibiting the employment of illegal aliens.

California's Proposition 187 subject to review

The debate on California's Proposition 187[93] has reopened the discussion about the constitutional status of illegal immigrants residing in the country. The issue has not yet triggered a Supreme Court decision and may never do so if, as seems likely, it is finally solved by settlement. Regardless of this, California's measure has provided a perfect occasion for discussing in a more thorough and encompassing way the general constitutional status of illegal immigrants. Hence the usefulness of reproducing here the terms of the debate. Briefly, this legal measure which was approved by popular referendum declared illegal aliens' ineligibility for public services and benefits including state-funded social services, access to state schools and universities and health care (with the exception of urgent medical assistance). It also provided for an intricate system of verification and notifications to the Immigration and Naturalization Service of apparent status of illegality both to the persons affected and to the federal immigration agencies, which involves California law enforcement agencies as well as social service agencies, schools and medical care providers.

[93] *Proposition 187: Illegal Aliens – Ineligibility for Public Services – Verification and Reporting*, 1994 Cal. Adv. Legis. Serv. B-39, B-3, '5–8.
   To follow some of the legal debate surrounding the adoption of Proposition 187 see, among others, Abriel 1995; Boswell 1995; Johnson 1995; Legomsky 1995a; Motomura 1994; Neuman 1995; Reich 1995.

Proposition 187 has to be set in its proper context. It took place in the midst of a public debate on a whole range of immigration issues which has taken on a harder edge, irrespective of the affected aliens' ties or length of residence in the country (Boswell 1995: 1478).[94] Anti-immigrant organizations have been flourishing lately, and elected officials have been increasingly resorting to harsh rhetoric and restrictive legislation. Significant is the fact that a great number of bills have been introduced in Congress lately to tighten the immigration laws or make English the nation's official language (Legomsky 1995a: 1453). Such a debate seems to confirm the predictions that during times of generally perceived economic uncertainty and hardship, such as the early nineties, immigrants are likely to become an easy target (Boswell 1995: 1476; Johnson 1995: 1541). In particular, illegal immigrants, against whom the recent state efforts to restrict public benefits have been aimed and who are often seen as 'criminal aliens' (Johnson 1995: 1531) or discriminated against because of their national origin or ethno-cultural background, become the easy scapegoat (Neuman 1995: 1451), and the target of measures of doubtful efficacy and economic interest.[95] No wonder that the movement started in California, one of the states that is most directly affected by the federal government's lack of efficacy in the enforcement of immigration laws. To the surface have come again the fairness-related arguments raised by *Plyler*. In this context some have recalled that the United States has historically made conscious decisions to attract undocumented alien labour to meet important economic needs (Legomsky 1995a: 1496) and that undocumented aliens have played an integral role in the nation's economic and social system (Reich 1995: 1588–94). For some, 'examination of history, federal statutes and regulations and enforcement

---

[94] America's immigration debate has been more ardently felt in California than elsewhere because half of the estimated total of illegal immigrants resides here. However, California epitomizes more general problems of contemporary immigration to the USA. Among them is the fact that this immigration is extremely concentrated and that disproportionate costs are incurred by some state governments and municipalities, while the main benefits in terms of federal taxes and social security payments are reaped by the federal government.

[95] Thus, even though California's Proposition 187 represents to a large extent a political reaction to the perception that public benefits and services were widely available to undocumented persons, in fact undocumented aliens have always been excluded from the main federal and state benefits programmes (see Johnson 1995: 1528, 1558; Legomsky 1995a: 1460). Also, the fact that participation in a programme could cause the undocumented person's later disqualification from permanent residence or enhance the risk of deportation has acted as a deterrent (Boswell 1995: 1497–8; Johnson 1995: 1529). Finally, it is questionable that banning undocumented aliens from social benefits and public services will make illegal entry into the country less alluring, at least as long as the employment opportunities (clearly, the main magnet) remain available and the desire to join their families remains a very strong motivation (Boswell 1995: 1469; Johnson 1995: 1558).

practices reveals a complete set of federal policies toward undocumented labor, which over the years might have promoted illegal migration more than what is acknowledged by federal decision makers' (Aleinikoff et al. 1998: 602–3). Others have argued that the denial of benefits to un-documented persons is justified: they broke the law to get into the country. From this one can deduce that they never intended to become a part of the social community (Johnson 1995: 1531–42). Public opinion seems to experience the 'cognitive dissonance' of 'admiring illegal immi-grants' tenacity, hard work and resourcefulness (at least the majority who do not commit crimes in the United States)' while at the same time resenting 'their furtive success in penetrating U.S. territory, working in U.S. jobs, earning (and exporting) dollars, and securing legal status – even the ultimate prize, citizenship – for themselves and their families' (Schuck 1997: 7). Also, the debate on the instrumental and/or non-instrumental protection due to undocumented resident aliens (i.e. pro-tection for their own sake versus protection for the well-being of the general society) has once more become relevant as people become aware that many of those who are targets of the restrictive measures are likely to remain in the country.[96]

The Proposition was injuncted as soon as it came into effect and a federal court decision has invalidated most of its provisions.[97] Several factors seem to increase the chances that this time, if it ever reached the Supreme Court, the Court would decide that this state measure is an intrusion into federal powers on immigration and thus, strike it down on pre-emption grounds, reducing the exploration of the demands based on equal protection claims to a minimum. First of all, the Proposition is much closer to an attempt to give a global answer to the problem of illegal immigration than were the provisions at stake in *De Canas* or in *Plyler*. In fact, Proposition 187 presented itself as a systematic programme for 'driving illegal aliens out of California'. Also, the federal government has since adopted measures to curb the phenomenon of illegal immigration and its negative effects on the draining of public resources, such as the

---

[96] The instrumental rationality stresses the threat that measures like Proposition 187 can pose to the public welfare. See, for example, Legomsky 1995a: 1465 (warning against the creation of a permanent, uneducated underclass and the accompanying potential for long-term catastrophe, as well as against the risks to public health intrinsic to prohibiting publicly funded facilities from immunizing immigrants against even life-threatening contagious diseases); Reich 1995 (arguing that 'most courts adjudicating alien benefit questions have recognized that the undocumented population is so symbiotically connected to the larger society that depriving the former would harm rather than protect the latter'). See also Boswell 1995: 1478, 1506 (denouncing the restrictive proposals from both an instrumental and a non-instrumental perspective which judges them 'wrong because immoral, punitive, and inhumane').

[97] See *League of United Latin American Citizens v. Wilson*, 908 F. Supp. 755 (C.D. Cal. 1995).

1986 Immigration Control and Reform Act and the Illegal Immigration Reform and Immigrant Responsibility Act of 1996, measures that might be interpreted as portraying Congress's intent to occupy the field and to finally give a homogeneous answer to a problem which affects not only California (Abriel 1995: 1619). Finally, these attempts to fight illegal immigration can also help to cast away the fear expressed in *Plyler* that the toleration of the phenomenon constitutes in reality a hypocritical *de facto* immigration policy, or, at least, an attitude of federal complicity in the exploitation of undocumented workers.[98]

As for the provisions denying undocumented aliens access to public benefits and the concern with equal protection, the Proposition is a direct challenge to *Plyler* as far as undocumented children's access to school education is concerned. In fact, many saw in it an attempt to offer a more conservative Court the chance to overrule this precedent. This would not even be necessary if, in the meantime, the federal government passed a bill allowing states to deny free public education to the children of illegal aliens.[99] The chances that this may happen seem, as of today, rather small. The Welfare Reform Act expressly left basic public education under the rulings of *Plyler*. In any event, having relied very strongly on the vital importance of school education and on the children's innocence in *Plyler*, it is not clear that the Court would interpret equal protection as expanding its fairness constraints to cover also responsible adults, or access to those other public benefits the Proposition refers to, not even regarding those who are permanently settled in the country, especially now that the federal government has embraced a restrictive policy in the field. Some voices claim that it should (Abriel 1995: 1623–4; Neuman 1995: 1448–9). So does the claim to full inclusion.

Alienage and the difference that residence makes: competing foundations for inclusion

We have been referring to the constitutional status of aliens as it has been developed to accommodate mostly immigrants. However, we have not specifically mentioned the difference that actual residence and the social

---

[98] As a matter of fact in *League of United Latin American Citizens v. Wilson* most of Proposition 187's provisions were invalidated on pre-emption grounds relying on the doctrine set in *De Canas*.

[99] Before the elections of November 1996 this possibility was actually discussed in Congress and strongly supported by the Republican presidential candidate Robert Dole. On 25 September the House passed the so-called Gallegly Amendment (named after its sponsor, California Republican Elton Gallegly), which would permit states to deny free public education to children of illegal aliens and thus turn into national law California's Proposition 187. The Senate did not consider the amendment and President Clinton threatened in August 1996 to veto any bill that would send children out of school.

integration that generally comes with it make in triggering the constitutional protection of aliens. Testing the normative claims might recommend that we do so now. It might therefore be interesting to stop thinking about the contrast of citizens versus aliens for a while and focus, first, on a contrast between aliens inside the country versus aliens outside the country and second, on the extent to which increasing duration of residence has triggered an increasing constitutional protection in the case of resident aliens.

Concerning the first, the Supreme Court has traditionally referred to aliens within the territorial jurisdiction of the United States when recognizing their entitlement to constitutional protection.[100] As we just saw, this has also included aliens who were unlawfully present. Also, the Court has protected the property rights of aliens not territorially present in the United States with regard to actions taken in the USA.[101] However, there is no consistent doctrine on the governmental action outside the borders of the country. Whereas it is now widely accepted that citizens do enjoy constitutional protection in those circumstances,[102] in 1990 the Supreme Court held that the search and seizure of non-resident aliens' property located outside the USA did not have to comply with the Fourth Amendment's Warrant Clause.[103]

So presence within the territorial jurisdiction of the USA is what apparently includes aliens within the general scope of constitutional protection. This is why the decisions on who is allowed to enter the country are so relevant even though, lying in the core of the country's immigration policy, such decisions have generally been left to the full discretion of Congress under the plenary power doctrine.[104] No constitutionally relevant liberty interest has been recognized as assisting entry applicants, not even when they were seeking entry to join citizens or resident aliens who are family members.[105] So, the first thing to say is that being in the country does have a clear triggering effect as regards the constitutional protection of aliens. Nevertheless, the underlying rationale

[100] *Yick Wo v. Hopkins*, 118 US 356 (1886); *Wong Wing v. United States*, 163 US 228 (1896).
[101] See *Asahi Metal Indus. Co. v. Superior Court*, 480 US 102 (1987); *Russian Volunteer Fleet v. United States*, 282 US 481 (1931). This protection was nevertheless subject to special rules for enemy aliens in time of war.   [102] See *Reid v. Covert*, 354 US 1 (1957).
[103] *United States v. Verdugo-Urquidez*, 494 US 259 (1990) (distinguishing the case from *Reid* on the basis that *Reid* applied to citizens only). On the discontent generated by this doctrine see, e.g., Neuman 1996 (defending the thesis that the protection of the Constitution should assist aliens outside the US in those instances where the US government seeks to subject aliens to its laws, claiming a legitimate authority to do so).
[104] Admission to the country has always been understood as a privilege and not as a right (Neuman 1996: 125). The constitutional charter of rights does not imply by itself a right to access the country in order to exercise those rights (*United States ex. rel. Turner v. Williams* 194 US 279, 292 (1904)).   [105] *INS v. Phinpathya*, 464 US 183 (1984).

behind this notion of 'physical presence' varies according to scholars and cases. Sometimes its significance seems to rest in the fact that it determines aliens' subjection to the laws and to the public authority of the country of residence (this we could call the 'subjection thesis').[106] On other occasions physical presence serves as a proxy for the ties and connections that possibly bind aliens to the country of residence (this we could call the 'significant ties thesis').[107] But one can also find it related to a more subtle and consensualist meaning which refers to having been formally accepted by the community with a more or less complete membership status which would eventually lead to citizenship as the last step (this could be called the 'membership thesis').[108] Finally, in some cases a purely geographical meaning and no further justifying rationale appears to back the inclusion (this would be the 'strictly territorial thesis').[109]

Let us focus now on the relationship between increasing residence and increasing constitutional protection. According to our theoretical claims, resident aliens' interest in remaining in the country is related to the extent to which they feel integrated, with their home, family, friends and businesses. It is in this light that the words of the Supreme Court, stating that deportation may result in the loss of 'all that makes life worth living',[110] should probably be read. Presumably, resident aliens' degree of interest in preserving their residence within the country is larger than that in gaining it initially (Neuman 1996: 162) and depends to some extent on the time they have already been there, since this may be taken as an indicator of the degree of attachment and the amount of investment they may have developed and undertaken in it. There is some rhetoric by the Court pointing in this direction. For instance, the Court has acknowledged that 'once an alien gains admission to our country and begins to

---

[106] Some cases specifically connect aliens' presence within the territory to their subjection to the law (see *Plyler v. Doe*, 457 US 202, 211–12 (1982) (all those who, in a geographical and territorial sense, are ordinarily subject to the state's laws enjoy the Fourteenth Amendment's equal protection of the laws)). See also *United States v. Verdugo-Urquidez*, 494 US 259 at 284 (1990) (Brennan, J. dissenting).

[107] Some judicial decisions have stressed the relevance of a progressive insertion of the alien into the community of residence. See, e.g., *Mathews v. Diaz*, 426 US 67, 78–9 (1976) and *Landon v. Plasencia*, 459 US 21, 29 (1982).

[108] See, e.g., *Johnson v. Eisentrager*, 339 US 763 (1950) ('The alien, to whom the United States has been traditionally *hospitable*, has been *accorded* a generous and ascending scale of rights as he increases his identity with our society' (ibid. 770) (emphasis added).

[109] There is some case law supporting the doctrine that mere presence in the territory entitles one to some degree of constitutional protection. See, e.g., *Mathews v. Diaz*, 426 US 67, 78–9 (1976) (stating that '[e]ven one whose presence in this country is unlawful, involuntary, or transitory is entitled to [Fifth Amendment] protection'); *Kwong Hai Chew v. Colding*, 344 US 590, at 597 n.5 (1953) (the constitutional protection of aliens stems from 'the alien's presence within [the] territorial jurisdiction') quoting *Johnson v. Eisentrager*, 339 US 763, at 771 (1950).

[110] *Ng Fung Ho v. White*, 259 US 276, 284 (1922).

develop the ties that go with permanent residence, his constitutional status changes accordingly'.[111] Some authors have taken this as a sign reflecting the Supreme Court's more general conviction that once aliens reside in the USA and establish substantial ties there, their residential status, as well as their general constitutional status, is substantially improved (Bosniak 1994: 1126 n. 331). So, although the Court has not developed any coherent theory thus far, some scholars have taken it to support a model of immigration as a process of growing attachment and gradual insertion of the alien into the United States (Aleinikoff 1990: 18).

If we want to leave aside the rhetoric and look for more concrete evidence, we would probably check the constitutional protection that assists aliens, as integrated residents, in their claims to continued residence. We know that residence is the essential precondition for the enjoyment of other constitutional rights and duties. Hence, the special significance of its protection. What difference does accomplished residence make for determining the degree of protection of resident aliens' interest in remaining in the country?

We should start by saying that such a difference has been both statutorily and constitutionally portrayed. Under US law, the grounds for deportation have traditionally been narrower than the grounds for exclusion, and it has often been easier for the government to deport more recently arrived immigrants than those who have resided there for any length of time. Even short-term or illegal residence has traditionally made a difference in the degree of constitutional protection against the government's attempt to end it. Unlike initial entrants, who enjoyed only an extremely precarious constitutional status under the exclusion procedures, residents have generally been covered by the larger constitutional guarantees that must accompany deportation procedures. Among them, and under the Fifth Amendment's Due Process Clause,[112] the Supreme Court has indicated that it would disapprove of any deportation order based on secret information as to which the alien was given no hearing.[113] Also, although as a matter of statutory interpretation, it has

---

[111] *Landon v. Plasencia*, 459 US 21, 32 (1982). See also *Mathews v. Diaz*, 426 US 67 (1976) ('[T]he class of aliens is itself a heterogeneous multitude of persons with a wide-ranging variety of ties to this country' (ibid. 78–9); 'Congress may decide that as the alien's ties grow stronger, so does the strength of his claim to an equal share of [the government's] munificence' (ibid. 80)); *Johnson v. Eisentrager*, 339 US 763, 770 (1950) ('The alien ... has been accorded a generous and ascending scale of right as he increases his identity with our society').

[112] US CONST. Amend. V: 'No person shall be . . . deprived of life, liberty, or property, without due process of law.'

[113] *Kwon Hai Chew v. Colding*, 344 US 590, 596–8 (1953). Note that Congress has recently enacted special procedures for the deportation of 'terrorists' which will test this proposition (new 8 USC ' 1530 *et seq.*)

required the government to prove grounds for deportation by 'clear, unequivocal, and convincing evidence'.[114]

This is no panacea if we recall the still reigning tradition that regards Congress, under the plenary power doctrine, as enjoying the largest discretion in selecting deportation grounds, deportation grounds which, we saw, can even have retrospective effects regardless of how long the implicated aliens had lived in the United States or how long ago the offending conduct had occurred. Also, this same tradition refuses to see deportation as a punishment for a crime, and insists that, literally, 'deportation is simply a refusal by the Government to harbor persons whom it does not want',[115] even though, just as with criminal convictions, deportation often implies stigmatization and separation from personal associations (Note 1971: 805–8).

So consolidating residence does not appear to alter the status of aliens as much as it should. As long as resident aliens are substantially vulnerable to the possibility of deportation, there inevitably remains a huge difference between aliens and citizens in terms of constitutional status (Aleinikoff 1990: 27 n. 67). No single answer exists as to why the whole set of substantive constitutional norms does not also apply to the regulation that burdens resident aliens, allowing for the standard balancing of the individual's countervailing interests in each case. In this respect, one can only hope that the current tendency of some lower courts to apply substantive constitutional standards of review such as equal protection and First Amendment standards to deportation cases will prosper (Legomsky 1995a: 930–4).[116] On the other hand, we should not minimize the importance of the protection that does assist resident aliens (whether physically present or re-entering the country) against deportation, especially if we consider that this is the only consolidated exception of a tradition, condensed in the plenary power doctrine, that allows the federal government the most absolute discretion on practically everything having to do with immigration.

Whatever its insufficiencies, the system of gradual consolidation of constitutional equality which is reflected in the Court's rhetoric and case law seems to rest on several foundations. In fact, more or less the same range of options that justify the constitutional protection of aliens as they

---

[114] *Woody v. INS*, 385 US 276, 286 (1976).

[115] See *Bugajewitz v. Adams*, 228 US 585, 591 (1913).

[116] See, for instance, *American-Arab Anti-Discrimination Committee v. Reno*, United States Court of Appeals, Ninth Circuit, 1995, 70 F. 3d 1045 (stating that aliens who reside within the jurisdiction of the USA are entitled to the full panoply of First Amendment rights of expression and association, even in deportation proceedings, and expressly rejecting the objection based on the plenary power doctrine of Congress in immigration matters).

initially come to the country compete now in the case law and in the scholarly debate as possible explanations as to why, with increasing residence, the degree of protection also has to increase.

In favour of the thesis that values the existence of ties and voluntary connections binding the alien to the country (whatever their immigration status) speaks the fact that, as we saw, some aliens who, under the traditional nomenclature, were formally defined as excludable aliens (e.g. resident aliens re-entering the country and thus, physically outside the country), have either enjoyed the same procedural guarantees in their exclusion procedures as they would have in deportation procedures,[117] or else benefited from the fiction that because they had never really left the country they were deportable and not excludable aliens, their exits having been regarded as not meaningfully interruptive of their residence in the USA.[118] This substantive conception of gradual protection is also supported by the fact that, unlike aliens seeking first entry, illegal residents, who are the paradigmatic example of non-formally admitted members, have traditionally enjoyed procedural guarantees in deportation hearings,[119] as well as the protection of other constitutional provisions.[120] Moreover the Court has recently recognized that legal but merely incidental presence in the country does not indicate sufficient substantial and voluntary connection with it to trigger the Fourth Amendment guarantees against the search and seizure by United States agents of property located in a foreign country.[121] For a substantive conception speaks also the fact that the Court has, at least on one occasion, upheld residence requirements for access to social benefits as allowing for an assumption of greater affinity to the country.[122] Finally, also telling is the fact that, on

---

[117] See *Landon v. Plasencia*, 459 US 21, 32 (1982). After the 1996 reform a returning permanent resident is not regarded as 'seeking admission into the United States' and hence, in principle, enjoys the same protection against removal as if she had not left the country (see INA & 101 (a) (13)).

[118] See *Kwong Hai Chew v. Colding*, 344 US 590, 596 (1953); *Rosenberg v. Fleuti*, 374 US 449 (1963).

[119] See *Yatamaya v. Fisher* 189 US 86 (1903) (illegal aliens enjoy the protection of deportation procedures); *Wong Yan Sung v. McGrath*, 229 US 33, 49–50 (1950) (admitting that the relevance of the fact that the entry into the country was initially clandestine for the determination of the adequate procedural guarantees in deportation proceedings can dissipate with time). Although the 1996 immigration statute provides now that aliens who enter without inspection are subject to exclusion proceedings rather than deportation proceedings it is telling for our purposes that such a status does not apply for illegal aliens who were admitted and then overstayed.

[120] See *Mathews v. Díaz*, 426 US 67, 78–9 (1976); *Plyler v. Doe*, 457 US 202, 210–15 (1982).

[121] See *United States v. Verdugo-Urquídez*, 494 US 259 (1990) (referring, by contrast, to the protection of illegal resident aliens in *Plyler* and expressly indicating that aliens with substantial ties through family and work form part of the 'national community' (ibid. 265)).

[122] See *Mathews v. Díaz*, 426 US 67, 83 (1976). The *Welfare Reform Act* of 1996 exempts certain groups of aliens from its restrictive provisions. Among them, aliens who have

some occasions, the Court has expressly rejected the sufficiency of certain formal immigration statuses (e.g. non-immigrant status, deportability status) as a self-sufficient explanation for certain discriminations which were unjustified when looking at the real situations and commonalities between the affected aliens and other kinds of aliens or citizens.[123]

There is also the thesis which valued membership and stressed the importance of having the community define itself on the important issue of membership, judging permanent residence relevant only to the extent that it is accompanied by a formal immigration status reflecting the process of gradual acceptance of newcomers which presumably ends with naturalization.[124] In other words, the consent of the receiving community is the determinant factor. In the light of this thesis one may justify the traditional inclusion, among the group of excludable, rather than deportable aliens, of some classes of aliens who have actually been living on the national territory for a long period of time, but still hold a provisional or undefined immigration status. Also, one should observe that most cases concerning aliens' constitutional status and stressing the commonalities between citizens and resident aliens refer to aliens who have been accepted into the country as immigrants. Thus, only immigrant aliens have thus far been treated as a suspect class under the Fourteenth Amendment's Equal Protection Clause. Finally, as we saw, the Court has been quite strict in its statement that the fact that an alien may be in the country illegally, and hence, without the permission of the community can never be regarded as a 'constitutional irrelevancy'[125] because it would question the state's capacity to sovereignly decide who is allowed into the country.

been working in the country for ten years without receiving federal means-tested benefits. The district court which upheld the statute in *Abreu v. Callahan* interpreted this as a justified exception for people who presumably have stronger ties and substantial connection to the national community.

[123] See *Elkins v. Moreno*, 435 US 647, 665–7 (1978) (recognizing that the 'non-immigrant' classification is by no means homogeneous and stressing the relevance of the plaintiffs at stake having the possibility of adjusting their status in consideration of elements such as family ties, hardship and length of residence so as to avoid deportation once their temporary legal status was no longer valid); *Plyler v. Doe*, 457 US 202, 226 (1982) (simple deportability is an insufficient ground on which to deny undocumented children access to education, among other reasons, because the record showed that many of them would remain in the country indefinitely, and some would become lawful residents or citizens of the United States).

[124] Note, however, that these two conceptions are often interrelated. Thus, for example, the alien's investment to achieve a certain immigration status (e.g. formal status of immigrant, or eligibility for naturalization) or the alien's degree of identification or attachment to the country *as a result* of a certain immigration status cannot be neglected. See, e.g., Hertz 1976: 1044 ('the immigrant who has devoted years to obtaining his immigrant visa and the more years to meeting residency requirements in the United States has interests that need to be balanced against the nation's interest in deciding who shall be granted membership in the American community and who shall not').

[125] *Plyler v. Doe*, 457 US at 219 n. 19.

Finally, the focus can be on aliens' subjection to the law, ordinary residence being important to the extent that such a subjection becomes permanent and, in practical terms, implies the inclusion of resident aliens in the net of reciprocal rights and obligations which generally binds resident citizens.[126] We have seen that the inclusion of resident aliens within the fairness-based scheme of reciprocal rights and duties has indeed played an essential role in deciding the protection that resident aliens could derive from the Equal Protection Clause and has been at the core of two of the most progressive cases on the constitutional protection of aliens: *Graham v. Richardson*, which decided the inclusion of alienage as a suspect classification,[127] and *Plyler v. Doe*, which decided the need to include illegal immigrants ordinarily residing in the country among those who, for certain purposes at least, deserve a heightened protection.[128]

In the scholarly debate the above-mentioned distinctions are reproduced, though not always in a consistent manner. Several authors have embraced, or at least recognized, the system of gradual consolidation of constitutional protection, but not many have taken a clear stand on the grounds on which such a system rests or should not rest. This becomes most evident when we look at the degree of constitutional relevance different scholars have been willing to grant to the community ties developed through residence by the paradigmatic case of non-formally accepted members: illegal resident aliens.[129] For our purposes what matters

---

[126] See 70 F.3d 1045 at 1064 (9th Cir. 1995) quoting Madison ('[a]s [aliens] owe, on one hand, a temporary obedience, they are entitled, in return, to their protection and advantage') to sustain the thesis that aliens within the country participate in a reciprocal relationship of societal obligations and correlative protection.

[127] See *Graham v. Richardson* 403 US at 376.

[128] See *Plyler v. Doe*, 457 US 202, at 213, 218–19.

[129] Martin strongly defends a system of complex and multi-layered constitutional membership in the form of concentric circles, stressing the relevance of aliens' developing a sense of community identity and community ties through continued residence (Martin 1983: 198, 201–2, 214). Yet at the same time, he has supported a view that stresses status, as a reflection of the polity's self-determination, over actual connections of the individual to society. Thus, he admits that the mere fact of common residence, even illegal residence, establishes a certain, though only a minimal, measure of community membership (ibid.: 202). However, he excludes the possibility that his theory of gradual membership be generally used to embrace long-term illegal residents. Connecting the membership and mutuality of obligations approach, he argues that community ties may give rise to stronger claims of constitutional protection only *because* they reflect the polity's understanding of the mutual and reciprocal obligations that are entailed in community relationships, a mutuality that illegal immigrants typically fail to respect when they evade the system the polity has established for deciding about membership as a key element of its process of self-definition (ibid.: 231).

Aleinikoff, who has advocated that, if useful at all, the concept of constitutional membership has to include permanent resident aliens also, has nevertheless been ambiguous as to where exactly his claim was grounded (Aleinikoff 1990: 10). In one place, just like Martin, he argues that 'it is hardly obvious why due process requires that

most is that permanent subjection to the law and societal integration have been recognized by the Court as autonomous grounds for inclusion in that they do not conceptually depend on the notion of consent. Hopefully, with time, they will deploy their inclusive potential even further, even if this is at the expense of undermining the consensualist notions that the Court has also occasionally embraced, when, instead of facilitating, they get in the way of the full inclusion of non-formally accepted permanent resident aliens.

Constitutional constraints on the definition of the national community: inclusion through citizenship

We have explored the current possibilities of the path of disentangling rights from citizenship for the sake of granting full constitutional equality to resident aliens. We have seen that alienage is increasingly becoming less of a self-explanatory ground for the exclusion of individuals from the realm of constitutional equality. On the other hand it is clear that we are still far away from having resident aliens enjoy full constitutional equality as aliens. It is time now to focus on the secondary claim of automatic membership and to analyse the possibilities that the US constitutional order offers in this respect. If aliens do not enjoy constitutional equality as such, what are the constitutional guarantees and constraints conditioning the path from alienage to citizenship? Do they come close to meeting the claim of automatic membership? In addressing this question the focus will first be on the constitutional constraints on naturalization, and then

we acknowledge the "ties" established by an alien who has entered the country without inspection' (Aleinikoff 1989: 867). While acknowledging elsewhere that a strong claim to the equal treatment of lawful residents and undocumented aliens cannot be sustained without questioning congressional authority to adopt immigration regulation (something he is obviously not willing to do), at the same time he admits that 'at some point, however, undocumented aliens may have lived here long enough to have developed substantial ties; indeed, their day-to-day existence may be quite similar to that of lawful resident aliens and citizens... It may be sensible to assimilate the status of such long-term undocumented aliens to that of permanent resident aliens' (Aleinikoff 1990: 27).

An evolutionary path towards an increasingly substantive conception seems to have characterized Rosberg's work. Initially, he defended the transcending of differences in the legal treatment of resident aliens and citizens, the first, however, meaning only aliens with the formal status of immigrant (Rosberg 1977a). In some of his later work, Rosberg has nevertheless reinterpreted the notion of 'resident alien' along more substantive lines to include not only non-immigrant legal residents but also illegal residents, as possible 'domiciliaries' of the state (Rosberg 1983: 401). This has not led him to deny the fact that aliens' unlawful conduct can be taken as a basis for classification for some purposes. Rather, he has argued that what this implies is only the irrelevance of those individuals' *alienage status* as a justificatory cause for their distinctive constitutional treatment (ibid: 407).

on birthright citizenship as a constitutional mechanism to ensure the automatic incorporation of the descendants of resident aliens born on the national territory, because the automatic granting of nationality to resident aliens who were born outside the country has not been contemplated by the laws of the constitution and is generally disregarded by the legal scholars too.

Naturalization: state sovereignty versus individual rights

No 'right' to be naturalized that assists resident aliens has ever been recognized as a matter of constitutional law.[130] The Constitution vests Congress with the power 'to establish an Uniform Rule of Naturalization'.[131] This competence has traditionally been considered to belong exclusively to the federal legislative powers[132] and to be virtually unrestricted. The congressional ability to define the classes of eligible aliens and the conditions for naturalization has never been significantly limited by the Supreme Court.[133] And although one can find some rhetoric to the contrary,[134] the Supreme Court has traditionally referred to naturalization mostly as a gift[135] or a 'privilege' to be granted at discretion and on such conditions as Congress sees fit to set.[136]

Nevertheless, in spite of this terminology, the fact is that naturalization in the USA has traditionally been a matter of statutory entitlement, rather than of administrative discretion, at least for all those who have complied with the required conditions. Furthermore, as a classical immigration country the USA has often perceived naturalization as the intended end of the immigration process, aliens being therefore not only allowed but actually expected to naturalize (Aleinikoff 1990: 17).[137] As a matter of fact, the recent curtailment of social benefits to resident aliens is often justified as a way of re-evaluating American citizenship by encouraging resident

---

[130] See *Petition of Ferro*, 141 F. Supp. 404, 408 (M.D. Pa. 1956); *United States v. Ginsberg*, 234 US 462, 475 (1917). *United States v. Macintosh*, 283 US 605, 615 (1931).

[131] Art.I, § 8, cl. 4.

[132] See *United States v. Wong Kim Ark*, 169 US 649, 701 (1898).

[133] See *United States v. Macintosh*, 283 US 605, 615 (1931); *Schneiderman v. United States*, 320 US 118, 131–2 (1943).

[134] See *Girouard v. United States*, 328 US 61 (1946) (stating that the power of Congress to set the standards for naturalization is very large but not absolute, and refusing to construe as mandatory a requirement made by Congress that a petitioner for naturalization swear to support the Constitution by taking up arms in defence of the country because otherwise the statute could have been declared unconstitutional).

[135] See *Maney v. United States*, 278 US 17, 22 (1928).

[136] See *Schneiderman v. United States*, 320 US 118, 131–2 (1943).

[137] See *Hampton v. Mow Sun Wong*, 426 US 88, 104 (1976); *Harisiades v. Shaughnessy*, 342 US 580, 585 (1952).

aliens to naturalize (Schuck 1997: 12).[138] The expectation that aliens would naturalize has been related to the country's interest in preserving some degree of national affinity,[139] or to ensuring a general attitude of allegiance to the USA on the part of resident aliens.[140] This has had its constitutional relevance. The fact that resident aliens could rely on the possibility of naturalizing (even if this was not depicted as a constitutional right) has been more or less explicitly recognized as a relevant fact in judging the severity of the exclusion of aliens from the full enjoyment of rights and benefits from a constitutional point of view. As a status from which the individual can withdraw herself, alienage has been judged as less likely to cover legislative discriminatory intent (Rosberg 1977a: 302). Also, the democratic and constitutional relevance of the permanent exclusion of resident aliens from the right to vote has been judged from the awareness that alienage is a status the individual can change more or less at will after no more than five years (Neuman 1992: 310 n. 324). It would be interesting to see to what extent these assumptions have 'constitutionalized' resident aliens' right to naturalization in spite of the rhetoric of the Court to the contrary. How the rest of the system would have to be adjusted if the laws on naturalization were substantially restricted remains therefore an open question. Presumably, making access to citizenship more difficult would force more serious consideration of the possibility of completely disentangling constitutional equality from citizenship.

Still, the Court's vague, unprincipled and old formulation of Congress's limitless power on naturalization has been rightly criticized. The same arguments brought up to discuss the plenary power doctrine in immigration matters have been used to criticize the equally broadly defined judicial deference in naturalization cases (Note 1971: 770; Note 1965: 1097). Underlying the criticism of Congress's unfettered power with regard to naturalization is a concern with maintaining a governmental system of generally constrained powers. In such a system, the general argument goes, specific attention has to be granted to the individual interests which can be at stake in the naturalization process, such as, typically, suffrage and residential stability. Also, just as with residence, naturalization needs to be instrumentally protected if resident aliens, many of whom can be assumed to be willing to naturalize, are to enjoy effectively the whole set of constitutional rights and freedoms granted to

---

[138] Note that this was one of the governmental interests advanced to justify the constitutionality of the Welfare Reform Act of 1996 in *Abreu v. Callahan.*

[139] *Nyquist v. Mauclet,* 432 US 1, 10.

[140] See *United States v. Rossler* (144 F.2d. 463, 465 2d Cir. 1944) ('Naturalization expresses the alien's voluntary initiation into the new society of his choice; his change of allegiance may be dictated by any purpose, however personal and selfish, so be it is not inconsistent with a willingness to throw in his lot with that society and make its fate his own').

them. Congress should not penalize or discourage resident aliens' legitimate exercise of rights by evaluating the manner in which they exercise their rights to determine their 'worthiness' for naturalization (Note 1971: 786 n.76, 789).[141] In other words, in a constitutional scheme where neither the powers nor the rights are absolute, the courts need to engage in a balancing process to ensure that the government's or the individual's interests do not automatically prevail (Note 1971: 773).

Moreover, if the importance of the individual interests at stake depends on the consolidation of societal membership, as I claimed it ought to, then the state should at least show a compelling interest in denying naturalization to socially integrated aliens and the narrow tailoring between the means of either denying naturalization or making it conditional and the public interests it intends to fulfil. The problem of qualifying naturalization indistinctly as a privilege instead of a right is that this helps to exonerate the conditions and requirements set in the laws on naturalization from judicial scrutiny even when they apply to socially integrated aliens. Granted, although not expressly sanctioned in the wording of the Constitution, some discrimination criteria in naturalization practices are said to be currently outlawed in a global vision of the constitutional practice. Among them are race or national origin (Karst 1989: 196–7). The Supreme Court and some lower courts have subjected access to citizenship by descent to serious review when these could infringe upon the Bill of Rights.[142] And at least as a matter of statutory obligation, the

---

[141] It is for these reasons that ideological qualifications for naturalization, which penalize political speech and action protected by the First Amendment, have been judged as a troubling speech-based restriction on the exercise of the constitutional freedoms of speech, association and thought (Neuman 1994: 256; Note 1971: 787–8, 791). Such qualifications have varied over time, excluding different groups at different times, ranging from the exclusion of those who did not want to renounce nobility titles, to anarchists, polygamists, persons who believed in the overthrow of the US government or were affiliated with organizations advocating these proscribed ideas, and persons who supported the Communist Party and the 'economic, international and governmental doctrines of world communism'.
      Although in 1990 an Immigration Act reform cut back sharply on ideological grounds for exclusion and deportation it maintained many of them as naturalization qualifications. Among other things current law bars from naturalization those who advocate or affiliate with an organization that advocates opposition to all organized government (8 USC ' 1424 (a) (1) (1988)); those who affiliate with the Communist Party of the United States or of any foreign state, or other totalitarian parties (8 USC ' 1424 (a) (2) (Supp. V 1993)); those who advocate the 'economic, international, and governmental doctrines of world communism' (8 USC ' 1424 (a) (3) (1988)); those who advocate the overthrow by force of the US government, the propriety of killing or unlawfully assaulting government officers, unlawful injury to property, or sabotage (ibid. 1424 (a) (4)); and those who knowingly write or circulate publications advocating any of these ideas, or who affiliate with an organization that does so (ibid. 1424 (a) (5)–(6)).

[142] See *Miller v. Albright*, 118 S. Ct. 1428, 140 L. Ed. 2d 575 (1998). See also *Wanchope v. US Dep't of State*, 985 F 2d. 1407 (9th Cir. 1993). But see *Price v. INS*, United States Court

right to become a citizen cannot currently be denied on the basis of sex or marital status either.[143] However, only pondering the seriousness of the individual interests at stake in the different situations might lead to a rejection of naturalization requirements, not as inherently contrary to the spirit of the Constitution (e.g. race-based requirements) but rather as applied to certain categories of aliens, such as those who have a stronger claim to inclusion because they have lived in the country for many more years than those generally required for ordinary naturalization. For them, anything but a fully unconditional and optional naturalization (if not the automatic granting of citizenship) might be what is constitutionally required. It is time for the inclusiveness of the US naturalization practice to cease to be described as a graceful sign of the generosity of the sovereign and for the individual interests at stake to be adequately pondered and fully recognized as right claims.

The birthright citizenship debate: setting additional obstacles to automatic incorporation?

Inclusion through birthright citizenship has always enjoyed a more solid constitutional ground in the USA. The Fourteenth Amendment's Citizenship Clause provides that '[a]ll persons born or naturalized in the United States, and subject to the jurisdiction thereof, are citizens of the United States and of the State wherein they reside'. Together with a generous naturalization practice, this *ius soli* citizenship has played a basic role in ensuring inclusive definitions of the political community, narrowing the concern about civic incorporation to the first generation of aliens. The principle was originally taken as part of the common law inheritance and has remained central to the American tradition, even if in practice it has nevertheless always been supplemented by statutory *ius sanguinis* elements to permit US citizenship to descend to children born abroad to citizen parents.

of Appeals, Ninth Circuit, 1992, 962 Fd 836, cert. denied 510 US 1040, 114 S. Ct. 683, 126 L. Ed. 2d 650 (1994) (stating that, as far as First Amendment rights are concerned, resident aliens willing to naturalize have the same minimal protection as aliens willing to enter the country). Note however, that these cases are somewhat different from naturalization cases even if they all imply the judicial review of rules set by Congress to determine access to American citizenship. In the cases dealing with *ius sanguinis* there is always a US citizen (the one purporting to pass her US citizenship onto her child) or at least a potential US citizen (the one claiming a right to inherit US citizenship from her parent(s)).
    This may also explain why the Supreme Court insisted so firmly on applying normal First Amendment standards when outruling in *Schneiderman v. United States*, 320 US 118 (1943) the denaturalization of the plaintiff because of his affiliation to the Communist Party of the United States twelve years after his naturalization.
[143] See § 311, 66 Stat. 239, 8 USC § 1422.

In the beginning, the incorporation of a constitutional definition of citizenship sought the extension of the principle that had governed American citizenship for persons of European descent to the black population, and to the newly freed slaves. A previous Supreme Court decision, *Dred Scott v. Sanford*, had denied citizenship to blacks on the grounds that whites did not consider them appropriate partners in the political community.[144] The Fourteenth Amendment's Citizenship Clause intended to overrule this outrageous doctrine by reaffirming the old principle of citizenship on a racially neutral basis (Neuman 1992: 496; Karst 1977: 14).

Although the primary purpose of the Fourteenth Amendment was thus to address the exclusion of blacks from the political community, in the 1890s, amid the heyday of an American nationalism identified with racial Anglo-Saxonism, in the decision *United States v. Wong Kim Ark*,[145] the Supreme Court affirmed that the Fourteenth Amendment also guaranteed the citizenship of children born to Chinese parents in the United States, notwithstanding Congress's anti-Chinese immigration and naturalization policies of the time.[146] By doing so, the Court was actually sanctioning a constitutional mechanism for automatic incorporation, placing it outside of the realm of the community's legislative self-determination and thus beyond the laws which express the country's self-perception as a country of intentional immigration.[147]

In a time of large-scale and long-term illegal immigration, the Fourteenth Amendment Citizenship Clause is playing a fundamental role in ensuring the incorporation of yet another vulnerable group of people who have not been welcomed by the laws as full members of the American society. These are the native-born children of illegal entrants. Concerned with what they saw as an encouraging effect of the Fourteenth Amendment's Citizenship Clause, as well as with the damages to the welfare state allegedly posed by the never-ending flow of illegal immigrants to the country, two scholars Peter Schuck and Rogers Smith published in 1985 their book *Citizenship Without Consent* (Schuck and Smith 1985). They were opening what has since been a highly disputed debate on the

---

[144] See *Scott v. Sanford*, 60 US 393, 407–9 (1857). Writing for the Court, Justice Taney held that blacks could not be citizens because they had not been included among 'the People of the United States' mentioned in the Preamble to the Constitution (ibid. 404–5). They had been excluded from membership in the national community, the Court stated, because they had been 'considered as a subordinated and inferior class of beings, who had been subjugated by the dominant race, and, whether emancipated or not, yet remained subject to their authority . . .' (ibid. 404–5). 'They [were] so far inferior, that they had no rights which the white man was bound to respect . . .' (ibid. 407).

[145] 169 US 649 (1898).

[146] See, for example, Chinese Exclusion Act (Act of May 5, 1892, ch. 60, 27 Stat. 25).

[147] *Wong Kim Ark*, 169 US 649, 703 (1898).

relevant interpretation of the constitutional Citizenship Clause in connection with the current phenomenon of illegal immigration. Eventually,
the debate reached the political arena. California governor Pete Wilson
called for a constitutional amendment to exclude children of illegal aliens
from the Citizenship Clause and California representatives introduced
amendments in Congress. Not surprisingly, ending birthright citizenship
for the children of illegal aliens became a plank in a sector of the Republican platform in the electoral campaign of the 1996 presidential elections.

Reproducing the main lines of the discussion is important in that it
shows how consensualist notions can compete with subjection and deep
affectedness as grounds for defining the boundaries of constitutional
equality through citizenship, as well as the serious exclusionary potential
of those notions. In summary, Schuck and Smith argued in their book
that in the light of the political theory and constitutional history of the
American polity, ascriptive citizenship on the basis of the accident of birth
was inconsistent with a polity whose chief organizing principle is the
liberal, individualistic idea of consent. According to them, the legislative
history of the Citizenship Clause of the Fourteenth Amendment demon-
strated precisely the incorporation of a consensual element in the inherited ascriptive rule of citizenship by birthplace. The consensual element
was incorporated through the clause 'subject to the jurisdiction' which, to
them, meant both a more or less complete and direct power by the
government over the individual, as well as a reciprocal relationship between government and the individual at the time of birth, the government
consenting to the individual's presence and status and offering him or her
complete protection (Schuck and Smith 1985: 86). So, they claimed, the
Constitution mandated citizenship only for children born within United
States territory to parents who are either citizens or permanent resident
aliens, the latter because admitting their parents as lifelong members
entails the nation's tacit consent to citizenship for their future offspring
(ibid.: 117–18). Accordingly, they claimed, Congress enjoyed the ultimate
authority to decide which native-born persons, other than those born to
citizens or to permanent resident aliens, should be eligible for citizenship.[148] Mandating citizenship for undocumented children, they argued,

---

[148] The authors observed that in the course of the Senate debates, the framers of the
amendment sought to exclude implicitly from its scope a few groups who were
identifiable as *not subject to the jurisdiction* of the United States. Such was the case of
Indians living under tribal authority who, as members of dependent nations (Indian
tribes), did not come within the Fourteenth Amendment's citizenship provision even
though they were born within the US territory. Their exclusion from American
citizenship was made express in the Civil Rights Act and was later confirmed by the
Supreme Court in *Elk v. Wilkins* (112 US 94 (1884)). This exclusion was made obsolete
by a statute in the 1920s which declared Indians born within the United States to be
American citizens.

impaired the nation's right of political self-definition (ibid.: 99).

Schuck and Smith's policy considerations were unsurprising. On their proposed interpretation of the constitutional Citizenship Clause, they defended a congressional policy of denial of automatic citizenship to children born in the USA to illegal aliens as a way to better preserve the society's right to consent. This, the authors claimed, would prevent the Citizenship Clause from being one of the main attractions to illegal immigration, together with the enjoyment of public services and social benefits (ibid.: 103–15). Additionally, recommended policy measures included more effective enforcement of existing immigration laws; a system of realistic, credible employer sanctions to remove the chief incentive to most illegal immigration; and more generous legal admission policies (ibid.: 5).

Schuck and Smith's public policy recommendations, as well as their arguments concerning political theory and constitutional interpretation, have since been severely criticized and the authors themselves seem to have changed their view on the matter.[149] Thus, it has been argued, there is no evidence that denying birthright citizenship can be of significant value in curtailing the flow of illegal immigrants or in relieving state and local governments of financial burdens (Note 1994: 1041–2; Martin 1985: 278). If the other recommended measures were taken with the expected result that far fewer children were born to illegal aliens, restricting birthright citizenship might not even be necessary (ibid.: 282). More importantly, if the birthright citizenship amendment was adopted but the other measures to fight illegal immigration were not implemented or failed to have an appreciable impact, then the USA might end up with a caste of undocumented resident aliens who, as they grow up, 'exhibit hostility and defiance' towards a society that 'denies them equal treatment at birth' (Note 1994: 1041–2) and excludes them from the common status of citizenship. Interestingly, the possible costs of exclusion (in terms of the possible damage to the integrative capacity of the USA) were often exemplified by pointing at the phenomenon of second- and third-generation immigrants which resulted from Europe's labour recruitment policies (Martin 1985: 283–4). At the present time, Congress seems to have abandoned whatever intentions it might have had to go along that path in its fight against illegal immigration.

Just as strongly criticized were Schuck and Smith's theoretical and constitutional arguments. Their attempt to read 'consensual' discretion

---

[149] See *Hearings Before the Subcomm. On Immigration and Claims and on the Constitution of the House Judiciary Comm.*, 103d Cong. (1995) (statement and letter of Peter Schuck); Peter H. Schuck and Rogers M. Smith, Letter to the Editor, *New York Times*, 11 August 1996, at A14.

into the constitutional language has not succeeded. '[S]ubject to its jurisdiction' should preserve a natural reading as referring to the actual subjection to the law-making power of the state (Neuman 1987: 493). Granted, at the time Indians were excluded but this was precisely because they were living under tribal quasi-sovereignty (ibid.: 286). The Fourteenth Amendment does not set out a theory of citizenship but rather sets out a rule for determining who is a citizen (Neuman 1996: 169). The original Constitution had failed to determine any precise rule on who was to be a citizen, thereby leaving the door open for the outrageous *Dred Scott* decision. By adopting the Fourteenth Amendment Citizenship Clause, the Reconstruction Congress had sought to remedy this. But the Fourteenth Amendment did not only seek to stabilize the resolution of the African slavery question. The amendment's architects deliberately chose language that went well beyond prohibiting racial discrimination (Karst 1977: 14, 17). Its greater ambition was confirmed by *United States v. Wong Kim Ark*. In that case the central argument of the dissenting opinion had been precisely that the government had explicitly refused to allow people of Chinese descent to become naturalized citizens and had admitted them with that restriction clearly in view. It could not reasonably be supposed to have agreed to granting citizenship to children who happened to be born in the United States while denying it permanently to their parents.[150] And yet the majority opinion rejected this reasoning and interpreted that the Fourteenth Amendment had placed the citizenship of native-born children beyond the power of Congress.[151]

Bringing up a concern which seems related to deep affectedness Martin argued that the consensual account of political membership on which Schuck and Smith's argument was built reflected 'an incomplete view of the wellsprings of both community and legitimacy' (Martin 1985: 291) and did not sufficiently ponder the exclusionary and repressive potential of consensualism when this consensualism is dogmatically supported, as was the case in *Elk v. Wilkins* or *Dred Scott v. Sanford*, the decisions sanctioning the two disheartening historical episodes of the exclusion of Indians and blacks from USA citizenship. Ascriptive but not irrevocable citizenship rules serve to anchor choice in a realistic and protective framework (ibid.: 292–3). Realistic in that it recognizes 'that time and familiarity weave their way into the complex relationship we call citizen-

---

[150] *United States v. Wong Kim Ark*, 169 US 649, at 729–32.
[151] Moreover, Neuman has argued, a category of illegal immigrants already existed at that time. These were the African slaves who continued to be imported even after such importation had expressly been banned by Congress. Most significantly, although this category of 'illegal aliens' was not mentioned in the debates, the framers made it clear that guaranteeing citizenship to *all* native-born blacks was their central purpose in the Fourteenth Amendment Citizenship Clause (Neuman 1987: 498).

ship' (ibid.: 292) and that most of us are simply born into some of our most basic affiliations (nation, family and religion), which are therefore anterior to choice, even though a person may decide to change some of those affiliations and it is precisely consent that allows one to do so. Protective in that, just as the notion of human rights, ascription serves to place certain claims beyond the reach of another individual's will (ibid.: 293). Consensualism's exclusionary and repressive potential is most pronounced when society excludes those who realistically have no home elsewhere and therefore deserve the status of member in the only national society to which they are actually connected (ibid.: 295).

Schuck and Smith's thesis is thus a perfect example of the problem that underlies the consensual approach to inclusion, namely, that it tends to assume who the negotiating parties are. The Fourteenth Amendment's birthright citizenship is a mechanism which incorporates the demands of a liberal democratic order into the Constitution. It is especially significant because the Constitution does not provide for the full inclusion in the realm of constitutional equality of resident aliens as aliens nor for their unconditional and optional right to citizenship. Throughout its history, it has enabled the incorporation into the realm of civic equality of those who were most likely to develop significant connections to the community and to be permanently and pervasively subject to its legal order even when these were not judged as 'suitable' partners by the politically empowered majority. It has thus avoided the process of second- and third-generation immigrants and the democratic legitimation concerns which such a process entails. As a constitutional commitment, it frames the reach of action within which the national community can legitimately exercise its right to self-definition. And it does so precisely by forcing the community to a certain degree of inclusiveness, or, in other words, by redefining what should be comprehended by the term 'national' when we talk about 'national community'. Those who, as a result of this, are included need no further consent, since, if anything, they belong to the 'consenters' and not to the 'consented'.

Summary

We have seen that in the USA it is residence, rather than national citizenship, which allows the enjoyment of a comprehensive constitutional status, with the significant exception of the core political rights such as suffrage. Non-resident aliens enjoy only context-specific protection (e.g. protection of their property in the country). Practically no protection at all covers their initial claims of entry from a constitutional point of view. Also, we have seen that with increasing residence there comes a strengthening of aliens' constitutional status and that both the fact that they develop ties with the country and that they are permanently subject to its laws have been decisive for such a purpose. At the same time, however, neither residence, nor even long-term residence, has been sufficient to place citizens and aliens on an equal constitutional footing as I claimed it ultimately should.

In the USA, the federal structure of government has authorized the schism between political and societal membership in the law. The concern with the political dimension of the national community has prevailed at a federal level, allowing resident aliens to be viewed mainly as members of other states. Following traditional notions of state sovereignty, it has been regarded as a matter of political discretion whether or not, and on what conditions, aliens were accepted into the country, allowed to naturalize and to remain there, even after they had set roots in the country. All of these decisions have been regarded as elements pertaining to the country's widely conceived immigration policy and hence, as falling under the exclusive province of the federal government. In this respect, increased residence has not sufficiently triggered a correspondingly strengthened constitutional status. Most regrettably, the Supreme Court has not yet overruled its doctrine granting the federal powers broad discretion on the deportation of even well-settled immigrants. In contrast, at state level, the societal dimension has been much more important. Here the Supreme Court has stressed the position of resident aliens as people who participate, contribute and are generally subject to the law and thus deserve in fairness to be treated with a concern equal to that of resident citizens. Most courageously, the Court has even been willing to extend some of this equal treatment doctrine to illegal immigrants, recognizing them, at least to some extent, as *de facto* societal members. The Court has been willing to make up for resident aliens' exclusion from political rights by subjecting the legislation affecting resident aliens to strict scrutiny. However, bringing again to the surface the split between socioeconomic and political membership, an exception has been formed allowing for lenient judicial review in the strictly political sphere, where only citizens are allowed to exercise those functions which are strictly related to representative government.

To judge properly the relevance of these constitutional elements it is important to relate them to the country's immigration policy. As we know, the USA has perceived itself as an immigration country and has traditionally admitted aliens, granting them from the beginning a status which enabled them to settle in the USA, and setting them generally on the route to a quite accessible and 'as-of-right' naturalization. This has clearly underscored the practical effects of the constitutional doctrine that allowed for such a broadly defined political discretion on the matter. It may also explain why settled immigrants' lack of full residential security or political rights and, more recently, their exclusion from the social safety net, has not been so worrisome in practical terms, doctrinally objectionable as it may be. The underlying belief is that resident aliens can always naturalize to overcome these obstacles to equality.

Relevant in this regard have probably also been other elements of the US constitutional culture on the subject. On the one hand, there is the Birthright Citizenship Clause. As we have seen, generation after generation, this constitutional provision has enabled the automatic granting of citizenship to the children of immigrants born in the territory. It has therefore been crucial in preventing the democratic legitimation gap from becoming an intergenerational problem. On the other hand, although naturalization has been constitutionally described as a discretionary act of the state, one common justification for the exclusion of aliens from the enjoyment of equal rights and freedoms as aliens (which reflects the country's generally extensive naturalization practice) has been that alienage in the USA is far from being an involuntary or immutable status. There is nothing better than these two elements to reflect the relationship between the two paths for the incorporation of resident aliens into the sphere of civic equality: full inclusion and automatic membership.

The future remains uncertain. There are promising signs that the doctrine of plenary powers of the federal government in its treatment of aliens will finally decay together with the outdated notions of state sovereignty on which it rests. The fact that it is starting to do so with relation to deportation is clearly a sign of the recognition of the constitutional relevance of the societal integration of a significant sector of the country's ordinary population, the non-citizen sector. Unfortunately, the decay of this doctrine will probably come about much more gradually than many had anticipated. Probably, its spirit is still quite alive when the federal government feels as free as it does to pass measures such as the recent restriction on permanent residents' access to social benefits, measures that are clearly much more related to domestic concerns than to the country's immigration policy. Also, to the extent that full equality is reserved for citizens only one would expect the naturalization of resident aliens to stop being portrayed as a privilege and, in accordance with how it actually functions, to be depicted more as a right assisting resident aliens. The larger hope is that the whole set of constitutional guarantees and fairness-based considerations which have proved so relevant at the state level under the equal protection doctrine will gradually gain recognition in relation to the federal powers as well, especially when their action affects settled immigrants. This might be of extreme importance now that the federal government has started to seriously restrict not only illegal but also legal immigrants' access to social benefits and federally funded programmes.

Equally important for resident aliens' effective constitutional protection is that the heightened protection that the Supreme Court has granted both legal and illegal resident aliens at state level, recognizing them as participants in the social scheme in which benefits and burdens are shared, does not become undermined either by exceptions in the name of more or less clearly defined interests of the state as a political entity, or by the thesis that everything having to do with aliens in some way or other has to be considered part of the country's immigration policy and hence, either reserved for the federal government's discretion or conditioned to the degree of generosity of the federal policy of the moment. We can only hope that the Court will not cease to act as a guardian of resident aliens' interests until the root cause of this special protection is addressed and resident aliens are granted an equal status of rights, including political rights, as the claim to full inclusion says they should.

The coming years will probably also see the end of the dispute raised by the Birthright Citizenship Clause amendment initiative. The solution of this debate will determine whether the clause is confirmed as a constitutional mechanism of vital importance in keeping the liberal democratic commitment relevant by forcing the polity to a certain degree of inclusiveness (something which the clause has accomplished in the past with regard to other vulnerable and victimized sectors of the population), or as one more instrument fully at the disposal of the country's most diverse interests. Only if the first interpretation wins out, as it has done thus far, can one reasonably expect that the practice of granting citizenship automatically at birth will not be given up now that it is facilitating the incorporation through citizenship of undesired and unconsented members who are nevertheless permanently subject to the laws as well as deeply affected by them.

8   The constitutional debate in Germany

The German case presents both relevant differences and similarities with that of the USA. They both share the challenge that a permanent non-national population residing in the country currently poses to constitutional liberal democracies. However, as we saw, Germany's immigration tradition is much more recent. Therefore, the time-frame of the country's constitutional response that I will analyse will be more limited. This will be particularly Germany's postwar era immigration experience, an experience Germany has denied and continues to deny is integral to its national identity. We are talking about how the German Basic Law, which also dates from the postwar period, and the scholars and judges who have interpreted it have been responding to such an experience and to the changes in Germany's social composition that have accompanied it.

Aliens and the residential community: the inclusive potential of the Constitution's liberal democracy

Aliens and the German Basic Law

Unlike the US Constitution, the 1949 German Basic Law (henceforth GBL) contains a systematic demarcation between the rights reserved to Germans and the rights which apply to everyone. The universal scope of the rights is naturally seen as the rule and the restrictions on some of them as the exception (Isensee 1974: 74).[1] In this, the GBL is a reaction against the positivist tendencies of a recent past which had led to the horrendous atrocities of the Nazi regime.[2] Recognizing human dignity as the supreme

---

[1] It is hard to determine how truly aware the German constituent was of the choice it was making and of its implications. In the Constituent Assembly of 1948 there had been little controversy on the issue of aliens as holders of fundamental rights, and the little there was centred more on justifying the restriction of some rights to Germans than the extension of all the others to everyone (see *Jahrbuch des öffentlichen Rechts der Gegenwart*, Band I, 1951: art. 3, 71 ff).

[2] The constitutional project of the 1849 *Paulskirche* Assembly had established the initial

constitutional value in its opening provision,[3] the GBL presented the list of fundamental rights as direct expressions of this recognition.

Thus, on the one hand, there are the so-called 'human rights' (*Menschenrechte*) or, to use a phrase more common in German legal discourse, 'everyone's rights' (*Jedermanrechte*), which are the general rule, and which do not discriminate on the basis of the holder's nationality. On the other hand, as exceptions to the rule, we find what are commonly termed 'Germans' rights', which I will call 'citizen rights', which have been expressly reserved for Germans only. Among them, the freedom of assembly,[4] the freedom of association,[5] the freedom of travel and movement,[6] the freedom to choose a profession,[7] the right not to be deprived of German citizenship,[8] the right not to be extradited,[9] the right to resist the overthrow of the government,[10] the guarantees of equal access to the public service[11] and of equal status of rights in all the *Länder*.[12] To these rights, most scholars add the right to vote at federal, regional and local level,[13] as a natural consequence of the principle of democracy according to which state authority emanates from the German people.[14]

This classification contained in the GBL 'has freed the judiciary from the task of continuously adjusting its doctrine to contemporary conditions' (Neuman 1990: 79–80). However, as we know, the country's immigration experience came after the GBL was approved. This explains why so many doctrinal debates among constitutional scholars in Germany have been on how to interpret the constitutional provisions properly so as to adjust them to the new realities. To understand this, it is important to observe, from the start, that the issue of whether and to what extent resident aliens may hold individual claims based on the list of constitutional rights has not completely covered the question of their constitutional status in Germany. In Germany, apart from the list of basic rights, individuals can also derive some indirect constitutional protection from certain constitutional principles which sanction the basic conditions for the legitimate exercise of power, and even from the list of constitu-

---

pattern. Rejecting the Enlightenment ideal of natural and inalienable rights, it had favoured a positivist conception of the constitutional provisions. In its view of rights as positive provisions in the relationship between a historically situated people and its government, the Constitution included a list of rights recognized for the German people only. This view was later inherited by the Weimar Constitution of 1919. 'The Fundamental Rights and Fundamental Duties of Germans' were mostly expressly limited to German citizens. However, already at that time, there was a vivid scholarly debate as to whether the Constitution's fundamental rights were to be seen as expressions of personality rather than of nationality and, accordingly, interpreted as embracing aliens as well.

[3] Art. 1.1 GBL. [4] Art. 8 GBL. [5] Art. 9 GBL. [6] Art. 11 GBL.
[7] Art. 12.1 GBL. [8] Art. 16.1 GBL. [9] Art. 16.2 GBL. [10] Art. 20.4 GBL.
[11] Art. 33.2 GBL. [12] Art. 33.1 GBL.
[13] These rights have only been indirectly contemplated in arts. 38.1.1 and 28.1 GBL.
[14] Art. 20.2 GBL.

tional rights, when, more than as rights, strictly speaking, these are seen as embodying a coherent system of objective constitutional values which limit the public authorities whenever they act. As Neuman has put it, the legal effects of constitutional rights in Germany have gone further than in the USA. In Germany, 'the design of public and private institutions is judged against the constitutional goal of effectuating and protecting basic rights' (ibid.: 40). As we will see, this so-called objective function of the basic rights is often conceptually connected to the constitutional commitment to a state which is based in the rule of law (*Rechtsstaat*).[15]

The protection of aliens in the sphere of citizen rights

To appreciate the current relevance of this constitutional classification, it is, first of all, useful to see how the constitutionally sanctioned differences have transcended the legal status of aliens. As a general rule, the classifications have been interpreted as allowing for, but not as requiring differences in the treatment of aliens. A 'may' and not a 'must'. In fact, in some respects, the law has narrowed the constitutional distinctions, depriving them of practical significance.[16]

On the other hand, whatever its translation into the law, the literal demarcation between everyone's and citizen rights is no longer sufficient to determine the constitutional status of aliens under the GBL. Rather, both the Federal Constitutional Court (FCC) and the constitutional commentators have invoked those constitutional provisions which contain the basic premises of Germany's liberal democracy to fill the constitutional vacuum left for aliens in the sphere of citizen rights, a vacuum which affects some of immigrants' most common interests as societal members, such as the freedom to remain in the country and to work there.

The effort to interpret the GBL so as to derive some protection for aliens in the sphere of citizen rights is specially significant for our purposes as it reflects the specific concerns raised by those aliens who have made Germany the centre of their existence. No wonder that the scholarly discussion gained in importance from the early seventies onwards, as it became increasingly clear that Germany's restrictive system of naturali-

---

[15] Art. 20.3 GBL refers to Germany as a *Rechtsstaat*. The various interpretations of the *Rechtsstaat* principle include: a state which is founded on and subject to the rule of law, a state respecting and conforming to the rule of law, a state governed by the rule of law, government under law and the supremacy of law. See Foster 1993: 111.

[16] Thus, for instance, as a matter of statutory regulation, the freedom of assembly has been accorded to everyone on equal tems. And with the exception of some grounds of dissolution which apply to aliens' associations exclusively, the same can be said about the freedom of association. Completing this regulation, the new Aliens Act of 1990 has provided for the occasional prohibition or limitation of aliens' political activity.

zation and of citizenship by descent (*ius sanguinis*) was likely to perpetuate the reality of Germany's permanent population of settled immigrants at a time when most immigrants were showing little willingness to return to their countries of origin. Such a discussion shows how a commitment to basic legitimation principles has forced some significant constitutional changes in Germany, to allow it to adapt to the social circumstances of an increasingly post-national order, even though, as we will see, these changes have not yet fully met the requirements of the claim of automatic incorporation.

Inclusion in the name of freedom   Article 2 GBL's general freedom of action (henceforth the general freedom clause), also read as the right to the free development of one's personality, has been the main mechanism on which the FCC has relied in granting resident aliens some weaker rights analogous to citizen rights so as to facilitate their full inclusion as societal members.[17] From the very beginning the FCC had interpreted the general freedom clause in the broadest sense. It had referred to it as an *Auffanggrundrecht* ('residuary' or 'encompassing' fundamental right) holding a subsidiary relationship to the other constitutional rights and freedoms. This means that the clause was to cover all spheres of freedom which, not being those traditionally violated by public powers, had not been expressly preserved in more specific constitutional provisions.[18] In spite of scholarly disagreement, the clause came also to close the gaps left by the exclusion of aliens from the constitutionally defined citizen rights, mainly by enabling resident aliens to claim, as a subjective right and before the FCC, the application of some objective constitutional principles, such as those deriving from the *Rechtstaatsprinzip* (principle of the rule of law) in the spheres of aliens' otherwise unprotected freedoms.[19] This is why many have seen the general freedom clause as a mechanism allowing for an up-to-date interpretation of the system of fundamental rights in the GBL, which enables it to face the social reality of a permanent non-national population (Rittstieg 1983: 2746; Isensee 1974: 80; Zuleeg 1973: 362).

More specifically, there are several constitutional constraints that the FCC has derived from the general freedom clause in relation to the *Rechtstaatsprinzip* to protect aliens in the spheres of citizen rights. Two are the most relevant for our purposes. The first has to do with the principle

---

[17] Art. 2.1 GBL states that everyone shall have the right to the free development of his personality in so far as he does not violate the rights of others or offend against the constitutional order or public morality.   [18] See BVerfGE 6, 32: 37.

[19] On the freedom of movement see BVerfGE 35, 382 (18.7.1973); on the freedom to choose a profession see BVerfGE 78, 179 (10.5.1988).

of the protection of legitimate expectations. Such a principle has been occasionally invoked to limit the executive discretion on aliens' residential status. Most significantly, the FCC has recognized that the administrative practice of routine and unconditional renewal of a residence permit may establish a ground for the legitimate individual trust in the continuation of such a practice, so that after long-term and regular residence in Germany, aliens may not be denied the permission to remain in the country, even if the permits had always been granted for limited time periods only.[20] There is also some case law by the lower courts pointing to the fact that the protection of legitimate expectations needs to be taken into account to decide on an alien's right to exercise a certain professional activity.[21]

The second is the principle of proportionality. In general, such a principle states that an impingement on individual liberty has to be necessary for the protection of a public interest, that the chosen means have to be reasonably related to the goal to be achieved, and that the public interest has to be balanced against the private interests of the individual. As we will see, the principle of proportionality has been most significant in limiting the exercise of public authority concerning aliens' residential status. It is through this principle that the concrete interest an alien may have in developing her personality in Germany has been accommodated.[22] It has also played a significant role in the lower courts' case law on aliens' right to work and to choose a profession in Germany.[23]

Inclusion in the name of human dignity and equality   There have been interesting scholarly proposals on the possibility of calling on the other two pillars of Germany's constitutional democracy, human dignity and equality, to derive from them some additional constitutional protection for resident aliens. However, the FCC has thus far not expressly accepted them. First, human dignity. When made, the claim has basically been that the human dignity clause[24] reserves a sphere of rights for every person in which no distinction is legitimate and no exception is accepted (Bleckman 1985: 112; Dürig et al. 1976: Rdnrs. 84–5). This 'human right content' (*Menschenrechtgehalt*) derives directly from the human dignity clause; it can be found in both the rights and freedoms for everyone and for citizens, and it has to be granted to aliens as well as to Germans (ibid.:

---

[20] BVerfGE 49, 168.   [21] See, for example, BVerwGE 45, 162: 172 (21.5.1974).
[22] See BVerfGE 35, 382 (1973).
[23] See, for example, BVerwGE 36, 45 (1970); BVerwGE 45, 162 (21.5.1974); BVerwGE 58, 291 (13.11.1979); BVerwGE 65, 19 (4.2.1982); BVerwGE 74, 165 (9.5.1986).
[24] Art.1.1 GBL provides that human dignity is inviolable and that to respect and to protect it is a duty of all the public powers.

Rdnr. 85). So, for instance, even though the art. 12 freedom to choose a profession is a citizen freedom, a regulation indefinitely forbidding resident aliens to work would not withstand constitutional challenge. Such a regulation would condemn aliens to depend on public care, reducing them to mere objects of the action of public powers and hence, violate their human dignity (ibid.: Rdnr. 66). However, in practical terms, the FCC has not been willing to check whether, when interfering with aliens' rights, political branches respected such a nucleus.

As for the equality principle, the German Basic Law contains several guarantees of non-discrimination. The most significant for our purposes are those of art. 3.1, according to which 'all persons shall be equal before the law', and art. 3.3 whereby 'no one may be prejudiced or favoured because of his sex, his parentage, his race, his language, his homeland and origin, his faith, or his religious or political opinions'. The FCC doctrine and the mainstream scholarly opinion have been that discrimination on the basis of alienage does not come under any of the specific discrimination grounds that art. 3.3 refers to, and so, deserves no heightened scrutiny. Rather, the general understanding is that such discriminations must be measured against the general equality principle of art. 3.1, which the courts read as forbidding 'arbitrary' discrimination only (Sachs 1981: 1133).[25]

However, when seen only as a prohibition of arbitrariness it is not clear what the equality principle can add in terms of constitutional protection, at least with regard to the spheres of protection covered by citizen rights. After all, the general claim goes, equality has to be interpreted as a command to accord equal treatment to what is equal in nature and to treat differently what is essentially different.[26] And the constitutional classification between everyone's and citizen rights seems to portray the constitutional judgement that, with regard to citizen rights, aliens do not deserve equal concern. It is therefore not surprising that the FCC has not relied on art. 3.1 as a supplementary provision to decide on the constitutional protection of resident aliens in the realm of citizen rights.

The attempt to derive some constitutional protection for aliens in citizen rights from the equality clause would probably make sense only in two cases. First, if we admitted, as has not commonly been done, that in distinguishing between everyone's and citizen rights the 1949 constituent

---

[25] See also BVerfGE 51, 1: 30; BVerwGE 22, 66: 70. But holding the contrary thesis see Zuleeg 1973: 363–4. According to Zuleeg, discrimination on the basis of alienage actually implies discrimination on the basis of parentage (because German nationality law follows primarily *ius sanguinis*); homeland (if nationality is seen as expressing the territorial connection between the alien and her homeland); or origin (if nationality is taken to express no more than the social integration of the individual).

[26] See BVerfGE 1, 14; 3, 240; 18, 46; 20, 33; 49, 65; 84, 157.

ignored the most basic notions of fairness, and hence, acted arbitrarily.[27] And second, if we argued, as has occasionally been done, that whether or not the constitutionally sanctioned differences were meaningful at the time they were made, given the profound transformation of the German society since, they have lost their constitutional function now (Zuleeg 1974: 341–2; 1973: 361; Schwerdtfeger 1980: 34).

However, stressing membership concerns, most scholars have considered that, in spite of Germany's transformed population, the constitutional distinction is still relevant in that it basically portrays the constitutional commitment to the preservation of the German nation or, at least, of the German state where only citizens are full members, even in the socioeconomic realm. In the international context, far from being nobody's land, Germany is a land which has to serve, first of all, as a setting for the full social and political development of German citizens (Quaritsch 1992: 716–18; Stern 1977: 1028–9). The constitutional exclusion, far from reflecting a merely neutral position, reflects the historical responsibility of public powers towards the German nation (Hailbronner 1983: 2112–13). Being an alien means more than simply not being a German; it means being a national of another country, a country which is in principle responsible for guaranteeing rights and freedoms to its own citizens (Isensee 1974: 57). The GBL's unwillingness to assume the whole responsibility for its resident aliens and treat them with equal concern follows from this.

Only a few scholars have maintained that the relevant question is not so much that of judging whether the constitutional distinctions are valid in themselves and conceived in abstract terms. The extent to which aliens may claim a legal status equal to that of nationals, I think, should not depend on the literal constitutional description but rather on the legitimacy of certain ends and on the adequacy of certain classifications to achieve them.[28] Under this more substantive approach, which would lead us to something more similar to the US equal protection doctrine on

---

[27] This should not be regarded as a totally absurd hypothesis. Reacting against positivism and against the excesses of the German national socialist experience, the recognition of fundamental rights in the GBL has been linked to the recognition of some principles, such as those of human dignity and equality before the law, as pre-positive principles against which even the constitutional provisions have to be checked (see BVerfGE 1, 18; 1, 208: 233; 23, 98: 106; 5, 205). However, even if theoretically possible, the FCC has recognized that it would be highly unlikely that the 1949 constituent had engaged in such infringements against the most basic sense of fairness. Rather, according to the FCC, the equality principle needs to be interpreted in a global and unitary manner that incorporates both the general principle and the express constitutional exceptions, such as those affecting aliens.

[28] See also, *Kommentar zum Grundgesetz für die Bundesrepublik Deutschland*, art. 3 Zr.39, art. 3 Zr.94; Rüfner 1950: art. 3.1 Rdnr 135–7.

alienage, the place in which the concerned individuals are actually developing their existence would probably play a more important role than the purely formal concept of their nationality and we would have to distinguish between the different kinds of aliens according to their degree of integration in Germany. However, the rigid wording of the GBL has partly prevented this flexible interpretation from becoming a more widespread one. In this respect, the GBL's clear-cut distinction between everyone's rights and citizen rights, which some scholars have celebrated as a way to avoid 'the textual ambiguity that has plagued American debates on the constitutional rights of aliens' (Neuman 1990: 79–80), might have had the paradoxical effect of creating certain obstacles to the adjustment to a new order in which basic assumptions, which probably held true in the immediate postwar period, are now proving increasingly inadequate. So what we have here is maybe clarity purchased at the price of inflexibility. Among the increasingly obsolete assumptions is the idea that only nationals belong to the country's, so to say, 'ordinary population' (Isensee 1974: 59).

This is not to say that the equality principle has become completely superfluous outside the realm of citizen rights and as applied to resident aliens. Rather, it has had an autonomous 'filling out' function which has enabled it to prevent arbitrariness in those spheres which are not expressly covered by either citizen or everyone's rights. Most significantly, the FCC has said that it applies in relation to the social state principle (which is sanctioned in universal terms) and which forces the state to grant some social rights, benefits and services as a way to ensure that the rights and freedoms of the GBL can be effectively enjoyed by the bulk of the population.[29] Art. 3.1's right to equal treatment has thus been a relevant parameter to judge upon classifications concerning aliens' status of social rights and public benefits.[30] Nothing similar to the US plenary power

[29] The social state principle is generally interpreted in universal terms, requiring equal treatment of all those who reside in the country and even of those who, residing outside, have significant connections to the country which place them under the state's responsibility (e.g. having exercised a professional activity and contributed to the social security).

[30] In 1971 the FCC scrutinized, but upheld, a discrimination in compensation for pretrial detention when the prosecution led to an acquittal or to a dismissal of charges. The measure was upheld on grounds of reciprocity, and under a very lenient standard of review. Basically, the Court contented itself with ensuring that the legislation was backed by a legitimate end, such as that of guaranteeing a similar treatment for Germans abroad. It did not require that the measure be the most rational, reasonable or fair to achieve such an end (BVerfGE 30, 409: 414 (1971)). Only a few years later, applying a much more demanding scrutiny, the FCC struck down, as offending against art. 3.1 GBL, an act providing that the pension payments to a former employee or to the widow or widower of a former employee would be suspended only for non-EC aliens, during any period of voluntary residence outside the Federal Republic, unless reciprocity applied. See BVerfGE 51, 1 (1979). In its reasoning, the majority rejected the argument that

doctrine has prevented this judicial control, whether or not the measures were enacted by the federal powers. In Germany, no governmental or legislative measure concerning aliens, including the ones most clearly related to the country's concern with immigration, has been regarded straightaway as immune from judicial scrutiny. Even though the FCC has not ignored the fact that the connection of aliens to another state introduces international dimensions, nor the broader political implications of the subject, it has concentrated on the internal considerations of immigration policy, rather than perceiving immigration and alienage cases as essentially connected to the country's foreign policy.[31]

Also, it has been generally interpreted that as soon as Germany consented to aliens' entering those spheres which are in principle reserved for citizens, it had to ensure aliens' equal treatment within them and therefore was no longer free to discriminate on the basis of alienage as a matter of consistency and basic fairness (Hailbronner 1983: 2111; Schwerdtfeger 1980: 41–2; Isensee 1974: 81–5). The clearest example may be the exercise of a professional activity in relationship with the duties and rights normally linked to it. The state may not be obliged to grant an alien a work permit, or to allow her to exercise a certain profession. And as a

discrimination could be justified by Germany's higher social obligations to its citizens and to aliens residing within its borders. The Court was willing to admit that both territoriality and nationality principles were to some extent relevant to the determination of the constitutional duties of the public powers (ibid.: 27). However, unlike the dissenting opinion (ibid.: 38–9), it held that this could only justify *some* discrimination against aliens residing abroad, but not the total suspension of payments without any restitution of the contributions.

31 To understand why, in Germany, there has not been anything like the dichotomy that we saw in the USA concerning the standards of constitutional review of state and federal action, we also have to keep in mind that, in Germany, the control of aliens has always been a shared responsibility of federal and state governments. The German Basic Law has given the federal government exclusive legislative power over immigration, but only concurrent legislative power over the residence and the establishment of aliens (see arts. 73.3 and 74.4 GBL). If foreign affairs and the control of the border are federal functions, aliens' agencies have been local agencies under *Länder* authority (Neuman 1990: 82). The German *Länder* have been responsible for the implementation of German immigration law and have even had subsidiary policy-making functions in the field (Esser and Korte 1985: 202–4). Thus, nothing like the division between state level/residential community versus federal level/political community we saw in the USA would have made sense in Germany.
    Also, when comparing the different degrees of judicial scrutiny of measures affecting aliens in the USA and in Germany, one should not forget the different realities that may hide under the same label of 'alien'. In the USA, naturalization and *ius soli* birthright citizenship have limited the reach of American 'immigration policies' if one means policies dealing with aliens. Given Germany's much more restrictive incorporation mechanisms, we find that a system with low standards of judicial review of measures affecting aliens would have actually implied the exclusion of a large sector of the ordinary population from constitutional protection in quite significant areas. And this would have been at odds with Germany's constitutional design.

matter of fact, aliens are subject to significant restrictions as to the kinds of professional activities they can undertake in Germany. However, when the state allows the alien to exercise a certain profession, it is obliged, as a matter of fairness, to provide that she enjoys the same working status as any other citizen worker (e.g. equal freedom to unionize; equal treatment in the payment of taxes linked to the activity such as the social security contribution; or equality in the enjoyment of social rights such as unemployment benefits or pensions). This duty of consistency and fairness is of essential relevance for aliens' equal enjoyment of social rights, since many of the benefits of the welfare state rest on the condition of the individual as a worker.

Underlying this, therefore, is a system of gradual inclusion of resident aliens in the socioeconomic realm of constitutional equality as societal members in both the USA and Germany. In the USA the crucial decision has been that of accepting aliens as immigrants from the beginning and so the fairness logic starts to apply from that moment even though the federal government has been exempted from those constraints in the name of the plenary power doctrine. It is different in Germany, where there has been more than one frontier to cross to achieve equality. Gaining access into the territory has not been enough. Rather, some rights are directly achieved through access into the territory while others are not. The GBL establishes the criteria. Among those which are not directly obtained on entry are the rights to remain in the country and to freely exercise a professional activity in it, two rights which are essential to ensuring the full acceptance of resident aliens as members of Germany's social tissue. Precisely to make up for the constitutional exclusions in those realms the courts have called on the general freedom clause, offering a more updated reading of the GBL which takes into account Germany's changed social composition after the immigration experience that the constituents could not foresee. The updated reading of the GBL has not gone as far as the complete cancellation of the constitutional distinctions between citizens and resident aliens. Neither the general freedom nor the equality clause has been interpreted as an adequate mechanism to overcome the conceptual difference between citizens and aliens that the GBL's distinction between everyone's and citizen rights is taken to embody. On the other hand, the GBL's commitment to a social-state order and basic demands of fairness linked to the notion of equality have implied that resident aliens are in principle entitled to enjoy a full status of social rights and benefits, even if those rights are connected to the exercise of a professional activity to which resident aliens have in principle no constitutional right. Once the state decides to allow aliens into the reserved spheres of rights and freedoms, it is obliged to ensure progressively their equal treatment within each of them as a matter of fairness. In other words, Germany's constitutional commitment to being a social state which is based on the rule of law has allowed for a significant, if not a full, inclusion of resident aliens in the sphere of constitutional equality, at least as far as socioeconomic membership is concerned.

The political status of resident aliens: limits to inclusion

Things have been quite different in the political realm, where the basic constitutional premises of Germany's constitutional democracy have been predominantly read as requiring the exclusion of resident aliens, rather than as requiring or even allowing for their inclusion. Let us describe how this has come about. The political status of aliens and, in particular, alien suffrage was vividly debated during the eighties in Germany. The movement for alien suffrage was linked to two phenomena. On one hand, the debate was carried on in the framework of the European integration process, as the idea of transcending a merely economic coalition for the sake of a closer political union was gradually gaining force (Neuman 1992: 264). Germany's coming to terms with the reality of the *de facto* immigration of guestworkers was the other relevant fact (ibid.: 263). Immigrants came to be seen as a permanent segment of the population, but neither they nor their descendants found the path to German citizenship easy, given Germany's restrictive naturalization policies and predominantly *ius sanguinis* birthright citizenship. Under these circumstances, democratic legitimacy concerns necessarily had to arise. That a large proportion of the ordinary population would, generation after generation, remain indefinitely disenfranchised seemed to violate basic postulates of a liberal democratic order. The living conditions of this population and the tensions in its relationship with German co-residents were also sources of concerns. In this context, the possibility of enfranchising resident aliens was essentially debated as a means to help immigrants' integration.

To some extent, the debate was encouraged by the GBL's lack of a coherent position on aliens' political status. The GBL reserves for Germans only the freedoms of assembly and association, both of which are essential to the exercise of political activity in the country. However, the no less significant freedom of expression, the rights to unionize and to petition have been granted to everyone without distinction.[32] As for the core political rights, namely the right to vote and the right to hold a public office, the relevant constitutional provisions do not refer to the concrete

---

[32] See arts. 8, 9, 5, 9.3 and 17 GBL.

position of aliens.[33] The provisions on suffrage are simply expressed in vague terms.[34] Apart from mentioning the fact that the federal president needs to be a German,[35] nothing concrete is added in the GBL as to the possibility of aliens exercising public offices or occupying important elective or non-elective positions.[36] The Constitution provides for the equal access of *citizens* to the public function[37] but it does not contain an express sanction of the requirement of being German to have access to any public office, not even to those which imply the exercise of public authority and to which the GBL expressly refers.[38] So much for the constituent's attempt to set a clear dividing line between citizens' and everyone's basic rights.

The possibility of aliens becoming public officers has not been discussed nearly as much as alien suffrage. In general, it has been accepted that, unlike suffrage and important elective positions, working for the state as a public officer implies the exercise of derivative, removable and guided public power rather than originary and sovereign power (Isensee 1974: 95). This explains why although the GBL refers only to the citizens' right to equal access to the public function, the statutory regulation according to which aliens need not but can be accepted as civil servants in the case of urgent need has generally not been said to offend against the Constitution (Zuleeg 1973: 368; Dolde 1972: 79), at least for the cases in which there is no exercise of sovereign authority at stake (Quaritsch 1992: 724). As to why aliens need not be accepted as civil servants on equal

---

[33] See arts. 38, 28 and 33 GBL.

[34] Concerning the right to vote in national elections, art. 38 provides that '[t]he deputies to the German *Bundestag* shall be elected in general, direct, free, equal, and secret elections. They shall be representatives of the whole people, not bound by orders and instructions, and shall be subject only to their conscience' (38.1 GBL). 'To be entitled to vote, one has to have attained the age of eighteen years; to be eligible, one has to have attained full legal age' (38.2 GBL). 'Details shall be regulated by a federal law' (38.3 GBL).

As for *Länder* and municipal elections, art. 28 GBL reads as follows: 'The constitutional order in the *Länder* must conform to the principles of republican, democratic and social government based on the rule of law, within the meaning of this Basic Law. In each of the *Länder*, counties [*Kreise*], and communes [*Gemeinden*], the people must be represented by a body chosen in general, direct, free, equal and secret elections. In the commune the assembly of the commune may take the place of an elected body' (28.1 GBL).

[35] Art. 54.1.2 GBL.

[36] There is disagreement as to how narrowly one has to interpret art. 54.1.2's exclusion. Most scholars have argued for its extension to cover the other political positions to which the GBL has referred only in vague terms (deputies, chancellor, etc.) (Isensee 1974: 95–6). Others have instead interpreted the provision rather restrictively, admitting the possibility that aliens have access to all the positions from which they have not been expressly excluded (Dolde 1972: 79).   [37] See art. 33.2 GBL.

[38] Art. 33.2 GBL provides that every German has an equal right to qualify for each public service according to his qualifications, capacities and expertise. Art. 33.4 GBL provides that the exercise of public authority generally refers to civil servants who are bound by their public duty to serve the public interest and behave loyally.

terms with citizens, it is generally assumed that the constitutional reference to citizens only implicitly allows for it. Often, the difference in
treatment is defended on the grounds of the political nature of the rights
at stake and on the loyalty bond which is generally presupposed for access
to public service. In this respect, some arguments are similar to those
around which, as we will see, the alien suffrage debate has centred (ibid.:
723 n. 275).[39] In any event, the fact that the constitutional provision
defining the right to choose a profession as a citizen right (art. 12 GBL)
could by itself justify the disparity in the treatment of aliens regarding
their professional aspirations probably explains why there has not been
any need for the FCC to develop something similar to the US Supreme
Court doctrine to separate the political functions in the strict sense from
the others.

In general, access to both political functions and suffrage has been
related to citizens' *status activus* or, in other words, to citizens' capacity to
act for the state as a state organ.[40] Most constitutional commentators have
therefore considered, as a matter of course, that only citizens had to be
guaranteed equality in their enjoyment (Stern 1977: 1028). More than to
the construction of Germany as a liberal or a social state around a more or
less universal concept of equality, the right to exercise political rights and
functions has been specifically connected to the structural features of
Germany's political order, which, as constitutionally sanctioned, are said
to circumscribe the sphere of political equality to the state and its citizens.

Most significantly, art. 2's general freedom clause, so relevant in filling
out the gaps in those citizen rights which could affect resident aliens as
members of Germany's residential community, has not been used to
strengthen aliens' political status (Von Mangoldt 1987: 660). The main
objection against applying the general freedom clause to strengthen alien
suffrage and aliens' access to public service has been that, rather than just
personal freedom, political rights express a qualified freedom which is
connected to the constitutional conception of the political community.
The legitimate exercise of these kinds of rights depends on the relationship of the individual to the political community. And what that relationship is cannot be decided without taking into consideration the more

---

[39] A different matter is that of defining the jobs and positions which art. 33.2 covers. For
many authors the constitutional provision covers not only civil service (*Beamtentum*) in
the narrow sense, but rather, public offices in a broader sense, meaning those offices which
imply the exercise of public authority, such as those of judge and public notary from which
aliens are currently banned (Franz 1989: 155).

[40] See Jellinek's classical distinction between *status activus*, *negativus* and *positivus* in Jellinek
1950: 94 ff and 130 ff. See also BVerfGE 83, 60 II (1971). The *status positivus* rights refer to
those which imply political participation and hence are generally said to presuppose
membership of the people of the state. They are said to be limited to the state community
and hence, by nature, to assist citizens only (see Stern 1977: 70 II 7, 1027–8).

specific constitutional provisions on the organization of Germany's political community (Schwerdtfeger 1982: 16). This is how the schism between individual freedom which applies to the socioeconomic realm and political freedom which applies to the political realm is generally established. When deciding on the distribution of political rights, the starting point is said to be the state as a political unit, and not the individual as a holder of natural freedom, equality or human dignity. But let us specifically see how these assumptions have appeared in the alien suffrage debate.

The alien suffrage debate

The legal debate on alien suffrage in Germany has embraced a wide variety of positions, ranging from those who have defended the view that granting suffrage to resident aliens was constitutionally required, to those who have argued that it was constitutionally prohibited (indeed that its prohibition was entrenched in the GBL). At the core of the debate has been the interpretation of the principle of popular sovereignty which, as constitutionally sanctioned, provides that '[a]ll the state authority emanates from the people [*Volk*] and shall be exercised by the people in elections and through specific legislative, executive, and judicial organs'.[41]

Pro-alien suffrage constitutional scholars have always been a minority and most of them have defended it as a constitutionally permissible option. Only exceptionally has it been argued that alien suffrage was constitutionally required (Bryde 1989: 257; Zuleeg 1988: 20).[42] Proponents of alien suffrage have rested particularly on a conception of democracy as a system of government which is intimately linked to respect for individual autonomy. In it, the concern for the safeguard of human dignity and individual freedom requires that all those affected by the laws and subject to the authority of the state legitimate such state authority through their active participation in the political process (Bryde 1994: 322; Frank 1990: 302; Zuleeg 1987: 155; Behrend 1973: 376). The popular sovereignty clause of art. 20.2, whereby 'every state authority emanates from the people', has been said to support alien suffrage. If the notion of a

---

[41] Art. 20.2 GBL.

[42] Even among those who have defended alien suffrage as a constitutionally permissible option, there has generally been a basic distinction between municipal or sub-state elections, on the one hand, and *Länder* and national elections, on the other. Whereas granting aliens voting rights in the former, they claimed, required only a change in the pertinent laws, recognizing their voting rights at state or national level required a constitutional amendment.

Summarizing the arguments which refer specifically to voting rights at a municipal level, see Neuman 1992: 274–6. One should note here that only the more limited option of local suffrage has thus far been on the political agenda.

sovereign people presupposes a subject capable of will and decision, then the individual capacity of will must be at the basis of it (Kurz 1965: 163–80). The principle of popular sovereignty results naturally from fitting the concept of autonomous individuals with a human right to self-determination into a political community holding the claim of having found the form of state government that complies best with the essence of the individual (Frank 1990: 298, 302; Birkenheier 1976: 54). In this sense, 'people' is another term for 'persons' (Bryde 1994: 322). The principle of popular sovereignty is more concerned with sanctioning a rule of legitimation of power to outlaw any kind of absolutist or tyrannical power contrary to the enlightened idea of natural freedom and equality of all individuals, than with entrenching a nationalistic version of political community which keeps the monopoly on political power for German citizens (Bryde 1989; Rittstieg 1981: 59–60). Scholars defending alien suffrage have therefore tended to stress the contingency of the historical argument linking the democratization process to the consolidation of nation-states and thus, making the link between national citizenship and political participation.[43] Even if the 1948 Constituent Assembly had assumed as a matter of course that the 'people' from which all the state authority emanated would only be the national citizenry, the alien suffrage advocates argued, the demographic changes resulting from the *de facto* immigration of guestworkers required an up-to-date reading of the legitimacy clause so as to overcome the new challenge posed by the presence of a large population of aliens permanently established in Germany (Frank 1990: 297; Kämper 1989: 96; Rittstieg 1981: 64). This conception of democracy was defended as best fitting the constitutional scheme given the prevalent position of human dignity, personal freedom and equality as values resoundingly proclaimed in the opening constitutional provisions, values to which the recognition of the other fundamental rights is linked. Telling in this respect was also said to be the FCC case law connecting these values to the democratic form of government in general.[44]

[43] Rather, they have argued, the revolutionary aspect of the citizenship concept emerging from the French Revolution rested on its overruling of the personalistic and non-autonomous concept of the holder of political rights. Since, generally, all the people residing in the state were recognized as citizens, citizenship could not be seen as a privileged status. Nevertheless, that the egalitarian spirit that animated this movement did not deplete itself in the conquest of citizenship, as a homogeneous criterion embracing all the population of the state, is shown by the fact that only much later was the actual enjoyment of political rights attached to citizenship, regardless of gender and economic position. In this regard, see Grabitz 1970: 25 ff (claiming that democratic participation is not bound to the idea of citizenship even if it has evolved in the framework of the national state).

[44] See BVerfGE 2, 1: 12–13; BVerfGE 5, 85: 204–5. Note, however, that even the strongest proponents of alien suffrage arguments have seen it as a task of the legislator to implement the demands of the constitutionally sanctioned rule of democracy interpreted in the light

Together with these notions which focus strongly on the moral relevance of aliens' subjection to the laws, basic notions of social justice were also called upon to defend alien suffrage under the constitutional social state clause. Invoking fairness for inclusion, it was argued that the contribution of resident aliens to the German economy was difficult to reconcile with their lack of political voice (Deubler 1988: B 24, 36; Zuleeg 1974: 348). Their exclusion would ultimately threaten social justice by making an already socially underprivileged class into a permanent underclass (Zuleeg 1987: 160, 183). Not surprisingly, underlying the usual counter-argument was the need to distinguish between the socioeconomic and the political spheres (Schink 1988: 423). Thus, it was generally said that these duties (such as tax and social security contributions) are not an exchange for the specific protection the state grants to its citizens, but rather, a compensation for the enjoyment of the services it offers, from which both citizens and resident aliens actually profit (Birkenheier 1976: 68).

Rejecting the above-mentioned arguments, the majority opinion was that, far from leaving it open, the GBL had decided that the 'people' of its democracy were the 'people of the German state' or the German citizenry (Ruland 1975: 9; Döhring 1974: 7 ff.; Isensee 1974: 92; Sasse 1974: 17; Behrend 1973: 376; Dolde 1972: 72; Tomuschat 1968: 57). When winding its way into modern constitutionalism, the principle of popular sovereignty was influenced by French Revolutionary thought which had taken the nation to be the locus of sovereignty (Huber 1989: 534; Bleckmann 1988: 437–8). This explains why national citizenship and political rights appeared so closely linked to each other (Quaritsch 1983; Rittstieg 1981: 50 ff; Grawert 1973). This should not be regarded now as a historical relic.

Several constitutional provisions were then commonly invoked to offer a reading of the GBL that would favour the interpretation of the 'people' (the *Volk* the popular sovereignty clause refers to) as the Germans. Often, such interpretation rested on merely grammatical grounds.[45] More

of the constitutional set of liberal values. Neither individual freedom (art. 2 GBL) nor human dignity (art. 1 GBL) or equality (art. 3 GBL) has, by itself, been judged as adequate to cover resident aliens' individual claims to suffrage (Zuleeg 1987: 179–80; 1974: 349).

[45] Among the most quoted provisions were those which refer to the 'German people', an expression that was taken to refer to an ideal political unity legitimating state authority (Huber 1989: 535; Bleckmann 1988: 438–9; and Schink 1988: 420–1). Also the right to resist the overthrow of the government, constitutionally reserved for Germans, was brought into the discussion (Rupp 1989: 365; Bleckmann 1988: 438–9; Quaritsch 1983: 4) (see art. 20.4 GBL). It would be contradictory if the state authority was said to flow both from Germans and resident aliens but only the former had a right to defend the constitutional order in critical times. The very distinction between citizens' and everyone's rights in the GBL and, more specifically, the restriction of political freedoms to citizens only, were also interpreted as expressions of the constitutional option to exclude aliens from full political membership (Bleckmann 1988: 440; Ruland 1975: 10). Finally, also the constitutionally sanctioned oath of the public powers to act in the interest of the

importantly, underlying this reading of the Constitution was a specific democratic theory: the 'no democracy without a demos' theory. As a form of collective self-determination, alien suffrage opponents said, democracy presupposes the demos or the people who are to decide jointly about the future of the community according to its understanding of itself and its own interests (Hailbronner 1989: 75–6; Huber 1989: 534–5). The national community formed by the citizenry as a whole, and not the individual, occupies the central place. Since citizenship is the key to the political community, democratic equality, which applies conceptually to all the members of the political community, can only be an attribute of citizens (Isensee 1973: 741). The idea of the national community as the proper locus for democratic legitimation was then given several interpretations ranging from the more legal and political one (the state as a legal and political unity in a universe divided into different state actors) to a more pre-political one (the national community as a cultural, religious or ethno-linguistic community) (Quaritsch 1983: 1, 8; Schachtenschneider 1980: L150). Rather than of all those who are affected by the laws of a country – a criterion which was criticized for the degree of uncertainty it would introduce (Birkenheier 1976: 60) – democratic equality needed to be predicated of those bound by the legal relationship of citizenship. Citizenship, and not human equality or freedom, was determined as defining the proper realm of democratic accountability. First the polity, then the individual.

Furthermore, reproducing some of the arguments we analysed when exploring the 'fairness objection', it was argued that citizenship as membership defines a sphere of equal rights and duties ensuring basic internal fairness: the idea of granting aliens the rights which, like voting, have been typically reserved for citizens, without imposing on them equal duties, was presented as seriously threatening equality. The possible solution of imposing on aliens the same set of duties as on citizens was generally rejected. After all, given the state's obligation to allow aliens to leave, these could always escape whatever duties are imposed on them by actually leaving the country (Birkenheier 1976: 64; Isensee 1974: 94; Thieme 1951: 63). Also, it was argued, citizens' specific and exclusive situation in the political community of the state is precisely symbolized by a certain kind of duty, such as military service and defence of the state, for the sake of which only citizens are expected to sacrifice themselves and even to risk their lives (Isensee 1974: 94; Döhring 1963: 181; Thieme 1951: 76). Ultimately, only citizens are indissolubly bound in a commu-

whole *German* people was mentioned (see art. 56 GBL): it would make little sense that the interests of part of the electorate did not deserve an adequate recognition (Huber 1989: 535; Bleckmann 1988: 440).

nity of fate (*Schicksalgemeinschaft*) from which, unlike aliens, they cannot simply leave, abandoning thereby their political responsibility (Karpen 1989: 1013; Isensee 1973: 93). Hence, they argued, full loyalty can be presumed of citizens only (Quaritsch 1983: 7, 15; Ruland 1975: 11; Döhring 1974: 34–37).

The Federal Constitutional Court's decision on alien suffrage

At last, the time came for the FCC to take an interest in this controversial debate. Two *Länder*, Schleswig-Holstein and Hamburg, had taken legislative action to confer on aliens the right to vote and to run for office at the local level. In the case of Schleswig-Holstein, where suffrage was also restricted to nationals of some European countries, specific requirements for the access to the franchise were those of having lived in Germany for five years and that their countries provided for reciprocal arrangements. In the case of Hamburg no distinction was made as to the alien's nationality. However, it was required that they had been residing in Germany for eight years and either held a residence permit or were stateless.

On the same day the Court invalidated both these statutes.[46] According to the Court the democratic legitimation that the popular sovereignty principle refers to could only flow from the people of the state, meaning the German people as they are defined in art. 116 GBL, hence German citizens and those assimilated categories of Germans.[47] The Court then argued that the kind of democratic legitimation which is required in national elections is the same required at *Land* and local levels (including the submunicipal borough assemblies that were at stake in the case of Hamburg). As structural elements of the German state these local entities also exercised sovereign power at least to the extent that they had the power to pass resolutions.[48]

The Court argued that the state must be conceived as a community, bound in a unity. The constitutional mandate had to be interpreted as referring not only to the principle of popular sovereignty in abstract terms. Rather, it had to be read as determining also who are the people who are supposed to exercise the state authority and these are the people of the state who form the Federal Republic of Germany.[49] 'As a democratic state [the German Federal Republic] cannot be conceived without

---

[46] See BVerfGE 83, 60 II (20.2.1989) and BVerfGE 83, 37 II (31.10.1990). For our concerns BVerfGE 83, 60 II refers essentially to the reasoning in BVerfGE 83, 37 II.

[47] BVerfGE 83, 37 II: 50 ff. Art. 116.1 GBL ascribes the condition of German both to German citizens and to those who 'have been admitted to the territory of the German *Reich* within the frontiers of 31 December 1937 as a refugee or expellee of German stock or as a spouse or descendant thereof'. These have been identified as 'Status-Germans'.

[48] Ibid. 53 ff.   [49] Ibid. 50.

a collection of persons that is bearer and subject of the public authority it exercises through its organs'[50] and from a systematic reading of the GBL, the Court concluded that the people from which the state authority emanates could only be the national citizenry.[51]

This is how the Court removed the individual and, instead, placed the national citizen in the central position of the democratic legitimation argument. It expressly relegated the concern with subjection and affectedness to second place. Referring to the clause sanctioning the principle of popular sovereignty, the Court literally stated that it could not 'mean that the state authority decisions have to be legitimated by those who are affected by them; rather, state authority requires its subjects to be identified with a group of human beings bound into a unity'.[52] In what can be read as an express rejection of the constitutional validity of the path of full inclusion, as far as political inclusion is concerned, the Court argued that membership within the people is mediated by citizenship as a legal condition for the enjoyment of a full status of rights and duties.[53] This applied especially to those rights which, like the franchise, are the clearest paths for the expression of democratic authority. No subsequent change in the circumstances brought about by immigration could be said to have changed the meaning of the popular sovereignty clause.[54]

This did not mean, the Court further argued, that the long-term exclusion of resident aliens who are permanently subject to the state authority was not democratically relevant in a liberal order. Connecting full inclusion and access to nationality as alternative paths for democratic incorporation, the Court argued that if the legislator felt the need to solve the democratic legitimation gap it would have to do it through the ruling on the acquisition of citizenship. And this, according to the GBL, would be a task of the federal and not the state legislator. What one could not break was the link between belonging to the state people, as the holder of state authority, and the condition of being a German.[55] This is all the Court said.

However, some scholars have interpreted the thesis sanctioned in the decision whereby the demos in Germany's democracy can include only German citizens and Status-Germans as deriving only in part from the

---

[50] Ibid. 51.
[51] Relevant to the Court's interpretation were the Preamble and Article 146 which mentions the *German people* as the constitution-giving power; art. 33's GBL guarantee of equal rights to *Germans* in every *Land*; and art. 56's official oath binding executive officials to serve the interest of the *German people*.   [52] BVerfGE 83, 37: 50.
[53] Ibid. 51. See also BVerfGE 37, 217: 239: 'citizenship expresses the basic relationship between the group of members legally bound and the community of the German state. Out of citizenship derives a constitutional status whereby some rights, and the guarantees for equal enjoyment of some others, are reserved for Germans.'
[54] BVerfGE 83, 37: 52.   [55] Ibid.

political theory which takes the state as a collective actor. Underlying this, they say, is also the particular historical development of nationhood in Germany during the nineteenth century where linguistic and cultural nationalism preceded the territorial consolidation of the German state, so that nationality, in this substantive sense, rather than residence, became crucial to define the political community (Neuman 1992: 291). I do not think this has to be seen as the only possible interpretation of the decision. Granted, the Court appeared to start by expressly embracing the 'no democracy without a demos' thesis and added little to justify the assumption that democratic legitimation can only be conferred through the exclusive participation of citizens in elections. But the decision needs to be set in context and appreciated for both what it said and what it did not say. Thus, none of the arguments on inescapability and community of fate, none of the concerns with fairness in the distribution of rights and duties or with aliens' alleged disloyalty, all of which the parties had put forward and the scholarly debate had been discussing for years, were brought up.[56] The Court did stress the constitutionally sanctioned state nature of the German polity and referred to citizenship not as a strong nationalistic membership status, but rather as a status binding those who share in the realm of civic equality within the state. Such a status had to be preserved for citizens. The path of full inclusion was therefore not constitutionally possible.

Nevertheless, the Court admitted the relevance of our main concern: the democratic legitimation gap resulting from the exclusion of resident aliens who are permanently subject to the state authority. Indeed it recommended the alternative path for inclusion: a more inclusive regulation of citizenship, a regulation pertaining to the federal and not the state legislator. Literally, 'the regulation on citizenship is thus the appropriate sphere for the legislator to take into account the change in the composition of the population of the Federal Republic and its implications on the exercise of political rights'.[57] It did not refer to this as a duty of the legislator which resulted from a systematic reading of the democratic principle in the GBL. We may think that it ought to have done so, especially since through its decision it was foreclosing full inclusion as an option for allowing resident aliens to enter the realm of civic equality. But we know that constitutional courts are rather cautious about giving the legislator specific commands as to what it needs to do. However, it could

---

[56] According to Neuman the abstractness of the decision and the lack of references to disloyalty, solidarity and 'community of fate' were rather chosen by the Court for its European audience to avoid the idea that German reunification, which had been accomplished precisely between argument and decision, created insecurities about the role of a strengthened Germany in Europe (Neuman 1992: 291).

[57] BVerfGE 83, 37: 52.

not escape the Court, nor the general audience, that, after all, the restrictive definition of the path to gain citizenship was precisely at the root of the
denounced situation. Finally, the Court was careful enough to emphasize
that this did not mean that a constitutional amendment to introduce local
alien suffrage was prohibited.[58] In fact, the Court expressly referred to the
discussion about alien suffrage in the framework of the European Community, anticipating political events, and sanctioning the path Germany
would take in 1992 to introduce local suffrage for EU nationals residing in
Germany after the signing of the Maastricht Treaty.[59]

Alienage and the difference that residence makes

This leads us to explore access to citizenship as an alternative path to civic
equality. But before we do so, it might be interesting to analyse on what
grounds the inclusion of resident aliens as aliens, to the extent that there
has been such an inclusion, has proceeded. In other words, we want to
check whether permanent subjection to the law and deep affectedness
have been recognized as grounds for inclusion in the German experience.

The constitutional status of non-resident aliens

The question of when the German Basic Law starts to protect aliens has
also been debated in Germany. The competing explanations for aliens'
initial constitutional protection that we identified in the US debate have
been more or less reproduced in the German context: subjection to the
law, acceptance or consent by the national community[60] and significant
connections with it.[61] In 1987 a family reunification decision gave the

[58] Ibid. 59.
[59] After the reform, a new paragraph, art. 28.3 GBL, was added. It provides that, as far as
county and commune elections are concerned, citizens from other EC Member States
may qualify for the right to vote and be eligible according to the EC legal system. See
BGBl.I 24.12.1992, 2086.
[60] In chapter 7 we identified the consent-based account as the 'membership model'. As
Germay does not recognize itself as a country of immigration, the idea that resident aliens
are to be seen as members of the national community has not been commonly held there.
Still, what I will call in this chapter the 'consensualist model' shares its foundational
grounds with what I identified as the 'membership model' in the previous chapter. In both
cases the protection granted to aliens results from the national community's act of consent
or acceptance which generally takes the form of the granting of some specific legal status
to aliens (typically, that of 'immigrant' in the USA, and that of 'permanent resident' in
Germany), whether or not one sees this as expressing also an act of the community's
self-definition.
[61] One exponent of the subjection thesis in Germany is Isensee for whom access to the
territory places aliens under the jurisdiction of the state, entitling them to global
constitutional protection. Only with residence comes the subjection to the law and hence,
the protection of the law (Isensee 1974: 61–2, 69). Just as in the US debate, when

FCC a wonderful occasion to take a stand on the topic as it was mainly concerned with the initial granting of residence permits.[62] Its analysis is especially meaningful for our purposes since it reflects the contrast with the US Supreme Court's stand on the matter. But let us first place the decision in its political context and summarize its content.

Since the German government stopped recruiting foreign workers in 1973, family reunification of first- and second-generation immigrants became one of the few remaining sources of immigration from outside the European Community, the other two being the immigration of ethnic Germans and of asylum claimants. In 1981 the federal government called upon the *Länder* to limit family reunification, recommending that first-time residence permits be denied to spouses of second-generation resident aliens unless the resident spouse had reached the age of eighteen, lived continuously in the Federal Republic for eight years and been married for at least one year. Although most *Länder* simply implemented this recommendation, others strengthened or weakened it. Most significantly, Baden-Würtemberg imposed the requirement of three years of marriage rather than one, before both first- and second-generation aliens could bring in their spouses.

In the decision the Court found that the family connection between the aliens seeking to reside in Germany and the resident aliens enabled not only resident but also non-resident aliens to assert their rights under art. 6 of the GBL, dedicated to the protection of the family. The Court denied the possibility that art. 6 conferred by itself a right of entry assisting non-resident aliens seeking to be reunited with their families. Ultimately, the constitution had granted a wide discretion to the political branches to determine in what numbers and under what conditions aliens could be admitted to the territory as something related to political estimations on the future development of the country's economic and social conditions. Nevertheless, the Court recognized that, apart from a subjective right, art. 6 embodied also the state's general duty to promote and protect the family. On such a duty rested the obligation of the administration and the

combined with these notions of strict territoriality, subjection as the foundation of constitutional protection often becomes entangled with consensualist notions. Isensee's thesis is precisely an example of this, as in other passages, he connects aliens' presence to the country's right to self-definition (ibid.: 69). We should mention Zuleeg (1974: 346) as an example of those who have instead been more sensitive to the existence of ties binding the alien to the national community to determine the moment at which the constitutional protection is triggered (whether or not these ties result from residence in the country). Defending a composite scheme under the label of 'sufficiently concrete relationship with the country', which includes presence within the territory, nationality, having a constitutionally protected good within the country such as property or family, or having a link which derives from a prior residence in the country, see Quaritsch 1992: 700 ff.

[62] BVerfGE 76, 1 (12.5.1987).

judiciary to take into account the family ties of the applicant for a residence permit. Expressly denying the extraterritoriality thesis, the FCC held that the lack of a territorial contact between the aliens and Germany was not an obstacle to the application of the constitutional right if those aliens had links to people who were themselves connected to the German territory in a constitutionally significant way and who could not be expected to give up their social and economic position as well as their personal links in Germany.

On this basis the FCC concluded that asking second-generation aliens for an eight-year residence period was in conformity with the GBL in that it furthered a legitimate end (ensuring the economic and social incorporation of further family members) and the eventual harm to the family interests was not too serious. Before that time the family could still be expected to flourish in the country of origin. However, the state's three-year waiting period after marriage produced a disproportionate and unacceptable injury to the constitutionally protected sphere of liberty. It could have far too destructive effects on young married couples who might underestimate the seriousness of such a lengthy separation during the early years of marriage.

The two most striking features of the decision are probably the rejection of the extraterritoriality thesis and the prevalence of the significant ties model of constitutional protection. Admittedly, one could say that in this case the applicant aliens were physically inside the country. They had been admitted temporarily as visitors and were in the country when stating their claims. However, the Court discarded this fact as irrelevant, equating the applicants' position, as soon as their visa expired, to that of any other family member waiting outside the border. The case also shows that not even the decisions on the entry of aliens into the country, which can be said to be at the core of the country's immigration policy, and whose political implications the Court did not hide, are, in Germany, simply left to the discretion of the political and executive branches.

Increasing protection through residence and societal integration

Even though the constitutional position of aliens and citizens has been established in the GBL, we have seen that both the FCC and the scholarly doctrine have favoured a more dynamic interpretation of the constitutional status of aliens which allows it to be redefined as resident aliens' substantive similarities to resident citizens increase. Unlike in the USA where, at least at the state level, the general rule has been that of equality and, therefore, differential treatment has required justification under more or less demanding scrutiny, we know that in Germany, the general rules have derived from the constitutional distinction between citizens' and everyone's rights. It is advancing from this baseline towards a progressive equalization between aliens and citizens that has required a special justification.

In the doctrinal debate, it has generally been accepted that with increasing residence and, more generally, with increasing social integration (of which ordinary residence, consolidation of family ties and of a professional status are usually taken as relevant signs) aliens are to enjoy a stronger constitutional status overall, including those rights initially reserved for citizens. One of the clearest advocates of this thesis has been Schwerdtfeger. His thesis seems to rest implicitly on the notion of deep affectedness.

According to Schwerdtfeger, in the beginning, aliens do not need to develop their personality in Germany and it is their countries of origin that hold direct responsibility for them (Schwerdtfeger 1980: 31). However, with increasing residence and societal integration things change. Whether or not aliens remain emotionally bound to their country of origin, eventually, Germany becomes the only place in which they can reasonably develop their personality (ibid.: 19–20). Thus, after fifteen years of residence (or as a second- or third-generation alien) one can say that an alien's substantive constitutional status should be almost identical to that of a citizen because the alien has presumably become inevitably bound to Germany (ibid.: 32). Even though it was the Constituent Assembly's express choice to privilege German citizens in the enjoyment of some constitutional rights and freedoms it is necessary to make an updated reading of the GBL, in the light of Germany's changed social circumstances (ibid.: 33–4).

The existing statutory regulations on aliens' residence, but also on work and family rights, have partly supported the thesis of incremental protection. These statutes foresee some reduction of the administrative discretion, as time passes and resident aliens become socially rooted in Germany, concerning decisions such as ending the right to residence, limiting the realm of activities aliens may engage in while in the country, or treating their desire to bring in family members as deserving less concern than that of citizens (Quaritsch 1992: 734). The FCC has also recognized the importance of societal integration for the enjoyment of different rights, including constitutionally defined citizen rights. It has granted constitutional relevance to the fact that aliens establish their life centre (*Lebensmittelpunkt*) in Germany. And this has been essential to allow resident aliens to consolidate their residential status in a country which was officially determined to endlessly regard them as temporary guestworkers.

Maybe the most relevant case in this regard was BVerfGE 49, 168, 1978. It was a crucial decision to end a tradition whereby, in spite of long-term and regular residence in the country, aliens could be denied the permission to remain in Germany simply because Germany did not consider itself an immigration country with a political interest in increasing its permanent population or citizenry through immigrants. At stake was the case of an Indian national who had been living in Germany for over twelve years, combining study and working periods, and had married an Indian woman with whom he was living in Germany. They were living together with a child born to them in Germany. Having renewed residence permits for both training and working purposes for over eleven years, at one point the administrative authorities decided not to renew the permit any longer on the grounds that the training in Germany had finished and so the goal for which the alien had originally requested a residence permit had been accomplished. The authorities further argued that the alien's intention to settle in Germany for life was not acceptable since it offended Germany's interest in remaining a non-immigration country and contradicted Germany's foreign policy of aid to development based on receiving citizens from developing countries for professional training only.

The Court recognized the seriousness of the individual interests at stake and linked them to the economic and social integration of the alien in Germany. It then called on the principle of protection of legitimate expectations to invalidate the decision that denied the extension of the residence permit. According to the Court, the administrative practice of routine and unconditional renewal of a residence permit established a ground for reliance on the continuation of such a practice. A reversal in the country's immigration policy would not justify the expulsion of foreign workers after the government had induced their *de facto* settlement. Although the Court stressed the need to protect legitimate expectations, it also underlined the importance of the alien's societal integration. The essential fact was that the local agency's routine renewal of the complainant's residence permits had induced the latter to rely on the possibility of staying, and thus, facilitated his economic and social integration in Germany. The Court paid no attention to the fact that the permits had always been granted for limited time periods only. And yet this limitation is sometimes taken as a proof that aliens are not being allowed to plan on staying in the country and thus, cannot legitimately claim an interest in the protection of reliance (Isensee 1974: 72 n. 56).[63]

---

[63] Isensee has argued that only the recognition of a permission to stay indefinitely can ground aliens' legitimate expectation to be allowed to remain indefinitely in the country, not the routine renewal of time-limited residence permits. If anything, Isensee argues, this

The relevance the FCC gives to aliens' societal integration for deciding their constitutional protection can also be illustrated through BVerfGE 35, 382 of July 1973. In it, the FCC struck down the expedited execution of a deportation order on two Palestinian students whose active involvement in a Palestinian students' organization (the General Union of Palestinian Students) was seen as grounds for suspicion of collaboration in terrorist actions. The deportation orders took place in the wake of the terrorist attack on Israeli athletes at the 1972 Munich Olympics. Applying the principle of proportionality, the FCC argued that not enough weight had been granted to the damage that the provisional expulsion would cause to the complainants. Both complainants were students of medicine who needed their residence permits to complete their degrees in Germany and one of them was also married to a German citizen. The Court also pondered the difficulty that an expedited expulsion would add to their defence against the deportation measure. Since the students were not accused of having supported terrorist acts in the past, the Court argued, the mere suspicion that they might do so during the time the appeals were pending was not sufficiently important to justify their immediate deportation.

Ever since that decision the proportionality test has played a significant role in the constitutional review of deportation measures and administrative discretion has accordingly been restrained. The Court has stressed that, when exercising its administrative discretion, the executive body has to keep in mind the specific interests of the alien. It has taken such interests to be in direct proportion to the degree of societal integration and has repeatedly relied on criteria such as the period of residence, the consolidation of family ties, and of a professional and/or an educational project to measure the alien's stake in preserving societal membership, and hence, the harm deportation would imply.[64] Against the weight of such individual interests the FCC has measured the importance of the public interest in having aliens leave the country in each case, as well as the possibility of finding less burdensome means to achieve the same purpose. Hence, unlike the US Supreme Court, the FCC has had no problems reviewing the constitutionality of the deportation of settled aliens on both procedural and also substantive grounds, even though the right to reside in Germany is one of those the GBL defines as a citizen right and, what is more important, even though its control implied a clear

last practice should make them aware of their precarious status and of the fact that they should not expect to be allowed to remain permanently (Isensee 1974: 71–2). Note that Isensee's argument ultimately reflects the problems which I argued were intrinsic to the protection of legitimate expectations as a ground for inclusion.

[64] See BVerfGE 35, 382: 404–7; 49, 168: 189; 50, 166: 177; 51, 386: 399–400; 69, 220: 228–9; 76, 1: 68–9.

interference with the government's official position on immigration matters.

In spite of this promising case law, the gap between the strongest version of the equalization thesis I defend and some weaker versions that have been defended by some scholars in Germany, on the one hand, and the official doctrine of the FCC, on the other, still remains quite wide. Thus, with regard to residential status, the Court has never gone as far as those authors who have argued that, eventually, aliens' interests should be considered completely equivalent to those which citizens may have in remaining within the country (Schwerdtfeger 1980: 32). Nor has the FCC embraced the idea that, as time passes, even the possibility of subjecting the right to remain in the country to certain conditions, such as work-related conditions, loses its legitimacy (Rittstieg 1983: 2947; Zuleeg 1973: 368).

As for the citizen freedom to choose a profession (art. 12 GBL), it has also been suggested that with increasing residence and social integration, aliens achieve exactly the same constitutional status as citizens (Franz 1989; Schwerdtfeger 1980: 32). This implies several things. It implies that aliens cannot indefinitely be denied a working permit, have their residence indefinitely made dependent on the continuation of a certain professional relationship (Zuleeg 1973: 368), or be indefinitely prevented from exercising certain professions (Franz 1989: 155), from changing profession, or from doing nothing but salaried employment (Zuleeg 1973: 368). Yet the truth is that many laws that discriminate in the exercise of certain professions have still gone constitutionally unchallenged and apply, to a larger or smaller degree, to long-term resident aliens just as they do to recently arrived aliens. Only German citizens can become civil servants unless there is a compelling public interest supporting the recruitment of aliens. Public notaries and judges have to be German citizens. Aliens' access to the medical professions has also been restrictively regulated and this includes the professions of doctor, dentist, veterinary surgeon and pharmacist. On one occasion the FCC expressly refused the 'equalization' claim.[65] In general, the FCC has not taken a stand on most of these issues. However, to accept the 'equalizing claims' it would have to overrule a long tradition of the lower courts and, in particular, of the highest administrative court, the Federal Administrative Court (*Bundesverwaltungsgericht*). This Court has never admitted a complete equalization or a complete cancellation of the administrative discretion, even though it has recognized that the longer the personal and professional

---

[65] See BVerfGE 78, 179 I: 197.

integration of the aliens at stake, the greater the weight to be given to their interests in developing a certain profession under the proportionality test through which the countervailing public interests are to be measured.[66]

When we enter the political realm things change. They change because, as far as political membership is concerned, not only the FCC but even the strongest defenders of the equalization thesis among the German scholars draw back. Most scholars have opposed the equalization through residence and social integration in this realm (Franz 1989: 155; Schwerdt-feger 1982: 16; Isensee 1974: 91 ff). Only a few have argued that long-term residents should be allowed to have an equal right to vote, at least in municipal elections, given that long-term residence ensures that aliens will be affected in similar ways to citizens. Only occasionally has it been maintained that democratic equality should not depend on the statutory regulation of nationality. Denouncing the artificial split between social and political membership, Zuleeg has argued that it goes against the principle of a social state not to allow those who are affected by the political process to have a voice in it, so as to fight against whatever social disadvantages they may be subject to (Zuleeg 1973: 370). However, in general, as we know, democratic equality has been said to constitute an essential attribute of citizens only, from which aliens, no matter how well integrated, are necessarily excluded. And we know that the FCC has also sanctioned this thesis. Thus, the progressive equalization thesis has, once again, only helped resident aliens consolidate their status as societal members. But it has done so even against Germany's express will, as defined in its ordinary political life where Germany has consistently denied having become an immigration country.

Competing foundations

To the extent to which it has been accepted, we would want to know what exactly the legitimating foundations of the thesis of progressive equaliz-ation have been. All in all, it seems that most crucial has been societal integration in itself, the consolidation of ties and the fact of being increas-ingly bound to develop one's existence in Germany. Neither resident aliens' being permanently subject to the law and, thereby, sharing to-gether with citizens in the sphere of rights and duties, nor the fact of having been more or less expressly accepted with a status of whole or partial membership by the German community, the other two possible justifications that we have consistently explored, has been generally relied

[66] See BVerwGE 36, 45: 48 (1970); BVerwGE 74, 165: 173–4 (1986); BVerwGE 45, 162: 167–8 (1974); BVerwGE 58, 291: 293–4 (1979); BVerwGE 65, 19 (1982).

upon by either the scholars or the FCC.[67] Thus, as we just saw, the Court has generally concentrated on the actual harm that deportation or non-renewal of residence permit decisions could imply for an alien, taking into account the period of residence of the alien in the country, the consolidation of family ties and the possibly negative effects of abandoning the country for the alien's professional life or educational project.[68] Just like the scholars supporting the significant ties model (Schwerdtfeger 1980: 19–20; Zuleeg 1973: 366), the FCC has expressly distinguished between aliens' emotional and cultural ties to their homeland, and their increasing societal integration and actual dependency on Germany as something which generally comes with long-term residence.[69] These scholars have relied on notions similar to those of deep affectedness. Thus, the expression 'community of fate' has been used by them to refer to those who, as permanent residents and not only as citizens, might have become dependent on the possibility of remaining within the country to have a meaningful chance to develop their personalities (Zuleeg 1988: 16). Even if the alien's residence permit is expressly renewed only for limited periods at a time, in the long run, residence will inevitably result in the consolidation of ties in the new environment, whether or not the alien remains emotionally bound to her homeland (Schwerdtfeger 1980: 19–20; Zuleeg 1973: 366). These ties must be taken into account before deciding to terminate the authorization to reside in the country. It is not

[67] Regarding the first, it has generally been assumed that subjection to the law implies protection by the law, but the law itself, in this case, the GBL, provides for an unequal protection of citizens and aliens. By making this classification, it is assumed that the GBL incorporates a judgement which portrays a legitimate commitment to the preservation of the German state as a setting for the full social and political development of German citizens only (Quaritsch 1992: 716–18; Hailbronner 1983: 2112–13). The most common argument is that there is a bond of inescapable dependency which links the citizen to the state (*unentrinnbare Staatsabhängigkeit*) and binds the whole of the citizenry in a common and unavoidable legal fate (*Rechtschicksal der Unentrinnbarkeit*). This does not apply to aliens who can always return to their homeland. And this is what renders the state primarily responsible for its own citizens' well-being (Isensee 1974: 58–9, 79).

As for the consensual or the membership account, it is not surprising that it has not played an essential role in Germany. In Germany, apart from naturalization, there have not been other clear ways to identify the formal acceptance by the community. Having traditionally refused to define itself as a country of immigration, the decision to allow aliens in could not have the same meaning it has had in the United States. In Germany, the common practice has instead been the discretionary extension of temporary residence permits which would only create a 'residence entitlement' after a long period of time. And naturalization in Germany has been treated as an exceptional measure. In the two last decades, guestworker families were actually discouraged from seeking it. It is therefore hard to attach the increase in constitutional protection that comes through residence to the community's willingness to admit aliens into the country and to set them progressively on the route to full membership.

[68] See BVerfGE 35, 382: 404–7; 49, 168: 189; 50, 166: 177; 51, 386: 399–400; 69, 220: 228–9; 76, 1: 68–9.   [69] BVerfGE 76, 1: 55.

legitimate to force the alien to perceive her existence in Germany as a precarious condition indefinitely.

It is far from clear that the FCC would however be willing to extend this approach to grant constitutional relevance to the ties that illegal immigrants can generate through time and residence. Often the FCC has introduced consensualist notions, in the form of preconditions, for the generation of constitutionally relevant ties. For instance, when considering, under the proportionality test, a socially integrated alien's interest in developing her existence in Germany, the Court has taken into account that such an integration and the consolidation of ties that went with it had been the natural result of lawful and unobjectionable residence in the country.[70] Explaining the notion of the central place for the development of one's existence, the Court has also considered that only when aliens had been granted residence permits or were entitled to them could one assume that they had established their life centre in Germany, thereby relegating the alien's subjective intent to second place.[71] Also relevant is the fact that the Court has considered the constitutional position of aliens who are physically present in the country but lack the legal entitlement to be so, to be equivalent to that of aliens outside the country.[72] It is therefore uncertain whether, for constitutional purposes, the degree of societal integration that illegal aliens can achieve through their illegal residence in the country would be considered relevant.

Constitutional constraints on the definition of the national community: inclusion through citizenship

We have explored the possibilities and limitations that have been read out of the GBL concerning the inclusion of resident aliens in the sphere of constitutional equality as aliens. It is time to focus now on the alternative path for inclusion: inclusion through citizenship. Hence, the need to look at the Constitution and at the constitutional debates to find out to what extent Germany's commitment to the legitimation principles of a liberal democratic order are forcing inclusion regardless of Germany's immigration and citizenship policies.

As a country which has systematically refused to define itself as an immigration country with an interest in enlarging its citizenry through immigrants, Germany has consistently held on to restrictive mechanisms of incorporation through naturalization and birthright citizenship. Still in force, the 1913 Nationality Act[73] rules that the acquisition of German citizenship at birth, including that acquired through multiple generations

---

[70] See BVerfGE 49, 168: 185.   [71] See BVerfGE 76, 1 II: 55.   [72] Ibid. 46, 71.
[73] *Reichs- und Staatsangehörigkeitsgesetz* from 22.7.1913 (RGBl., 583).

abroad, follows exclusively the criterion of descent, either from a German father or from a German mother as long as the parents have not lost their German nationality either by express renunciation or by voluntary naturalization abroad.

The 1913 Nationality Act also governs access to citizenship through naturalization, a naturalization which, for most cases, is conceived as an exceptional discretionary act of the state (even when the applicant meets the statutory criteria for it).[74] This has allowed a naturalization practice which is known for its large administrative discretion under vaguely defined legal provisions. As a general rule, these provisions contained only the minimum requirements enabling (though not obliging) the administrative authorities to naturalize. Before the 1990 reform, this large discretion was only limited by a set of federal administrative guidelines which dictated the policy that has been followed from 1977 onwards.[75] The courts in Germany have consistently sanctioned the principle contained in the 1977 Administrative Guidelines, whereby in the exercise of discretion on naturalization Germany's public interests are the only determinant. Nothing like a balancing of individual versus public interests has been required. In deciding on naturalization applications, the

[74] Article 8 of the Nationality Act provides the framework for the general case. It authorizes, but does not recognize, a legal entitlement to the naturalization of aliens who reside within the Federal Republic, have a fixed place of residence and are able to support themselves and their dependents. The condition that they lead an irreproachable way of life was replaced in 1993 by a reference to particular grounds of deportation. See Hailbronner and Renner, 1991, 8 RuStAG, 167, Rdnr. 13 ff.

[75] The 1977 Federal Administrative Guidelines start off by recognizing that the personal and economic interests of the applicant are not sufficient to justify naturalization unless it is also supported by public interests (Guideline 2.2). They also assert that the Federal Republic is not a country of immigration and thus does not seek to increase the number of German citizens through naturalization (ibid. 2.3). Other criteria for discretionary naturalization are the fact that the individual has to prove a voluntary and lasting orientation to Germany (ibid. 3.1.1); oral and written mastery of German (ibid. 3.1.1); knowledge of the form of government and loyalty to the free democratic order (ibid. 3.1.2); and adaptation to living conditions in Germany, which is generally presumed after ten years of residence in the country (ibid. 3.2.1), with the exception of children who may naturalize simultaneously regardless of length of residence and a spouse who may be naturalized simultaneously on the basis of five years' residence (ibid. 3.2.2.4; 3.2.2.5). Political activity regarding homeland affairs is taken as a sign against the required orientation to Germany (ibid. 3.1.1) and the years spent living in special housing for foreigners do not count as contributing to the integration into German living conditions (ibid. 3.2.1). Naturalization should also be denied if it can offend against foreign policy goals, including the avoidance of a brain drain from developing countries (ibid. 5.1; 5.2). Multiple citizenship is particularly undesirable and, in order to preserve the unity of nationality within the family, naturalization is not advised when some close family members of the applicant retain their foreign nationality (ibid. 4.1; 4.3). Finally, it is also required that naturalization applicants achieve legally effective release from their prior nationality (ibid. 5.3.1). The guidelines have been reprinted in Hailbronner and Renner 1991: 624.

authorities were to ponder whether, due to their personal assets, naturalization applicants could be a worthy contribution to the population or whether other general political, economic and cultural considerations spoke for naturalization. In principle, there was no acknowledged interest in increasing the size of the population. Thus, naturalization had to be conceived as an exceptional and individualized measure.[76]

In 1990, the 1965 Aliens Act was finally reformed and a further naturalization reform was negotiated as part of the so-called Asylum Reform Compromise of December 1992, introducing 'as-of-right' naturalization in the strict sense.[77] Since then, naturalization has lost its discretionary nature for certain categories. In spite of this, naturalization is still very demanding in terms of the period of residence required as a condition, as well as of other naturalization criteria, such as the divestiture of prior nationality. This may explain why, in spite of the reforms undertaken, naturalization rates have not yet increased as much as they were expected to.[78] In 1990 German reunification finally satisfied the Federal Republic's

---

[76] See BVerwGE 4, 298: 300; BVerwGE 7, 237: 238; BVerwGE 49, 44: 46; BVerwGE 64, 7: 9; BVerwGE 67, 177: 179.

[77] Focusing on the guestworker generation, the 1990 Aliens Act foresees that aliens who have resided lawfully in the Federal Republic for fifteen years can apply for naturalization under relaxed criteria and it severely limits the official discretion to deny naturalization (see § 86 in the 1990 version of the Aliens Act). Naturalization in this case can only be denied due to exceptional circumstances of the particular case. The eligibility criteria include renouncing prior nationality, being free of criminal convictions and being able to support oneself and one's family without relying on welfare or unemployment benefits, unless the inability results from reasons for which the alien cannot be held responsible (see § 86 (1; 1, 2, 3) in the 1990 version of the Aliens Act).

As for the later generations, a rule has been created giving aliens the opportunity to apply for naturalization under relaxed criteria upon reaching maturity. Among the eligibility requirements, the alien applicant must be between sixteen and twenty-three years old, give up her prior nationality, have been lawfully residing in Germany for eight years, of which at least six should have been spent attending school (four of these years have to be in general education) and be free of criminal convictions. Also the new law lowered the previously extremely high costs of naturalization to a symbolic sum and granted exceptions to the previously strict prohibition of double citizenship.

After the Asylum Reform Compromise, § 86 of the new Aliens Act, which had not initially been conceived as a permanent rule for later generation immigrants but only as a transitional rule for first-generation immigrants who had to apply before December 1995, was changed into a permanent provision relaxing naturalization rules after fifteen years of residence for aliens who arrived in Germany before 1980. Also, the remaining discretion to deny naturalization was eliminated from both § 85 and § 86 (Renner 1993b: 127)

[78] The debate on the reasons accounting for low naturalization rates in Germany remains quite controversial. There is almost general agreement that the main deterrent is the obligation to give up the previous citizenship, something which appears to be linked to a set of both practical and psychological disadvantages for aliens. Among the practical disadvantages are the difficulty of entering or returning to the country of origin, to acquire or sell property and to inherit in their home countries (see Wollenschläger and Schraml 1994: 228). Psychologically damaging may be the loss of national identity which may result from renunciation (see Zuleeg 1987: 186), especially if one takes into account that, in a society that is not very welcoming to immigrants, these are likely to preserve a strong

claim to be a single German state with a single German citizenry. One would have expected that, after that, the interest in preserving the old 1913 Nationality Act as the basis for a common citizenship among West and East Germans would finally cease, allowing for the long-awaited global revision of nationality regulation (Renner 1993a: 25). The violent actions against immigrants in 1992 and the Asylum Reform Compromise which was achieved in the same year between the different political forces highlighted the need to make advances in the incorporation of resident aliens into the national citizenry (Blumenwitz 1993: 155).[79]

Since 1993 the political forces have been discussing the possibility of further facilitating the access to German citizenship, mainly in two ways. Neither of them is as ambitious as the claim to automatic membership but both would imply advancing towards a more inclusive citizenry. The first was to allow applicants to retain their prior nationality and the second, to include some *ius soli* elements in the definition of birthright citizenship, so as to facilitate the incorporation of second or third generations. Thus far, these attempts have failed. Nevertheless, the issue of nationality in Germany remains a relevant political issue (Bryde 1989: 258). As a matter of fact, Germany's Social Democrat–Green coalition government which resulted from the September 1998 elections has announced that it will undertake the long-awaited reform.[80] But is it all a question of democratic self-definition that needs to be decided through the ordinary political process? Is it all a matter of deciding which are Germany's interests on the subject? Are there any fundamental commitments in the GBL which set constitutional constraints in this respect and allow our normative discussion a say in constitutional interpretation? Do they encourage or discourage the inclusion of resident aliens through citizenship?

sense of national identity binding them to their home societies as an essential element for their self-esteem.

Other authors have relied on the thesis of the overall devaluation of citizenship (Karpen 1989: 1017; Quaritsch 1983: 14) and some others have claimed that low naturalization rates are no mystery given the fact that immigrants have not generally come to Germany in search of a new home, their ties to the country of origin and to their co-nationals in Germany proving sufficient to satisfy their need for a homeland (Quaritsch 1989: 743–4).

Note that this may be undergoing a process of change. It has been noticed that the naturalization rate of Turks has almost tripled between 1993 and 1995 (Joppke 1999b) and recent surveys have found a great increase in the intention of Turks to naturalize.

[79] See *Asylkompromiss Gesetz* from June 28, 1993, BGBl. IS. 1002.
[80] As of March 1999 it seems that the most likely reform of Germany's citizenship law will consist of an 'option model' that would come into force starting on January 2000 and would allow persons born in Germany of foreign long-term residents to gain German citizenship at birth and ask them to choose to become exclusively Germans or lose their German nationality by the age of 23 unless the person has serious difficulties in releasing herself from her prior citizenship. The reform also contemplates a reduction of the minimum time required for naturalization from fifteen to eight years. However, unless they have lived in Germany more than thirty years, aliens taking up naturalization would still be required to renounce their previous citizenship.

Nowhere in the GBL is there a functional definition of citizenship or, unlike in the US Constitution, any specification of the general criteria by which this status is acquired. The GBL basically makes the federal legislator responsible for fleshing out the concept of citizenship. And it is generally admitted that this applies both for citizenship at birth and through naturalization.[81] That aliens may have a subjective claim to be admitted as citizens as a result of the GBL has almost unanimously been denied.[82] In the absence of more specific constitutional provisions, one might have expected the constitutional pillars of the liberal democratic order (art. 1's human dignity clause, art. 2's general freedom clause or art. 3's equality principle) to work as supplementary mechanisms to support, at least to some extent, the claims of aliens seeking inclusion through citizenship, as we know they have done in other instances. But this has not been the case, and not even the most progressive commentators have seriously explored this path.[83] Sanctioning the split between societal and political membership, the thesis of aliens' strengthened fundamental rights position through increasing residence has been said to apply to the residential domain and not to aliens' claims to naturalization as the door to political membership (Stein 1984b: 183; Schwerdtfeger 1980: 126).

[81] See arts. 73.2 and 116 GBL.

[82] Maybe the only exception to this would be, according to art. 116.2 GBL, former Germans and their descendants who, between 30 January 1933 and 8 May 1945, were deprived of their nationality on political, racial or religious grounds. As for former East Germans their case was somewhat different. The GBL had not granted them a right to acquire German citizenship. Rather, the FCC had interpreted that, as constitutionally sanctioned (arts. 16 and 116 GBL), German citizenship referred to the whole of Germany and not only to the Federal Republic citizenship (see BVerfGE 36, 1). This applied not only to those who were Germans at the time the GBL was enacted, but also to those who were recognized as Germans by the DDR authorities thereafter (see BVerfGE 77, 137 (21.10.1987)). There is finally the category of Status-Germans or *Volkszugehörige* contemplated in art. 116.1 GBL, which refers to those who 'have been admitted to the territory of the German *Reich* within the frontiers of 31 December 1937 as a refugee or expellee of German stock or as a spouse or descendant thereof'. Although they are 'Germans' within the meaning of the GBL, this does not mean that they are automatically ascribed German nationality in the strict sense. Rather, they have a statutory claim to acquire it upon request.

[83] Art. 1's right to human dignity has only rarely been brought up in the discussion, and when it has, only in extremely vague terms. The Federal Administrative Court has explicitly rejected the thesis that the practice of not weighing the individual interests of the applicant against the public interests at stake necessarily implied that the person was being treated as a mere object and thus, having her human dignity violated (see BVerwG, Bay VBl. 1980, 727 = InfAuslR 1980, 311 and BVerwG, decision from 11.10.1985 -1B 102.85-= DVBl. January, 1986, 111). More often, one finds art. 2's general freedom clause in the debate (Rittstieg 1980: 312; Zuleeg 1974: 344). However, its negative freedom nature is usually brought up to deny its usefulness to ground aliens' subjective claim to naturalization (Von Mangoldt 1987: 660).
    Art. 3's equality principle has been almost as fruitless. Just as the right to equality was judged inadequate to support the claim of an equal status of rights outside the framework of citizenship (e.g. through the equal recognition of voting rights), it has also been generally regarded as insufficient to ground a claim to incorporation through naturalization or through facilitated naturalization (Ziemske 1994: 229; Uhlitz 1986: 149).

Here again, the underlying assumption has been the alleged difference between someone's personal equality as an individual and someone's political equality, as a member of a political community.

We have therefore that the GBL makes the federal legislator competent to rule on the conditions for access and loss of nationality and that individuals cannot derive right claims on the field from the GBL. However, this does not mean that there are no constitutional limits on the laws ruling on citizenship. In fact, as early as 1974 the FCC left no doubts on both the need for the regulation of citizenship to comply with constitutional constraints and the FCC's own power to review the constitutional validity of the pertinent laws.[84] At stake in the 1974 decision was the gender equality guarantee of art. 3.2 GBL which the FCC thought was violated by the 1913 Nationality Act whereby the legitimate child of a German father and a foreign mother was granted German citizenship, but not the legitimate child of a German mother and a foreign father, who was granted German citizenship only if the child would otherwise become a stateless person.[85] Thus, reluctant to derive individual claims to nationality directly from the GBL's list of fundamental rights, the FCC has nevertheless admitted that such fundamental rights embody a system of objective values useful to guide the legislator and the administrative authorities in their exercise of discretion. Applied to naturalization, this has implied that although naturalization policies have been said to respond to the public interest almost exclusively, respect for fundamental rights and for the system of constitutional values has been interpreted as part of the public interest and has accordingly set some constraints on the administrative discretion in the field (Deibel 1984: 322). So, for instance, under art. 6's right to the protection of marriage and family, the convenience of preserving a unitary treatment of the family as far as the national-

---

[84] BVerfGE 37, 217 (21.4.1974).

[85] In the passage which is most relevant for our purposes the FCC sanctioned the need to set limits on the legislator in the definition of the citizenry, limits which are related to the constitutionally sanctioned democratic order. Literally: 'the thesis, dominant at one time and in part, still currently relevant, whereby the recognition of nationality is an act to define the people of the state taking into account political order considerations which the state can make at its discretion, with no more limits than those of not acting arbitrarily, does not accord to the democratic and social *Rechtsstaat* portrayed in the German Basic Law . . . Rather [the state the GBL refers to] is characterized by the fact that in it all state authority flows from the people (art. 20.2 GBL) so that the will formation process goes from the people to the state, rather than from the state to the people . . . The claim that the decision on the acquisition of such a significant status [the German nationality] could depend on the free will of the state organs is thus unacceptable. The establishment of a systematized regulation on the matter would not be sufficient either. Rather, this regulation would also have to comply with the fundamental decisions [and system of values, it adds later] of the Basic Law, as they have found expression mainly in the constitutional rights' (ibid. 239–40).

ity of its members is concerned has been taken to embody a public interest, and art. 3's equality clause has been the basis of the principle whereby, unless some special circumstances arise, the administrative authorities are bound by their own consolidated practice. This is how fundamental rights have indirectly gained a certain recognition in the resolution of naturalization applications and the constitutional design of constrained powers has been saved.

Nevertheless, since what is at stake here is the shaping of the political community it can hardly be a surprise that much of the juristic debate on the regulation of citizenship, which the mentioned reform proposals have triggered, has not started out from the individual, their constitutional rights and their role in a liberal democracy, but rather focused on the community, the state, as a point of departure. So, as in the debate on the political status of aliens, the central question has been with regard to the kind of political community that is shown by a systematic reading of the GBL. For one thing, the state form of the Federal Republic appears as a constitutional presupposition. The GBL refers to what have been considered the three classical elements of the state under public international law (territory, organized structure of government and citizenry)[86] and makes references to Germany as being integrated into the international community of sovereign states.[87] Subject to more dispute has been whether the acceptance of the preconstitutionally existing state order implies also a constitutional entrenchment of the historical form of the nation-state. The constitutional validity of advancing towards more inclusive definitions of the national citizenry has been said to depend partly on this factor.

It is therefore not surprising that the political debate around the possibility of including *ius soli* and dispensing with the renunciation of prior nationality as a naturalization requirement, has been accompanied by a constitutional discussion. From a constitutional perspective, most scholars have simply qualified these reforms as options falling within the sphere of legislative discretion: as one possible and legitimate outcome of the community's right to self-definition. A few have actually advocated these reforms as required by a systematic reading of the constitutional principles and values, thus perceiving them as limits to the community's right of self-definition to satisfy Germany's required degree of inclusiveness as a liberal democracy. Finally, some opponents have claimed that the reform proposals fall outside the constitutionally permitted range of

---

[86] See old art. 23 GBL and new Preamble after the constitutional reform following German reunification; arts. 20.1, 116 and 73.2 GBL. Also presupposing citizenship see arts. 16.1, 73.2, 74.4, 74.8 and 19.3 GBL.
[87] See the Preamble, first sentence; arts. 9.2, 22, 24, 25, 26, 32, 59 GBL; and section Xa.

options, thereby setting limits to self-definition in the name of the constitutionally required limits to inclusion. Common to most opponents has been the alleged constitutional unacceptability of the proliferation of cases of dual or multiple citizenship which both proposals would inevitably bring about.

The FCC has not taken an interest in the discussion as the pertinent statutes have not yet been approved. Given that it has foreclosed the principle of full inclusion through its rejection of the possibility of disentangling voting rights from citizenship, it is of utmost importance to the claim to inclusion that it does not also preclude the subsidiary path by adhering to the thesis whereby what is constitutionally sanctioned is an ethnically and/or culturally burdened notion of nation-state, a notion which requires that the German citizenry remains as restrictively defined as it has traditionally been.

A 'nationalistic citizenship' constitutionally sanctioned?

It is widely acknowledged that, with its emphasis on cultural, linguistic and even ethnic components, nationalism played an essential role in the very definition of the German polity at the beginning of the nineteenth century, contributing most significantly to the later creation of the German state (Hailbronner 1989: 73–4; Quaritsch 1983: 7). Those who defend the constitutional sanctioning of the German national state have also defended a theory of citizenship whereby citizenship implies not only a formal legal relationship binding the individual to one of the states in the international order. Rather, the nationalistic or 'völkish' conception of citizenship advocates that citizenship presupposes membership of the German people, and presents peoplehood as resting on both subjective socio-psychological and objective organic elements which can be observed empirically and which ensure the spiritual unity of the state and a certain homogeneity of its people (Bleckmann 1990: 1399). Among the subjective manifestations of peoplehood there are references to a sense of social cohesion, solidarity, shared destiny and collective self-identity which result in and deserve loyalty (Weiler 1995: 8–9). These subjective manifestations are supported on at least some of the following objective elements: common language (Kirchhof 1987: 745), common history, common cultural habits, common ethnic origin and/or common religion (Isensee 1993: 122).

Nation-states, it is claimed, are an international reality as the revolutions of 1989 and 1990 in Germany and Eastern Europe prove. The atrocities of national socialism against which the GBL has strongly reacted do not discredit the scheme of the nation-state in itself but only the ideological regime it embodied at that time (Quaritsch 1992: 718–19). Admittedly, today's nation-states are not based on the idea of completely independent sovereign states which reigned before the world wars. However, the structural features remain. Among them, most importantly, is the recognition of the relevance of nationality as a legal status which helps to draw an essential distinction between national citizens and aliens. Central to this approach are the concerns about homogeneity and loyalty that I analysed in chapters 3 and 4. Generally, these concerns are brought up with no support from empirical evidence and generally no attempt is made to distinguish among the class of aliens those who, as permanent residents or as second or third generations, might have more in common with resident Germans than with non-resident nationals of their countries of nationality.

Two decisions of the FCC have been sometimes brought into the discussion as supporting the described political theory. The first is the 1989 alien suffrage decision that I analysed above (see pp. 203–206). Some people have read this decision as sanctioning the nexus between the demos, in an ethno-cultural sense, and democracy (Weiler 1995: 13). If only German people can democratically legitimate the political process it must be because only Germans can be trusted to be loyal to the interests of the German people which representatives are supposed to serve (Bleckmann 1988: 439–41). But this reading of the decision is not conclusive. We saw that the decision can be and has been interpreted in several different ways. Together with this nationalistic reading, it could be seen as sanctioning only Germany's state form and encouraging the federal legislator to facilitate the incorporation of resident aliens to the state community through a facilitation of naturalization which actually 'denationalizes' the concept of German citizenship and opens it up to the pluralism of the country's current population (see also Joppke 1999a: 19). Ultimately, the decision only says that, if resident aliens want to vote, they have to naturalize first. What the requirement of prior naturalization really stands for depends on what naturalization is taken to express and inevitably leads to two different readings of the alien suffrage decision. Only for those for whom belonging to the state community implies a prior integration within the national and cultural community, naturalization implies the dedication of the 'newcomers' to Germany and their complete cultural identification with it, more than just the formal and legal inclusion within the citizenry. It is therefore not surprising that among those who have argued that naturalization is the only path for aliens to achieve the full equality of rights, some have argued for making naturalization requirements and procedures less demanding (Karpen 1989: 1018; Birkenheier 1976: 96) while others have defended restrictive and highly selective naturalization practices (Bleckmann 1990: 1399; Quaritsch 1988: 481).

The other decision is the 1993 Maastricht decision which reviewed the constitutional validity of the German law passed to ratify the Maastricht Treaty approved in 1992 in the framework of the European Union building process.[88] Essential to the resolution of the complaint was the question of whether Europe could serve as an adequate locus for democratic deliberation and decision making or whether the process of democratic legitimation had to remain strictly linked to a national framework. According to the Maastricht decision, as it stands now, the European Union's authority derives mainly from the national parliaments. Presumably, as the development of the European Union progresses, democratic legitimation flowing directly through the European Parliament will become increasingly important. However, to achieve this, besides an institutional adaptation, a certain set of extra-legal conditions for democracy should be fulfilled. And these, the Court thought, were still lacking at a European level. Among them, the FCC included a common European public opinion, the transparency of the political aims of the Union and the opportunity for every citizen of the Union to communicate in her native tongue with any public authority to which she is subject. Until these conditions are given, the Court argued, it is important that the national parliament retains 'sufficiently rich spheres of competence for the state people to develop and articulate itself through a legitimate political process of will formation which allows for the legal expression of what is relatively homogeneous in the sense of spiritually, socially and politically linked'.[89]

This last reference quoted the German liberal scholar Herman Heller[90] and has been taken to endorse a 'völkish' conception of the political community which makes social homogeneity a prerequisite for a democracy and reproduces it at a European level (Weiler 1995: 35; Bryde 1994: 321). The Court has been accused of demagogically quoting a Jewish liberal author to sanction a thesis which fits much better the doctrine of far more conservative constitutional scholars (Weiler 1995: 5). However, once again, I think that the decision does not conclusively establish an objectionable conception of the demos. To a great extent the FCC seemed to be concerned with the necessary conditions for the practical functioning of liberal democratic institutions and with the guarantees of minimally effective political equality. Whether or not we think the FCC was right when judging the degree of social and political development of the Union, I think that the concerns the Court raised are legitimate concerns in a liberal democracy. A different issue is whether such con-

---

[88] BVerfGE 89, 155 (12.10.1993).   [89] Ibid. 184–6.
[90] In *Politische Demokratie und soziale Homogenität*, Gesammelte Schriften, 2 Band, 1971, 427 ff.

cerns might also be justified when applied to resident aliens or to second or third generations, and whether, in general, they necessarily require exclusion.

Those authors who have defended the constitutional sanctioning of a nationalistic conception of citizenship based on a common German culture, language, history or even ethnic background have called upon some specific constitutional provisions to strengthen their thesis. Among these are the provisions which constitutionalize national symbols, such as the national flag (Frank 1990: 295). Most quoted has also been the old Preamble's commitment to the preservation of the German state and national unity, as the main constitutional basis for the now achieved reunification of the country (ibid.; Bleckmann 1988: 440–1; Uhlitz 1986: 145–6). Although in the relevant decisions the FCC insisted on the idea of reunification of the *German state* rather than of the *German nation*,[91] it has been argued that the very idea of a German reunification presupposed a German people, or a German nation, for the sake of which the new state order had to be achieved (Bleckmann 1988: 440; Uhlitz 1986: 145–6). The ascription of the condition of 'Germans' to the so-called Status-Germans (*Volkszugehörige*) as refugees or expellees of German stock and their descendants, has also been regarded as a relic of a nationalist past (Neuman 1992: 291; Hailbronner 1989: 73–4), and sometimes, more specifically, as a sanction of the *ius sanguinis* rule of citizenship.[92] Some authors take it as still endorsing, today, this nationalistic conception of citizenship (Blumenwitz 1993: 153; Uhlitz 1986: 145–6). This is reinforced when the legal definition of *Volkszugehörige* (which makes reference to those united by a common descent, language and culture) is read into the Constitution.

Clearly, not everyone agrees with deriving such a nationalistic concep-

[91] See BVerfGE 36, 1: 17, 25 (31.7.1973). In the decision, the FCC maintained the thesis of West and East Germany as two parts of a continuing state, descendant of the old German Empire, lacking, however, the political structure required to act internally and internationally as a single state (ibid. 16 f., 23). The decision defended a common German citizenship for both West and East Germans. The lack of a common German state in the full sense at the time has induced some people to think about a 'German people' or 'nation' as a necessary substratum of that common citizenship.

[92] See art. 116.1 GBL. Several arguments are put forward to justify the view that the Status-Germans provision endorses the *ius sanguinis* rule of citizenship. For one thing, descent is included among the statutory signs which define their belonging to the people of German stock. Also, the constitutional provision refers to the people of German stock *and to their descendants* (Ziemske 1994: 229). However, strictly speaking Status-Germans are entitled only to a statutory right to naturalization upon request, a right which has been statutorily restricted since 1990.

Similar conclusions have been derived from art. 116.2. GBL., since the right to the reacquisition of German nationality contained in this provision applies also to the descendants of the expatriates during the national socialist regime (Von Mangoldt 1994: 39).

tion of citizenship from the GBL. Some authors have recalled the fact that the GBL is precisely a reaction against the excesses to which an ethnically burdened conception of citizenship led under the Nazi regime. Only as this kind of reaction can one read the GBL's effort to reverse the expatriation of those Germans who during such a regime had been deprived of their citizenship due to political, racial or religious reasons. For this scholarly sector the constitutional provisions referring to Status-Germans and to the expatriated, as well as to the commitment to German reunification, must be contemplated as directly linked to the postwar situation, and hence, as purely transitory in nature (Birkenheier 1976: 28). These commentators justify the special status for Status-Germans in relation to their persecution in a number of Eastern European states after 1945 and the responsibility of the German state for their fate, as for other direct and indirect consequences of the Nazi regime.[93] The GBL's commitment to a liberal and pluralistic democracy with universalist vocation, they claim, needs to be held against the temptation of imposing a concept of national homogeneity on a heterogeneous social reality (Oberndörfer 1989: 8–9). In the GBL, cultural freedom, as well as freedom of belief, of conscience and of religious practice have been safeguarded, and discrimination on the basis of race, language and origin has been expressly forbidden (Frank 1990: 294; Oberndörfer 1989: 12). Also, the patterns of the truly German culture are difficult to define. Cultures are continuously changing and, today more than ever, necessarily subject to myriad external influences (ibid.). As far as the regulation of citizenship is concerned, it is highlighted that the Basic Law has entitled the legislator to rule freely on the acquisition of citizenship and has avoided imposing any nationalistic requirements. Although the Constituent Assembly saw no need to define citizenship in a more precise way, one cannot conclude that it thereby intended to entrench the statutory *ius sanguinis*-based system existing in 1949 and still in force as *the* constitutional option (Birkenheier 1976: 27;

---

[93] This would explain why, as their states are becoming fully democratic, the special rights of Status-Germans are expiring and also why some non-German victims of the Nazi regime have also been granted special admission, such as Russian Jews. Indeed, successive legislations have chipped away the priority status of ethnic Germans. The Integration Adjustment Law of 1989 reduced the social benefits granted thus far to them. The Resettler Reception Law of 1990 forced would-be resettlers to file their applications from abroad (Joppke 1999a: 96). Finally the Law on Removing the Consequences of the War of 1993 reversed the burden of proof, determining that the existence of expulsion pressure (i.e. the repression endured for one's Germanness) would no longer be automatically assumed. Except for ethnic Germans from the former Soviet Union, it would no longer be the task of the government to disprove that an applicant had suffered from expulsion-type repression. Rather, the applicant would have to credibly demonstrate the existence of such a repression. Also, this statute set the date of its coming into force (January 1993) as a limit for applying for the status of *Aussiedler*. Finally, the law imposed an annual quota (see Alexy 1993: 1171; Gaa-Unterpaul 1993: 2080).

Isensee 1974: 59, n. 22). Ultimately, the express constitutional commitments to international cooperation, to the achievement of worldwide
peace and to the strengthening of the European integration process must
be interpreted as commitments to a form of open statehood which is
contrary to organicist conceptions of German nationhood (Frank 1990:
297; Zuleeg 1987: 158).

Probably the most convincing hypothesis is that, as a result of Germany's history, its Constitution was born with a structural tension – a
tension between 'creedal postnationalism' and a 'perpetuated ethno-
cultural nationhood' (Joppke 1999a: 188). With the Nazi experience in
mind, the former took the shape of a commitment to the ideal of an open
republic based on universal human rights and friendly to newcomers. The
commitment to reunification and the construct of an 'all-German' citizenship embracing also all ethnic Germans who were then living under
communism embody the latter (Hailbronner 1989: 73). Whether or not
one accepts the premise that 'nationalistic citizenship' was indirectly
sanctioned, it seems that with the breakdown of communism and national reunification there is not even an indirect constitutional sanctioning of
it. With unity completed in 1990 and the ethnic diaspora problem now
obsolete, Germany is no longer an incomplete nation-state. With the
accomplishment of reunification the idea of a 'pre-political' German
people appears to have served its primary function, namely, supporting
West Germany's claim to reunification and facing its responsibility for the
consequences of its Nazi regime. 'No more unity mandate or homeland
responsibilites . . . For the first time since the end of the war, Germans are
free to rethink the meaning of membership in [their] nation-state'
(Joppke 1999a: 200).

Naturalization and nationality reform debates

Not surprisingly, a specific constitutional debate has arisen around the
proposals for the reform of the naturalization and nationality laws, between those who read the GBL as sanctioning a historically formed
nationalistic conception of citizenship, and those who see the Constitution primarily as establishing the framework for the legitimate exercise of
power in a liberal pluralistic democracy. The former have opposed the
inclusive tendencies of the reform proposals, as possibly undermining
both the ethno-cultural basis of the community and the feeling of exclusive loyalty and commitment to the country by the citizenry. The latter
have argued for inclusion as the proper way to overcome the democratic
legitimacy gap posed by Germany's new social reality, especially now that
the FCC has expressly foreclosed the path of full equality of rights for

long-term resident aliens. This debate shows the relevance of the normative assumptions from which one starts on constitutional interpretation.

Those defending the constitutional sanction of the national state have
strongly opposed the introduction of *ius soli* elements to complement the
traditional *ius sanguinis* nationality rules. Germany is not an immigration
country seeking to increase its population with new immigrants, they
claim, and this is connected to the constitutional sanction of the national
state (Uhlitz 1986: 148). Introducing *ius soli* would end up weakening the
ethnic, cultural and spiritual homogeneity which the transmission of
nationality through descent is said to ensure (Von Mangoldt 1994: 40–1;
Ziemske 1993: 334; Bleckmann 1990: 1399). If access to citizenship was
facilitated in an increasingly mobile society without ensuring first certain
assimilation or integration guarantees the polity would run the risk of
becoming a 'community of chance' (Uhlitz 1986).

Nevertheless the fact is that *ius soli* is nowhere constitutionally forbidden (Wollenschläger and Schraml 1994: 226; Hailbronner 1992: 37, 39).
As we said, the Basic Law does not specify any of the requirements for
gaining or losing nationality. The question is whether some element of *ius
soli* is now constitutionally required, given Germany's changed composition (Zünkler and Findeisen 1991: 252). Some commentators have
criticized the currently existing *ius sanguinis* citizenship rules as ethnically
burdened (Bryde 1994: 313; Habermas 1992: 144–5) and hence, of far
more dubious constitutional validity than would be those inspired by the
principle of *ius soli* (Hailbronner 1992: 37; Oberndörfer 1989: 11). *Ius soli*
would imply the automatic inclusion at birth and thus, the end of the
phenomenon of second- and third-generation immigrants. And this cannot possibly lead to anything like a 'community of opportunism'. If
anything, the reform would ensure the connection of the new members to
Germany. It is far more questionable that descent rules can by themselves
indefinitely do the same (Wollenschläger and Schraml 1994: 228). Recognizing the difficulty of separating the socioeconomic from the political
spheres of membership some authors have argued that the protection of
the economic interests of the German elite actually offers a much more
realistic explanation for the exclusion of long-term resident aliens from
nationality (Rittstieg 1991: 1397). After all, this allows for their more
precarious residential status as well as for their reduced status of social
benefits and political rights.[94]

---

[94] It is not clear which position the FCC would take on the matter. In spite of its long
tradition in German law, the FCC has not yet taken a clear stand on the constitutional
ranking of the *ius sanguinis* principle. Only in passing, in an *obiter dictum*, the FCC once
sanctioned *ius sanguinis* as a valid criterion for ascribing nationality. As a justification, the
Court stated only that the principle of descent ensures the individual attachment to the
German people and to Germany's legal order and culture and hence, to the German state

Very much criticized has also been the alternative path for increasing the level of incorporation: facilitating naturalization by allowing for the retention of prior nationality. The objections here generally start from the assumption, which I have questioned from a normative point of view, according to which naturalization, far from implying the simple acceptance of the civic obligations of citizenship, requires the profession of undivided loyalty to Germany as well as the embracing of German national identity understood in a deep cultural sense: a true cultural assimilation and the obliteration of other loyalties and identifications (Quaritsch 1983: 14–15). Divestiture of prior nationality becomes thus the proof of full identification with the German community and of renunciation to prior cultural and national identities (Uhlitz 1986: 150).

Among the more concrete objections against giving up the divestiture requirement, the one which has deserved most attention has been that springing from the undesirable, yet inevitable, fact that this modification would result in a multiplication of the cases of dual or multiple nationality. Understandably, this objection has also been made against the incorporation of *ius soli* elements for this too would result in the proliferation of cases of multiple citizenship (Von Mangoldt 1994: 41; Ziemske 1994: 231). Apart from the manifold practical inconveniences which are said to come with multiple nationality, its rejection has been connected to possible conflicts of loyalty of doubtful validity and democratic relevance. If people are not willing to give up their prior nationality, the argument goes, it is presumably because they have preserved strong and effective ties to their countries (Von Mangoldt 1994: 41) and thus, are not in the position to offer a guarantee of full loyalty and permanent dedication to Germany (Hailbronner 1992: 14; Zünkler and Findeisen 1991: 253; Karpen 1989: 1018). Pointing to fairness-related concerns, it has also been argued that multiple citizenship would introduce disruptive elements in the state order, especially when nationality is understood as a package of rights and duties. It would generate a situation in which some nationals, but not others, are inextricably bound to the national community (Ziemske 1994: 231; Quaritsch 1983: 12), and some nationals (dual or

(BVerfGE 37, 252 (1974)). Moreover, being a part of the close relations between parents and children, the attachment to a common state community contributed to strengthen the cohesiveness of the family (ibid. 246). The Court briefly questioned whether it would be valid to completely replace the *ius sanguinis*-based system with another system which was exclusively based on *ius soli* (ibid. 248–9). Yet at the same time the decision was based on the assumption of the usual case, namely, that in which the citizen ordinarily resides in her own country. Thus, the Court stressed that the value of citizenship lies in its function of linking the individual to the legal system with which she is most familiar, since 'citizenship expresses a lasting personal connection with the state' (ibid. 243). Presumably, familiarity and connection are more likely for second- and third-generation immigrants, than for Germans who have been living abroad for generations.

multiple nationals) are privileged, enjoying greater personal and professional freedom, greater geographic mobility, a double set of political rights, and, eventually, a more limited set of obligations or, at least, the possibility of evading their political responsibility or their obligations by leaving the country (Ziemske 1994: 230–1; Löwer 1993: 157–8; Uhlitz 1986: 150).

Central to the argumentation of reform opponents has been the 1974 decision on gender discrimination and birthright citizenship that we discussed before.[95] In this decision the Court sanctioned in passing the so-called *Übeldoktrin* describing multiple nationality as an 'evil' (Blumenwitz 1993: 154; Ziemske 1993: 336). According to the *Übeldoktrin* multiple or dual nationality has to be regarded, both domestically and internationally, as an evil to be avoided in the interests both of the state and of the affected individuals. The state seeks the exclusivity of its nationality to be sure about the reach of its personal jurisdiction and about the exclusive loyalty of those who, eventually, might be asked to die for it. The state also has an interest in avoiding conflicts with other states, conflicts which can derive from imposing duties (e.g. military duty) and making exertions on behalf of its citizens (e.g. diplomatic protection) without taking into account the other nationality ties they may have. Some of the problems would also affect third states which would not know to which country's administrative and judicial authorities' claims they should give priority. Finally, avoiding subjection to multiple duties (e.g. military duty) and avoiding loyalty conflicts would also be to the advantage of the affected citizens. Given all of this, the general argument goes, not even the concern with democratic legitimation is sufficient to justify the multiplication of cases of dual citizenship (Ziemske 1994: 230; Uhlitz 1986: 149).

Reform proponents have strongly refuted these objections. Their counterarguments will sound familiar to the reader who has followed our normative discussion. The constitutionally sanctioned liberal order, the claim goes, requires no cultural homogeneity whatsoever, democratic pluralism being one of its essential pillars (Bryde 1994: 310–11, 322; Oberndörfer 1989: 12). Stressing the connection between cultural identity, individual self-esteem and human dignity (Rittstieg 1991: 1388; Zünkler and Findeisen 1991: 253), it has been argued that the expectation of citizens' full commitment, identification and undivided loyalty to the state rests on absolutist and obsolete notions about the state, or as some people have put it, on feudal notions anchored in nineteenth-century political thought which have not been constitutionally sanctioned (Rittstieg 1991: 1385–8; Zünkler and Findeisen 1991: 253). After all, nowhere

---

[95] BVerfGE 37, 217 (21.4.1974).

does the GBL refer to the duty of loyalty as such (Hailbronner 1992: 36; Zünkler and Findeisen 1991: 253) or to the need for aliens to give up their prior nationality before they can gain the German one (Renner 1993a; Hailbronner 1992: 17). Newly naturalized aliens retain, along with their old nationality, the possibility of returning to their home countries. And this may be essential for them if xenophobic outbursts against them do not cease in Germany (Rittstieg 1991: 1386).

As for multiple nationality, it has been noticed that the toleration of dual nationality is already widespread in Germany, and this is only likely to increase (Von Mangoldt 1993a; Renner 1993: 23; Hailbronner 1992: 17). In fact, it is increasingly common in the whole of Europe, where the fears of loyalty conflicts, so frequent in the narrative about multiple citizenship, have not yet been verified (Frowein 1994: 101). Since the state already has to rule out the difficulties which may come along with multiple citizenship for the many cases that the system already allows for, there would hardly be any additional costs in extending that regulation to new citizens (Wollenschläger and Schraml 1994: 228). The *Übeldoktrin* is inconclusive, even if not wrong, at least in as far as it endorses the theory that multiple citizenship infringes international law (Frowein 1994: 102; Rittstieg 1991: 1388). The FCC decision in which the doctrine was sanctioned is also inconclusive. In it, the Court started by admitting how common multiple citizenship was already in Germany.[96] In fact, the decision itself abolished a case of gender discrimination in the passing of birthright citizenship admitting that, as a consequence, there would be even more cases of multiple citizenship at birth. The Court recognized this fact and still argued that this was not a sufficiently compelling public order interest to justify the violation of the constitutionally required equal treatment of mothers and fathers in nationality law. As far as the individual is concerned, the Court recognized that both disadvantages and benefits are attached to multiple citizenship, so that fairness objections against multiple citizenship could always be raised from two different perspectives. Some scholars have argued that it should be ultimately up to the individual to decide whether the disadvantages outweigh the benefits Zünkler and Findeisen 1991: 253). In any event, what is really crucial is that there does not seem to be any problem with multiple nationality (including these fairness-related concerns) which cannot be resolved by statute or international agreement if there is sufficient political will to do so (Renner 1993a: 25). The Court itself recognized that the eventual harm of multiple citizenship depended only on the laws of the country and on the existence of international agreements dealing with it. And in this

[96] Ibid. 255.

respect one can only stress, as the Court did, the increasing importance of the notion of effective nationality, generally the nationality of the country of ordinary residence, for the resolution of the possible conflicts deriving from multiple nationality both domestically and internationally (Frowein 1994: 101; Zünkler and Findeisen 1991: 251).[97] The likelihood that the new German government will finally undertake the long-awaited reforms introducing some kind of *ius soli* element as well as increasing the tolerance of dual citizenship may reinforce the obsoleteness of the constitutional reading supporting the survival of Germany's nationalistic citizenship.

Summary

With a Constitution which reacted against the excesses of positivism declaring its utmost commitment to human dignity, individual freedom and equality, the rights reserved for citizens in Germany have been expressly and restrictively defined. Still, among the privileges which have remained attached to nationality, we find the right to reside in the country and to freely choose a professional activity there, as well as the right to exercise some political freedoms and, above all, the core political rights. None of these can be regarded as insignificant for the status of permanent resident aliens.

At the same time, given the constitutional commitment to a system of generally restrained powers in what is portrayed as a social state subject to the rule of law and expressed in universal terms, resident aliens have been recognized as entitled to social rights and benefits, and supplementary mechanisms have been authorized by an activist judiciary to control the exercise of administrative discretion in the spheres of freedom otherwise covered by citizen rights only. This has especially been the case when the aliens concerned were people who had developed significant ties with the country and established the basis of their personal, social and professional lives there. Although full equalization has not been reached through aliens' continued residence, the development of constitutional mechanisms to protect aliens' legitimate expectations and freedom interests in remaining and working in the country has contributed to keeping the Constitution relevant and adjusted to the new social circumstances of Germany, even though Germany has never officially accepted itself as an immigration country. Unlike in the USA, the fear of interference with politically sensitive areas such as the country's immigration policy has not led to the measures concerning aliens being regarded as inappropriate objects of judicial scrutiny, regardless of which authority they emanated from.

---

[97] Ibid. 243–4, 256–7.

However, the mechanisms of progressive equalization have developed exclusively in the social and civil realms. The split between the societal and the political spheres of membership has most strikingly materialized in Germany around the dichotomy between, on the one hand, personal and social freedom and equality, and, on the other, political freedom and equality. The former, being central to Germany's commitment to a social state based on the rule of law, have been said to attach to individuals as such and the effort to grant resident aliens some protection, even in the sphere of citizen freedoms, has been connected to it. The latter, however, have been perceived as essentially connected to Germany's commitment to a democratic state order and have applied exclusively to citizens as such. Opposing the attempts of two *Länder* to grant local suffrage to resident aliens, the Federal Constitutional Court has expressly rejected the path of full inclusion and, more specifically, the possibility of disentangling the full enjoyment of rights from citizenship. No change in the circumstances brought about by the immigration phenomenon has, therefore, been sufficient to undermine the exclusion of resident aliens from the sphere of political equality sanctioned in the German Basic Law. And although a constitutional reform was adopted in 1992, it only applies to local voting rights and to nationals of European Union Member States.

As it stands now the only alternative to solve the democratic legitimacy dilemma, as the Federal Constitutional Court has expressly recognized, remains that of facilitating the incorporation of resident aliens by modifying the rules on the acquisition of citizenship, something which seems a priority in the political agenda of Germany's new elected coalition government. This takes us to the subsidiary claim: access to civic equality through citizenship. From a constitutional point of view, with due respect towards the general constitutional design of constrained powers, the Federal Constitutional Court has recognized that the statutory regulation and administrative practice on the access to citizenship (including naturalization) have to comply with constitutional constraints. Unlike in the USA, in Germany there has not been any constitutional rhetoric defining access to citizenship as a privilege falling within the sovereign political discretion of the state. Yet at the same time, nothing like a constitutional right to naturalization has helped permanent resident aliens. Neither have the pillars of Germany's constitutional democracy (the human dignity, general freedom and equality clauses) played a supplementary role here supporting resident aliens' claims to inclusion through citizenship. And this has been aggravated by the Basic Law not containing anything like the US Birthright Citizenship Clause, but rather making the federal legislator fully responsible for deciding the criteria by which citizenship is to be acquired both at birth and through naturalization. The practical relevance of this can only be fully appreciated by recalling the aggravating fact of Germany's traditionally restrictive laws on access to citizenship. As we know, the system of birthright citizenship has been exclusively based on descent and naturalization has traditionally been conceived as the exception rather than the rule: something that requires from the applicant a complete break with old identities and loyalties; a matter of administrative discretion, where public interests necessarily prevail.

The future is uncertain. The 1990 Aliens Act significantly reduced the sphere of administrative discretion regarding aliens' residential, family reunification and working status. And after the reforms resulting from the 1992 Asylum Compromise, as-of-right naturalization of well-settled immigrants and their descendants is a possibility too and does not require proof of cultural assimilation. On the other hand, the foreclosing of the possibility of granting resident aliens suffrage has put some additional pressure on the need to facilitate further resident aliens' incorporation through a more automatic and unconditional access to nationality. In the alien suffrage decision the Court pointed to this connection between the alternative mechanisms of incorporation, and there is an ongoing discussion as to how constitutionally urgent is the long-awaited reform of the old 1913 Nationality Act. The statutory reform proposals over recent years, first, to alter the definition of German citizenship by introducing some *ius soli* elements into the system and, second, to facilitate naturalization mainly by allowing naturalization applicants to retain their prior nationality, seem good ways to advance in the required direction. They have not succeeded yet though there are signs that they may at least in part do so.

Underlying this is the tension between those who have seen such a reform proposal as simply falling within the range of possibilities for the community's self-determination in the matter of membership and those who, instead, have seen it as falling outside the realm of political self-determination. Among the latter, some have conceived it as the expression of a constitutionally required inclusion and others of a constitutionally forbidden one. At stake is the sanctioning of two competing visions of Germany. The first focuses on the German nation-state as the foundational political community and as the ultimate locus of democratic sovereignty which cannot be eroded through inclusive reforms that will surely undermine national homogeneity and the citizenry's sense of exclusive loyalty. The second instead sees Germany as foundationally committed to a liberal and pluralistic democracy, and to an open form of statehood which is sanctioned in the Basic Law and which, given the circumstances, demands the redefinition of German national citizenship in more inclusive terms, especially now that, with completed unity and the increasing obsolescence of the ethnic diaspora problem, Germany is more at liberty to rethink its immigration and citizenship laws.

9   Summary and final remarks

Postwar processes of economic globalization have been a major stimulus to human and labour mobility across frontiers. Restrictive naturalization practices and territorially exclusive definitions of national citizenship centred around the idea of common descent, as well as a persistent resistance to disentangling the full enjoyment of rights and freedoms from nationality, as a membership status, have generated a split in those countries which are most affected by immigration between what one could call their societal and their political communities. Throughout this book, I have criticized this split as posing serious democratic legitimacy concerns which make us wonder whether nationality will become a privileged status of the modern world, dividing the ordinary population of the state into first- and second-class citizens and allowing only the former into the realm which defines the boundaries of democratic membership. There are reasons to believe that this concern will be with us for some time in the future.

As a matter of fact, there have already been some reactions to the new order of things. Thus, some Western countries have granted permanent resident immigrants almost all of the rights citizens enjoy, including civil and economic freedoms, social rights, a rather secure residential status and, occasionally, a comprehensive status of political rights, such as the right to vote in local elections. However, at the same time, there are still movements which call into question the apparent stability of the situation reached, like the current curtailment of social benefits to permanent resident aliens in the USA. Also, almost nowhere have aliens been granted core political rights. Voting for the national parliament and holding a public office continue to be rights generally attached to citizenship. And the same applies, in a way, to full residential security. No matter how secure the residential status of immigrants, deportation is always a threat. What this means is that, ultimately, only nationals are allocated a geopolitical space for their personal and economic development in a system of states that divides the world's territory and population into competing political units. Equal political rights and residential status are not the only but certainly among the most strongly consolidated privileges of national citizenship.

As for naturalization, most countries have actually liberalized their naturalization policies and thereby increased the rate of civic incorporation. Only a few have maintained a restrictive naturalization practice, judging inclusion into the political community, membership in the nation and the resulting full enjoyment of rights and duties in the state as something deeper than the inevitable outcome of mere physical and social coexistence. Still, cultural and political assimilation, economic self-sufficiency, moral virtue and exclusive allegiance (mostly expressed in the form of requiring the renunciation of prior citizenship and allegiances) are among the conditions that most Western states still set at some stage or other in aliens' paths to full inclusion, no matter how long they have been residing in the country. More importantly, however liberally designed, naturalization policies are still generally affirmed as expressions of state sovereignty and of the national community's right to self-determination in the important field of defining membership. The tendency of immigrants to lose interest in full membership as soon as they reach the status of permanent residents and, with it, the access to a secure residential status and most civil freedoms and social rights, has also increased the risk of widening the gap between society and the political community.

Finally, also, the phenomenon of illegal immigration is triggering the permanent coexistence of citizens and non-citizens in less than full equality of rights. Already widespread in the USA, it would be worrisome if this reality of people living with an absolutely precarious residential and working status, which prevents them from effectively enjoying even those minimal rights attached to their common humanity, were to reach similarly high levels in other Western countries. And yet the fact that these countries continue to restrict their immigration and asylum rules, plus the prevailing economic and demographic disparities and the political instability in a world where communications and transportation are increasingly facilitated, make this concern a vivid one. It is highly unlikely that the alternative, mass deportation, will be considered a legitimate or politically advisable measure in most Western democracies today.

Given all of this, it seems that, ultimately, Western constitutional democracies face a dilemma. On the one hand, they can insist on preserving a privileged position for national citizens as full members of their historical communities. This would require them to strengthen further both their domestic and external borders and would probably trigger the dynamics of exclusion. Alternatively, Western states may decide to reinforce their compromise with a foundational commitment to a liberal and democratic order, as an order which is essentially connected to the recognition of equal rights as an expression of equal human dignity. Doing so obliges them to face the new challenge of inclusion posed by the current social and economic realities.

Facing this challenge requires, among other things, that Western democracies come to regard as full members of their organized political communities all those who reside in their territory on a permanent basis, being subject to the decisions collectively taken in it and dependent on its protection and recognition for the full development of their personalities, be they legal or illegal resident aliens. This they could do by ensuring that after no longer than ten years resident aliens are included in the sphere of enjoyment of equal rights. To the extent that in our world of states compelling reasons can be identified for preserving the full enjoyment of rights and duties within the state attached to the formal status of national citizenship, a second alternative was recommended. According to it, with time, permanent resident aliens should automatically and uncondi- tionally be recognized as citizens of the state even if, as a result of this, they become dual or multiple citizens.

The duty to include permanent resident aliens results from taking into account the moral relevance of at least two facts. First, their long-term subjection to the laws and public authority of the state. And second, the likelihood that with residence (and the societal integration that generally follows from it) they will increasingly come to depend on the possibility of continuing residing in the country in order to lead a meaningful life. This would recognize that the social ties and attachments, and maybe also the cultural and political context that allows for their relevant interpretation, can be essential for such a life. With time the issue of the initial right or intent of aliens to establish those links of dependency and attachment becomes irrelevant. A liberal society which is committed to a conception of individuals as capable of continuously questioning and redefining their life projects in the light of new experiences and information, cannot view a fraction of the population as being indefinitely committed to a predefined and limited set of purposes, whatever these may be. Much less can it actually impose such limits.

Therefore, the main thrust of the argument is that a liberal democratic society should look at all of its permanent residents as if they were potential citizens, equally dependent on it for the protection of their rights and the development of their persons, rather than relegate some of them indefinitely to a specific function or set of purposes, such as that of indefinitely being merely workers. This requires the recognition of per- manent resident aliens as equally entitled to aspire to whatever life options the society generally allows for and presents as meaningful. Whether these aliens actually start to conceive of the country of residence as the relevant framework to measure their status of political equality will partly depend on a self-perception which, in turn, will inevitably be largely influenced by their experience in the country of residence as a new social and cultural space.

This might well imply that it is time to abandon some more of the old assumptions of the nation-state construct. Among them, most importantly, the idea that nationality, as sovereignly defined by each state, necessarily closes the circle of the democratically relevant sphere of political accountability since democracy requires the legitimation of power to flow from the people to the state and not the other way round. Also, presumably, nationality will increasingly become a thinner concept, with the old aspiration of a homogenous body of citizenry united by a common ethno-cultural background and a feeling of deep and exclusive loyalty ever more difficult to sustain. But this is just the natural result of Western countries' taking their commitment to liberal democracy seriously and adjusting accordingly to the realities generated by human and labour mobility in a world where territorially organized power structures still predominate. That these structures of power will be increasingly inter-related and become far less mutually exclusive than they once were seems thus inevitable.

This might also imply that the time has come to abandon the merely instrumentalist logic which often lurks in the discussions on the legal status of illegal resident aliens. When millions of illegal immigrants are permanently settled and actively present in the labour market and in public institutions such as education and health systems, the perpetuation of their exclusion and inequality gains relevance as a proper concern related to the legitimate exercise of power in liberal democratic societies. It is not only a question of how granting or not granting them certain rights or benefits can affect the general interest of society, though this is a legitimate concern too. That the exclusion of illegal resident aliens has thus far not been a main concern in studies on immigration and political justice shows how deeply entrenched are the assumptions about national and territorial sovereignty. More specifically, it shows how often it is taken for granted that membership, according to the liberal tradition, requires mutual consent. On the other hand, as we have seen, there is an increasing dissatisfaction with confining the debate on the status of aliens to consent-based arguments which assume, more than discuss, who the legitimate consenting parts really are. Along this line, my attempt to show that illegal resident aliens share with legal resident aliens sufficiently compelling moral grounds to claim inclusion should lead to the recognition that, in consensualist terminology, illegal residents are also part of the would-be consenters rather than the would-be consented.

Neither fairness-based considerations resulting from the perception of states as mutual benefit societies, nor concerns with the preservation of the liberal democratic institutions where they already have a foothold are, in principle, sufficient to justify the long-term coexistence of nationals and non-nationals in conditions of less than equal rights. And this applies, in principle, to both legal and illegal resident aliens.

In summary, we have seen that the fairness objection to the claim of automatic incorporation of aliens starts out from the image of state communities as mutual benefit societies within which a fair balance between the distribution of benefits and burdens must be preserved. While resident aliens are supposed to share in the benefits and burdens of social and economic membership, only citizens can share in the benefits and burdens of political membership. The link between resident aliens and their country of nationality prevents the state from possibly accommodating, on the side of burdens, the expansion that full political inclusion would entail on the side of benefits.

Two sources of inequalities have been commonly alleged in this respect. One is the 'citizen prerogative' that immigrants have to return to their countries of origin. The second has to do with some duties with which, being typically 'citizen duties', the country of residence cannot expect immigrants to comply for the sake of a community other than that of their country of nationality. This is sometimes referred to as citizens' duty of loyalty to their state, and the greatest and most concrete expression of such an expected loyalty is the duty to contribute to the military defence of the state. Allowing immigrants to co-participate in deciding the political destiny of the state, the fairness objection goes, would give equal power to those who are always free to evade their political responsibility by leaving the country and cannot be asked to sacrifice themselves to the same extent for the sake of the state.

In dealing with this objection I have shown that the position of resident aliens and that of citizens as groups regarding duties and prerogatives are generally not so different from a social or legal point of view. Moreover, whatever the legal differences, their practical significance is often minimal. Finally, the alleged impossibility of the state rendering the position of resident aliens equal to that of national citizens (either by imposing the same duties on them directly, or else by granting them nationality) has been based on international impediments of doubtful validity or on unproved assumptions about resident aliens' inconvenient internal disposition (e.g. assumed disloyalty).

I have also briefly explored the possibility of invoking fairness on the other side. In doing so, the current situation was confronted with a hypothetical claim according to which, until the equal recognition of the rights of resident aliens is granted, fairness cannot be done, as citizens would be 'free riding' on immigrants' contribution. In this regard I have expressed doubts as to the possibility of having separate economic and political schemes of cooperation peacefully coexisting. This attempt often represents a purely theoretical and far from neutral approach which neglects the political relevance of immigrants' contribution to the societies of residence as well as the economic relevance of their political exclusion.

As far as illegal residents are concerned, we have explored the most common claim whereby illegal residents, generally portrayed as 'outsiders', cannot possibly belong to the same social scheme of cooperation as citizens and/or legal resident aliens. First of all, it is questionable whether illegal immigrants benefit the community of residence and second, it is not clear that, when given, such benefits can be relevant to tie illegal immigrants, on the one hand, and citizens and legal immigrants, on the other, in one single scheme of cooperation.

Although it was recognized that generalizations are inadequate, I have explained how the dangers and costs associated with the presence of illegal aliens are frequently overemphasized in the public debate. The claim here has been that, at least as long as the community of residence derives some advantages from the massive presence of economically integrated undocumented immigrants, we should carefully check that it is really true that these advantages have not been sought or tacitly accepted by the benefited society. In doing so, we should look for signs which allow us to conclude that the community has been actively fighting against the use and exploitation of illegal immigrants mainly as cheap and non-complaining labour.

More serious than the fairness-related concerns is what I have called the 'democratic objection' to the claims to inclusion. This objection expresses the worries with regard to the limits of the integration capacity of the liberal state, and the fears raised by allowing immigrants to gain civic equality without ensuring that they first acquire sufficient knowledge and that they prove the kind of internal disposition and willingness which the functioning of the liberal institutions requires (e.g. loyalty to the state, knowledge of the dominant language, commitment to the laws and institutions, sense of a common identity, etc.).

In dealing with it, we have seen that although the main concern that animates this objection is a legitimate one, the accuracy of many of the assumptions on which it commonly rests is doubtful. Modern states are seldom homogeneous nation-states, and the phenomenon of multiple identifications and mixed identities is the norm in modern societies and affects both citizens and resident aliens. Moreover, immigrants generally have an interest in being law-abiding to remain within the country and long-term residence usually implies a process of acculturation and political resocialization for them. Finally, citizenship is a bad proxy for exclusive loyalty to the state since many citizens lack a sense of exclusive allegiance to their states, naturalized citizens generally preserve their ties with the societies of origin even when they give up their old nationalities, and resident aliens generally have a stake and thus can be presumed to be committed to defend the interests of the countries in which they ordinarily live, especially if they are treated as equals. Leaving aside these factual assumptions, I have discussed their democratic relevance and, connected to it, the legitimacy of the most common conditions set for the full incorporation of permanent resident aliens. Concerning cultural assimilation requirements the main argument has been that the principle of toleration in democratic societies requires respect for diversity, and hence, accommodation, rather than repression, of cultural pluralism. Any other option would question the 'equal citizenship' of dissident citizens and national minorities and makes us wonder why, if found compelling for the survival of the democratic order, the requirements for inclusion should not be imposed on native-born citizens as well.

There is also a concern with resident aliens' political attitudes and with the preservation of the integrity of the state or of its constitutional order. However, we have seen that dual allegiance, as applied to resident immigrants, often entails nothing more than strong affection or dual identity and is no serious threat to the law or the defence of the state. Also, loyalty to the state and to its constitutional order do not necessarily go together. Only when they do, can immigrants' or citizens' disloyalty to the state pose a true 'democratic threat'. Finally, even if some concerns still seem justified, an effort should be made to look for less-restrictive means of protection than those of general exclusion. Typically, every state has a legal order which contemplates repressive mechanisms to deal with lawbreakers.

Finally, the possibility of inclusion as a path to integrate differences and ensure cohesion has been explored. The starting assumption was that often the alternative to full inclusion is that immigrants will remain in the country in perpetual exclusion. We have seen why this is not an appealing alternative. Briefly, it might generate a dynamics of exclusion which, in the long run, has a more disruptive effect overall than the full inclusion of insufficiently qualified members. It has also been emphasized that, usually, unlike national minorities seeking their own separate institutions, it is recognition within the institutions of the state, and hence, accommodation of their differences within the mainstream society that immigrants long for and would presumably dedicate their political efforts to. And this is why measures which respond to their needs cannot be expected to be seriously divisive for the residential society.

As applied to illegal resident aliens, the democratic objection presents certain specificities. Legal resident aliens have at least overcome some scrutiny when allowed into the country and granted the legal entitlement to live in it on a permanent basis. Presumably, the country of reception takes these decisions in the awareness that they might imply a choice on the future composition of the society and hence, has a chance to ensure, already at this stage, that the joining newcomers will not set too heavy strains on the absorptive capacity of the liberal state and its institutions. What distinguishes illegal immigrants is precisely the fact that they do not pass this initial scrutiny. Also, one has to take into account the additional strains on the political and economic systems of the country of residence that their inclusion can imply, given that illegal immigrants often belong to an economically and educationally deprived population and that their inclusion calls into question the overall credibility of the country's immigration policy and can, ultimately, encourage further illegal entries.

Although all of these objections raise legitimate concerns none of them is considered sufficient to justify long-term exclusion. This is partly because the system's credibility is already and most severely affected by the *de facto* consolidation of a second-class citizenship, but also because, ultimately, excluding illegal resident aliens from civic equality does not imply excluding them from society. More than anything else, it is the actual opportunities that the different job markets offer to them that have an encouraging effect on other would-be illegal entrants. Also, it is important to recall that it is not the right to adopt coercive measures to enforce one's immigration policy that has been questioned, but only the possibility of enforcing them with no time limit. Finally, whatever the additional strains and dangers associated with illegal immigrants, these are probably more closely related to their presence in the country than to their eventual inclusion in the realm of civic equality. Hence the need to ponder, even more seriously than in the case of legal immigrants, the costs of exclusion and the possible impact of such exclusions on the lower edge of the national population.

Throughout this book there has been a concern that political inclusion might not be sufficient to ensure the adequate functioning of egalitarian democratic institutions. This is why I have argued that the state should actively encourage those people who have had fewer chances to gain the cultural and political skills which they need to enjoy their rights and freedoms effectively, to acquire them both for their own sake and for the well-being of the wider society. This applies especially to illegal resident aliens. Unfortunately, too often it is economic domination and oppression that prevent immigrants from stepping out from marginalized and criminal activities, and from gaining access to the dominant social institutions, and encourage them to retain their culture or even to construct a different one.

It has been another central aim of this book to explore the relationship between the path of full inclusion, as a main claim, and the more novel path of granting resident aliens nationality automatically, as a secondary claim. To support this second alternative as a more freedom-enhancing one altogether than that of allowing optional naturalization, two conditions have been set. First, that automatic membership should only come into play if there are major concerns which make it compelling that the status of full and equal rights and duties remains attached to nationality as a membership status. Among such concerns might be the need to preserve a bond of commonality which ensures solidarity and cohesion and binds the polity internally and externally. As a second condition, it was argued that nationality has to be granted automatically, as an additional nationality, and regardless of the degree of cultural or political assimilation achieved by resident aliens. Since the validating condition that the previous nationality not be taken away requires the connivance of both the state of origin and that of residence, I recommended prudence against following the path of automatic ascription of second nationalities until multiple citizenship becomes more generally accepted, as I claimed should be the case.

It is possible that quite a few people will show an initial resistance against the idea of granting resident aliens nationality automatically. Nevertheless, I have argued that the automatic granting of nationality should not be seen as a freedom-restricting imposition on resident aliens, especially when multiple citizenship becomes the rule. As birthright citizenship generally does, ascriptive nationality serves a protective function by ensuring inclusive communities of citizens and avoiding the vulnerability generated by either statelessness or the holding of merely nominal citizenship. Moreover, automatic nationality does not have to be seen as imposing a certain identity on resident aliens as long as nationality is previously redefined to deal with the existing plurality of identities, attachments and loyalties. Admittedly, automatic membership may have some freedom-restricting implications for resident aliens, as it does for native citizens. For instance, it may result in the imposition of some unwanted duties. But to the extent that the reasons for binding civic equality to national membership are valid, they should be conceived as restrictions on the freedom of individuals which are necessary for the preservation of the framework of the liberal democratic state. Also when it works against resident aliens, cohesion and solidarity should not be selectively safeguarded.

Doubts were also raised as to whether unconditional and automatic membership might be the best way to respond to the concerns supporting the marriage between civic equality and nationality, especially if compared with the alternative of optional naturalization for long-term resident aliens, be it conditional or unconditional. More specifically, the worry was brought up that a nationality status, which can be based on nothing more than coexistence within a territorially organized political community, might not be adequate to promote both the subjective attitudes and the objective conditions that the proper functioning of liberal institutions requires.

These concerns may well be legitimate. However, the main problem with a system of conditional access to nationality which allows the community to decide what is necessary in order to preserve the basis of understanding, solidarity and cohesion, even *vis-à-vis* long-term resident aliens, is that it often assumes commonalities binding the citizenry or important differences on the part of settled immigrants which do not actually exist. In practice it ensures 'commonality' only selectively. Moreover, it typically ignores the eroding effects of the alternative of permanent exclusion. Finally, it relies too heavily on the 'transformation power' of naturalization.

There is also the option of making naturalization optional but unconditional as a path for the expression of individual commitment to the legal and political institutions of the state. But the main problem with this alternative is that, if some rights are preserved until after naturalization, then an instrumental rationality might dominate the thinking of naturalization applicants, undermining whatever value naturalization might have had as an expression of individual commitment. On the other hand, if there is no success in making naturalization appealing enough, the levels of self-exclusion would increase. The question becomes, then, whether the symbolic value of the expression of commitment should be sacrificed for the sake of more inclusive results.

Finally, I have briefly analysed and rejected some feasibility objections from the point of view of international law. In doing so, it was recognized that states are fully sovereign to define who their nationals are. There is no reason why the stable connection of settled immigrants to the country should not be sufficient to legitimate their recognition as nationals. All of this will certainly have a multiplying effect on the cases of multiple citizenship. But in the modern world this phenomenon is bound to become increasingly common anyway. There is no general principle in international law opposed to it. And even the European countries with high rates of immigration, which in the sixties and seventies were most concerned about multiple citizenship, are showing now a positive interest in its re-evaluation.

The main thrust of the argument is that we can preserve the concept of national citizenship if we think it still has a great potential in our world of states, but prevent it at the same time from remaining essentially attached to increasingly outdated notions such as that of exclusive loyalty. The concept of national citizenship should thus become more open and inclusive, and adequately take into account the social reality posed by the new forms of residential communities. The underlying idea has been that, if such a concept was indeed framed in sufficiently broad terms, the automatic recognition of nationality would not necessarily have to be seen as an imposition on individuals. Yet again, this requires first that the concept of nationality be redefined and 'democratized' to accommodate the recognition of the new members and their cultural and political specificities.

I am not pretending that the implementation of the claims to automatic incorporation advanced here may not be accompanied by many difficulties and specific problems. And this is why prudence was recommended so as to adapt these normative claims to the specificities of each actual situation which no normative approach which purports to be general can possibly take into consideration. But specific problems require specific solutions. Overbroad generalizations and extremist examples will not do. Often, they are simply brought up as ways to hide discriminatory intents. So, for example, one might say, 'If your claims were implemented, a spy from an enemy country could sneak into the country illegally, wait ten years until she becomes a citizen and work her way through the public service so as to eventually reach a position from which she can affect the national security. Also, a terrorist could sneak into the country illegally, wait until she has fully consolidated her residential status, then, as a citizen, devote the rest of her life to terrorist actions.' I am not saying that such situations are literally impossible though they appear to be extremely unlikely. There just seem to be faster and more efficient ways to get a spy filtered into the system and it seems unlikely that someone will need a passport to start undertaking terrorist actions. For that purpose, clandestinity is generally preferred. Be it as it may, it seems that these situations can be addressed by specific solutions, solutions similar to those adopted to deal with terrorists or spies in general. I am assuming that in most countries there is a highly selective screening process which applies to all of those who gain access to national security related positions. Also, citizenship entitles one to vote and to remain in the country, but not to undertake terrorist actions. Granted, keeping people in jail instead of sending them back to their country of nationality might turn out to be more expensive. But then we should be talking about saving money instead of animating phantoms through a rhetoric which calls on the need to preserve the peaceful coexistence in society. And, ultimately, we should decide whether or not avoiding the additional costs that these rather rare situations would entail justifies the wholesale exclusion of the millions of resident aliens who are neither spies nor terrorists.

Whatever the concrete difficulties and problems related to the implementation of the claims, we cannot avoid mentioning here some general concerns that such implementation would probably raise. A first concern, which was mentioned in passing, would be that with the possible effects of internal inclusions on external inclusions. In other words, can we expect the inclusion of resident aliens into the realm of civic equality to come at the price of making it more difficult for those externally excluded to overcome the borderline exclusion? I think the answer is 'not necessarily'. Intuitively, the following statement seems rather appealing and realistic: 'the more they get once they are in, the harder it will become to get in initially'. But from a liberal perspective this does not really need to be so. Internal inclusions will not inevitably enhance external exclusions. A practice of domestic toleration of differences and solidarity towards resident immigrants may prepare the population to overcome prejudice and lose 'cultural fears' from the outside world as well as to realize that social solidarity can no longer be limited to the 'national club' simply as a matter of course. Also, increased awareness that immigrants cannot be treated as a cheap commodity and that immigration pressure is unlikely to stop as long as economic and political imbalances between countries persist, and as long as our globalized economic order requires relatively open and permeable borders, might oblige the more prosperous states to take more seriously their joint responsibility to attack the root causes of migration movements.

The fact that exclusions of aliens who are outside the territory have not been affected by my claims, nor generally been the subject of this book, is by no means to suggest that it is a morally neutral concern whether the state has an unlimited power to decide which persons it lets into its territory or whether the outsiders may also hold some kind of claims against it.[1] Nor is it to ignore that, from a commitment to a liberal democratic ethos, some exclusion or inclusion priorities affecting those who are not present in the territory might be either recommended, or doubtful. Among the latter we would probably find exclusion or inclusion priorities based merely on racial or gender considerations. The normative claims discussed here are not an effort to indicate the global attitude that Western liberal democracies should have towards current immigration

---

[1] To follow the discussion in this respect see also van Gunsteren 1988; Miller 1988: 647; Carens 1987: 251; Walzer 1983: 31–63.

pressure from neighbouring and less well-off countries. In regulating immigration issues there are three possible points of intervention: at the border, domestically, or in the country of departure. I have almost entirely concentrated on domestic inclusion. However, in a world in which economic resources and political stability are unequally distributed, one can hardly defend the view that the commitment to egalitarian liberalism allows states to face moral obligations only to those who are already within its jurisdiction.

Therefore, limiting the scope of the claims to the inclusion of those who are already located within the national borders does not deny the usefulness of engaging in a broader project, and, in fact, my hope is that some of the reflections in this work would also be relevant in such an enterprise. For instance, if we take the notion of deep affectedness seriously, it is clear that the country of origin should be the main target of our efforts. Leaving one's country implies generally a break with ties and attachments as well as with the cultural idioms that feed the meaningfulness of one's life projects. Certainly, with time, people may become socially and culturally embedded somewhere else and this is what grounds the need that they be eventually recognized as full members of the country of residence. However, if the process of resocialization and cultural assimilation is generally so costly and painful that we cannot expect people to be endlessly ready to undertake it, the question becomes: why should we expect people to experience it even once? In other words, to the extent that it is possible, people should have the choice to preserve their social and cultural bonds to the places of their primary socialization and this should be taken into consideration when deciding what are the moral obligations that we have towards neighbouring and less well-off countries.

On the other hand, I am not suggesting that the internal inclusions defended here *necessarily* have to be regarded as a cautious step towards open borders. Clearly, for some liberal scholars nothing but complete freedom of movement will do to accommodate the liberal premise of equal dignity and freedom to a modern world in which the most basic goods are unequally distributed (see Carens 1987). Nevertheless, many important reasons, of a more or less transitory nature, have been put forward by authors (many of whom present themselves as committed liberals) against open borders.[2] What the specific limitation of the scope

[2] Among the great variety of arguments we could cite the following: the fact that national communities have to be preserved because people value their freedom not only in abstract terms but mainly in cultural and socially bounded spaces (Kymlicka 1995); the fear that excessively heterogeneous societies may not be able to allow for the degree of civic virtue, understanding and sense of solidarity that the working of liberal institutions requires, especially when they are committed to a scheme of distributive justice (see Ackerman 1980, referring to the possible limits of absorption of the liberal institutions; Whelan 1988:

of this book suggests is only that the exclusion of aliens who are permanently settled in a society presents morally relevant specificities which
need to be addressed.

This is not to deny that external and internal exclusions might be, not
only morally connected, but also practically interrelated. As a matter of
fact, the very possibility of establishing the relevant links of social membership on which the claim to automatic incorporation rests, depends on
the state's permission, or at least tolerance, of the alien's residence and
employment within the state and, as we have seen, is greatly facilitated
when the immigrant acquires permanent legal residence. However, this
does not make the state's tacit or express consent in admitting the alien
the main basis of legitimation of the claim. Whether social membership is
encouraged, tolerated or even opposed by the receiving state, the fact
remains that its very existence is democratically relevant and hence,
sufficient to ground the claim of inclusion. In other words, the duty to
accept newcomers into the country needs to be specifically addressed. I
do not think it is morally acceptable to trade off full inclusion for more
open borders or, put in other terms, to allow people in on the condition
that they will always remain second- or third-class citizens. In the long
run, this would clearly undermine the premise of coexistence in equal
political freedom to which Western democracies are foundationally committed.

The same applies for a related temptation, namely, that of facilitating
full inclusion at the expense of undermining the content of what inclusion
means in terms of legal entitlements linked to citizenship. At risk would
be the most basic social rights and benefits that have come to be part of
the commitment to social justice defining citizenship in Western democracies. It is not surprising that the largest support for open borders has
come from ultra-libertarians speaking for a fully free labour market with
no state interference. Here, facilitated inclusion of resident aliens or even
non-resident aliens would come at the price of embracing a less socially
inclusive notion of citizenship with marginalizing effects on the most
culturally and economically deprived. Both the trade-off of 'letting more
people into the country' but allowing for the consolidation of different
classes of citizenship, and that of 'letting more people into citizenship' but
detracting from the notion of citizenship some of the rights which are now
seen as essential to preserve political equality are unacceptable. Ensuring

16–23, referring to the need to compromise certain liberal principles in practice so as to
ensure that in a non-ideal world these get preserved wherever they already have a
foothold); the fear that newcomers may directly threaten the liberal order and institutions
if they are not sufficiently committed to them (see Habermas 1992, for whom the only
legitimate exclusions are those which aim to protect the basis of the democratic order
against direct threats).

that those who are inside will be treated with equal concern and respect is essential to preserve the 'cherished' liberal democracies, especially when these are committed to a redistributive conception of justice. The risk of doing otherwise is that we may end up undermining the liberal democratic institutions there where they already have a foothold. And if we did, we would lose one of the most powerful arguments for not having to fully question, from a liberal morality, and, eventually, to decide from anew, the allocation of people and political membership to states which are differently endowed in terms of the most basic goods, such as peace, health, work and wealth.

The constitutional analysis carried out in this book illustrates the difficulties involved in and obstacles to, but also the hopes for, the required constitutional adaptation to the new order in two Western countries, Germany and the USA. Both of them have significant non-national populations mainly as a result of their immigration experiences and, for different reasons, will probably continue to do so in the future. It has been my aim to show here how the constitutional case law and doctrinal discussions on the status of resident aliens and on their access to nationality in both these countries portray the tensions of the denounced split between societal and political membership, and reflect the interrelation between full inclusion as aliens and access to nationality as alternative paths to overcome it. These tensions have taken different forms in Germany and the USA, but the vivid constitutional debates raised by these issues in two countries with such different immigration and nation-building traditions support the thesis that setting the boundaries of the political community by defining who gets recognition as a full member is not only the product of a country's perception of its self-interest and identity, but is also related to its foundational legitimation principles, as constitutionally expressed. I have focused here on the USA, a country which has traditionally seen itself as an immigration country, welcoming newcomers and setting them soon on the route to citizenship, and Germany, a country which, in spite of its continuous and diversified receptions of aliens, has always perceived such receptions as temporary and contingent rather than as portraying Germany's wish to enlarge its social and political tissue with new external members. In spite of this difference, clearly linked to their different traditions of nationhood, we have seen that in both of them the daily political battles giving birth to naturalization, immigration and citizenship laws and policies have been accompanied by a permanent constitutional debate of courts and scholars as to whether or not the degree of inclusiveness of the different policies and statutes was sufficient to match the demands of constitutionally sanctioned liberal democracies committed to human dignity, personal freedom and equality as foundational values.

As a matter of fact, in both of these countries, with some important exceptions, the higher courts have taken very significant steps towards the recognition of the constitutional relevance of the societal integration of a non-citizen population, thus questioning the status of citizenship as self-explanatory grounds for constitutional discrimination. Granted, they are still far from offering a single and coherent explanation as to why, more and more, residence and not only national citizenship should open the way to the enjoyment of a comprehensive constitutional status and, more importantly, far from overcoming some of the old and outdated assumptions on state sovereignty and the nation-state construct that would need to be given up before the claims to inclusion defended here could be fully enforced. This is especially true for all that has to do with the strictly political realm, still largely conceived as the domain of citizenship. Hopefully, some of the arguments and insight provided here will be useful in questioning the underlying split between the political and the socioeconomic spheres of membership and contribute to reaching the coherent and relevant constitutional interpretation that both the USA and Germany need in order to face some of the related issues on their political agendas. Presumably, this interpretation would help these countries and many others faced with similar questions to update their commitments to a liberal democratic order with universalist vocation in an increasingly postnational order.

As neatly encapsulated in the title of one of Habermas's most recent books *Faktizität und Geltung* (1992), law is a phenomenon permanently torn between the conflicting demands of normativity and facticity. Our case studies, in Germany and United States, are vivid examples of the basic tension between the factual situation in modern democracies and their moral aspirations. Those of us living in Western democracies, looking at the 'stranger' in our midst, must decide a fundamental question: should our political institutions, constitutional law and moral beliefs serve merely to idealize our current realities, or should they serve to implement our self-proclaimed ideals?

Bibliography

Abriel, E. G. 1995, 'Rethinking Preemption for Purposes of Aliens and Public Benefits', *University of California at Los Angeles Law Review* 42: 1597.

Ackerman, B. A. 1980, *Social Justice in the Liberal State*, New Haven: Yale University Press.

Aleinikoff, T. A. 1986, 'Theories of Loss of Citizenship', *Michigan Law Review* 84: 1471.

  1989, 'Federal Regulation of Aliens and the Consultation', *American Journal of International Law* 83: 862.

  1990, 'Citizens, Aliens, Membership and the Constitution', *Const. Commentary* 7: 9.

Aleinikoff, T. A., Martin, D. A., and Motomura, H. 1998, *Immigration and Citizenship: Process and Policy*, 4th edn. America Casebook Series, St. Paul, Minn.: West Group.

Alexy, H. 1993, 'Zur Neuregelung des Aussiedlerzuzugs', *Neue Zeitschrift für Verwaltungsrecht* 12: 1171.

Alexy, R. 1989, *A Theory of Legal Argumentation: the Theory of Rational Discourse as Theory of Legal Justification*, trans. N. MacCormick, Oxford: Oxford University Press.

Barbieri, W. A. 1998, *Ethics of Citizenship*, Durham and London: Duke University Press.

Bauböck, R. 1994a, *Transnational Citizenship*, Aldershot: Edward Elgar.

  1994b, 'Changing the Boundaries of Citizenship', in *Redefining the Status of Immigrants in Europe*, ed. R. Bauböck, Aldershot: Avebury: 199.

Behrend, O. 1973, 'Kommunalwahlrecht für Ausländer in der Bundesrepublik', *Die Öffentliche Verwaltung* 11/12: 376.

Berber, F. 1975, *Lehrbuch des Völkerrechts*, 2 Auf. Munich: Beck.

Bernsdorff, N. 1986, *Probleme der Ausländerintegration in verfassungsrechtlicher Sicht*, Frankfurt am Main: Peter Lang.

Bickel, A. 1975, *The Morality of Consent*, New Haven and London: Yale University Press.

Birch, A. H. 1993, *The Concepts and Theories of Modern Democracies*, New York: Routledge.

Birkenheier, M. 1976, *Wahlrecht für Ausländer-zugleich ein Beitrag zum Volksbegriff des Grundgesetzes*, series Schriften zum öffentlichen Recht, Berlin: Duncker und Humblot.

Bleckmann, A. 1985, *Staatsrecht II*, Cologne: Heymann.

1988, 'Das Nationalstaatsprinzip im Grundgesetz', *Die Öffentliche Verwaltung* 41: 437.

1990, 'Antwartschaft auf die deutsche Staatsangehörigkeit', *Neue Juristische Wochenschrift* 43: 1397.

Blumenwitz, D. 1993, 'Territorialprinzip und Mehrstaatigkeit', *Zeitschrift für Ausländerrecht und Ausländerpolitik* 13: 151.

Bosniak, L. S. 1988, 'Exclusion and Membership: the Dual Identity of the Undocumented Worker under the United States Law', *Wisconsin Law Review*: 955.

1994, 'Membership, Equality, and the Difference that Alienage Makes', *New York University Law Review* 69, 6: 1047.

Boswell, R. A. 1995, 'Restrictions on Non-citizens' Access to Public Benefits: Flawed Premise, Unnecessary Response', *University of California at Los Angeles Law Review* 42: 1475.

Brubaker, W. R. (ed.) 1989a, *Immigration and the Politics of Citizenship in Europe and North America*, New York: University Press of America.

1989b, 'Membership without Citizenship: the Economic and Social Rights of Non Citizens', in *Immigration and the Politics of Citizenship in Europe and North America*, ed. R. Brubaker, New York: University Press of America: 145.

1992, *Citizenship and Nationhood in France and Germany*, London: Harvard University Press.

Bryde, B. O. 1989, 'Ausländerwahlrecht und grundgesetzliche Demokratie', *Juristische Zeitung* 6: 257.

1994, 'Die bundesrepublikanische Volksdemokratie als Irrweg der Demokratietheorie', *Staatswissenschaften und Staatspraxis* 3: 305.

Carens, J. H. 1987, 'Aliens and Citizens: the Case for Open Borders', *Review of Politics* 49, 2: 251.

1989, 'Membership and Morality: Admission to Citizenship in Liberal Democratic States', in *Immigration and the Politics of Citizenship in Europe and North America*, ed. W. R. Brubaker, New York: University Press of America: 39.

Dagger, R. 1985, 'Rights, Boundaries, and the Bonds of Community: a Qualified Defense of Moral Parochialism', *The American Political Science Review* 79: 143.

Dahl, R. A. 1956, *A Preface to Democratic Theory*, London: University of Chicago Press.

1989, *Democracy and its Critics*, New Haven: Yale University Press.

de Groot, G. R. 1989, *Staatsangehörigkeitsrecht im Wandel. Eine rechtsvergleichende Studie über Erwerb- und Verlustgründe der Staatsangehörigkeit*, Cologne: Carl Heymans Verlag.

Deibel, K. 1984, 'Deutsche Staatsangehörigkeit und Grundrechte', *Die Öffentliche Verwaltung* 8: 322.

de Tocqueville, A. 1963, *Democracy in America*, New York: Alfred A. Knopf.

Deubler, M. 1988, 'Der Ausländer als Untertan – ein Dauerzustand?', in *Politik und Zeitgeschichte*, Beilage zur Wochenzeitung 'Das Parlament', B 24: 36.

Döhring, K. 1963, *Die allgemeinen Regeln des völkerrechtlichen Fremdenrechts und das deutsche Verfassungsrecht*, Cologne and Berlin: Heymann.

1974, 'Die staatsrechtlichen Stellung der Ausländer in der Bundesrepublik

Deutschland', *Veröffentlichungen der Vereinigung der Deutschen Staatsrechtslehrer (VVDStRL)* 32: 8.

Dolde, K. 1972, *Die politische Rechte der Ausländer in der Bundesrepublik*, Berlin: Duncker & Humblot.

Dürig, G., Herzog, R., and Maunz, T. 1976, *Grundgesetz Kommentar*, Munich: Beck.

Dworkin, R. 1986, *Law's Empire*, London: Fontana.

Dyzenhaus, D. 1993, 'Law and Public Reason', *M'Gill Law Review* 38: 336.

Ely, J. H. 1980, *Democracy and Distrust: a Theory of Judicial Review*, Cambridge, Mass.: Harvard University Press.

Esser, H., and Korte, H. 1985, 'Federal Republic of Germany', in *European Immigration Policy. A Comparative Study*, ed. T. Hammar, London: Cambridge University Press: 165.

Fitzheigh, W. W. and Hyde, C. C. 1942, 'The Drafting of Neutral Aliens by the United States', *American Journal of International Law* 26: 369.

Foster, N. G. 1993, *German Law and Legal System*, London: Blackstone.

Frank, G. 1990, 'Ausländerwahlrecht und Rechtstellung der Kommune', *Kritische Justiz* 23: 290.

Franz, F. 1989, 'Benachteiligungen des ausländischen Wohnbevölkerung in Beruf, Gewerbe und Gesundheitswesen', *Zeitschrift für Ausländerrecht und Ausländerpolitik* 4: 154.

1990, 'Der Gesetzentwurf der Bundesregierung zur Neuregelung des Ausländerrechts', *Zeitschrift für Ausländerrecht und Ausländerpolitik* 1: 3.

Frowein, J. A. 1994, 'Rechtliche Aspekte der Ausländerpolitik und des Staatsangehörigkeitsrechts', in *Migration und Integration in Brandenburg*, Potsdam: Brandenburgische Universitätsdruckerei und Verlagsgesellschaft: 100.

Gaa-Unterpaul, B. 1993, 'Das Kriegsfolgenbereinigungsgesetz und die Änderung für das Vertriebenenrecht', *Neue Juristische Wochenschrift* 46: 2080.

Gerety, T. 1983, 'Children in the Labyrinth: the Complexities of *Plyler v. Doe*', *University of Pittsburgh Law Review* 44: 379.

Grabitz, E. 1970, *Europäische Bürgerrecht zwischen Marktkbürgerschaft und Staatsbürgerschaft*, series Europäische Schriften des Bildungswerks Europäische Politik, 25, Cologne: European Union.

Grawert, R. 1973, *Staat und Staatsangehörigkeit*, Berlin: Duncker & Humblot.

Habermas, J. 1992, 'Staatsbürgerschaft und nationale Identität', *Faktizität und Geltung*, Frankfurt am Main: Suhrkampf Verlag.

Hailbronner, K. 1983, 'Ausländerrecht und Verfassung', *Neue Juristische Wochenschrift* 37: 2105.

1989, 'Citizenship and Nationhood in Germany', in *Immigration and the Politics of Citizenship in Europe and North America*, ed. R. Brubaker, New York: University Press of America: 67.

1992, *Einbürgerung von Wanderarbeitnehmern und doppelte Staatsangehörigkeit*, Baden-Baden: Nomos Verlagsgesellschaft.

Hailbronner, K. and Renner, G. 1991, *Staatsangehörigkeitsrecht: Kommentar*, Munich: Beck.

Hammar, T. 1985a, 'Citizenship, Aliens' Political Rights, and Politicians' Concern for Migrants: the Case of Sweden', in *Guest Come to Stay*, ed. R. Rogers, Boulder: Westview Press: 85.

1985b, 'Dual Citizenship and Political Integration', *International Migration Review*, 19, 3: 438.

1989, 'State, Nation, and Dual Citizenship', in *Immigration and the Politics of Citizenship in Europe and North America*, ed. R. Brubaker, New York: University Press of America: 81.

1990a, *Democracy and the Nation State*, Aldershot: Avebury.

1990b, 'The Civil Rights of Aliens', in *The Political Rights of Migrant Workers in Western Europe*, ed. Z. Layton-Henry, Modern Politics Series 25, London: Sage Publications: 74.

1994, 'Legal Time of Residence and the Status of Immigrants', in *Redefining the Status of Immigrants in Europe*, ed. R Bauböck, Aldershot: Avebury: 187.

Hart, H. L. A. 1955, 'Are There Any Natural Rights?', *Philosophical Review* 64: 185.

Heckmann, F. 1985, 'Temporary Labor Migration or Immigration? "Guest Workers" in the Federal Republic of Germany', in *Guest Come to Stay*, ed. R. Rogers, Boulder: Westview Press: 69.

Hertz, M.T. 1976, 'Limits to the Naturalization Power', *Georgetown Law Journal* 64: 1007.

Himmelfarb, G. (ed.) 1963, *Essays on Politics and Culture*, New York.

Hirschman, A.O. 1970, *Exit, Voice and Loyalty*, Cambridge, Mass.: Harvard University Press.

Huber, P. M. 1989, 'Das "Volk" des Grundgesetzes', *Die Öffentliche Verwaltung* 22: 531.

Hull, E. 1983, 'Undocumented Alien Children and Free Public Education: an Analysis of *Plyler v. Doe*', *University of Pittsburgh Law Review* 44: 409.

Isensee, J. 1973, 'Leitsatz 18b', *Die Öffentliche Verwaltung*: 741.

1974, 'Die staatsrechtliche Stellung der Ausländer in der Bundesrepublik Deutschland', *Veröffentlichungen der Vereinigung der Deutschen Staatsrechtslehrer (VVDStRL)* 32: 49.

1993, Nachwort 'Europa - die politische Erfindung eines Erdteils', in *Europa als politische Idee und als rechtliche Form*, eds. J. Isensee, H. Schäfer and H. Tietmeyer, Berlin: Duncker & Humblot.

Jacobson, D. 1996, *Rights Across Borders*, Baltimore and London: Johns Hopkins University Press.

Jellinek, G. 1950, *System der subjektiven öffentliche Rechte*, 2 Aufl., Tübingen: Mohr.

1992, *Allgemeine Staatslehre*, 3rd edn., Berlin: Springer Verlag.

Johnson, K. R. 1995, 'Public Benefits and Immigration: the Intersection of Immigration Status, Ethnicity, Gender, and Class', *University of California at Los Angeles Law Review* 42: 1509.

Joppke, C. 1999a, *Immigration and the Nation-State: the United States, Germany and Great Britain*, Oxford: Oxford University Press.

1999b, 'How Immigration is Changing Citizenship: a Comparative View', *Ethnic and Racial Studies* (forthcoming).

Kämper, F. 1989, 'Kommunalwahlrecht für Ausländer', *Zeitschrift für Ausländerrecht*: 62.

Karpen, U. 1989, 'Kommunalwahlrecht für Ausländer', *Neue Juristische Wochen-*

schrift 16: 1012.

Karst, K. L. 1977, 'Foreword: Equal Citizenship Under the Fourteenth Amendment', *Harvard Law Review* 91: 1.

1989, *Belonging to America: Equal Citizenship and the Constitution*, New Haven and London: Yale University Press.

Kirchhof, P. 1987, 'Deutsche Sprache', in eds. J. Isensee and P. Kirchhof, *Handbuch des Staatsrechts der Bundesrepublik Deutschland, Vol. I: Grundlagen von Staat und Verfassung*, Heidelberg: C. F. Müller Juristischer Verlag.

Klosko, G. 1992, *The Principle of Fairness and Political Obligation*, Lanham: Rowman & Littlefield.

Koh, H. H. 1985, 'Equality with a Human Face: Justice Blackmun and the Equal Protection of Aliens', *Hamline Law Review* 8: 51.

Kurz, H. 1965, *Volkssouveranität und Volksrepräsentation*, Cologne.

Kymlicka, W. 1995, *Multicultural Citizenship*, Oxford: Clarendon Press.

1996, 'Social Unity in a Liberal State', *Social Philosophy and Policy Foundation*: 105.

Layton-Henry, Z. 1990a, 'The Challenge of Political Rights', in *The Political Rights of Migrant Workers in Western Europe*, ed. Z. Layton-Henry, Modern Politics Series 25, London: Sage Publications: 1.

1990b, 'Immigrant Associations', in *The Political Rights of Migrant Workers in Western Europe*, ed. Z. Layton-Henry, Modern Politics Series 25, London: Sage Publications: 94.

1990c, 'Citizenship or Denizenship for Migrant Workers?', in *The Political Rights of Migrant Workers in Western Europe*, ed. Z. Layton-Henry, Modern Politics Series 25, London: Sage Publications: 186.

1991, 'Citizenship and Migrant Workers in Western Europe', in *The Frontiers of Citizenship*, eds. U. Vogel and M. Moran, London: Macmillan.

Legomsky, S. H. 1984, 'Immigration Law and the Principle of Plenary Congressional Power', *Supreme Court Review*: 255.

1994, 'Why Citizenship?', *Virginia Journal of International Law*, 35, 1: 279.

1995a, 'Immigration, Federalism and the Welfare State', *University of California at Los Angeles Law Review* 42: 1453.

1995b, 'Ten More Years of Plenary Power: Immigration, Congress, and the Courts', *Hastings Constitutional Law Quarterly* 22: 915.

Levi, D. F. 1979, 'The Equal Treatment of Aliens: Preemption or Equal Protection?', *Stanford Law Review* 31: 1069.

Levinthal, L. 1996, 'Welfare Reform and Limits on the Rights of Legal Residents', *Georgetown Immigration Law Journal* 10: 467.

Levison, S. 1986, 'Constituting Communities Through Words That Bind: Reflections on Loyalty Oaths', *Michigan Law Review* 84: 1440.

Lillich, R. B. 1984, *The Human Rights of Aliens in Contemporary International Law*, Manchester: Manchester University Press.

Lipjhart, A. 1997, 'Unequal Participation: Democracy's Unresolved Dilemma', *American Political Science Review* 91 (March): 1.

López, G.P. 1981, 'Undocumented Mexican Migration: In Search of a Just Immigration Law and Policy', *University of California at Los Angeles Law Review* 28: 615.

Löwer, W. 1993, 'Abstammungsprinzip und Mehrstaatigkeit', *Zeitschrift für Ausländerrecht und Ausländerpolitik* 13: 156.

Macpherson, C. B. 1977, *The Life and Times of Liberal Democracy*, Oxford: Oxford University Press.

Margalit, A., and Raz, J. 1990, 'National Self-Determination', *Journal of Philosophy*, 87, 9: 439.

Martin, D. A. 1983, 'Due Process and Membership in the National Community: Political Asylum and Beyond', *Pittsburgh Law Review* 44: 165.

    1985, 'Membership and Consent: Abstract or Organic?', *Yale Journal of International Law* 11: 278.

    1994, 'The Civic Republican Ideal for Citizenship, and for Our Common Life', *Virginia Journal of International Law* 35, 1: 301.

Michelman, F. 1988, 'Law's Republic', *Yale Law Yournal* 97: 1493.

Miller, D. 1988, 'The Ethical Significance of Nationality', *Ethics* 98: 647.

Mir Puig, S. 1995, *Derecho Penal: Parte General*, Barcelona: Promociones Publicaciones Universitarias.

Motomura, H. 1990, 'Immigration Law after a Century OF Plenary Power: Phantom Constitutional Norms and Statutory Interpretation', *Yale Law Review* 100: 545.

    1992, 'The Curious Evolution of Immigration Law: Procedural Surrogates for Substantive Constitutional Rights', *Columbia Law Review* 92: 1625.

    1994, 'Immigration and Alienage, Federalism and Proposition 187', *Virginia Journal of International Law* 35: 201.

Münz, R. and Ulrich, R. 1997, 'Changing Patterns of Immigration to Germany 1945–1995', in *Migration Past, Migration Future*, eds. K. J. Bade and M. Weiner, Providence: Berghahan Books.

Needelman, J. A. 1997, 'Attacking Federal Restrictions on Noncitizens' Access to Public Benefits on Constitutional Grounds: a Survey of Relevant Doctrines', *Georgetown Immigration Law Journal* 10: 467.

Neuman, G. L. 1987, 'Back to *Dred Scott?*', *San Diego Law Review* 24: 485.

    1990, 'Immigration and Judicial Review in the Federal Republic of Germany', *International Law and Politics* 23: 35.

    1992, '"We are the People": Alien Suffrage in German and American Perspective', *Michigan Journal of International Law* 13: 259.

    1994, 'Justifying US Naturalization Policies', *Virginia Journal of International Law* 35, 1: 237.

    1995, 'Aliens as Outlaws: Government Services, Proposition 187, and the Structure of Equal Protection Doctrine', *University of California at Los Angeles Law Review* 42: 1425.

    1996, *Strangers to the Constitution*, Princeton, N.J.: Princeton University Press.

Nino, A. 1993, 'A Philosophical Reconstruction of Judicial Review', *Cardozo Law Review* 14: 798.

Note 1965, 'Constitutional Limitations on the Power of Congress to Confer Citizenship by Naturalization', *Iowa Law Review* 50: 1093.

Note 1971, 'Constitutional Limitations on the Naturalization Power', *Yale Law Journal* 80: 768.

Note 1979, 'The Equal Treatment of Aliens: Preemption or Equal Protection',

Stanford Law Review 31: 1069.

Note 1980, 'State Burden On Resident Aliens: A New Preemption Analysis', *Yale Law Journal* 89: 940.

Note 1994, 'The Birthright Citizenship Amendment: a Threat to Equality', *Harvard Law Review* 107: 1026.

Note 1997, 'The Functionality of Citizenship', *Harvard Law Review* 110: 1814.

Oberndörfer, D. 1989, 'Der Nationalstaat –Ein Hindernis für das dauerhafte Zusammenleben mit ethnischen Minderheiten', *Zeitschrift für Ausländerrecht und Ausländerpolitik* 1:3.

O'Connell, R. and Rubio-Marín, R. 1999. 'The European Convention and the Relative Rights of Resident Aliens', *European Law Journal* 5, 1:4.

Olivas, M. 1994, 'Preempting Preemption: Foreign Affairs, State Rights, and Alienage Classifications', *Virginia Journal of International Law* 35: 217.

Pateman, C. 1970, *Participation and Democratic Theory*, Cambridge: Cambridge University Press.

Perry, M. J. 1983, 'Equal Protection, Judicial Activism, and the Intellectual Agenda of Constitutional Theory: Reflections on, and Beyond *Plyler v. Doe*', *University of Pittsburgh Law Review* 44: 329.

Pitkin, H. F. 1981, 'Justice: On Relating Private and Public', *Political Theory*, August 9: 327.

Quaritsch, H. (Discussion participant) 1980, 'Welche rechtliche Vorkehrungen empfehlen sich, um die Rechtstellung von Ausländern in der Bundesrepublik Deutschland angemessen zu gestalten?', *Verhandlungen des Dreiundfünfzigsten deutschen Juristentags Berlin 1980*, Vol. II, Munich: Beck: L 137.

1983, 'Staatsangehörigkeit und Wahlrecht', *Die Öffentliche Verwaltung* 1: 1.

1988, 'Einbürgerungspolitik als Ausländerpolitik', *Der Staat* 27: 481.

1989, 'Die Einbürgerung der "Gastarbeiter"', in *Staat und Völkerrechtsordnung: Festschrift für Karl Döhring*, eds. K. Hailbronner, G. Ress and T. Stein, Berlin: Springer Verlag: 740.

1992, 'Der grundrechtliche Status des Ausländer', *Handbuch des Staatsrecht*, eds. J. Isensee and P. Kirchhof, Vol. I, *Allgemeine Grundrechte*, Heidelberg: C. F. Müller: 663.

Raskin, J. 1993, 'Legal Aliens, Local Citizens: the Historical, Constitutional and Theoretical Meanings of Alien Suffrage', *University of Pennsylvania Law Review* 141: 1390.

Rawls, J. 1993, *Political Liberalism*, New York: Columbia University Press.

Reich, P. L. 1995, 'Environmental Metaphor in the Alien Benefits Debate', *University of California at Los Angeles Law Review* 42: 1577.

Renner, G. 1993a, 'Verhinderung von Mehrstaatigkeit bei Erwerb und Verlust der Staatsangehörigkeit', *Zeitschrift für Ausländerrecht und Ausländerpolitik* 13: 18.

1993b, 'Asyl und Ausländerrechtsreform', *Zeitschrift für Ausländerrecht und Ausländerpolitik* 3: 118.

Rittstieg, H. 1980, 'Entscheidungsrezension', *Informationsbrief Ausländerrecht*: 312.

1981, 'Wahlrecht für Ausländer', Königstein: Athenäum.

1983, 'Ausländerrecht und Verfassung', *Neue Juristische Wochenschrift*, 48:

2746.

1991, 'Doppelte Staatsangehörigkeit und Minderheiten in der transnationalen Industriellgesellschaft', *Neue Juristische Wochenschrift* 44: 1386.

Roh, C. E., and Upham, F. K. 1972, 'The Status of Aliens under United States Draft Laws', *Harvard International Law Review* 13: 501.

Rosberg, G. M. 1977a, 'The Protection of Aliens from Discriminatory Treatment by the National Government', *Supreme Court Review*: 275.

1977b, 'Aliens and Equal Protection: Why not the Right to Vote?', *Michigan Law Review* 75: 1092.

1983, 'Discrimination Against the "Nonresident" Alien', *University of Pittsburgh Law Review* 44: 399.

Rubio-Marín, R. 1996, 'La Protección Constitucional de los Extranjeros Ilegales en Estados Unidos', *Revista Española de Derecho Constitucional* 46: 107.

Rüfner, A. 1950, *Kommentar zum Bonner Grundgesetz*, Hamburg: Hausicher Gildenverlag.

Ruland, F. 1975, 'Wahlrecht für Ausländer', *Juristische Schulung*: 110.

Rupp, H. H. 1989, 'Wahlrecht für Ausländer?', *Zeitschrift für Rechtspolitik* 10: 363.

Sachs, M. 1981, *Neue Juristische Wochenschrift*: 1133.

Sasse, C. 1974, *Kommunalwahlrecht für Ausländer*, Bonn: Europa Union Verlag.

Scanlan, J. A., and Kent, O. T. 1988, 'The Force of Moral Arguments for a Just Immigration Policy in a Hobbesian Universe: the Contemporary American Example', in ed. M. Gibney, *Open Borders? Closed Societies? The Ethical and Political Issues*, London: Greenwood Press: 61.

Schachtenschneider, K. (Discussion participant) 1980, 'Welche rechtliche Vorkehrungen empfehlen sich, um die Rechtstellung von Ausländern in der Bundesrepublik Deutschland angemessen zu gestalten?', *Verhandlungen des Dreiundfünfzigsten deutschen Juristentags Berlin 1980*, Vol. II, Munich: Beck: L 149.

Schauer, F. 1986, 'Community, Citizenship and the Search for National Identity', *Michigan Law Review* 84: 1504.

Schink, A. 1988, 'Kommunalwahlrecht für Ausländer?', *Deutsches Verwaltungsblatt* 9: 417.

Schuck, P. H. 1984, 'The Transformation of Immigration Law', *Columbia Law Review*, 84, 1: 4.

1989, 'Membership in the Liberal Polity: the Devaluation of American Citizenship', in *Immigration and the Politics of Citizenship in Europe and North America*, ed. R. Brubaker, New York: University Press of America: 51.

1994, 'Whose Membership is it Anyway?: Comments on Gerald Neuman', *Virginia Journal of International Law* 35, 1: 321.

1995, 'The Message of 187', *The American Prospect*, Spring: 85.

1997, 'Re-evaluation of American Citizenship', *Georgetown Immigration Law Journal* 12: 1.

Schuck, P. H. and Smith, R. M. 1985, *Citizenship Without Consent*, New Haven and London: Yale University Press.

1998, *Citizens, Strangers and In-Between: Essays on Immigration and Citizenship*, Boulder: Westview Press.

Schumpeter, J. A. 1976, *Capitalism, Socialism and Democracy*, 5th edn., London:

Allen & Unwin.

Schwartz, W. F. (ed.) 1995, *Justice in Immigration*, Cambridge: Cambridge University Press.

Schwerdtfeger, G. 1980, 'Welche rechtliche Vorkehrungen empfehlen sich, um die Rechtstellung von Ausländern in der Bundesrepublik Deutschland angemessen zu gestalten?', *Verhandlungen des Dreiundfünfzigsten deutschen Juristentags Berlin 1980*, Vol. II, Munich: Beck, Gutachten A: A 119.

1982, *Einwanderungsland Bundesrepublik?*, Baden-Baden: Nomos Verlagsgesellschaft.

Shacknove, A. E. 1988, 'American Duties to Refugees. Their Scope and Limits', in *Open Borders? Closed Societies? The Ethical and Political Issues*, ed. M. Gibney, London: Greenwood Press: 144.

Simmons, A. J. 1979, *Moral Principles and Political Obligation*, Princeton, N.J.: Princeton University Press.

Soysal, N. Y. 1994, *Limits of Citizenship: Migrants and Postnational Membership in Europe*, Chicago and London: University of Chicago Press.

Spinner, J. 1994, *The Boundaries of Citizenship: Race, Ethnicity and Nationality in the Liberal State*, London: Johns Hopkins University Press.

Spiro, P. J. 1994, 'The States and Immigration in an Era of Demi-Sovereignties', *Virginia Journal of International Law* 35: 121.

1997, 'Dual Nationality and the Meaning of Citizenship', *Emory Law Journal* 46: 1411.

Starke, J. G. 1984, *Introduction to International Law*, 9th edn., London: Butterworth.

Stein, T. 1984a, *Kommentar zum Grundgesetz für die Bundesrepublik Deutschland*, Neuwied: Luchterhand.

1984b, 'Verwaltungsgerichtliche Kontrolle abgelehnter Ermessenseinbürgerungen?', *Die Öffentliche Verwaltungs*: 177.

Stern, K. 1977, *Das Staatsrecht der Bundesrepublik Deutschland*, Munich: Beck.

Thieme, H. W. 1951, 'Die Rechtstellung des Ausländers nach dem Bonner Grundgesetz. Ein Beitrag zur Auslegung des Gleichheitssatzes', (unpublished), Dis jur. Göttingen.

Tomuschat, G. 1968, *Zur Politischen Betätigung des Ausländers in der Bundesrepublik Deutschland*, Berlin and Zurich: Verlag Gehlen. Bad Homburg v. d. H.

Tung, R. K. 1981, *Exit-Voice Catastrophes: Dilemma between Immigration and Participation*, Stockholm: Department of Political Science, Stockholm University.

Uhlitz, O. 1986, 'Deutsches Volk oder "Multikulturelle Gesellschaft"?', *Recht und Politik*: 143.

van Gunsteren, H. R. 1988, 'Admission to Citizenship', *Ethics* 98: 731.

Verdross, A. 1984, *Universelles Völkerrecht*, Berlin: Duncker & Humblot.

Von Mangoldt, H. 1987, 'Die deutsche Staatsangehörigkeit als Voraussetzung und Gegenstand der Grundrechte', *Handbuch des Staatsrecht*, eds. J. Isensee and P. Kirchhof, Vol. I, *Allgemeine Grundrechte*, Heidelberg: C. F. Müller: 617.

1993, 'Öffentliche-rechtliche und völkerrechtliche Probleme mehrfacher Staatsangehörigheit aus deutscher Sicht', *Juristen Zeitung* 48: 965.

1994, 'Ius sanguinis- und ius soli-Prinzip in der Entwicklung des deutschen Staatsangehörigkeitsrechts', *Das Standesamt* 47: 33.

Walzer, M. 1983, *Spheres of Justice: a Defense of Pluralism and Equality*, Oxford: Robertson.

Weber, E. 1977, *Peasants into Frenchmen: the Modernization of Rural France 1870–1914*, London: Chatto and Windus.

Weiler, J. H. 1995, 'Demos, Telos and the German Maastricht Decision', *EUI Working Paper RSC no. 95/19*, Florence: European University Institute.

Weissbrodt, D. 1992, *Immigration Law and Procedure*, St. Paul: West Publishing.

Wengler, W. 1964, *Völkerrecht*, Berlin: Springer Verlag.

Whelan, F. G. 1988, 'Citizenship and Freedom of Movement: an Open Admission Policy?', in *Open Borders? Closed Societies? The Ethical and Political Issues*, ed. M. Gibney, London: Greenwood Press: 3.

Wihtol de Wenden, C. 1990, 'The Absence of Rights: the Position of Illegal Immigrants', in *The Political Rights of Migrant Workers in Western Europe*, ed. Z. Layton-Henry, Modern Politics Series 25, London: Sage Publications: 27.

Wollenschläger, M., and Schraml, A. 1994, 'Ius soli und Hinnahme von Mehrstaatigkeit', *Zeitschrift für Rechtspolitik* 27: 225.

Ziemske, B. 1993, 'Mehrstaatigkeit und Prinzipien des Erwerbs der deutschen Staatsangehörigkeit', *Zeitschrift für Rechtspolitik* 26: 334.

1994, 'Verfassungsrechtliche Garantien des Staatsangehörigkeitsrechts', *Zeitschrift für Rechtspolitik* 27: 229.

Zuleeg, M. 1973, 'Zur staatsrechtlichen Stellung der Ausländer in der Bundesrepublik Deutschland. Menschen zweiter Klasse?', *Die Öffentliche Verwaltung* 11/12: 361.

1974, 'Grundrechte für Ausländer: Bewährungsprobe des Verfassungsrecht', *Deutsches Verwaltungsblatt* 15 April/1 May: 341.

1987, 'Die Vereinbarkeit des Kommunalwahlrechts für Ausländer mit dem deutschen Verfassungsrecht', in *Ausländerrecht und Ausländerpolitik in Europa*, ed. M. Zuleeg, Baden-Baden: Nomos Verlagsgesellschaft.

1988, 'Juristische Streitpunkte zum Kommunalwahlrecht für Ausländer', *Zeitschrift für Ausländerrecht* 1: 13.

Zünkler, M. and Findeisen, M. 1991, 'Einbürgerung ist das Zeichen der Demokratie', *Informationsbrief Ausländerrecht* 13: 248.

Index

Index of Cases